Robotic Process Automation with Automation Anywhere

Techniques to fuel business productivity and intelligent automation using RPA

Husan Mahey

BIRMINGHAM—MUMBAI

Robotic Process Automation with Automation Anywhere

Publishing Product Manager: Pavan Ramchandani
Senior Editor: Hayden Edwards
Content Development Editor: Abhishek Jadhav
Technical Editor: Shubham Sharma
Copy Editor: Safis Editing
Project Coordinator: Kinjal Bari
Proofreader: Safis Editing
Indexer: Manju Arasan
Production Designer: Nilesh Mohite

First published: November 2020
Production reference: 1191120

Published by Packt Publishing Ltd.
Livery Place
35 Livery Street
Birmingham
B3 2PB, UK.

ISBN 978-1-83921-565-0

www.packt.com

Packt.com

Subscribe to our online digital library for full access to over 7,000 books and videos, as well as industry leading tools to help you plan your personal development and advance your career. For more information, please visit our website.

Why subscribe?

- Spend less time learning and more time coding with practical eBooks and Videos from over 4,000 industry professionals

- Improve your learning with Skill Plans built especially for you

- Get a free eBook or video every month

- Fully searchable for easy access to vital information

- Copy and paste, print, and bookmark content

Did you know that Packt offers eBook versions of every book published, with PDF and ePub files available? You can upgrade to the eBook version at packt.com and as a print book customer, you are entitled to a discount on the eBook copy. Get in touch with us at customercare@packtpub.com for more details.

At www.packt.com, you can also read a collection of free technical articles, sign up for a range of free newsletters, and receive exclusive discounts and offers on Packt books and eBooks.

Contributors

About the authors

Husan Mahey has been working in software development since 1991. He currently works as the Chief Technology Officer at SkySoft UK Ltd. Having worked with Automation Anywhere since 2016, he has been recognized by the Automation Anywhere University to be the first to gain all official Automation Anywhere certifications and accredited badges within 3 months. These accreditations include Certified Master RPA Professional and Certified RPA Trainer.

Husan has previously worked for several organizations across finance, pharmaceutical and education sectors, providing automated solutions in various capacities. In his current role, he provides RPA consultancy and training to organizations of all sizes.

About the reviewer

Aravind Krishnaswamy is the Practice Manager for Automation and Cognitive Solutions at D2M, a Division of DISYS. He has over 15 years of experience, including serving as a domain specialist at CSSCORP Pvt. Ltd. before joining DISYS. In this role, he managed a large datacenter and cloud infrastructures. Arvind specializes in automation technologies and has professional certification from Amazon Web Services, Microsoft, Automation Anywhere, and UiPath.

Packt is searching for authors like you

If you're interested in becoming an author for Packt, please visit `authors.packtpub.com` and apply today. We have worked with thousands of developers and tech professionals, just like you, to help them share their insight with the global tech community. You can make a general application, apply for a specific hot topic that we are recruiting an author for, or submit your own idea.

Table of Contents

Preface

1

About Automation Anywhere

2

Installing Automation Anywhere

3

Overview of Automation Anywhere Control Room

4

Overview of the Automation Anywhere Development Interface

5

Building Your First Bot

6

Introducing Variables in A2019

10
Working with XML Files

11
Automating Excel

12
Automation Using Word

13

Working with Emails

14

Working with PDF files

15

Working with Databases

16
Building Modular Bots and Sub-Tasks

17
Running External Scripts

18
Managing Errors

Other Books You May Enjoy

Index

Preface

With an increase in the number of organizations deploying **Robotic Process Automation (RPA)** solutions, RPA is quickly becoming the most desired skill set for both developers starting their career and seasoned professionals. This book will show you how to use Automation Anywhere A2019, one of the leading platforms used widely for RPA.

Starting with an introduction to RPA and Automation Anywhere, the book will guide you through the registration, installation, and configuration of the bot agent and Control Room. With the help of easy-to-follow instructions, you'll build your first bot and discover how you can automate tasks with Excel, Word, Emails, XML, and PDF files. You'll learn from practical examples based on real-world business scenarios, and gain insights into building more robust and resilient bots, executing external scripts such as VBScripts and Python, and adding error handling routines.

By the end of this RPA book, you'll have developed the skills to install and configure an RPA platform confidently and have a solid understanding of how to build complex, robust, and performant bots.

Who this book is for

This Automation Anywhere RPA book is for automation engineers, RPA professionals, and consultants who are looking to explore the capabilities of Automation Anywhere for building intelligent automation strategy for their enterprises. A solid understanding of programming concepts and exposure to the Automation Anywhere platform is necessary to get started with this book.

What this book covers

Chapter 1, About Automation Anywhere, will give you an understanding of what Automation Anywhere is and its place within the global market. We will also discuss the different versions available and why we will be using the Community Version for this book. You will also be guided on how to register an account with Automation Anywhere.

Chapter 2, Installing Automation Anywhere, will guide you on how to connect to Control Room, and prepare and configure the workstation so you are ready to log into A2019.

Chapter 3, Overview of Automation Anywhere Control Room, goes into the details of Control Room. You will get an understanding of the cloud based A2019 version, and you will navigate through various dashboards (from RPA activity to setting up devices).

Chapter 4, Overview of the Automation Anywhere Development Interface, introduces you to the development interface. This chapter will explore what packages and actions are. We will also take a quick look at variables and triggers.

Chapter 5, Building Your First Bot, guides you through building your first software bot through step-by-step instructions. The bot will be able to read and append CSV files, as well as perform some simple calculations.

Chapter 6, Introducing Variables in A2019, explores the different types of variables available in A2109 and how to convert data types. This chapter also has a practical walk-through that will use message boxes, prompts, and comments.

Chapter 7, Interacting with Applications, will help you understand how to automate tasks using windows and web applications, concentrating particularly on the screen controls such as text boxes and buttons.

Chapter 8, String Manipulation and List Variables, takes a closer look at the String type variables. You will learn how to manipulate a string using actions such as Trim, Sub-String, and Find, as well as using regular expressions. The chapter will also look at List variables and how to iterate through them.

Chapter 9, Working with Conditional Logic, Loops and the Filesystem, looks at the different types of loops and conditions available.

Chapter 10, Working with XML Files, will help you understand how we can automate tasks while working with XML files. The XML package will be explored, particularly the reading, deleting, and updating of different notes within XML files.

Chapter 11, Automating Excel, teaches you how Automation Anywhere A2019 can help automate tasks in Excel. You will learn about the different Excel packages available. The practical walk-throughs will include opening, closing, and saving workbooks, as well as reading data, writing data, and running Excel macros.

Chapter 12, Automation Using Word, teaches you how Automation Anywhere A2019 can help automate tasks in Word. You will learn about various actions that will help you in creating documents as well as inserting and replacing text.

Chapter 13, Working with Emails, looks at the automation of email tasks. This chapter will guide you through connecting to different type of mail servers, as well as sending and receiving emails from these servers.

Chapter 14, Working with PDF Files, examines the PDF package in Automation Anywhere A2019. We will look at features such as extracting text and images. We will also look at merging multiple documents, as well as splitting documents.

Chapter 15, Working with Databases, teaches you about connecting to different types of data sources, including SQL Server, Oracle, and Access. The walk-throughs include building a bot to run SQL statements, as well as updating and deleting commands.

Chapter 16, Building Modular Bots and Sub-Tasks, helps you understand how to design modular tasks and how to pass parameters between tasks. The practical walk-through includes building a main bot with three sub-bots.

Chapter 17, Running External Scripts, looks at calling scripts. We will also look at how to pass parameters between the bot and external scripts.

Chapter 18, Managing Errors, teaches you how to handle the errors. You will learn how to implement a robust error handling routine in this chapter.

To get the most out of this book

You don't need any special software installed to use Automation Anywhere A2019 as this is a cloud-based platform. All that's needed is an internet connection and a web browser. To fully explore all the practical walk-throughs, having a system with Windows 7 (or higher), MS Office 2016, Microsoft Excel, Access, Outlook, and a PDF reader would be useful.

If you are using the digital version of this book, we advise you to type the code yourself or access the code via the GitHub repository (link available in the next section). Doing so will help you avoid any potential errors related to the copying and pasting of code.

Download the example code files

You can download the example code files for this book from your account at www . packt . com. If you purchased this book elsewhere, you can visit www . packtpub . com/ support and register to have the files emailed directly to you.

You can download the code files by following these steps:

1. Log in or register at www.packt.com.
2. Select the **Support** tab.
3. Click on **Code Downloads**.
4. Enter the name of the book in the **Search** box and follow the onscreen instructions.

Once the file is downloaded, please make sure that you unzip or extract the folder using the latest version of:

*   WinRAR/7-Zip for Windows
*   Zipeg/iZip/UnRarX for Mac
*   7-Zip/PeaZip for Linux

The code bundle for the book is also hosted on GitHub at https://github.com/PacktPublishing/Robotic-Process-Automation-with-Automation-Anywhere. In case there's an update to the code, it will be updated on the existing GitHub repository.

We also have other code bundles from our rich catalog of books and videos available at https://github.com/PacktPublishing/. Check them out!

Conventions used

There are a number of text conventions used throughout this book.

Code in text: Indicates code words in text, database table names, folder names, filenames, file extensions, pathnames, dummy URLs, user input, and Twitter handles. Here is an example: "Mount the downloaded WebStorm-10*.dmg disk image file as another disk in your system."

A block of code is set as follows:

```
html, body, #map {
  height: 100%;
  margin: 0;
  padding: 0
}
```

When we wish to draw your attention to a particular part of a code block, the relevant lines or items are set in bold:

```
[default]
exten => s,1,Dial(Zap/1|30)
exten => s,2,Voicemail(u100)
exten => s,102,Voicemail(b100)
exten => i,1,Voicemail(s0)
```

Any command-line input or output is written as follows:

```
$ mkdir css
$ cd css
```

Bold: Indicates a new term, an important word, or words that you see onscreen. For example, words in menus or dialog boxes appear in the text like this. Here is an example: "Select **System info** from the **Administration** panel."

> **Tips or important notes**
> Appear like this.

Get in touch

Feedback from our readers is always welcome.

General feedback: If you have questions about any aspect of this book, mention the book title in the subject of your message and email us at customercare@packtpub.com.

Errata: Although we have taken every care to ensure the accuracy of our content, mistakes do happen. If you have found a mistake in this book, we would be grateful if you would report this to us. Please visit www.packtpub.com/support/errata, selecting your book, clicking on the Errata Submission Form link, and entering the details.

Piracy: If you come across any illegal copies of our works in any form on the Internet, we would be grateful if you would provide us with the location address or website name. Please contact us at copyright@packt.com with a link to the material.

If you are interested in becoming an author: If there is a topic that you have expertise in and you are interested in either writing or contributing to a book, please visit authors.packtpub.com.

Reviews

Please leave a review. Once you have read and used this book, why not leave a review on the site that you purchased it from? Potential readers can then see and use your unbiased opinion to make purchase decisions, we at Packt can understand what you think about our products, and our authors can see your feedback on their book. Thank you!

For more information about Packt, please visit packt.com.

1

About Automation Anywhere

Robot Process Automation (RPA) has attracted significant investment from many corporate organizations in recent years. This has opened up many opportunities for using RPA, whether you are an experienced developer wanting to gain additional valuable skills or you're thinking about starting your career as an RPA developer. Not only will you learn what commands and functionality **Automation Anywhere (AA)** has to offer; you will also gain practical experience of how to use them. You will put everything you learn into practice with plenty of walk-throughs.

In this chapter, we will summarize what Robot Process Automation is. You will learn about what AA is, what it does, and get some initial insights into their RPA tool. There are a number of versions available from AA, you will gain an understanding of the differences between them. This book is based on the latest Community Edition A2019. Besides being the latest version, there are several other reasons for learning RPA with this version. You will get an insight into why this version is ideal for providing actual hands-on experience and starting your journey in building software robots (bots).

Along with building bots, AA also has a number of additional features and components. These include IQ Bot, Bot Insight, Bot Store, Mobile Bot, and Automation Anywhere University. In this chapter, you will get insights into what these are and how you can benefit from these features and components.

We will cover the following topics in this chapter:

- What is robotic process automation?
- Overview of Automation Anywhere
- Automation Anywhere Versions
- Community Edition A2019

Technical requirements

In order to use AA A2019 Community Edition, the following requirements are necessary:

- Windows OS version 7 or higher
- A processor with a minimum speed of 3 GHz
- A minimum of 4 GB RAM
- Internet Explorer v10 or higher, or Chrome v49 or higher
- An internet connection with a minimum speed of 10 Mb/second

What is robotic process automation?

You probably already know what RPA is, but we will go through a quick overview here. The words *automation* or *robot* usually conjure up images of a physical machine performing repetitive tasks. We began to see this type of automation years ago, particularly in manufacturing. Physical robotic machines were built to help automate tasks usually done by humans. This form of industrial manufacturing automation was later adopted by many other industries including logistics, distribution, and packaging. This also led to automation being taught in universities at postgraduate level. Many new technology jobs were also created from this, including roles such as robotics engineer, designer, and maintenance operative, as well as automated programmable manufacturing tools such as CNC machinery. Since the widespread adoption of the internet, we have seen the concept of web-controlled automation also being introduced. As an example, large buildings often deploy internet-enabled CCTV, heating controls, and security systems, where all these systems can be managed remotely over the internet. You could have a very fulfilling career as a developer or engineer working in automation.

We can see the same thing happening with RPA. RPA is specifically designed to automate tasks that are performed by humans on desktops. Most jobs have an element that involves tasks that are high volume, repetitive, and tedious. Such tasks tend to drain the enjoyment out of our jobs. This is where RPA can be applied to automate these types of tasks.

We can build bots to perform these types of tasks, and this is specifically what RPA bots have been designed for. Having a bot can give you more time to spend doing the tasks that you actually enjoy and excel at. This in turn would deliver more job satisfaction.

You may be thinking, *well, what's the difference between RPA and traditional software development?* Well, with traditional development, the developer needs to be proficient in developing the application with it being automated as well. For example, to automate a task in Excel, you would expect the developer to have skills in VBA. To develop web applications, the developer may need skills in Java or HTML. The developer needs to understand how the application is executing the tasks as well as what the user needs to do. It would usually also involve a greater learning curve to master these skills and would involve writing lines of code to build the solutions. RPA is different. It doesn't really matter what application you are working with as it interacts with the user interface. The user only needs to understand how to operate the application they are working with without necessarily understanding how the applications executes the task, and this is all that RPA needs to know. So, no specific expertise is needed to work on multiple applications. It also does not require writing lines of code, as you can build a solution by designing a workflow or using pre-defined drag and drop commands. This makes it an ideal technology to rapidly learn how to build bots and doesn't require years of learning to become a bot developer. See the following comparison:

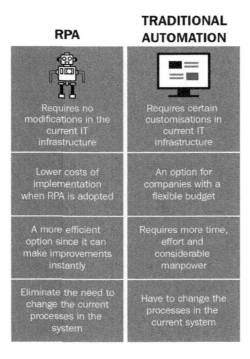

Figure 1.1 – Comparison of traditional automation against RPA

You can clearly see the benefits of having an RPA bot as opposed to building a new traditional-style software solution. So, what sort of tasks can a bot actually perform? Bots can pretty much do most tasks that involve a human using the desktop. This includes the automation of the tasks shown in the following diagram:

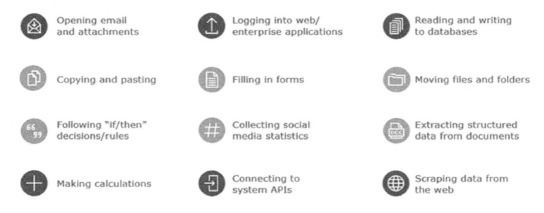

Figure 1.2 – Tasks that can be performed with RPA

You should now have a good understanding of what RPA is. This is a growing market with great demand for RPA skills. We know we can learn these skills far more quickly and easily than those required for traditional development. The scope of the types of tasks that can be automated with RPA is vast and not limited to specific industries.

The number of RPA vendors on the market is growing. As in most industries, only a few become recognized and reputable as market leaders, although we have seen a handful of industry leaders emerging over the last few years. One of the key players has been AA.

Overview of Automation Anywhere

The list of vendors that provide RPA tools is growing constantly. There are three main leaders in this technology. These are UiPath, Blue Prism, and **AA**. All these vendors provide RPA tools with pretty much the same functionality. You can see the top 10 RPA vendors of 2020 at the following link, created by **Horses for Sources**: https://www.horsesforsources.com/RPA_Top10_2020_012920.

Although the aforementioned top three do provide similar functionalities, there are some key differences. The following table shows a breakdown of the features available from each provider:

	BluePrism	UiPath	Automation Anywhere
Free Community Edition	No	Yes	Yes
Front Office Development	No	Yes	Yes
Back Office Development	Yes	Yes	Yes
User Friendly Interface	Yes	Yes	Yes
Drag & Drop Development Feature	Yes	Yes	Yes
Interface Recorder Development Feature	No	Yes	Yes
Certification Available	Yes	Yes	Yes
Training Academy	No	Yes	Yes
Cloud Based Development	No	Yes	Yes
Bot Store Marketplace	No	Yes	Yes

Figure 1.3 – Top vendors' features comparison

We can see that AA and UiPath have the most comprehensive tools and features when compared to Blue Prism.

In this book we will be using AA, as they were the first to release a fully cloud-based RPA tool. This eliminates the need to install AA on your desktops to build, manage, and deploy bots. AA has also won a number of prestigious technology awards and was recently named the *market leader* in RPA by a Forrester report.

AA also runs a number of annual events, where they host the *Bot Games*. Here, developers from around the world are challenged against each other to build specific bots. Maybe, once you have gained enough confidence in your own bot development skills, you can be part of these Bot Games.

The mission statement of AA, as published on their website at `https://www.automationanywhere.com/company/about-us`, is as follows:

"To enable companies to operate with unprecedented productivity and efficiency by automating any part of the enterprise that can be automated with the most intelligent and intuitive robotic process automation platform we call

- The Intelligent Digital Workforce"

We can break this statement down into three distinct elements:

- **What AA offers**: Giving organizations the opportunity to increase productivity and efficiency.
- **How they can offer this**: Creating the opportunity to automate any process within the organization by the deployment of intelligent RPA.
- **The outcome**: This results in building bots that make up the **Digital Workforce**.

When designing and building an RPA solution, it is essential that a statement relates to the purpose of why RPA is needed. The Digital Workforce has to add value within the organization. This can be measured in terms of cost savings, time reduction, or the reduction of effort. As a developer, understanding why automation is needed can help in designing a robust intelligent solution.

We will take a closer look at some of the additional features and components available with AA. This will show how AA stands out from the crowd of its competitors. We will look at the following features and components:

- The Digital Workforce
- IQ Bot
- Bot Insight
- Bot Store
- Mobile Bot
- Automation Anywhere University

Let's take a look at these in more detail.

The Digital Workforce

A bot is referred to by AA as a **Digital Worker** as it clones the actions of a human to perform a given task. A Digital Worker is a member of the team designed to carry out a process just the same as any human worker. In a working environment, a team can consist of both humans and bots, hence the bot being referred to as a Digital Worker. As more bots are built within an organization, you can see a Digital Workforce being created. These bots can work side by side with a human or can be deployed to run on their own. Decision-making is a key aspect when using RPA. RPA has the capability to perform condition-based decisions. This is when the outcome is purely based on a single condition or set of conditions.

For example, a condition-based decision could be, *do we order some keyboards?*

We would check our stock levels in the stock database, and if it is below our re-ordering threshold, then yes, we do; otherwise, we don't.

In some cases, condition-based decisions are not sufficient to get the correct outcome. There are occasions when decisions have to be made using **Artificial Intelligence** (**AI**) or by applying machine learning algorithms. This is where RPA needs to be used in conjunction with AI. AA allows us to train an RPA bot to perform complex decisions involving some machine learning algorithms and AI. This is achievable using the IQ Bot feature of AA.

IQ Bot

As well as utilizing condition-based decisions, more and more processes require a certain level of cognitive intelligence to make decisions. An example of this would be when dealing with unstructured data. A common scenario would be based on invoices, they all tend to have the same type of data such as supplier, items, costings, and dates, but the layout and format will vary between different suppliers. The consistency is not present when handling multiple suppliers. AA has developed a product called **IQ Bot**. This bot uses cognitive automation with RPA to learn how to handle unstructured data. This enables such processes to be automated from end to end without human intervention. It integrates AI technologies such as fuzzy logic, **Natural Language Processing** (**NLP**), computer vision, and **Machine Learning** (**ML**), all without the help of data scientists or highly trained experts.

We will look at IQ Bot later in the advanced commands section of this book and will give you the opportunity to create and train your own IQ Bot to handle unstructured data.

Bot Insight

Designing and building bots is not the complete story. AA has also developed a platform that produces real-time analytics about your Digital Workforce, processes, and business-level processes This is all a part of the Bot Insights tool, the RPA analytics tool for AA. Bot Insights is broken down into two categories: operational analytics and business intelligence.

As bots are deployed, as well as executing tasks, they also process data. This data is related to each specific process and can provide valuable insight. Bot Insight analyzes this data and transforms it into meaningful insights. It also captures operational data such as how well the bot is performing, tracking data as it is being processed. All this data can be presented in various formats including graphs, charts, and tables. It can also predict possible bot failures. It can be integrated seamlessly with other leading business intelligence platforms such as Tableau, ThoughtSpot, and QlikView. As an independent tool, Bot Insight provides a complete analytics solution without the need to integrate with other tools. It's simple to use; all it requires is tagging the data items that need to be analyzed and Bot Insight will do the rest for you.

> **Note**
>
> You can learn more about Bot Insight at `https://www.automationanywhere.com/products/bot-insight`.

Bot Store

AA is the first RPA vendor to have a fully operational Bot Store. Bot Store is an online store with a collection of Digital Workers. The bots available here are built by independent developers from all around the world as well as AA themselves. AA Bot Store won the Silver award in the 2019 Edison Awards for developing the world's first and largest enterprise automation marketplace.

These are complete bots out of the box that will perform a specific task or role. They are available as bots for specific applications, categories, or business processes. These applications include Microsoft, Google Cloud, CyberArk, and LinkedIn. You can pick specific bots for tasks such as converting speech to text or converting a QR code image to text. The bots on offer are continuously growing as more of them are added. Many of these bots are available for free, but there are some you will have to pay for.

Once you have mastered bot development, maybe you can submit your bots to be hosted on Bot Store. This is a great way to promote your skills as well as having the opportunity to sell your bots.

> **Note**
>
> You can learn more about Bot Store at `https://www.automationanywhere.com/products/botstore`.

Mobile Bot

AA has also released a mobile app to work with your bots. It allows you to manage your Digital Workers from your mobile device. Bot Insight is available on the mobile app. This app will give you live alerts on bot performance as well as business insights on bot data. You can control your bots from the app including starting and stopping them. It also provides a platform for you to connect with the wider AA RPA community.

> **Note**
>
> You can learn more about Mobile Bot at `https://www.automationanywhere.com/products/apps`.

Automation Anywhere University

AA also has an online university that provides many learning paths and opportunities to get a globally recognized certificate. You can gain many accreditation badges approved by AA by completing the online assessments. These assessments usually consist of multiple-choice questionnaires. In order to gain the Certified Master Professional accreditation, you will have to build three bots and submit them to the university. These will then be assessed to determine whether you qualify or not. There are many areas of AA that you can gain accreditation badges for, including Bot Developer, Business Analyst, IQ Bot Developer, Control Room Administrator, Solutions Architect, Technical Support Specialist, and RPA Program Manager.

You can attempt the accreditation badge assessments for free, but there is a cost for the certifications. The costs vary from 50 USD to 100 USD depending on the certificate.

These certifications are great ways to promote your RPA skills and I would recommend you to try the Automation Anywhere Certified Advanced RPA Professional certification after completing this hands-on book.

> **Note**
>
> You can learn more about the AA University at `https://university.automationanywhere.com/`.

Hopefully, you will now have a better insight into the features of AA. There is a distinct advantage of using AA for RPA over its competitors. We know that the AA platform offers far more than just bot development. It allows data analytics, a platform to showcase and generate revenue from our bots, a tool specifically designed to incorporate AI in our bots, as well as a path to gain recognized certifications for our skills.

Along with these features, there are three versions of AA available. We will now look at the differences between all three of them.

Automation Anywhere versions

As mentioned, there are three versions available from AA. We will learn what each version has to offer. Also, we will look at which version we will be using and why.

Each version is designed with a different user in mind. The following table shows you what these versions are and their main differences:

ENTERPRISE VERSION 11	ENTERPRISE A2019	COMMUNITY EDITION A2019
Designed as an on-premises enterprise level RPA platform	Designed as a cloud-based enterprise level RPA platform	Designed for the developer and student
Free trial for 30 days	Free trial for 30 days	Free for small businesses, developers, and students
Included components: Enterprise – RPA on-premises IQ Bot, Bot Insight, Bot Store, Mobile App	Included components: Enterprise – fully web-based RPA in the cloud IQ Bot, Bot Insight, Bot Store, Mobile App	Included components: Enterprise – fully web-based RPA in the cloud IQ Bot, Bot Insight, Bot Store

Figure 1.4 – AA versions

We will be using Community Edition A2019, the main reason being that it's totally free. Both the other two versions come with a 30-day free trial, after which you have to purchase an AA license to continue using them. Community Edition A2019 is specifically designed for students and developers. There is no limit to the number of bots you can build nor is there any limited functionality.

I am sure you can now see the benefits of using Community Edition A2019 as well as understanding what additional capabilities the other versions have to offer. In the next section, we will take a closer look at Community Edition A2019 as well as a walk-through on how to register with AA in order to start using it.

Community Edition A2019

AA Community Edition A2019 is the latest free version available and was released in November 2019. The version prior to this, AA v11.x, used a client-server architecture where the management was done through the web-based Control Room app while the bot development was done through a client application installed on the desktop.

Community Version A2019 is a fully cloud-based solution. The bot management and building are all done through the web application. No development client is installed on your desktop. Each device that you will run the bot on will need to download and install a **Bot agent**. Once installed, you build your bot, then connect to your device using a Bot agent, and then deploy.

Registration with Automation Anywhere

As Community Edition A2019 is free, you can start using it once we have registered with AA.

To register, follow these instructions:

1. Navigate to `https://www.automationanywhere.com/products/community-edition`.
2. Complete the appropriate details, including your **First Name**, **Last Name**, **Email Address**, **Country**, **Phone Number**, and **Company Name**.
3. Then submit your details.

You will shortly get a welcome email including your login credentials. The key details to note are the following:

- Your Control Room URL
- Your username
- Your password

You will need these credentials every time you launch AA so keep a note of them. You need to change the password when you first log in.

You are now ready to start your RPA journey using AA.

Summary

You will now have a good understanding of AA and its competitors as well as what AA's capabilities are. Having registered with AA to use the free Community Edition A2019, you must be keen to get AA up and running on your machine.

In the next chapter, you will be guided through the installation process of AA. This will be done through step-by-step instructions to get you ready to start taking a closer look at the AA interface.

2
Installing Automation Anywhere

The latest Community Edition of Automation Anywhere is a fully cloud-based platform. It is also available to students and small businesses for free. There is no limit on the number of bots you can build; the only limitation is that they can only be deployed to one device. This makes it ideal to learn how to start building RPA bots.

The basic components needed for any version of Automation Anywhere to run are **Control Room** and the **Client**. **Control Room** functions as a management tool. It is used to manage your user accounts, devices, bots, and schedules, as well as giving bot insights. In previous versions, the **Client** was the bot development interface, but this has been superseded in the latest Community Edition A2019 and all the development is now done from within **Control Room**. So, there is no need to install any client application.

The previous chapter showed how to register with Automation Anywhere. This registration process will create a user account for you and allocate your account to a control room. You will receive an email with the **Control Room** URL details as well as your login credentials.

In this chapter, we will get Automation Anywhere up and running, ready to start building bots. You will learn how to connect to the control room and update your profile, and we will move forward to setting up the machine you would run your bot on, known as a **device**. After creating the device, you will learn how to configure and set up any credentials needed to log in to the device. By the end of this chapter, you will have completed learning how to set up the environment and get ready for your RPA bot development journey using Automation Anywhere.

We will cover the following topics in this chapter:

- Connecting to **Control Room**
- Preparing your device
- Configuring profile and device credentials

Technical requirements

In order to install the Automation Anywhere A2019 Community Edition Bot agent, the following requirements are necessary:

- Windows OS version 7 or higher
- A processor with a minimum speed of 3 GHz
- A minimum of 4 GB RAM
- At least 100 MB hard disk space
- Internet Explorer v10 or higher, or Chrome v49 or higher
- A minimum screen resolution of 1024*768
- An internet connection with a minimum speed of 10 Mb/second
- Have completed the registration process with Automation Anywhere for Community Edition AA 2019

Connecting to Control Room

Continuing from *Chapter 1, About Automation Anywhere,* after your registration with Automation Anywhere is complete, you should have received an email with the following details:

- Your Control Room URL

- Your username

- Your password

Let's start by logging into **Control Room** and getting familiar with the interface.

Launching and logging into Control Room

As Automation Anywhere is 100% cloud-based, the platform is a totally web-based application. As such, we need to run Automation Anywhere from our web browser. I am using Chrome, but Internet Explorer can also be used to launch Automation Anywhere:

1. Copy the **Control Room** URL details from your registration email and enter this URL into your web browser address bar:

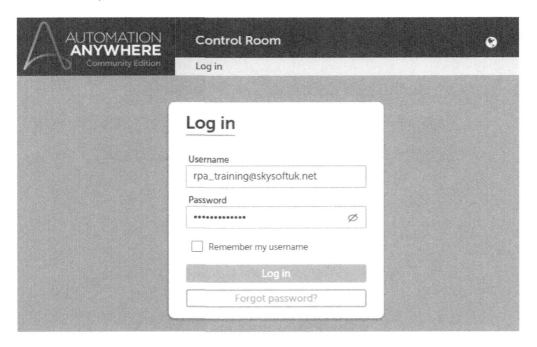

Figure 2.1 – Automation Anywhere Log in interface

2.   Next, enter the **Username** (this is usually your email address), followed by the **Password** sent in the email from Automation Anywhere.

3.   Click on the **Log in** button. When you have successfully logged in, you will be navigated to the **Home** page:

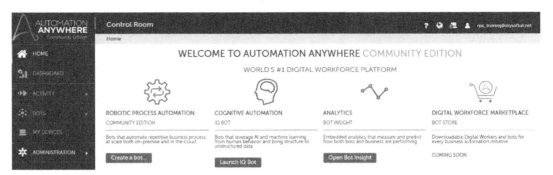

Figure 2.2 – Automation Anywhere Home page

You have managed to log in to Automation Anywhere **Control Room**. The top right shows the user details, while the left-hand pane has all the different sections of Control Room.

Updating your profile and password

The first thing you may want to do is update your profile and set a new password:

1.   In the top right-hand corner of the **Home** page, click on your profile icon:

Figure 2.3 – Profile icon

2.   From the dialog box, click on **Go to My profile**:

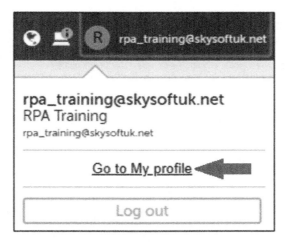

Figure 2.4 – Navigate to your profile details

3. This will take you to your profile details interface; to make any changes to your profile, click on **Edit**:

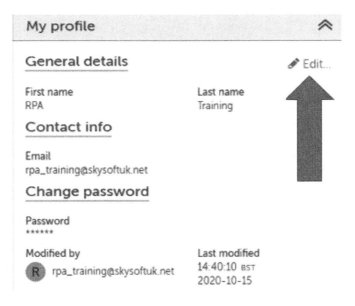

Figure 2.5 – Profile settings page

4. This will allow you to update your details. Here, you can update your **password**; once you have made your changes, click on **Save changes** to apply them:

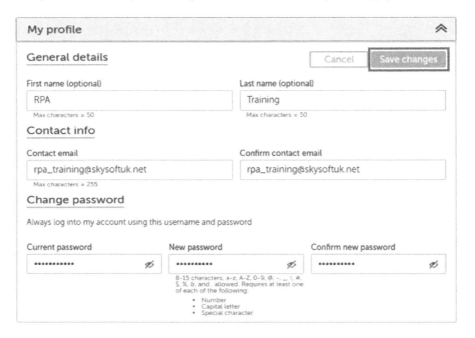

Figure 2.6 – Updating the profile settings

You are now successfully connected to **Control Room** and have configured it to your liking. Every time you want to launch Automation Anywhere, you will navigate via your browser to the URL given and use your credentials to log in. Now let's prepare your device.

Preparing your device

When bots are built, they need to be run on a device. This device can be a physical desktop, laptop, or even a virtual machine. We need to install and configure all devices that we may want to run a bot on. With this free edition of Automation Anywhere, we can add only one device.

To add a device, two stages are involved:

*   Installing a Bot agent
*   Enabling the extension

Let's go through each stage now.

Installing a Bot agent

The Bot agent is a small application that allows the device to communicate with the task bots. To install the Bot agent, follow these steps:

1. Click on **MY DEVICES** from the left-hand menu bar, then click on the **Add local bot agent** icon:

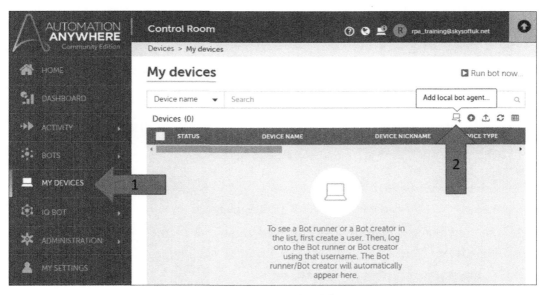

Figure 2.7 – Adding a local device

2. The connection wizard will pop up. Click on **Connect to my computer**:

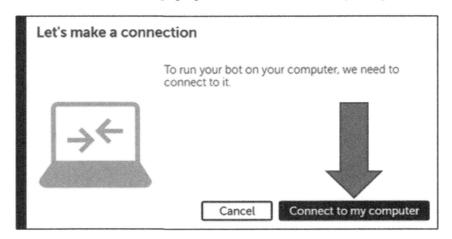

Figure 2.8 – Connecting to a local device

3. The wizard will start to download the Bot agent (into your default downloads folder) as shown in the following screenshot:

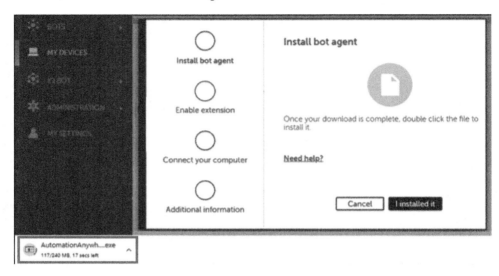

Figure 2.9 – Downloading a Bot agent to a local device

4. Once the Bot agent has been downloaded, right-click on the downloaded file's icon and select **Open**:

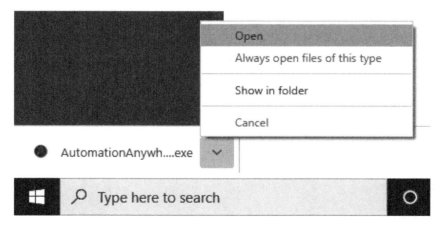

Figure 2.10 – Installing a Bot agent on a local device

5. This will initiate the Bot agent install wizard. Follow any onscreen instructions to install the Bot agent.

6. Once it has been installed, you will notice a green tick in the **Install bot agent** step. This green tick indicates the successful completion of that task:

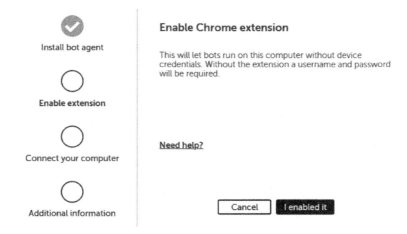

Figure 2.11 – Installation progress indicator

The wizard will automatically lead you into the next section for enabling the extension.

Enabling the extension

If you are using Google Chrome as your browser, Automation Anywhere will need to enable an extension for this. This allows Automation Anywhere to identify and interact with web-based objects for automating your bots. To enable the extension, you may need to download it from the Chrome Web Store. Follow these steps to enable the extension:

1. Click on the **I enabled it** button shown in *Figure 2.11*. This will tell you whether the extension is already enabled or not:

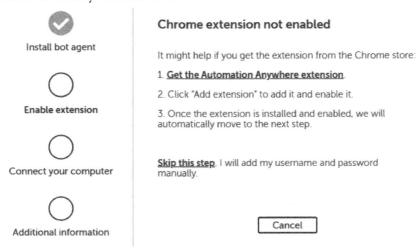

Figure 2.12 – Enabling the extension

2. Click on the **Get the Automation Anywhere extension** link to navigate to the Chrome Web Store:

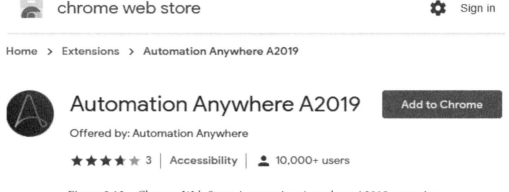

Figure 2.13 – Chrome Web Store Automation Anywhere A2019 extension

3. Click on **Add to Chrome** button and you will get the following prompt; click on **Add extension**:

Figure 2.14 – Extension installation prompt

4. This will install and enable the extension. To view or disable the extension in Chrome, navigate to **Settings | Extensions** and the Automation Anywhere extension should be visible:

Automation Anywhere A2019

Automation Anywhere A2019 extension to automate web applications in Google Chrome.

Details	Remove

Figure 2.15 – The extension in Chrome

5. Once the extension has been enabled, the progress indicator will be updated with further green ticks, shown as follows:

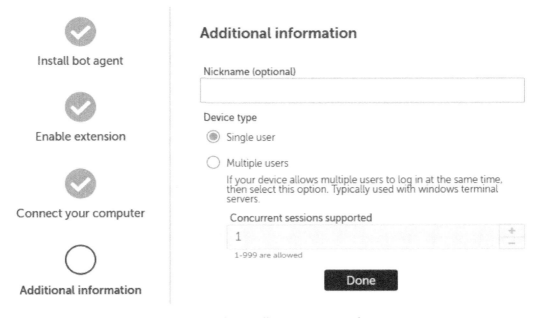

Figure 2.16 – The installation progress indicator

6. Finally, to complete the installation, click on the **Done** button. You can give your workstation a nickname in the **Nickname (optional)** text box if you wish.

7. Looking at **My devices** in **Control Room**, you will now notice your device listed:

Figure 2.17 – List of installed devices

8. The Bot agent should now be successfully installed on your device. You will also notice a little green tick against your local device icon on the top pane:

Figure 2.18 – Local device status icon

We now need to configure the device so that Automation Anywhere can log in to it, even if no one is logged in to that device or if it's locked.

Configuring profile and device credentials

Once your device is visible on the listed devices in **Control Room**, you may need to configure the user profile for that device. Imagine that we build a bot and deploy it to your device, but the device is locked or you are not logged in to it. Automation Anywhere will need to log in to the device. In order to achieve this, we need to set the login user credentials for the device.

This is achieved with the following steps:

1. Once in **Control Room**, from the **Home** screen, click on the local device icon, followed by **Update credentials**:

Figure 2.19 – Updating local device credentials

2. The dialog will allow you to update the **Device password**. Enter the user password for the device and click on **Update**:

Figure 2.20 – Updating the device's password

3. Your device has now been successfully configured.

Great work! We have now got our device all ready to start working with **Control Room**. **Control Room** is set up with a user profile and a device.

Summary

We are all ready to get going now. You will be comfortable in the future with setting up and configuring a device with Automation Anywhere Control Room, and can configure your device credentials as well as update your user profile. You could have a number of devices installed in **Control Room**. Once a bot is built, it can be deployed to any one of them or even a number of devices. Installing and configuring devices is an essential part of deploying and testing bots, and Control Room provides a centralized location to manage all your devices easily.

In the next chapter, we will look more closely at the **Control Room** features. We have already looked at setting up devices, but there is a lot more to it. We will learn about the dashboard, and how your bot is managed and monitored. This will get you more familiar with the **Control Room** interface used in Automation Anywhere.

3

Overview of Automation Anywhere Control Room

Understanding the **Control Room** interface is key when building, deploying, and managing bots. **Control Room** is used to perform all these tasks. It has a very *easy-to-use* intuitive interface. The interface is designed with a pane on the left-hand side used as a navigation bar, which lists the main sections and sub-sections of the control room. The main desktop area has all the functionality and features for each section.

In the previous chapter, you learned how to connect your device to the control room and get ready to start building bots. Before we actually build a bot, it is important that you have a clear understanding of the user interface.

In this chapter, we go greater into detail about the **Control Room** interface. Each section is explored, giving you hands-on experience with the interface. You will learn about the dashboard, monitoring bot activity, setting application credentials, device management, and user management.

As part of the cloud-based infrastructure, all actions are now done via the **Control Room** interface. We will look at this in more detail. It is key that you can confidently navigate through the **Control Room** interface. This interface is your single platform to design, build, and manage your RPA solution. We will cover the following sections of **Control Room** in this chapter:

- Exploring the home screen
- Understanding the dashboard
- Viewing RPA activity
- Managing bots
- Managing **My Devices**
- Managing user administration

Technical requirements

In order to install Automation Anywhere A2019 Community Edition, the following requirements are necessary:

- Windows operating system version 7 or higher
- A processor with a minimum speed of 3 GHz
- Minimum of 4 GB RAM
- At least 100 MB hard disk space
- Internet Explorer v10 or higher OR Chrome v49 or higher
- A minimum screen resolution of 1024*768
- An internet connection with a minimum speed of 10 Mb/sec
- Completed registration with Automation Anywhere A2019 Community Edition
- Logged on successfully to Automation Anywhere A2019 Community Edition
- A successfully registered local device

Exploring the home screen

The home screen is the first interface presented to you when you initially log on to **Control Room**. You will notice shortcuts to some of the exciting features available for you to explore:

Figure 3.1 – Home screen

There are a number of options and information available in the top-right panel. These are as follows:

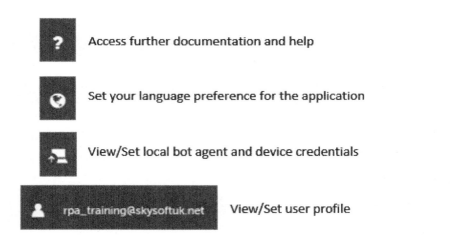

Figure 3.2 – Screen icons

The main navigation menu is on the left-hand side of the home screen. This will take you into the different sections of **Control Room**. We will explore each section further in this chapter.

On the main window of the home screen, there are four shortcuts available. These are for the following:

- **Create a Bot**: Launches the interface to quickly get you started in building your bots
- **Launch IQ Bot**: Launches the artificial intelligence and machine learning tool
- **Open Bot Insight**: Launches the data collection and analysis tool
- **BotStore**: When available, this will launch the platform to market and sell your bots to a wide consumer marketplace.

The home screen serves as the landing screen when you log on to the new Automation Anywhere platform. It provides you with an introduction to the features available to support your bot production and management.

Getting familiar with the **Control Room** interface is important so that you have a clearer understanding of how to best utilize all its features. We will explore all sections of **Control Room**. The next section is the dashboard, which shows more information on the status of your activity and bots.

Understanding the dashboard

The dashboard acts as the information and metrics section. It is split into two main sections: the top section contains a few shortcuts, while the bottom section shows bot metric data, as shown in the following screenshot:

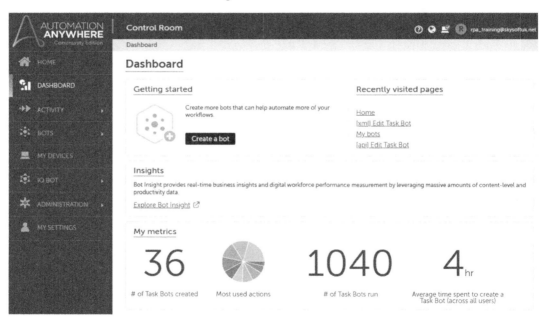

Figure 3.3 – Dashboard interface

The available shortcuts on the dashboard are as follows:

- Creating a new bot
- Launching bot insights
- Your recently visited pages

The metrics will display the number of bots you have created, data on the success and failures of these bots, as well as performance-related data. Other metric data is also available through bot insights, including return on investment analysis, transactions processed in terms of volumes and speed, and the efficiency of bots, to name a few. As we have not built any bots yet, the metrics data will be sparse.

The dashboard displays aggregated data for a period of time. We can view the activity of individual bots in the next section. The **Activity** section goes into a more granular level of detail about the metrics.

Viewing RPA activity

The **Activity** section shows the current and historic status of your bots and devices. This is in the form of a list. By clicking on the **ACTIVITY** option from the menu pane, you will see the following interface:

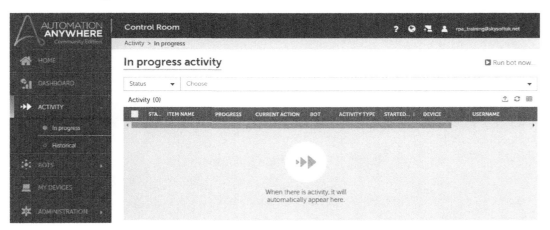

Figure 3.4 – Activity: In progress interface

You can quickly identify which bot is running on which device. A device is the desktop that bots are deployed to. In *Chapter 2, Installing Automation Anywhere*, we went through how to add, register, and connect your local device.

There are two sub-sections to the **Activity** page, showing **In progress** and **Historical**:

Figure 3.5 – Activity options

Both of these sub-sections display a list of your bots or devices. The **In progress** list shows the bots that are currently active, and the **Historical** screen lists bots with a completed status. It displays all bots and all devices that are managed within **Control Room**.

A number of options are available through the icons on the right, just above the activity list:

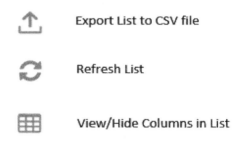

Figure 3.6 – List options

This list can be configured to show/hide different columns. A number of columns are available, including **STATUS, CURRENT ACTION, BOT, ACTIVITY TYPE, START TIME, USERNAME,** and **DEVICE,** to name a few.

For the purpose of routine management reporting or further analysis, the list can be exported as a CSV file. You can modify the columns you wish to view or export. Here, you can see all the columns that are available. Each one can be set to be visible or hidden:

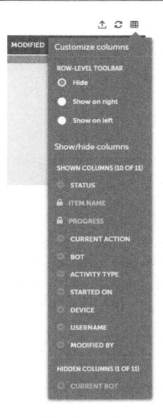

Figure 3.7 – All the columns that are available

You can also search and apply a filter to the list of bots or devices. The search and filter functions are available in the top part of each sub-section, as shown in the following screenshot:

Figure 3.8 – Search options

So far, all the sections we've seen really come into force once you have built and deployed some bots. They help monitor and manage your bots and deployment.

The next section we will look at is **BOTS**. This section concentrates more on bot development.

Managing bots

Bot management and deployment are performed in this section. This is broken down into four sub-sections, which are accessible from the main menu pane on the left:

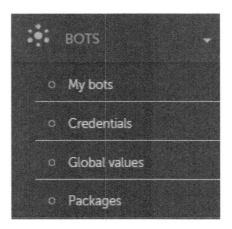

Figure 3.9 – Bot management options

The **BOTS** section is one of the key sections when it comes to building and managing bots. We will look further into each sub-section in greater detail.

My bots

All your bots are visible here. They are presented via folders and files related to your bots. Automation Anywhere A2019 uses a pre-defined file structure, the root folder being Bots. This folder structure is an exclusive storage area for your account. Within the root folder, you can create new folders, the standard practice being to create a folder for each individual bot or a bot category.

As you can see, the folder structure is displayed on the left pane and the contents on the right:

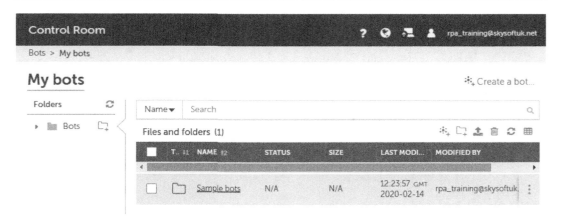

Figure 3.10 – The My bots interface

There are a few options available for each file and folder within this interface, as shown in the following screenshot:

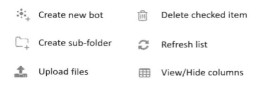

Figure 3.11 – My bots: icon options

There is also a search facility available to help find your bot files more easily.

As you build your bots, you may need to access secure desktop or web applications that need log-in credentials. The next sub-section describes a feature used to manage these credentials.

Credentials

For any application that requires credentials, it is recommended not to store these credentials within your task bots. For added security, all credentials should be secured in **Automation Anywhere's Credential Vault**. To achieve this, the following steps should be executed:

1. Create a credential with the required attributes; that is, a username/password.
2. Add this credential to a locker.
3. Grant the bot access to the locker.

The bot can now get this specific credential to access the application.

The **Credentials** sub-section has three tabs. These are **MY CREDENTIALS**, **MY LOCKERS**, and **CREDENTIAL REQUESTS**. All credentials are created under the **MY CREDENTIALS** tab. These can be grouped and stored within lockers. Grouping can be done for applications or a specific category. For example, a single application may need multiple credentials for various tasks. In this case, you would create individual credentials and put them all in one locker. The final **CREDENTIAL REQUESTS** tab is an informative tab showing all the requests that have been made for any credentials. You can see in the following screenshot the **Credentials** interface showing the three different tabs:

Credentials
MY CREDENTIALS
MY LOCKERS
CREDENTIAL REQUESTS
Search

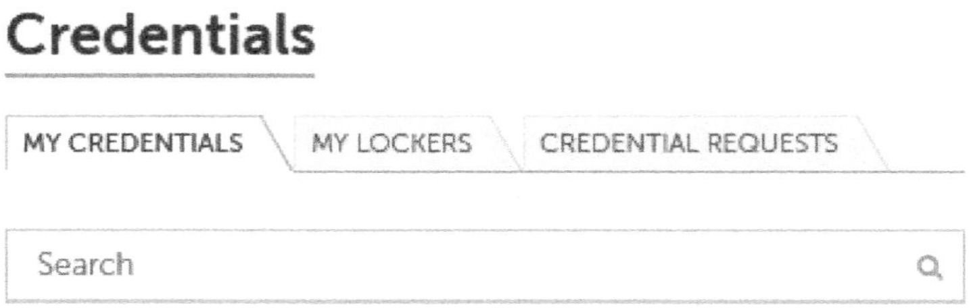

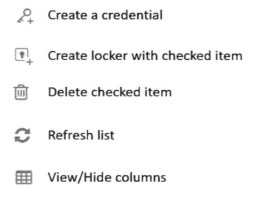

Figure 3.12 – Credentials tabs

The options available for credentials are shown in the following screenshot:

Create a credential
Create locker with checked item
Delete checked item
Refresh list
View/Hide columns

Figure 3.13 – Credential options

When we build a bot, it performs a series of actions. Automation Anywhere has hundreds of these actions available. They are all categorized into groups that are known as **packages**.

Global values

Global values is a way to configure constant values that can be used multiple times by multiple bots. This feature is not available with the Community version that we are using.

Packages

A package is essentially a group of actions available to build the tasks you want to perform. This list can be customized to view or hide columns as needed. A **Search** facility is also available to help find the required package, as shown in the following screenshot:

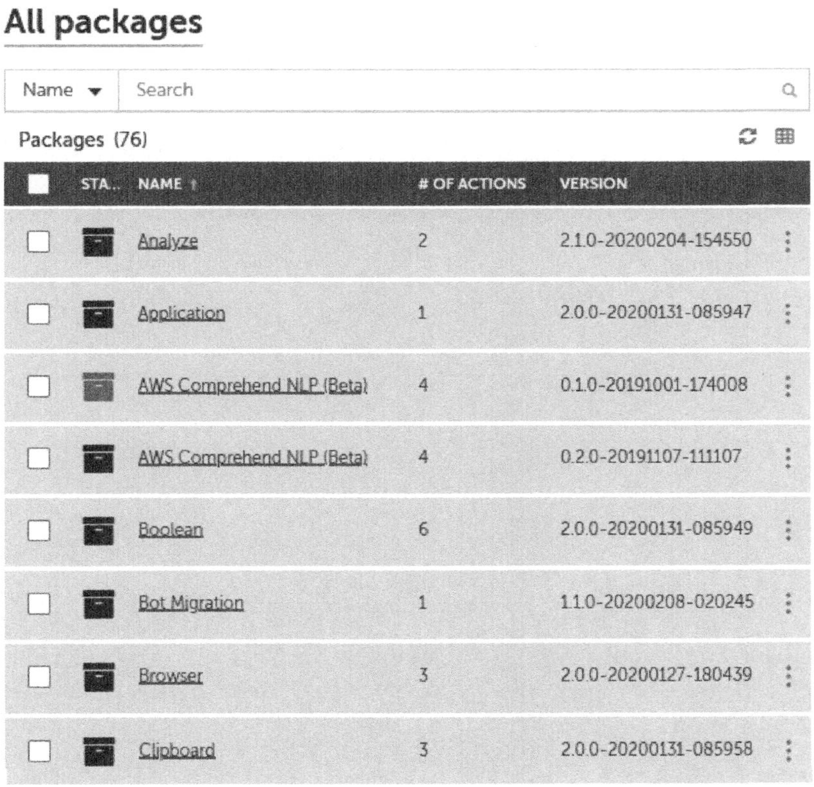

All packages

	STA..	NAME ↑	# OF ACTIONS	VERSION	
☐		Analyze	2	2.1.0-20200204-154550	⋮
☐		Application	1	2.0.0-20200131-085947	⋮
☐		AWS Comprehend NLP (Beta)	4	0.1.0-20191001-174008	⋮
☐		AWS Comprehend NLP (Beta)	4	0.2.0-20191107-111107	⋮
☐		Boolean	6	2.0.0-20200131-085949	⋮
☐		Bot Migration	1	1.1.0-20200208-020245	⋮
☐		Browser	3	2.0.0-20200127-180439	⋮
☐		Clipboard	3	2.0.0-20200131-085958	⋮

Name ▼   Search   🔍

Packages (76)

Figure 3.14 – Packages interface

Each package may have several versions. These can be managed, allowing specific versions to be used for each bot. From the preceding package list, you can see how many actions each package consists of. You will see the following options for each package:

- **Versions available**
- **Actions available**
- **Iterators available**

As new actions are added or old ones are superseded, any version of a particular package can be used. The version is selected via the drop-down version selection menu in the top pane.

The following screenshot shows the **Email** package as an example. The package details show the package version at the top, followed by actions and iterators:

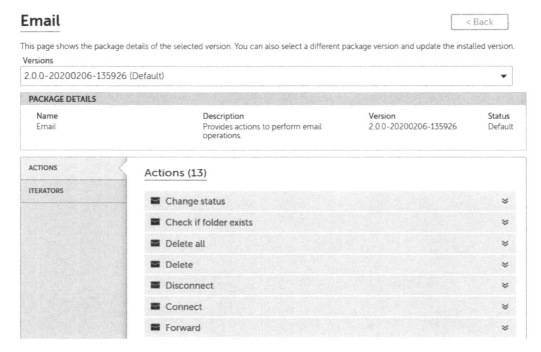

Figure 3.15 – Example of Email package versions

You can see the list of actions that the bot can use when working with email automation. This is a comprehensive list, including actions such as **Change status**, **Delete**, **Forward**, **Reply**, **Send**, and so on.

In the following screenshot, we can see that an iterator is also available to help with our bot:

Figure 3.16 – Iteration options

This means a pre-defined function is available that will loop through a specified mailbox. As packages are updated and new ones available, this will be presented here in the **Packages** sub-section. This is all done automatically, as Automation Anywhere is a cloud-based application.

Once bots are built, they need to be deployed to a device. In the next section, we will look at **My devices**.

Managing your devices

Building bots aside, we need to deploy them to desktops. These can come in the form of laptops, desktop machines, virtual machines, and so on. In this section, all your devices are listed. Every device that needs to be deployed should be on this list. By selecting the **MY DEVICES** option from the menu pane, you will see the following interface:

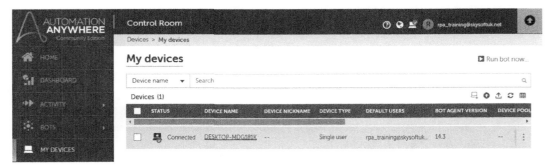

Figure 3.17 – The My devices interface

To set this up, a device needs to be installed with a Bot agent and registered and connected to the control room.

In the previous chapter, we went through the process of setting a device up and connecting it to the **Control Room**. All your devices that are available on the network can be set up in the same way.

After your devices are set up, the users need to be set up and configured. User setup is done through the administration section.

Managing user administration

This is the centralized location where all users are set up. You can set the type of user, as well as allocate the type of license for them. By selecting **Users** from the **ADMINISTRATION** option on the menu pane, you will see the following interface:

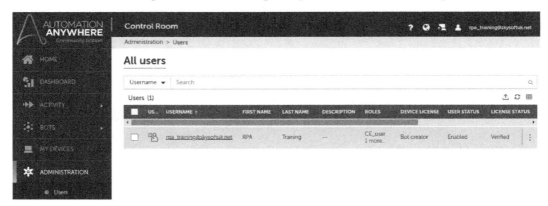

Figure 3.18 – Administration: Users interface

Each user can be configured and roles can be allocated. By selecting or creating a user, you can configure all the details shown in the following screenshot:

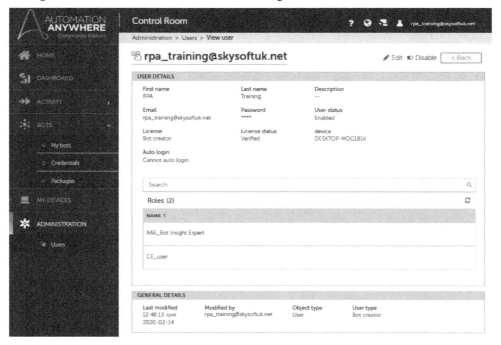

Figure 3.19 – User details

All users are managed here. You can assign a specific role to a user, such as Bot agent (Bot agents have no access to the underlying code but can only run a bot), bot creator, and custom-defined roles. Also, a different device can be allocated to each user.

The easy-to-use intuitive interface of Automation Anywhere **Control Room** makes managing bots, devices, and users very easy.

Summary

You should now be comfortable with Automation Anywhere's user interface, having a clearer understanding of all the configurations needed to design and support your bot. You will understand why features such as security, reusability, and a simple interface make Automation Anywhere an award-winning RPA tool and one of the industry leaders. You should now have an overview of the **Control Room** interface and its features.

In the next chapter, we will look at the development interface. You will learn how to navigate the hundreds of actions available, as well as the different methods available to build a bot. Automation Anywhere provides a graphical interface to map out a process as well as a drag-and-drop-based option. These are the three methods for building and designing a bot: *Flow*, *List*, and *Dual*. You will also understand bot packages in more detail, as well as dependencies and properties.

All this will set you up to start building your first working bot using Automation Anywhere A2019.

.

4

Overview of the Automation Anywhere Development Interface

With all software development platforms, it is vital that you understand the development interface. This interface is where you convert logical steps into instructional steps. In the past, most programming languages used some form of scripting. This is where you write your code while adhering to a very specific structure. The structure is dependent on the programming language used. Development in Automation Anywhere varies from this standard. It doesn't involve writing instructions using scripts. The Automation Anywhere development interface allows the developer to drag and drop instructions. These instructions have properties and attributes that are configured to perform specific actions.

In the previous chapter, you got an overview of the **Control Room** interface. Hopefully, you feel confident in navigating the different sections of Automation Anywhere. As you have learned about setting up users and managing bots, you must be keen to learn about actually building bots. In this chapter, you will learn about the development interface. We will take a close look at what functionality bots can perform, as well as how to deploy these actions. We will also look at the whole interface and what other tools are available to enhance and help with your bot development, including debugging and triggers. As well as the interface, we will also explore a number of basic programming techniques including variables, actions, and triggers.

In this chapter, we will cover the following topics:

- Bot development interface
- What can a bot do?
- Programming techniques using Automation Anywhere
- Variables and triggers
- Debugging and dependencies

Technical requirements

In order to install the Automation Anywhere Bot agent, the following is required:

- Windows OS version 7 or higher
- A processor with a minimum speed of 3 GHz
- A minimum of 4 GB RAM
- At least 100 MB of hard disk space
- Web browser: Internet Explorer v10 or higher *or* Chrome v49 or higher
- A minimum screen resolution of 1024*768
- An internet connection with a minimum speed of 10 Mb/sec
- Completed registration with Automation Anywhere A2019 Community Edition
- Successful logon to Automation Anywhere A2019 Community Edition
- Successful registration of a local device

Bot development interface

The development interface is where all the magic happens. This is where bots are created, edited, and debugged. In order to look at what it has to offer, you need to start by creating a new bot. Let's dive straight into creating a bot so that we can explore the development interface.

Creating a new bot

There are a number of shortcuts available to create a new bot. The following steps will guide you through the process of creating a new bot:

1. Log in to the **Control Room**.

2. Navigate to the **BOTS** section.

3. Select the **My bots** sub-section:

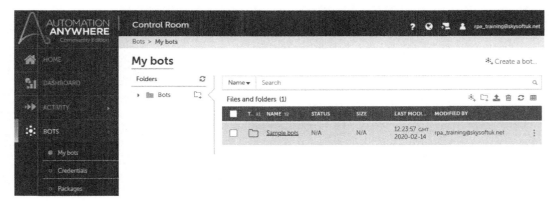

Figure 4.1 – The My bots interface

4. Click on the **Create a bot** icon from the icon options in the top-right corner:

Create a bot...
Create a bot...

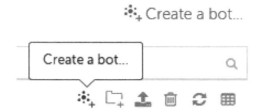

Figure 4.2 – Creating a new bot

5. The following bot properties dialog is presented:

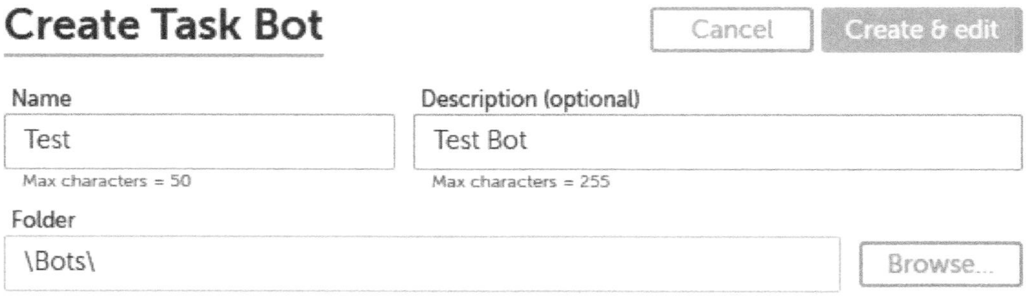

Create Task Bot
Cancel
Create & edit
Name
Test
Max characters = 50
Description (optional)
Test Bot
Max characters = 255
Folder
\Bots\
Browse...

Figure 4.3 – Bot properties dialog

6. Set the following properties for your bot:

   Name: `Test`

   Description (optional): `Test Bot`

   Folder: `\Bots\`

7. Click on the **Create & edit** button. This will open the development interface:

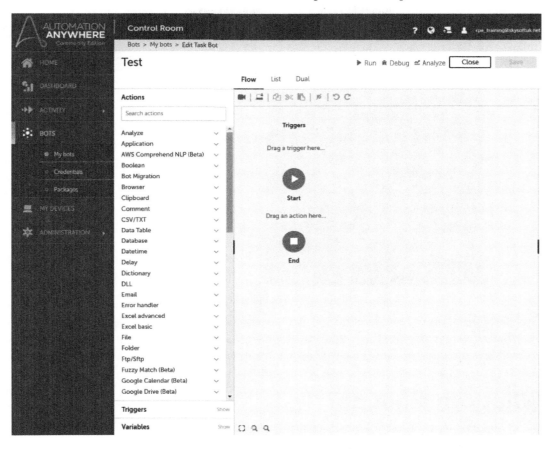

Figure 4.4 – Development interface

8. We can hide the sections menu pane in order to get a better view of the development interface. Just click on the collapse icon at the top of the screen.

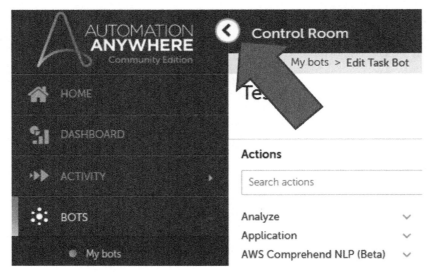

Figure 4.5 – The collapse icon

Great! You have now created a new bot and have access to the full development interface. So, what's the next step? In the next section, we will look at what functionality is available. You will learn about some of the key tasks your bot will be able to automate.

What can a bot do?

We are now ready to start looking at what functionality Automation Anywhere offers as regards bot development. There are hundreds of actions available to help automate your tasks. All the options are listed on the left pane. These actions are grouped into categories known as **packages**. Each package is a collection of individual actions. Here you can see the list pane showing all the available packages:

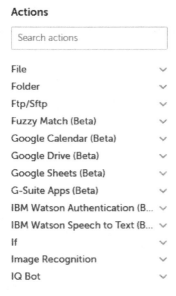

Actions

| Search actions |

File	⌄
Folder	⌄
Ftp/Sftp	⌄
Fuzzy Match (Beta)	⌄
Google Calendar (Beta)	⌄
Google Drive (Beta)	⌄
Google Sheets (Beta)	⌄
G-Suite Apps (Beta)	⌄
IBM Watson Authentication (B...	⌄
IBM Watson Speech to Text (B...	⌄
If	⌄
Image Recognition	⌄
IQ Bot	⌄

Figure 4.6 – The packages list pane

You can see all the packages and actions available in this list. This list is in alphabetical order and is searchable, allowing quick access to your actions. Each package can be expanded or collapsed to view or hide the actions available. As you can see, the usual functionality available in most programming languages is available, including the following:

- Working with files and folders

- Conditional logic operands, that is, if/else

- Iterations

- Text manipulation

In addition, there are packages with more advanced actions that are not always available as standard functions of most common programming languages. Some of these advanced packages include the following:

- IBM Watson Speech to Text

- Image recognition

- Fuzzy matching

- G-Suite apps

- MS LYUIS **NLP (Natural Language Processing)**

In the packages list pane, you'll find a comprehensive list of packages that will allow your bots to perform almost any foreseeable task. In some cases, we may come across an action that may not be available in the list. Automation Anywhere has thought of this and does have packages to help overcome this. You can call VBScript and Python scripts directly. This is a fully featured action allowing you to pass parameters to and from your scripts. If you need more functionality, Automation Anywhere also allows you to work directly with independent DLLs. You can use distributed DLLs as well as creating your own using a standard suitable development platform.

You can see now what actions your bot will be able to perform. In the next section, we will look at how to implement these actions using Automation Anywhere. There are a number of techniques available to deploy actions to build your bot functionality.

Programming techniques using Automation Anywhere

Building tasks for your bot using Automation Anywhere is comparatively easier than other scripting languages, such as VBScript, JavaScript, or Python. To make a bot perform a task, you give it a list of actions. These actions are executed in a sequential manner. To put it simply, the bot will run through a list of actions. These actions, put together, become a task. The complete list is what makes a taskbot.

There are three different ways to visualize your bot actions. These are Flow, List, and Dual. The default view is Flow when you initially create a bot. You can switch between the three ways by selecting the desired tab located on the top pane of the interface, as shown in the following screenshot:

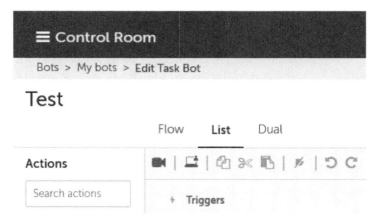

Figure 4.7 – Bot development visual aids

Let's explore the three views in more detail. Before we do this, we will add a simple action for the bot to perform. We will add a message box; the following steps will walk you through the process of adding a message box action:

1. Select the **List** view from the view selection tab at the top and expand the **Message box** package:

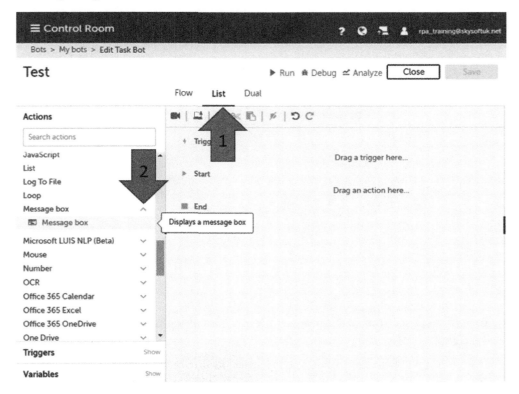

Figure 4.8 – List view

2. Drag and drop the **Message box** action to the development pane, between **Start** and **End**:

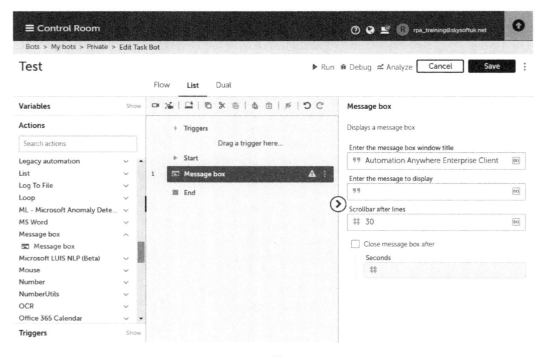

Figure 4.9 – Adding an action

3. You will now see your first action set for your bot along with the properties pane on the right.

4. This action needs to be configured by setting its attributes and properties. The properties available will vary depending on the type of action.

5. Set the following properties for the **Message box** action:

Figure 4.10 – Message box properties

6. As this action is the first instruction for your bot, it is set as instruction number 1. Every action you set will have a number. This is also referred to as a line number.

7. You can collapse the properties pane when you are not using it. Just hover over and click the collapse icon to hide it:

Figure 4.11 – The collapse icon

You have now created a bot that will perform a very basic task of displaying a **Message box**. We can take a look at the different views available to help us build our functionality further.

List view

You have used this so far to add the **Message box** action. In this view, all actions are listed, similar to a script. The line number provides the logical workflow of the task:

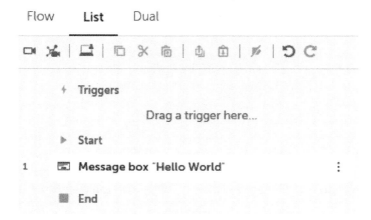

Figure 4.12 – Development interface – List view

You can also see the same task represented graphically. This is effected by using the **Flow** view.

Flow view

The **Flow** view shows your task actions as a flowchart. As you can see, this provides a more visual process flow of how your bot works through the workflow. The line numbers are omitted as they are not necessary:

Figure 4.13 – Development interface – Flow view

You can change the size of the flow diagram using the sizing options on the bottom left. These options are as follows:

Figure 4.14 – Flow view options

An alternative view is the **Dual** view. This is a combination of both the **List** and **Flow** views.

Dual view

You are shown both views here side by side. This gives the best of both worlds. The views are totally synchronized with one another. If you select an action on either view, it will also be selected in the other view. This makes navigation and editing much easier:

Figure 4.15 – Development interface – Dual view

By selecting any action on any view, the properties window will appear on the left to edit. To add actions while using the **Flow** view independently or in **Dual**, you simply drag and drop the action to the required position.

Whenever you want to execute a bot, it needs to be saved. A bot will always be executed from the last saved version. Let's test our bot so far:

1. Click on the **Save** button in the top-right pane:

Figure 4.16 – Bot options

2. Click on **Run** to execute the bot.

3. While the bot is executing, a progress window will appear in the bottom-left corner. This shows what line number the bot is currently running. This progress window gives a real-time view of what action is being performed. It is useful for testing and debugging your bot:

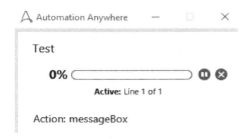

Figure 4.17 – Bot execution progress box

4. The **Message Box** should be displayed as your bot runs the action:

Figure 4.18 – Message box in action

5. Click on the **Close** button in **Message Box**. Once the bot has completed, you will be presented with the following:

Figure 4.19 – Successful execution message

Congratulations on building a simple bot and running it successfully! In the next section, we will be looking at variables and triggers. These are essential to any type of development.

Variables and triggers

As we build more functionalities, we will need to understand how to use the basics of programming. One of the key elements of programming is assigning and reading variables. Automation Anywhere A2019 can handle a variety of variable types, including numeric, string, list, array, date, and Boolean. We will demonstrate how to create, assign, and read a variable through the following walk-through:

1. Click on **Show** for the **Variables** tab from the option pane on the left:

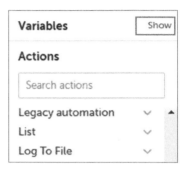

Figure 4.20 – Viewing variables

2. Click on the + icon to create a new variable:

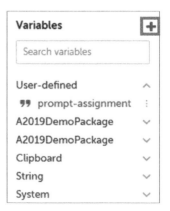

Figure 4.21 – Adding a new variable

3. This will launch the **Create variable** dialog box:

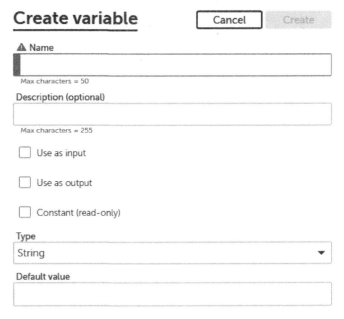

Figure 4.22 – The Create variable dialog box

4. You will notice from the **Type** variable drop-down list all the different data types that are available for your variables:

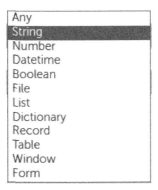

Figure 4.23 – Variable data types

5. Set the following properties to create a new variable:

    Name: strName

    Type: **String**

    Default Value: *(Enter your name)*

The **Create variable** dialog box should look similar to this:

Figure 4.24 – Create variable properties

6. Click on **Create** and then click on **Save**.

7. Select the **Message box** action on line **1** that we created earlier so the properties can be updated to include the `strName` variable value:

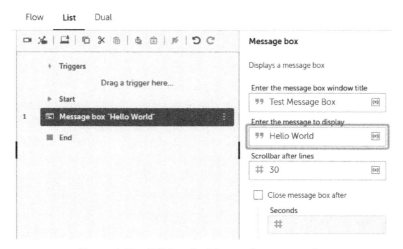

Figure 4.25 – Editing the Message box properties

8. Modify the following property value:

   Enter the message to display: `Hello $strName$`

9. The property value should look like this:

Figure 4.26 – Updated property value

10. Click on **Save**.

11. Now, let's run the bot by clicking on **Run**. You should get a **Message Box** with your name:

Figure 4.27 – Output message from the bot

You have successfully created a `String` type variable and assigned your name to it. The value was read by the bot and output to a **Message Box**.

We will now take a look at triggers. Once a bot is built, we may need to execute it when a specific event occurs. This is often when a specific file or folder is created, deleted, or modified. We will create a trigger, setting our bot to run when a specific file is modified. Perform the following steps to create this trigger:

1. Create the following folder: `C:\RPA\`.

2. Create a text file in this folder called `TriggerFile.txt`. We now have a file that can be used to initiate a trigger.

3. Click on **Show** on the **Triggers** tab from the option pane on the left:

Figure 4.28 – Viewing Triggers

4. Expand the **Files & folders** trigger group:

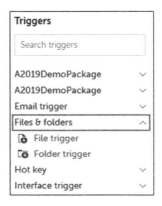

Figure 4.29 – Trigger groups

5. To create a new file trigger, select and drag the **File trigger** option to the **Triggers** section in your development window. Your interface should look like this:

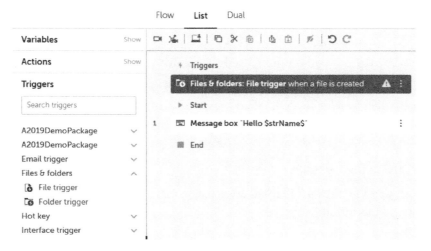

Figure 4.30 – Adding a file trigger

6. Set the following properties for the new **Files & folders: File trigger**:

   File: `C:\RPA\TriggerFile.txt`

   Start the bot when the file is…: modified

   The trigger properties should look similar to this:

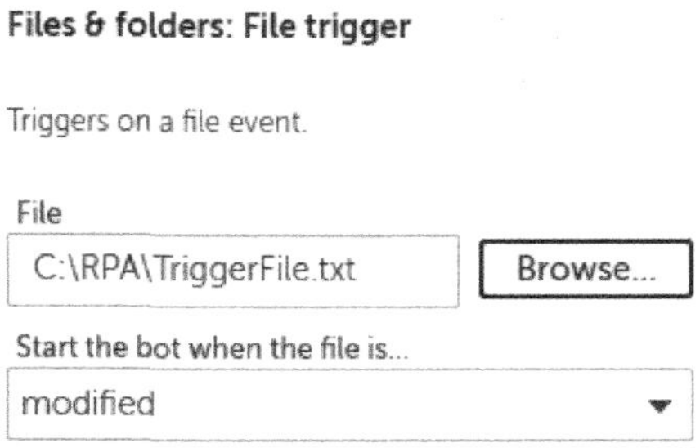

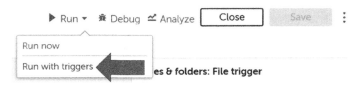

Figure 4.31 – File trigger properties

7. Click on **Save**.

8. To run the bot with triggers, click on **Run** and, from the dropdown, select **Run with triggers**:

Figure 4.32 – Running a bot with a trigger

9. The bot will be deployed to your device. It will then wait for the trigger event to be true. This is known as listening for triggers. The following message box should appear as it listens for the trigger:

Figure 4.33 – The Listening for triggers… message box

10. Open, edit, and save the `TriggerFile.txt` trigger file that we created. You will notice the bot start and execute once you have saved the file:

Figure 4.34 – Successful execution message

Great! You have now successfully added a trigger to your bot. You can add multiple triggers if required. In the next section, we will be taking a look at debugging and assigning dependencies to your bots.

Debugging and dependencies

Once we have built a bot, it needs to be tested. Being able to identify the root cause of any issue requires good troubleshooting skills. In order to help us troubleshoot, Automation Anywhere has a debugging tool. It allows you to go through each line one by one, so you can examine the taskbot status in more detail before moving on to the next line.

We will need to edit our current bot so that it flows end to end with no user interactions. Also, we need to add a few more actions as it only has one action at the moment. To make the message box automatically close without waiting for a user response, we can set a duration that we would like the message to be displayed for before it closes. To do this, perform the following steps:

1. Navigate to the properties of our **Message box** action on line **1** and update the following properties:

Figure 4.35 – Updated Message box properties

2. Click on **Save**.

3. We need to add more actions, so we will copy and paste the existing message box action three times. To do this, click on the three dots on the action line **1** and select the **Copy action** option:

Figure 4.36 – Copying action lines

4. Click on the three dots on the action line **1** again, and this time select **Paste after action**:

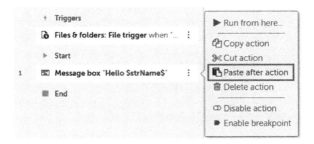

Figure 4.37 – Pasting action lines

5. Repeat step *4* two more times. The development interface should look like this:

Figure 4.38 – Development interface

6. Click on **Save** and run the bot without triggers by selecting **Run now**. The bot should go through the series of message boxes without any intervention from you.

7. Switch to debug mode by clicking on **Debug** from the top-right menu:

Figure 4.39 – Switching to debug mode

8. Once in debug mode, you can run the bot from the start icon above the development window, as shown in the following screenshot:

Figure 4.40 – Running the bot from debug mode

9. Again, the bot will run through all the message boxes without your intervention.

10. To help with debugging, we will add a breakpoint. A *breakpoint* is a flag on an action line that instructs the bot to pause. While it is paused, we can examine variable values. We will add a breakpoint to the **Message box action** on line **3**. To do this, select **Enable breakpoint** from the action line options:

Figure 4.41 – Adding a breakpoint

11. Click on **Save**.

12. Now run the bot and you will notice the bot pause at the breakpoint action:

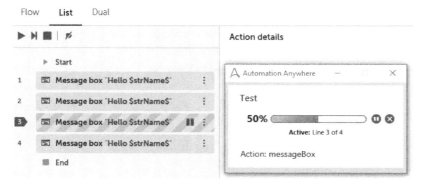

Figure 4.42 – Bot reaching a breakpoint

13. The breakpoint also allows you to view any values assigned variables during runtime:

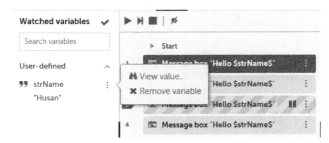

Figure 4.43 – Variable values at breakpoint

14. To continue, just click on the play button at the top. The bot will carry on executing to the next action.

15. Once the bot has completed, we can exit debug mode by clicking on **Exit debug** to take you back to the normal development interface:

Figure 4.44 – Exiting debug mode

16. The breakpoint will still be enabled even when the bot is not in debug mode. Remember to disable this. This can be done from the **Disable breakpoint** line option:

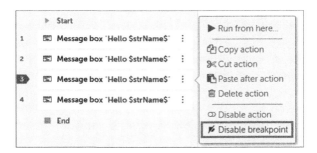

Figure 4.45 – Disabling a breakpoint

You should now have a clearer understanding of how to work with debugging your bot. Another element that may apply to your bot is dependencies. There may be certain files that need to be in place in order for your bot to perform its tasks successfully. These files are described as dependencies as the bot is dependent on them.

The following steps will walk through how to navigate to the dependency interface:

1. From the bot properties options menu in the top-right corner of the screen, select **Dependencies**:

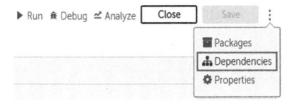

Figure 4.46 – Bot dependencies

2. The **Dependencies** interface is split into two sections – file selection on the left and selected files on the right. To select a file as a dependent file, you would navigate to it using the folder structure. Then, add it to the list on the right:

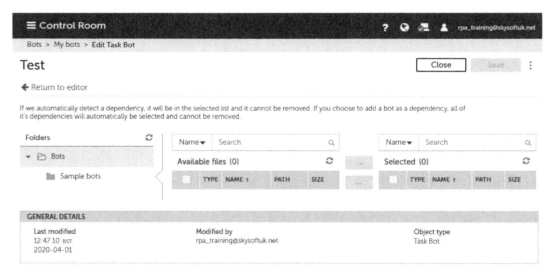

Figure 4.47 – Bot dependency interface

Once all dependencies are set, you can navigate back to the editor from the top-left icon. You should now be confident in using the different areas of the development interface and be comfortable in creating new bots and setting variables and triggers.

Summary

You should now be comfortable with the Automation Anywhere development interface. We have gone through creating a simple bot. You have created variables and triggers for your bot. In addition, you have also acquired some hands-on experience of using the debugging tool for Automation Anywhere. Having created your initial bot and gotten an overview of all the other actions available, you must be keen to start implementing more complex actions in your bot. You have also gained knowledge of how to use the different views while building a bot. Apply the view that works best for you.

In the next chapter, we will build a bot using a number of more complex actions. You will learn about working with data and files. This is just the start of your RPA development experience. It will use a practical step-by-step process to guide you. By the end, you will be confident in using Automation Anywhere to start building your bots.

5
Building Your First Bot

As a bot developer, you will use many of the different actions available to you. We have already looked at implementing a simple **Message box**. Although this shows how to apply an action, it doesn't really perform any task. In the real world, bots perform tasks that are usually done by humans. These tasks are often tedious, boring, and repetitive. To really learn how to build fully functional bots, we need a task that would be ideal for automation.

You should now be familiar with the development interface. In the previous chapter, we looked at the different views for visualizing your bot as you built it. You also got a glimpse of all the actions available to help automate your tasks.

In this chapter, we will expand on this knowledge. We will take a real-life business case, a relatively simple process, with the aim of fully automating it. The process will involve including, reading, and creating a CSV file, as well as carrying out some basic arithmetic calculations.

Such scenarios need sample data to work with. There is a GitHub repository available that contains all the sample data to accompany this book. It also has all the source code for reference. Before you start to build your bot, you are guided on how to download this repository from GitHub. This data will also be needed for the forthcoming chapters.

By the end of this chapter, you will have built your own RPA fully functioning bot. You will have learned how to take a user story and build a bot specification. With regard to bot functions, you will know how to make a bot perform actions such as reading and writing CSV files and performing calculations.

In this chapter, we will cover the following topics:

- Downloading sample data from GitHub
- Understanding your automation task
- Creating and reading a CSV file
- Performing basic arithmetic calculations
- Appending records to a CSV file

Technical requirements

In order to install Automation Anywhere A2019 Bot agent, the following is required:

- Windows OS version 7 or higher
- A processor with a minimum speed of 3 GHz
- A minimum of 4 GB RAM
- At least 100 MB of hard disk space
- Internet Explorer v10 or higher OR Chrome v49 or higher
- A minimum screen resolution of 1024*768
- An internet connection with a minimum speed of 10 Mb/sec
- Completed registration with Automation Anywhere A2019 Community Edition
- Successful login to Automation Anywhere A2019 Community Edition
- Successful registration of a local device

Downloading sample data from GitHub

GitHub provides a public repository for files and source code files. This is ideal for hosting the necessary accompanying files for this book. I would recommend you download the whole file structure to your root folder. I use my C:\ drive as my root folder. The book will be referring to this folder to help identify the location of files that will be needed. You do not need a GitHub account to download the repository.

To download the complete repository needed for this book, perform the following steps:

1. Navigate to the GitHub repository from your web browser using the following link: `https://github.com/RPA-Training/Hands-On-RPA-with-AA/tree/Sample-Data`:

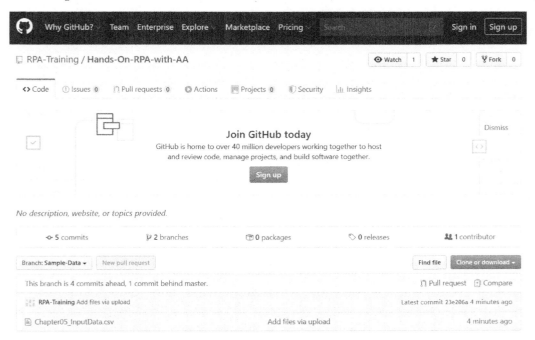

Figure 5.1 – GitHub repository

2. To download, click on the green **Clone or download** button. This will open a small dialog box, and then click on **Download ZIP**:

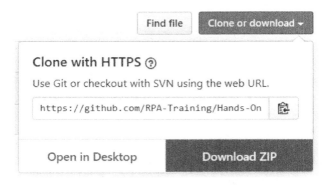

Figure 5.2 – Repository download dialog

3.   This will begin the downloading of the compressed `Hands-On-RPA-with-AA-Sample-Data.zip` file.

4.   Once the ZIP file has been downloaded, extract it all to your root folder. If you use `C:\` as your root folder, you will have the following path: `C:\Hands-On-RPA-with-AA-Sample-Data\`.

5.   Close the GitHub page.

You will now have the sample data file needed for your first bot. Before we build the bot, it is important that you understand the manual task that is to be automated. In the next section, we will get a good understanding of the steps we will need to automate for our bot.

Understanding your automation task

The purpose of using software robots is to make our life easier by freeing up valuable time. In this section, we will outline the manual process that will be used for our first bot. Mapping a step-by-step process of the manual task is known as a user story. This bot will execute the process end to end automatically. We will start by drafting a quick user story of this task.

This bot is based on a manual task performed by John, who works within a loans department of a finance company. The process executes as follows:

1.   John creates a new empty CSV file called `Chapter05_Output.csv`.

2.   A daily CSV file is available on a shared drive, `Chapter05_Input.csv`.

3.   John will open this file and read each record. This record has the following fields: `Reference`, `Amount`, `Years`, and `Interest`.

4.   John calculates the monthly payment by using the following formula: *(Amount + Interest)/ (Years x 12)*.

5.   John adds a record for each calculation in the new `Chapter05_Output.csv` file containing the following fields: `Reference` and `Monthly Payment`.

6.   The process ends.

This user story will be used as a process design for our bot. We can break this down to create a logical specification as follows using pseudocode. Pseudocode is used when you identify the logical steps of a process using simple plain English:

1. Create a new `Chapter05_Output.CSV` file.

2. Open the existing `Chapter05_Input.CSV` file.

3. Loop through all the records in the `Chapter05_Input.CSV` file.

4. Read the entire record to variables.

5. Calculate `Monthly Payment` using *(Amount + Interest)/ (Years x 12)*.

6. Add the new record to the `Chapter05_Output.CSV` file.

7. End looping.

8. Close the `Chapter05_Input.CSV` file.

In the next section, we will start building the bot. As we now have a design, we can start by building each step as a building block.

Creating your first bot

You will now start to build your first bot. Just follow the step-by-step instructions to guide you through the process. We know the tasks that the bot needs to perform. Before we apply this, it's always good practice to build a skeleton of the whole task using comments. This ensures that we won't miss any crucial functionality out and also acts as a template for all the actions.

Let's start by creating a new bot in **List** view:

1. Log in to **Control Room**.

2. Create a new bot and call it `Chapter 5 - FirstBot` in the `\Bot\` folder.

3. Add a **Comment** action as line **1**; we will use this as our bot description comment.

4. Set the **Comment** property's text as `"Task: Calculate Monthly Loan Payment to new CSV File"`.

5. Click on **Save**. The development interface should look like this:

> ▶ Start

1   📝 Comment 'Task: Calculate Monthly Loan Payment to new CSV File' ⋮

▦ End

Figure 5.3 – FirstBot initial comment action

6. Add a new **Comment** action as `"Create output csv file"` on line **2** and click on **Save**.

7. Add a new **Comment** action as `"Open csv file"` on line **3** and click on **Save**.

8. Add a new **Comment** action as `"Loop through records"` on line **4** and click on **Save**.

9. Add a new **Comment** action as `"Read record to variables"` on line **5** and click on **Save**.

10. Add a new **Comment** action as `"Calculate values"` on line **6** and click on **Save**.

11. Add a new **Comment** action as `"Add new record to output file"` on line **7** and click on **Save**.

12. Add a new **Comment** action as `"End Looping"` on line **8** and click on **Save**.

13. Add a new **Comment** action as `"Close csv file"` on line **9** and click on **Save**.

Your bot should look something like this:

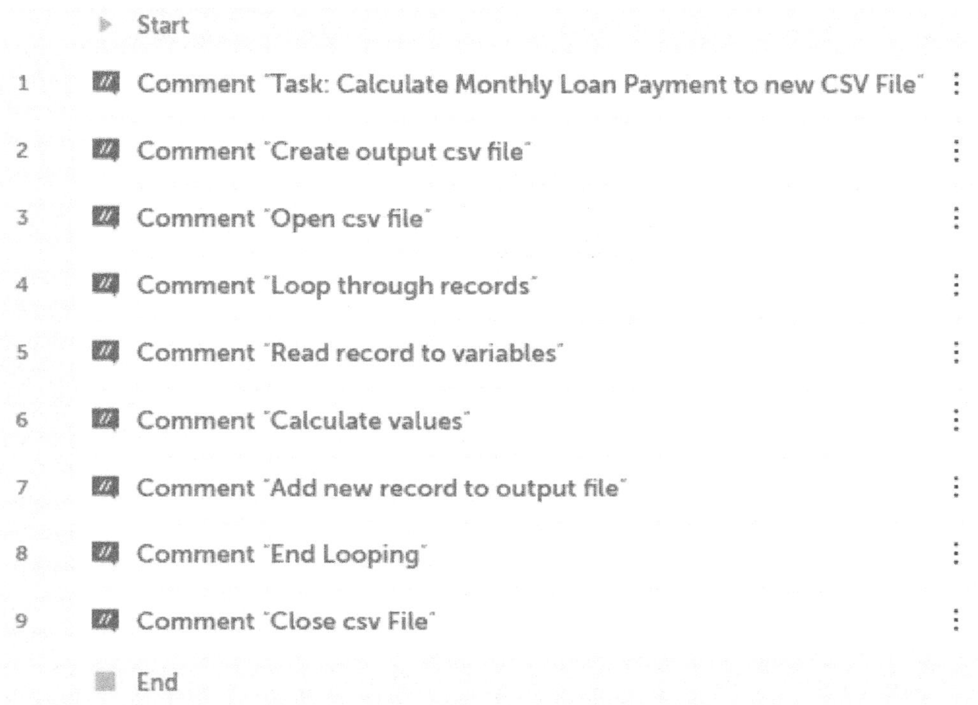

▶ Start

1   ▨ Comment "Task: Calculate Monthly Loan Payment to new CSV File"   ⋮

2   ▨ Comment "Create output csv file"   ⋮

3   ▨ Comment "Open csv file"   ⋮

4   ▨ Comment "Loop through records"   ⋮

5   ▨ Comment "Read record to variables"   ⋮

6   ▨ Comment "Calculate values"   ⋮

7   ▨ Comment "Add new record to output file"   ⋮

8   ▨ Comment "End Looping"   ⋮

9   ▨ Comment "Close csv File"   ⋮

▨ End

Figure 5.4 – FirstBot all the comment actions

The bot doesn't actually do anything yet, but we have used comments as a kind of map of what we need to develop and its sequence. The comments also make the bot more readable when it comes to understanding and troubleshooting.

Before we start to add any more actions, let's have a look at the structure our bot will take. From the specification, we can break the complete task down into sub-sections. This would look as follows:

1. Creating bot variables
2. Creating a CSV file
3. Opening and closing a CSV file
4. Looping through rows in a CSV file

5. Reading record values

6. Performing basic arithmetic calculations

7. Adding records to a CSV file

In the next section, we will start by creating the variables we need for our bot.

Creating bot variables

As we have a good understanding of the task for our bot, we are in a good position. This means that we can create all the variables our bot needs before we actually apply any further actions. A good design will always mean most, if not all, of the variables can be created initially.

When the CSV file is read, we will need variables to store the following: `Reference` (`string`), `Amount` (`number`), and `Years` (`number`). These values will be read from each record. A record is a row within the CSV file, so another variable will be needed to store this record. The data type used for this is called a `Record` in Automation Anywhere. We will also need variables to calculate and store `Monthly Payment` (`number`).

To create the variables, perform the following steps:

1. Click on the **Show** option for the **Variables** tab from the option pane on the left:

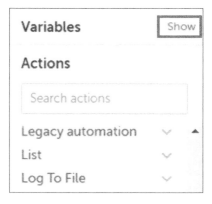

Figure 5.5 – Viewing the Variables tab

2. Click on the + icon to create a variable:

Actions
Show
Triggers
Create variable...
Variables
Search variables

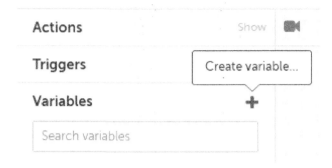

Figure 5.6 – Creating a new variable

The **Create variable** dialog will appear. Give your new variable the name `strRef`, set it as a `String` type, and then click on **Create**:

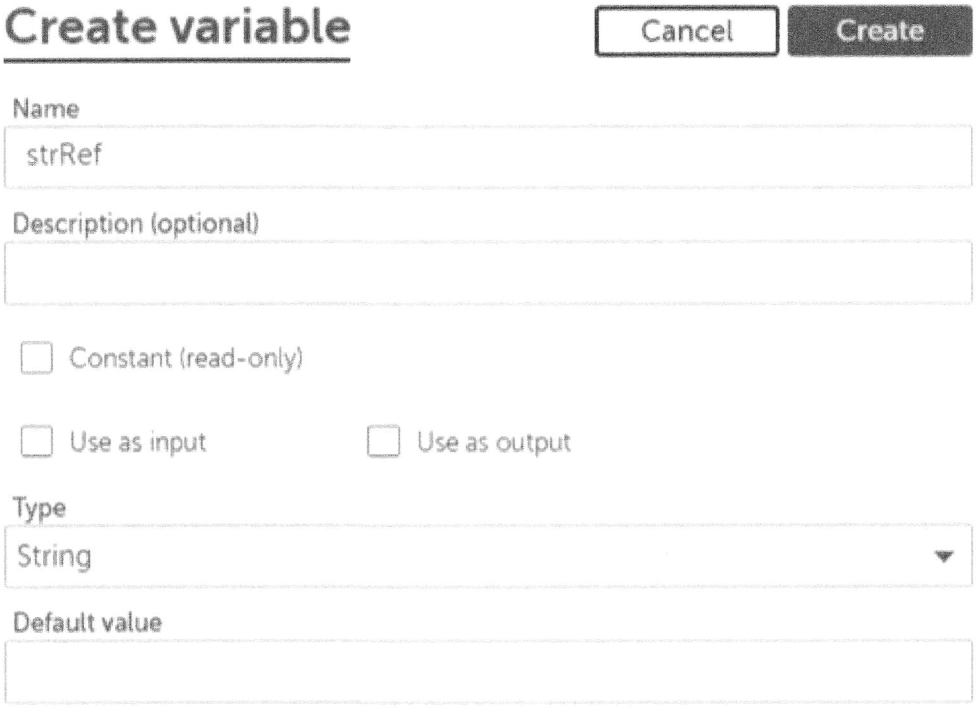
Create variable
Cancel
Create
Name
strRef
Description (optional)
Constant (read-only)
Use as input
Use as output
Type
String
Default value

Figure 5.7 – Creating a variable dialog

3. Create another new variable named numAmount as the Number type.

4. Create another new variable named numYears as the Number type.

5. Create another new variable named numInterest as the Number type.

6. Create another new variable named numMonthly as the Number type.

7. Create another new variable named strMonthly as the String type.

8. Create another new variable named recLoan as the Record type.

You should now have created the following seven variables:

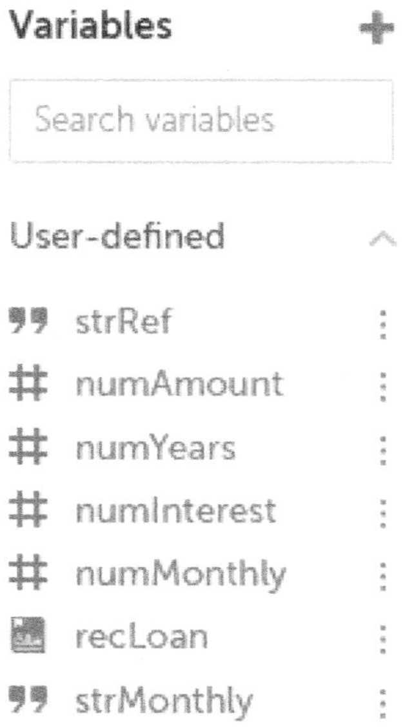

Variables   ✚

Search variables

User-defined   ⌃

" strRef   ⋮

numAmount   ⋮

numYears   ⋮

numInterest   ⋮

numMonthly   ⋮

▦ recLoan   ⋮

" strMonthly   ⋮

Figure 5.8 – List of created variables

All the required variables have now been created. We are ready to start giving the bot instructions to perform actions. Automation Anywhere uses **packages**, which are groups of actions. Each action is an instruction telling the bot to do something. In the next section, we will start building the actions for our bot.

Creating and reading a CSV file

From our comments, we can see that the first action the bot performs is to create an output CSV file. This is the file that will have Reference Number and Monthly Payment. A new record will be appended to this file every time new values are calculated. We create this file first because the bot will be in a loop when it is processing each record. The file only needs to be created once and we can add the headers in when we create it.

In this scenario, we can use the **Log to file** action as we will not be reading the output file, just creating and appending to it. This is the simplest action to achieve what we require.

To create the CSV file with headers, perform the following steps:

1. Drag the **Log to file** action just below line number **2**.

    Your bot development interface in **List** view should look like this:

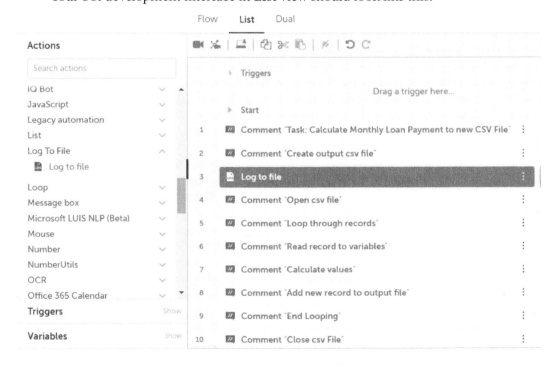

Figure 5.9 – Adding the Log to file action

2. Set the following properties for the **Log to file** action on line **3**:

File path: `C:\Hands-On-RPA-with-AA-Sample-Data\Chapter05_Output.csv`

Enter text to log: `Reference, Monthly Amount`

When logging: **Overwrite existing log file**

The action properties dialog should look like this:

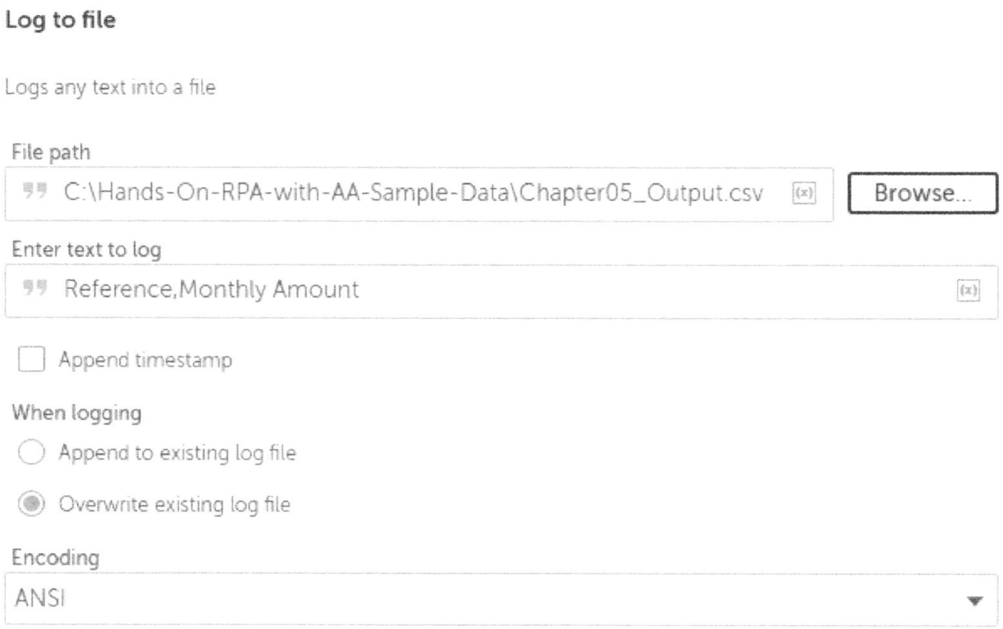

Log to file

Logs any text into a file

File path

`C:\Hands-On-RPA-with-AA-Sample-Data\Chapter05_Output.csv`   (x)   Browse...

Enter text to log

`Reference,Monthly Amount`   (x)

☐ Append timestamp

When logging

○ Append to existing log file

◉ Overwrite existing log file

Encoding

ANSI   ▼

Figure 5.10 – Log to file: The action properties dialog

3. Click on **Save**.

That's great! Your bot should now create a new CSV file with headers ready to have new records added. To test the bot, you can run it. Upon completion, the bot should create the `Chapter05_Output.csv` file.

Now we know how to create a simple CSV/text file. This can be used for creating a process log as well as a data file, as we have done in this instance. The next section is about opening and closing a CSV file.

Opening and closing a CSV file

From the design, we know we need to open the input CSV file. This is a file with some sample data and is available from GitHub. You should have the sample data already downloaded from GitHub and in your root folder. I am using the `C:\` drive as my root folder. You need to refer to the folder to which you downloaded the sample data.

To get the bot to open and close a specified CSV file with headers, perform the following steps:

1. Drag the **CSV/TXT: Open** action just below line **4**.

2. Drag the **CSV/TXT: Close** action just below line number **11**.

   Your bot development interface in **List** view should look like this:

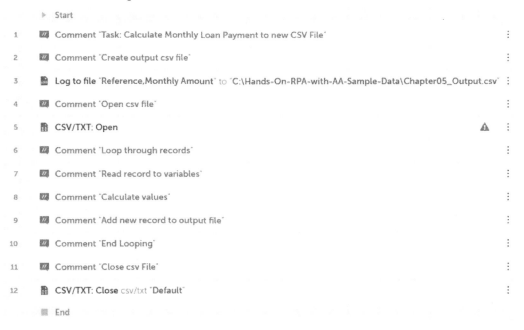

Figure 5.11 – CSV/TXT file opening and closing action

3. Set the following properties for the **CSV/TXT: Open** action on line **5**:

   Session name: `InputData`

   File path: Desktop file – `C:\Hands-On-RPA-with-AA-Sample-Data\Chapter05_InputData.csv`

   Contains header: *Checked*

Delimiter: **Comma**

Trim leading spaces: *Checked*

Trim trailing spaces: *Checked*

The action properties dialog should look like this:

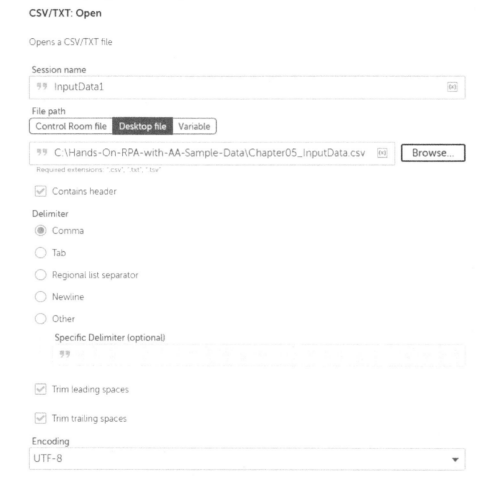

Figure 5.12 – CSV/TXT file opening properties dialog

4. Click on **Save** or use the shortcut, *Ctrl + S*.

5. Set the following property for the **CSV/TXT: Close** action on line **12**:

    Session name: InputData

6. Click on **Save**.

   Your bot development interface in **List** view should look like this:

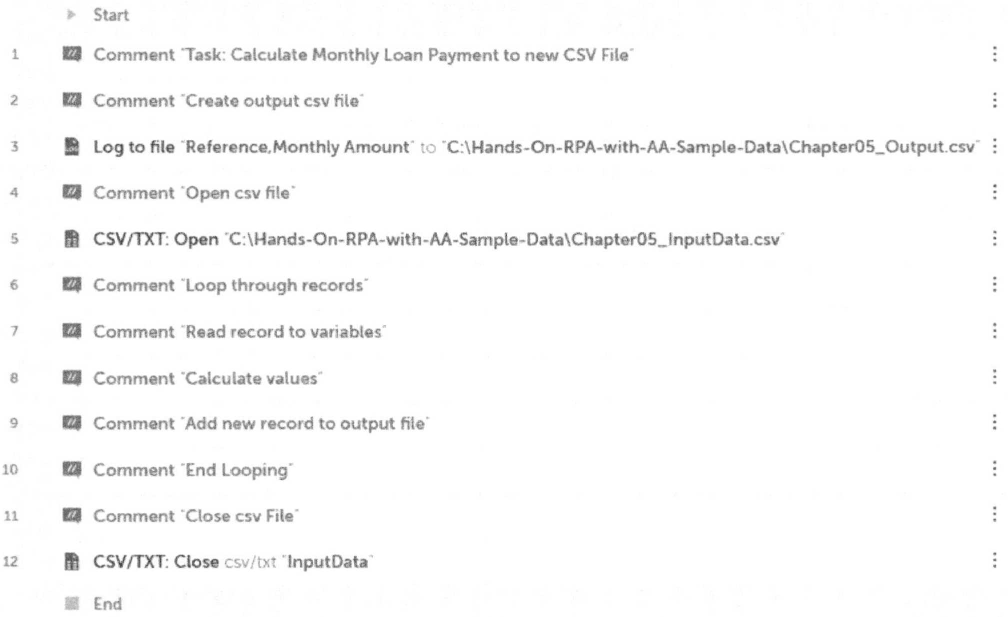

   ▷ Start

   1   💷 Comment 'Task: Calculate Monthly Loan Payment to new CSV File'   ⋮

   2   💷 Comment 'Create output csv file'   ⋮

   3   📄 Log to file 'Reference,Monthly Amount' to 'C:\Hands-On-RPA-with-AA-Sample-Data\Chapter05_Output.csv' ⋮

   4   💷 Comment 'Open csv file'   ⋮

   5   📊 CSV/TXT: Open 'C:\Hands-On-RPA-with-AA-Sample-Data\Chapter05_InputData.csv' ⋮

   6   💷 Comment 'Loop through records'   ⋮

   7   💷 Comment 'Read record to variables'   ⋮

   8   💷 Comment 'Calculate values'   ⋮

   9   💷 Comment 'Add new record to output file'   ⋮

   10 💷 Comment 'End Looping'   ⋮

   11 💷 Comment 'Close csv File'   ⋮

   12 📊 CSV/TXT: Close csv/txt 'InputData'   ⋮

   ▣ End

Figure 5.13 – Bot development so far

Your bot so far will now create the output CSV file. Then it will open the input CSV file that has the sample data. It will also close the input file once it's finished with it.

Looping through rows in a CSV file

Apart from opening and closing the input, it's not doing anything else with it. The bot needs to loop through each row in the sample data input file. Whenever you need to read from an external file, whether it's CSV, text, or Excel, a connection is created when this file is opened. The term used for this connection is **Session**. In this instance, we have called our session InputData. We will need to refer to this whenever we are working with the Chapter05_InputData.csv file:

To loop through the input CSV file, perform the following steps:

1. Drag the **Loop** action just below line **6**.

2. Set the following properties for the **Loop** action on line **7**:

   Loop Type: Iterator

Iterator: For each row in CSV/TXT

Session name: InputData

Assign the current row to this variable: recLoan - Record

The action properties dialog should look like this:

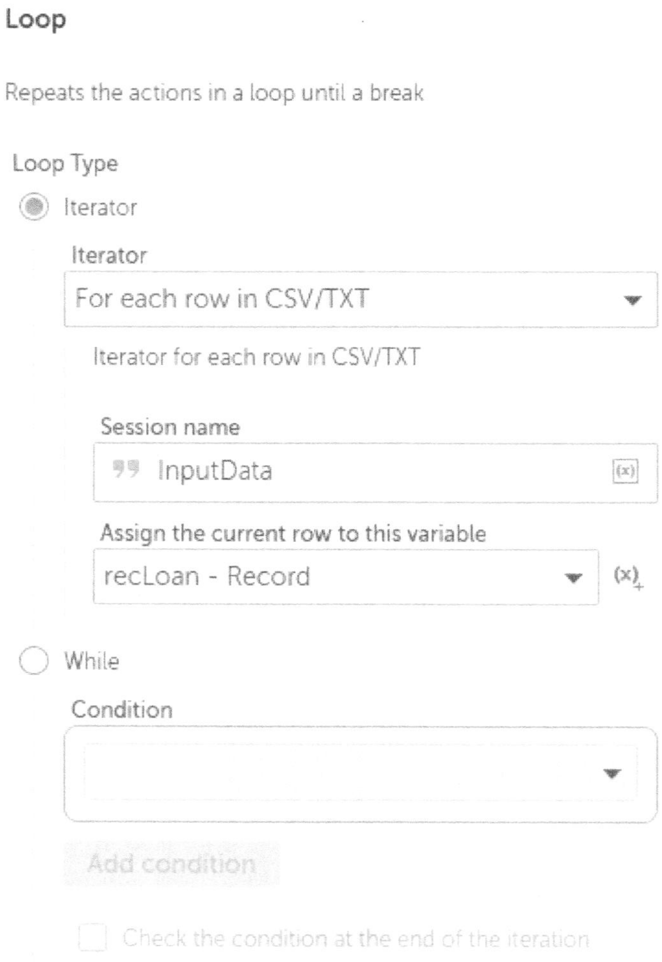

Loop

Repeats the actions in a loop until a break

Loop Type

⦿ Iterator

Iterator

For each row in CSV/TXT   ▼

Iterator for each row in CSV/TXT

Session name

🙶 InputData   (x)

Assign the current row to this variable

recLoan - Record   ▼   (x)₊

◯ While

Condition

[▼]

Add condition

☐ Check the condition at the end of the iteration

Figure 5.14 – The looping properties dialog

3. Click on **Save**.

4. Select the comments on lines **8**, **9**, and **10** (you select multiple actions by keeping the *Shift* key pressed) and drag them directly under line **7**, ensuring they are within the **Loop** action on line **7**.

5. Click on **Save**.

6. Your comments will now be indented within the loop.

    Your bot development interface should look like this:

Figure 5.15 – Bot development interface with Loop

The bot will now loop through every row in the input CSV file. The next stage will be to start reading the values for each record.

Reading record values

Each record we read is assigned to the variable called recLoan. We can work directly with the record values or we can assign them to variables. In our case, we will be reading the record and assigning the values to individual variables.

To read and assign the record value to variables, perform the following steps:

1. Drag the **String: Assign** action just below line **8**, ensuring it is within the **Loop** action on line **7**.

2. Set the following properties for the **String: Assign** action on line **9**:

   Select the source string variable(s)/ value (optional): $recLoan[0]$ (you can also use the *F2* keyboard shortcut to select a variable)

   Select the destination string variable: strRef - String

   The properties should look like the following screenshot:

Figure 5.16 – String: Assigning properties

3. Click on **Save**.

4. Drag the **Number: Assign** action just below line **9**, ensuring it is within the **Loop** action on line **7**.

5. Set the following properties for the **Number: Assign** action on line **10**:

   Select the source string variable/value: $recLoan[1]$

   Select the destination number variable: numAmount - Number

   The properties should look like the following screenshot:

Figure 5.17 – Number: Assigning properties

6. Click on **Save**.

7. Drag another **Number: Assign** action just below line number **10**, ensuring it is within the **Loop** action on line **7**.

8. Set the following properties for the **Number: Assign** action on line **11**:

    Select the source string variable/value: $recLoan[2]$

    Select the destination number variable: **numYears - Number**

    The properties should look like the following screenshot:

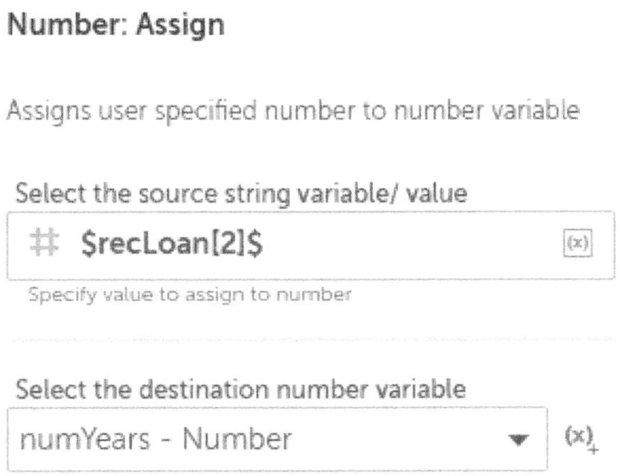

Number: Assign

Assigns user specified number to number variable

Select the source string variable/ value

    # **$recLoan[2]$**   (x)

Specify value to assign to number

Select the destination number variable

    numYears - Number   ▼   (x),

Figure 5.18 – Number: Assigning properties

9. Click on **Save**.

10. Drag another **Number: Assign** action just below line **11**, ensuring it is within the **Loop** action on line **7**.

11. Set the following properties for the **Number: Assign** action on line **12**:

    Select the source string variable/value: $recLoan[3]$

    Select the destination number variable: numInterest - Number

    The properties should look like the following screenshot:

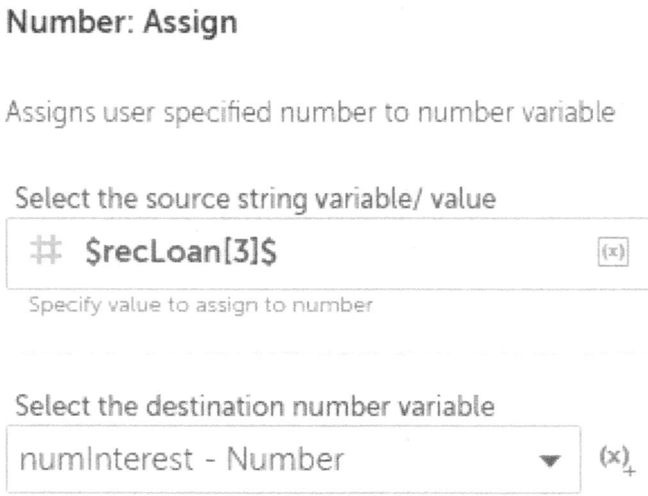

Number: Assign

Assigns user specified number to number variable

Select the source string variable/ value

    # $recLoan[3]$ (x)

Specify value to assign to number

Select the destination number variable

    numInterest - Number   ▼   (x)₊

Figure 5.19 – Number: Assigning properties

12. Click on **Save**. Your bot development interface in **List** view should look like this:

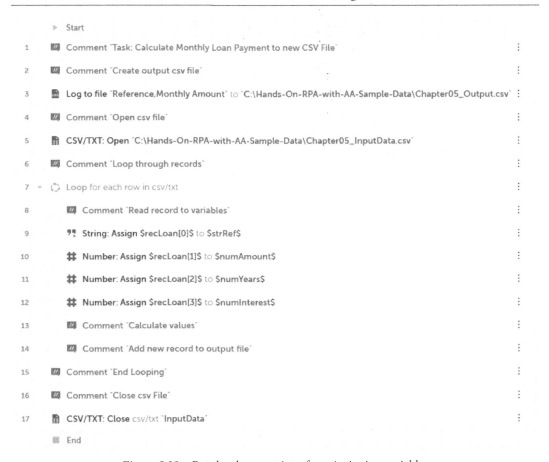

▷ Start

1   Comment "Task: Calculate Monthly Loan Payment to new CSV File"

2   Comment "Create output csv file"

3   Log to file "Reference,Monthly Amount" to "C:\Hands-On-RPA-with-AA-Sample-Data\Chapter05_Output.csv"

4   Comment "Open csv file"

5   CSV/TXT: Open "C:\Hands-On-RPA-with-AA-Sample-Data\Chapter05_InputData.csv"

6   Comment "Loop through records"

7 ▾ ○ Loop for each row in csv/txt

8   Comment "Read record to variables"

9   String: Assign $recLoan[0]$ to $strRef$

10   Number: Assign $recLoan[1]$ to $numAmount$

11   Number: Assign $recLoan[2]$ to $numYears$

12   Number: Assign $recLoan[3]$ to $numInterest$

13   Comment "Calculate values"

14   Comment "Add new record to output file"

15   Comment "End Looping"

16   Comment "Close csv File"

17   CSV/TXT: Close csv/txt "InputData"

     End

Figure 5.20 – Bot development interface: Assigning variables

The bot has all the values it needs from each record. The next step is to calculate Monthly Payment, and we will see how to do that in the next section.

Performing basic arithmetic calculations

We need to add actions to enable the bot to calculate Monthly Payment. We know the formula is *(Amount + Interest)/ (Years x 12)*.

We have all the values needed to perform this calculation already assigned to variables. For your bot to calculate this, perform the following steps:

1. Drag the **Number: Assign** action just below line **13**, ensuring it is within the **Loop** action on line **7**.

2. Set the following properties for the **Number: Assign** action on line **14**:

    Select the source string variable/value: `($numAmount$ + $numInterest$)/ (12 * $numYears$)`

    Select the destination number variable: **numMonthly - Number**

    The action properties dialog should look like this:

Figure 5.21 – Applying a calculation

3. Click on **Save**.

We are near the end now; you're doing really well! The next step is to write the results to the output CSV file we created earlier.

Appending records to a CSV file

We often need to add records or even logs to a CSV file. In this scenario, we will be writing the calculated results to a CSV file. Each row that we calculated will be a separate row in the output CSV file.

Your first bot has already been able to perform the following tasks:

1. Create a CSV file.

2. Read records from a CSV file.

3. Perform calculations for each row in the CSV file.

We have all the information that needs to be added to the output file. Before we actually add this, we will need to convert the numMonthly variable to a string. This is because we cannot output a numeric value as a string to the output CSV file.

To convert this variable and add the record to our output CSV file, perform the following steps:

1. Drag the **Number: To string** action just below line **15**, ensuring it is within the **Loop** action on line **7**.

2. Set the following properties for the **String: Assign** action on line **16**:

    Enter a number: $numMonthly$

    Enter number of digits after decimal: 2

    Assign the output to variable: strMonthly - String

    The action properties dialog should look like this:

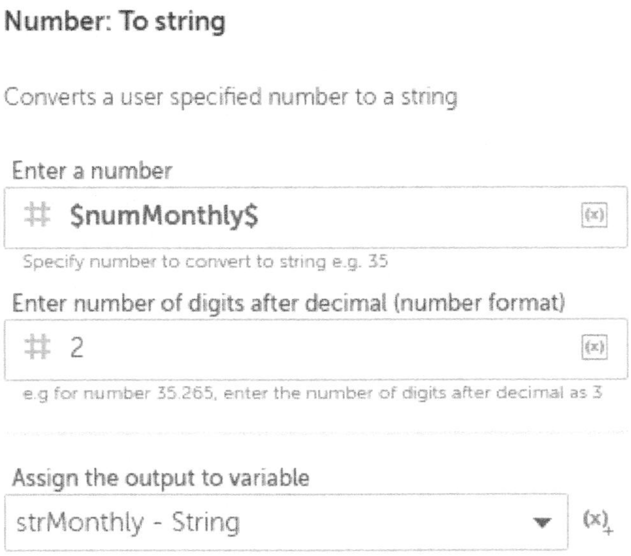

Number: To string

Converts a user specified number to a string

Enter a number

$numMonthly$ (x)

Specify number to convert to string e.g. 35

Enter number of digits after decimal (number format)

2   (x)

e.g for number 35.265, enter the number of digits after decimal as 3

Assign the output to variable

strMonthly - String   ▼   (x)₊

Figure 5.22 – Converting a numeric variable to a string

3. Click on **Save**.

4. Drag the **Log to file** action just below line **16**, ensuring it is within the **Loop** action on line **7**.

5. From the action properties pane, set the following values:

    File path: C:\Hands-On-RPA-with-AA-Sample-Data\Chapter05_ Output.csv

    Enter text to log: $strRef, $strMonthly$

    When logging: **Append to existing log file**

    The action properties dialog should look like this:

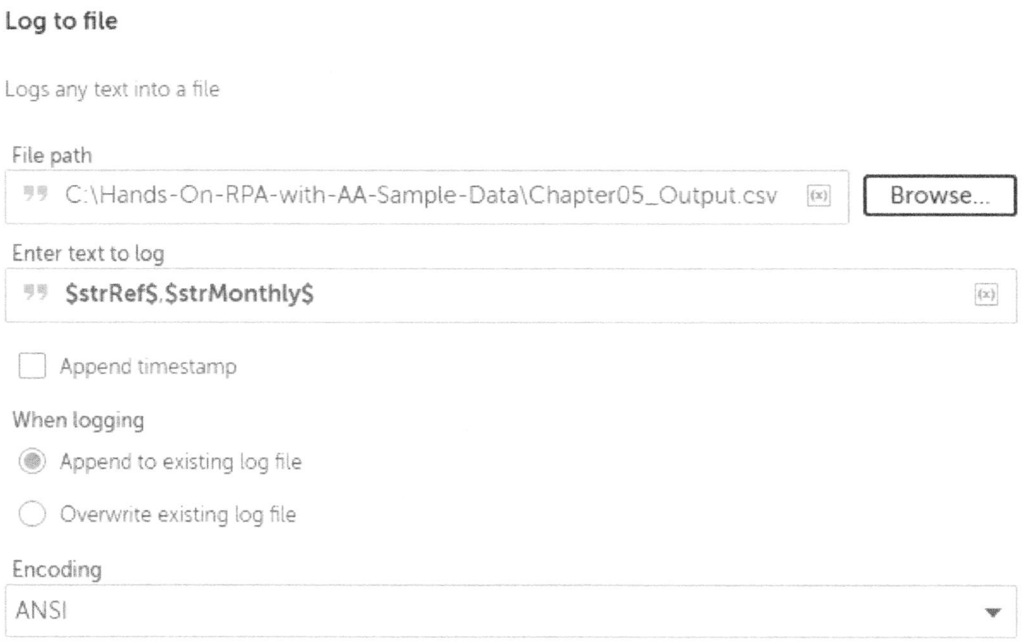

Log to file

Logs any text into a file

File path

    " C:\Hands-On-RPA-with-AA-Sample-Data\Chapter05_Output.csv   [x] | Browse... |

Enter text to log

    " $strRef$.$strMonthly$ [x]

☐ Append timestamp

When logging

◉ Append to existing log file

○ Overwrite existing log file

Encoding

ANSI   ▼

Figure 5.23 – Adding a new row to a CSV file

6. Click on **Save**.

7. This completes your first bot. The complete list of actions in the development window should look like this:

▶ Start

1   Comment "Task: Calculate Monthly Loan Payment to new CSV File"

2   Comment "Create output csv file"

3   Log to file "Reference,Monthly Amount" to "C:\Hands-On-RPA-with-AA-Sample-Data\Chapter05_Output.csv"

4   Comment "Open csv file"

5   CSV/TXT: Open "C:\Hands-On-RPA-with-AA-Sample-Data\Chapter05_InputData.csv"

6   Comment "Loop through records"

7 ▾ ↻ Loop for each row in csv/txt

8   Comment "Read record to variables"

9   String: Assign $recLoan[0]$ to $strRef$

10   Number: Assign $recLoan[1]$ to $numAmount$

11   Number: Assign $recLoan[2]$ to $numYears$

12   Number: Assign $recLoan[3]$ to $numInterest$

13   Comment "Calculate values"

14   Number: Assign "($numAmount$ + $numInte..." to $numMonthly$

15   Comment "Add new record to output file"

16   Number: To string convert $numMonthly$ to a string datatype and assign output to $strMonthly$

17   Log to file "$strRef$,$strMonthly$" to "C:\Hands-On-RPA-with-AA-Sample-Data\Chapter05_Output.csv"

18   Comment "End Looping"

19   Comment "Close csv File"

20   CSV/TXT: Close csv/txt "InputData"

▪ End

Figure 5.24 – Completing the bot actions

You have done some great work. Go ahead and run your first bot. Your first bot should create the output CSV file containing the calculated `Monthly Payments`. The output file should look like this in Excel:

	A	B
1	Reference	Monthly Amount
2	508-001	176.66
3	523-679	147.22
4	524-602	110.41
5	534-001	265.00
6	302-170	298.33
7	230-614	53.00
8	550-205	176.66

Figure 5.25 – CSV file output

Summary

You have built your first bot using Automation Anywhere. You are now a lot closer to becoming an RPA developer, having gained some valuable knowledge with the help of a real-life business process. You should be very comfortable with using actions to make your bot perform tasks. We have already looked at comma-separated files, in other words, reading, creating, and appending. You will have also increased your knowledge in terms of the use of variables, including strings, numbers, and even records.

You should now be comfortable with building and running bots. We just need to explore more actions that can be automated. In the next chapter, we will expand further on the Automation Anywhere actions. We will take a closer look at variables. You will be building a bot that uses different types of variables, from Boolean to dates. As well as creating variables, you will also gain some insight into performing calculations with dates and numbers. We will also look at prompts, message boxes, and using comments. Other useful elements in the next chapter include disabling/enabling actions and converting data types.

Again, congratulations on building your first fully functional Automation Anywhere bot!!

6
Introducing Variables in A2019

Having already built your first bot, you should now be very comfortable with navigating through the Automaton Anywhere interface. You should have no issues with logging on to the **Control Room** and creating a new bot. We have also looked at some of the actions the bots can perform, but there are many more actions available. The tasks a bot can perform are pretty much limited to your imagination. There really isn't much that a bot cannot be instructed to perform. A lot of this functionality is already available and grouped within packages using Automation Anywhere. In the next five chapters, we will be taking a closer look at the different packages and actions Automation Anywhere offers.

In this chapter, you will get hands-on experience with the basic essentials for developing with Automation Anywhere. You will be creating, assigning, and editing values stored in variables, and these variables will include Booleans, strings, numbers, and dates. We will also be using message boxes and prompts to act as inputs and outputs of our data. This chapter will also include the continuous use of comments to help us stick to our specifications. When working with variables and their values, as developers we often need to convert the data types of assigned values. You will also get an opportunity to convert some data types between variables.

Again, you will get a hands-on opportunity to build and execute bots using these actions through simple, step-by-step instructions. You will build various components throughout this chapter as we walk through the actions.

In this chapter, we will cover the following topics:

- Working with different variable types
- Using message boxes and prompts
- Converting data types

Technical requirements

In order to install the Automation Anywhere Bot agent, the following is required:

- Windows OS version 7 or higher
- A processor with a minimum speed of 3 GHz
- A minimum of 4 GB RAM
- At least 100 MB of hard disk space
- Internet Explorer v10 or higher OR Chrome v49 or higher
- A minimum screen resolution of 1024*768
- An internet connection with a minimum speed of 10 Mb/sec
- Completed registration with Automation Anywhere A2019 Community Edition
- Successful logon to Automation Anywhere A2019 Community Edition
- Successful registration of a local device
- The successful downloading of sample data from GitHub

Working with different variable types

We have already used some variables for our first bot. In this section, we will be taking a closer look at the following data types: `String`, `Number`, `Datetime`, and `Boolean`. You will also get to explore the specific packages and actions available for these types of variables. There are other data types available in A2019 and each type is represented by a specific icon. Here, you can see the icons for each type of variable:

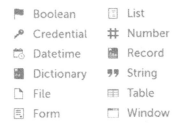

Figure 6.1 – A2019 icons that represent each data type

From the symbol, you will be able to quickly identify the variable type without relying on the variable name. When you select and use variables, they will all be displayed between the $ symbol. Like most development platforms, it is good practice to use a naming convention when crating variable names. This book will be using the following variable naming notation:

A2019 Data Type	Variable name Prefix
Number	num
String	str
Boolean	bln
Date\Time	dte
Record	rec
List	lst
Table	tbl
Dictionary	dct

Figure 6.2 – Naming convention

In the following section, we will take a walk-through of each variable type. This walk-through will show how to create, assign, use, and output each variable type. Although the process is similar for all variable types, they all use different Automation Anywhere packages. This will give you a clearer understanding of how to implement different data types using Automation Anywhere. We will be using comments and message boxes throughout the walk-throughs. This will also get you familiar with using comments to map out the process and message boxes to check each stage of the bot.

Using the String variable type

Learning how to use variables is key to pretty much all programming languages. A String type variable is used for alphanumeric values. String variables are required for most outputs in Automation Anywhere. This includes output to message boxes and log files.

In the walk-through that we will look at next, we will be performing the following tasks:

1. Creating three String variables – strFirstName, strSurname, and strFullname

2. Assigning values to strFirstName and strSurname

3. Merging both variables together and assigning them to strFullname

4. Showing the value of strFullname in a **Message box**

Let's start this walk-through by executing the following steps:

1. Log in to the **Control Room**.

2. Create a new bot and call it Chapter 6 - Variables in the \Bot\ folder.

3. Expand the **Variables** pane from the options on the left and select + to create a new variable:

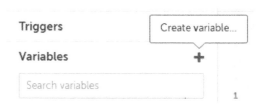

Figure 6.3 – Creating a new variable

4. The **Create variable** dialog will appear. Call this variable strFirstName and set it as a String type. Once the details are entered, click on **Create**. The dialog should look like this:

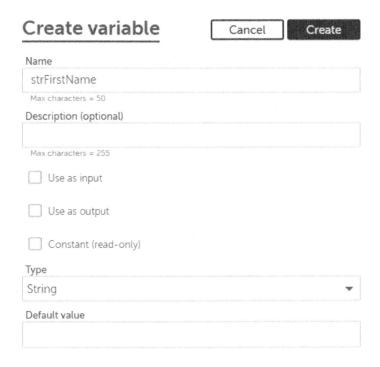

Figure 6.4 – Creating a variable dialog

You can give a description if you want. This is useful when you have multiple variables and the variable name does not clearly describe what it will be used for.

The **Constant (read-only)** checkbox is used to indicate a constant variable, one that is read only. This is very useful as reference data.

The **input** and **output** checkboxes relate to passing and receiving these variables between taskbots. We will cover this in more detail at a later stage.

You can also give this variable a **Default value**. This assigns it a value for the first time it is accessed.

5.   Create another new variable named strSurname as a String type.

6.   Create another new variable named `strFullname` as a `String` type.

Your variable list should appear as follows:

Figure 6.5 – Variables list

7.   Now that we have our variables, let's start by adding some comments to form the template guide for our bot. Expand the **Actions** pane from the options on the left.

8.   Add a **Comment** action as line **1**.

9.   Set the **Comment** properties text as `"String Variables"` and click on **Save**.

10.   Add a new **Comment** action as `"Merge variables"` on line **2** and click on **Save**.

11.   Add a new **Comment** action as `"Show Output"` on line **3** and click on **Save**.

12.   Add a new **Comment** action as `"- - - - - - - - - - - - - - - - - - - -"` on line **4** and click on **Save**. Your bot should now look like this:

Figure 6.6 – Development interface

13.   From the `String` package, drag the **Assign** action under line **1**.

14.   Set the following properties for the **String: Assign** action on line **2**:

Select the source string variable(s)/ value (optional): `John`

Select the destination string variable: strFirstName - String

The action properties dialog should look like this:

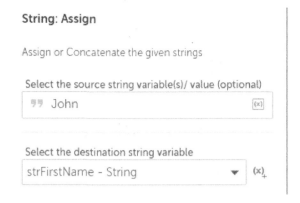

Figure 6.7 – String: Assign action properties

15. Click on **Save**.

16. Drag the **String: Assign** action just below line number **2**.

17. Set the following properties for the **String: Assign** action on line **3**:

    Select the source string variable(s)/ value (optional): Smith

    Select the destination string variable: strSurname - String

    The action properties dialog should look like this:

Figure 6.8 – String: Assign action properties

18. Click on **Save**.

19. Now we will merge the values of the strFirstName and strSurname variables and assign the results to the strFullname variable. Drag the **String: Assign** action just below line **4**.

20. Set the following properties for the **String: Assign** action on line **5**:

    Select the source string variable(s)/ value (optional): $strFirstName$
    $strSurname$

    Select the destination string variable: strFullname - String

    The action properties dialog should look like this:

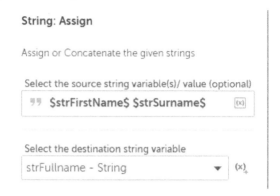

Figure 6.9 – String: Assign action properties

21. Click on **Save**.

22. To view the **strFullname** variable, add the **Message box** action just below line **6**.

23. Set the following properties for the **Message box** action on line **7**:

    Enter the message box window title: Merged variables

    Enter the message to display: $strFullname$

    The action properties dialog should look like this:

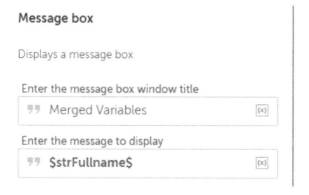

Figure 6.10 – Message box properties

24. Click on **Save**. The development interface should look something like this:

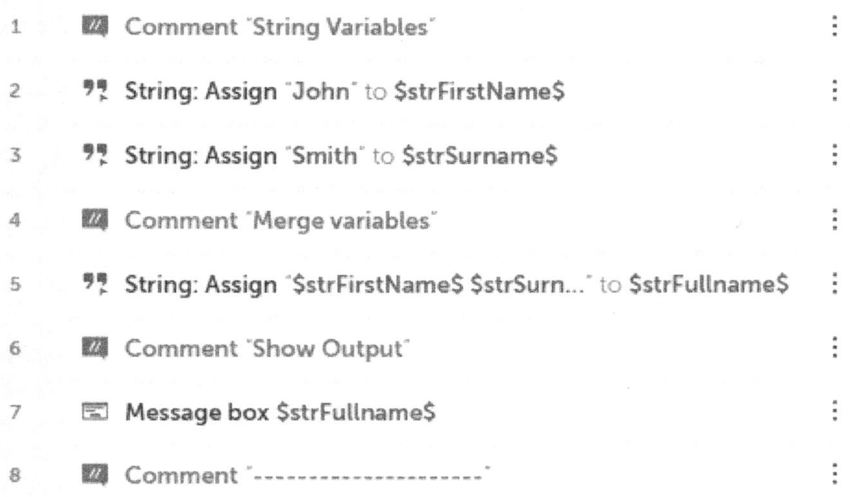

1	🖼 Comment "String Variables"	⋮
2	💬 String: Assign "John" to $strFirstName$	⋮
3	💬 String: Assign "Smith" to $strSurname$	⋮
4	🖼 Comment "Merge variables"	⋮
5	💬 String: Assign "$strFirstName$ $strSurn..." to $strFullname$	⋮
6	🖼 Comment "Show Output"	⋮
7	📧 Message box $strFullname$	⋮
8	🖼 Comment "---------------------"	⋮

Figure 6.11 – Development interface

In this walk-through, you have learned how to create **String** type variables and assign values to all of them. We also looked at how to merge the values of two variables and assign them to a single variable.

In the next walk-through, we will look at different data type variables, starting with the Datetime data type.

Using the Datetime variable type

A Datetime type variable is used for date and time values. It stores the date and time as a single unit. Dates can be tricky as the format can vary between different regions. That's why a time zone needs to be selected.

In this walk-through, we will be performing the following tasks:

1. Creating two Datetime variables – dteChristmas and dteChristmasPlus2Weeks

2. Creating a String variable, strDate, to store the output for the message box

3. Adding 2 weeks to the dteChristmas variable and assigning the result to dteChristmasPlus2Weeks

4. Showing the value of dteChristmasPlus2Weeks in a **Message box**

Let's start this walk-through by executing the following steps:

1. While still working on the same bot as before, expand the **Variables** pane from the options on the left and select + to create a new variable.

2. The **Create variable** dialog will appear. Set the following values:

    Name: dteChristmas

    Type: **Datetime**

    Default value: 12/25/2019 12:00 AM

    The dialog should look like this:

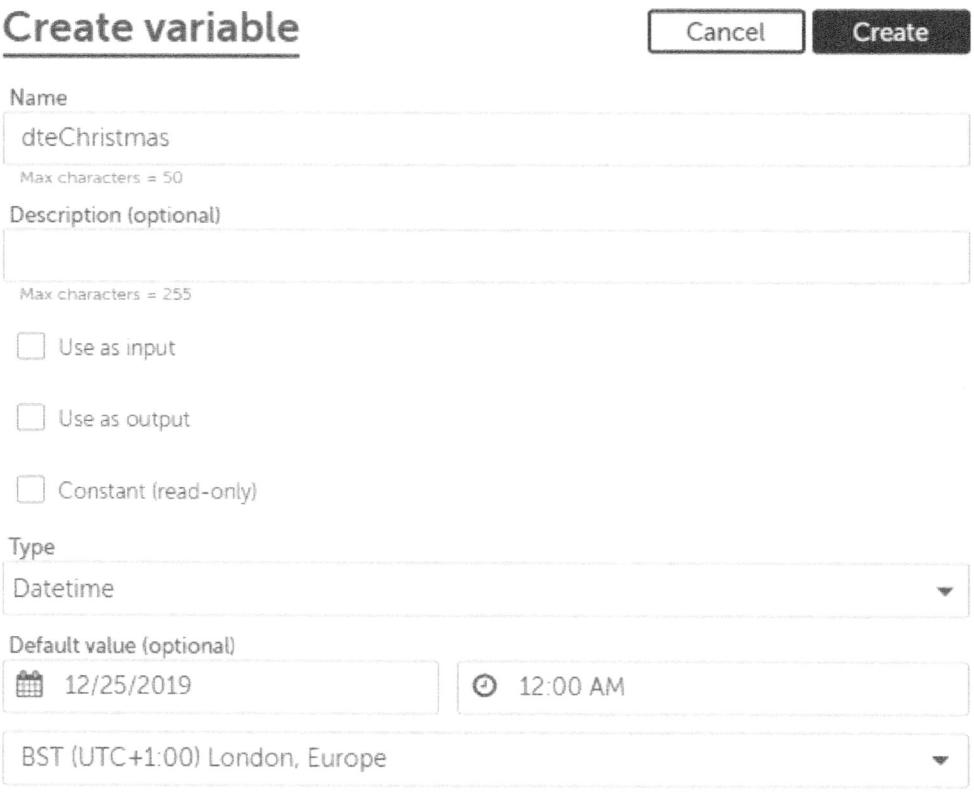

Figure 6.12 – Creating a new Datetime variable

3. Click on **Create**.

4. Create another **Datetime** type variable, set the values as follows, and then click on **Create**:

   Name: `dteChristmasPlus2Weeks`

   Type: Datetime

   Default value: *(Leave blank)*

5. Create a `String` type variable called `strDate` and then click on **Save**.

6. Now that we have our variables, we start by adding some comments to form the template guide for our bot. Add the **Comment** action as line **9**, set the comment property as `"Datetime Variables"`, and then click on **Save**.

7. Add a new **Comment** action as `"Add 2 Weeks to Date"` on line **10** and click on **Save**.

8. Add a new **Comment** action as `"Show Output"` on line **11** and click on **Save**.

9. Add a new **Comment** action as `"---------------------"` on line **12** and click on **Save**. Your bot should look like this:

9	Comment "Datetime Variables"	⋮
10	Comment "Add 2 Weeks to Date"	⋮
11	Comment "Show Output"	⋮
12	Comment "---------------------"	⋮

   Figure 6.13 – Development interface

10. To add 2 weeks to the `dteChristmas` variable, add the **Datetime: Add** action just below line **10**.

11. Set the following properties for the **Datetime: Add** action on line **11**:

    Source date and time variable: dteChristmas - Datetime

    Time value to add: 2

    Time unit to add: Weeks

    Assign the output to a variable: dteChristmasPlus2Weeks - Datetime

The **Datetime: Add** action properties should look like this:

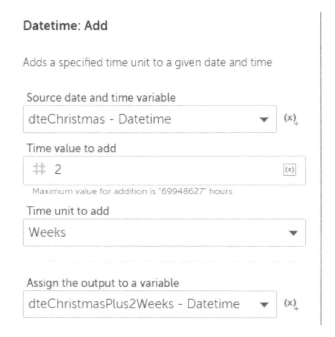

Figure 6.14 – Datetime: Add action properties

12. Click on **Save**.

13. To view the dteChristmasPlus2Weeks variable in a message box, it needs to be converted to a String variable. To do this, add the **Datetime: To string** action just below line **12**.

14. Set the following properties for the **Datetime: To string** action on line **13**:

    Source date and time variable: **dteChristmasPlus2Weeks - Datetime**

    Select date time format: **Custom format** – DD MM YYYY

    Assign the output to a variable: **strDate - String**

    The action properties should look like this:

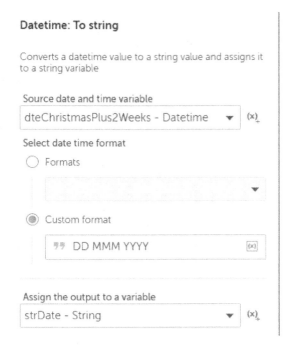

Figure 6.15 – Datetime: To string action properties

15. Click on **Save**.

16. To view the results, add the **Message box** action just below line **13**.

17. Set the following properties for the **Message box** action on line **14**:

Enter the message box window title: Datetime variables

Enter the message to display: $strDate$

The action properties dialog should look like this:

Figure 6.16 – Message box properties

18. Click on **Save**. The development interface should look something like this:

9	🖍 Comment `Datetime Variables`	⋮
10	🖍 Comment `Add 2 Weeks to Date`	⋮
11	🗓 **Datetime: Add 2** Weeks to **$dteChristmas$** and assign result to **$dteChristmas**...	⋮
12	🖍 Comment `Show Output`	⋮
13	🗓 **Datetime: To string** Convert **$dteChristmasPlus2Weeks$** and assign result to $...	⋮
14	✉ **Message box $strDate$**	⋮
15	🖍 Comment `---------------------`	⋮

Figure 6.17 – Development interface

In this walk-through, you have created two Datetime type variables and assigned a value to one of them. The walk-through also demonstrated how to add a time period to a Datetime type variable as well as converting it to a String variable.

In the next walk-through, we will look at another data type variable, the Boolean data type.

Using the Boolean variable type

A Boolean type variable is used as a **Flag**. This is represented as *True/False*, *Yes/No*, or *On/Off*. However, it is represented as the underlying value being either 0 or 1. There can only be one of the two states of the value of a Boolean variable at any given time. Usually, when a Boolean variable is created, it tends to be set as False by default. This can be set to True if required.

In the next walk-through, we will be performing the following tasks:

1. Creating a Boolean variable – blnLeapYear

2. Creating a String variable, strLeapYear, to store the output for the message box

3. Setting the blnLeapYear variable to True

4. Inverting the value of the blnLeapYear variable

5. Converting the value of `blnLeapYear` to a `String` variable and assigning it to `strLeapYear`

6. Showing the value of `strLeapYear` in a **Message box**

Let's start this walk-through by executing the following steps:

1. While continuing to work on the same bot as previously, expand the **Variables** pane from the options on the left and select + to create a new variable.

2. The **Create variable** dialog will appear. Set the following values:

   Name: `blnLeapYear`

   Type: **Boolean**

   Default value: **True**

   The dialog should look like this:

Figure 6.18 – Creating a new Boolean variable

3. Click on **Create**.

4. Create a **String** type variable called `strLeapYear` and click on **Save**.

5. Now that we have our variables, we start by adding some comments to form the template guide for our bot. Add the **Comment** action as line **16**, set the comment property as `"Boolean Variables"`, and click on **Save**.

6. Add another **Comment** action as `"Assign Boolean Value"` as line **17** and click on **Save**.

7. Add another **Comment** action as `"Invert Boolean Value"` as line **18** and click on **Save**.

8. Add another **Comment** action as `"Show Output"` as line **19** and click on **Save**.

9. Add another **Comment** action as `"--------------------"` as line **20** and click on **Save**. Your bot should look like this:

16	🏁 Comment "Boolean Variables"	⋮
17	🏁 Comment "Assign Boolean Value"	⋮
18	🏁 Comment "Invert Boolean Value"	⋮
19	🏁 Comment "Show Output"	⋮
20	🏁 Comment "--------------------"	⋮

Figure 6.19 – Development interface

10. To assign a `True` value to the `blnLeapYear` variable, from the **Boolean** package, drag the **Assign** action just below line **17**.

11. Set the following properties for the **Boolean: Assign** action on line **18**:

    Select the source Boolean variable/ value: Constant values

    Constant values: True

    Select the destination Boolean variable: blnLeapYear - Boolean

The action properties should look like this:

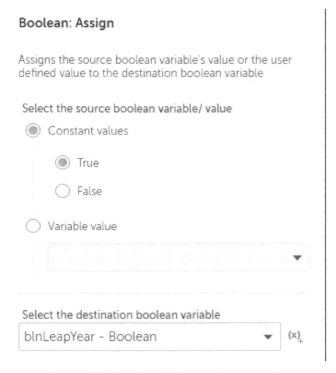

Boolean: Assign

Assigns the source boolean variable's value or the user defined value to the destination boolean variable

Select the source boolean variable/ value

⦿ Constant values

  ⦿ True

  ◯ False

◯ Variable value

  [▾]

Select the destination boolean variable

[blnLeapYear - Boolean   ▾] (x)₊

Figure 6.20 – Boolean: Assign action properties

12. Click on **Save**.

13. To invert the value of the blnLeapYear variable, from the **Boolean** package, drag the **Invert** action just below line **19**.

14. Set the following properties for the **Boolean: Invert** action on line **20**:

    Select the Boolean variable to be inverted: Variable

    Value: $blnLeapYear$

    Assign the output: blnLeapYear - Boolean

The Boolean: Invert action properties should look like this:

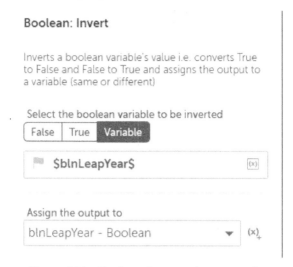

Figure 6.21 – Boolean: Invert action properties

15. Click on **Save**.

16. To convert `blnLeapYear` to a `String` variable, add the **Boolean: To string** action just below line **21**.

17. Set the following properties for the **Boolean: To string** action on line **22**:

    Select Boolean variable: **blnLeapYear - Boolean**

    Select the string variable to store the result: **strLeapYear - String**

    The action properties should look like this:

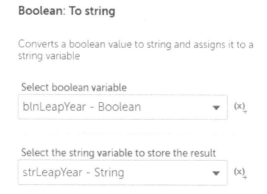

Figure 6.22 – Boolean: To string action properties

18. Click on **Save**.

19. To view the results, add the **Message box** action just below line **22**.

20. Set the following properties for the **Message box** action on line **23**:

    Enter the message box window title: `Boolean variables`

    Enter the message to display: `$strLeapYear$`

    The action properties dialog should look like this:

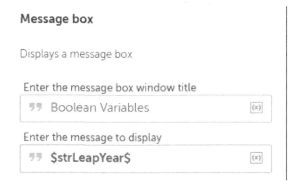

Figure 6.23 – Message box properties

21. Click on **Save**. The development interface should look something like this:

16	Comment "Boolean Variables"	⋮
17	Comment "Assign Boolean Value"	⋮
18	**Boolean: Assign** True to $blnLeapYear$	⋮
19	Comment "Invert Boolean Value"	⋮
20	**Boolean: Invert** value of boolean variable $blnLeapYear$ and assign result to $bl...	⋮
21	Comment "Show Output"	⋮
22	**Boolean: To string** $blnLeapYear$ and assign result to a $strLeapYear$	⋮
23	**Message box** $strLeapYear$	⋮
24	Comment "----------------------"	⋮

Figure 6.24 – Development interface

In this walk-through, you have created a `Boolean` variable and assigned a `True` value to it. Then this value was inverted using Automation Anywhere actions and the results shown in a message box.

The next variable type we will explore is the `Number` variable, probably one of the most commonly used data types.

Using the Number variable type

A `Number` type variable is used to store all numeric values. Automation Anywhere uses this single variable type to store any numeric type value, for example, an integer, currency, or decimal. We do not need to identify the type of number it is.

In this walk-through, we will be performing the following tasks:

1. Creating two `Number` variables – `numRandom` and `numResult`

2. Creating a `String` variable, `strResult`, to store the output for the message box

3. Assigning a random number between `1` and `100` to the `numRandom` variable

4. Applying a formula, *(Random/2) + 25*, and assigning the results to `numResult`

5. Converting the value of `numResult` to a `String` variable and assigning it to `strResult`

6. Showing the value of `strResult` in a **Message box**

Let's start this walk-through by performing the following tasks:

1. While still working on the same bot as before, create a `Number` type variable called `numRandom` and click on **Save**.

2. Create another `Number` type variable called `numResult` and click on **Save**.

3. Create a `String` type variable called `strResult` and click on **Save**.

4. Now that we have our variables, we start by adding some comments to form the template guide for our bot. Add the **Comment** action on line **25**, set the comment property as `"Number Variables"`, and click on **Save**.

5. Add another **Comment** action as `"Assign Random Value"` as line **26** and click on **Save**.

6. Add another **Comment** action as `"Apply Formula"` as line **27** and click on **Save**.

7. Add another **Comment** action as `"Show Output"` as line **28** and click on **Save**.

8. Add another **Comment** action as "- -" as line **29** and click on **Save**. Your bot should look like this:

25	🎟 Comment "Number Variables"	⋮
26	🎟 Comment "Assign Random Value"	⋮
27	🎟 Comment "Apply Formula"	⋮
28	🎟 Comment "Show Output"	⋮
29	🎟 Comment "---------------------"	⋮

Figure 6.25 – Development interface

9. To assign a random number to the numRandom variable from the **Number** package, drag the **Random** action just below line **26**.

10. Set the following properties for the **Number: Random** action on line **27**:

Beginning of range: 1

End of range: 100

Save the outcome to a number variable: numRandom - Number

The action properties should look like this:

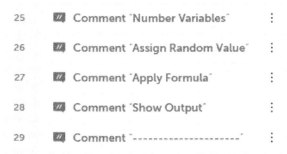

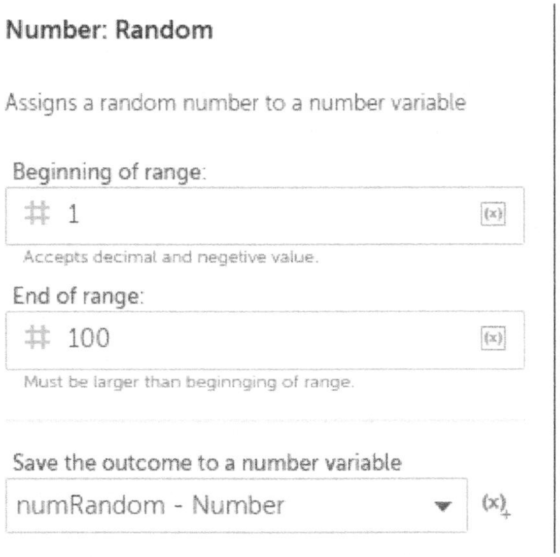

Figure 6.26 – Number: Random action properties

11. Click on **Save**.

12. To apply the formula *(Random/2) + 25* and save the outcome to the `numResult` variable, add the **Number: Assign** action just below line **28**.

13. Set the following properties for the **Number: Assign** action on line **29**:

    Select the source string variable: `($numRandom$/2) + 25`

    Select the destination number variable: **numResult - Number**

    The action properties should look like this:

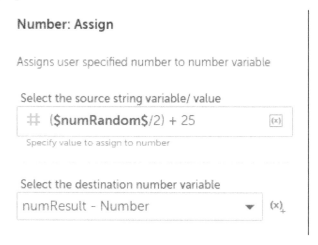

Figure 6.27 – Number: Assign action properties

14. Click on **Save**.

15. To convert `numResult` to a `String` variable, add the **Number: To string** action just below line **30**.

16. Set the following properties for the **Number: To string** action on line **31**:

    Enter a number: `$numResult$`

    Enter number of digits after decimal: 2

    Assign the output to variable: `strResult - String`

The action properties should look like this:

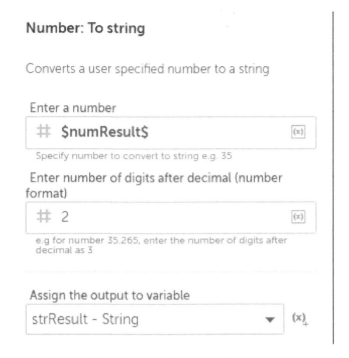

Figure 6.28 – Number: To string action properties

17. Click on **Save**.

18. To view the results, add the **Message box** action just below line **31**.

19. Set the following properties for the **Message box** action on line **32**:

    Enter the message box window title: Number variables

    Enter the message to display: $strResult$

The action properties dialog should look like this:

Figure 6.29 – Message box properties

20. Click on **Save**, and the development interface should look something like this:

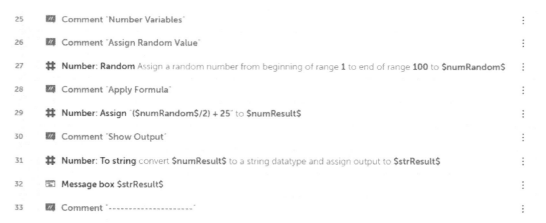

Figure 6.30 – Development interface

You should now have a clear understanding of how to create new variables as well as assign and re-assign values. There are more variable types available, such as `Window`, `File`, and `Record`. Covering the most common variables will give you a good start on your journey to becoming a bot developer. In the walk-throughs so far, you should now be comfortable with using the `String`, `Datetime`, `Boolean`, and `Number` variables. We will cover some of the other variables in the forthcoming chapters.

Although our bot so far is performing a number of calculations, we do not have any user inputs or any outputs. In the next section, we will add prompts to get user inputs and message boxes to output the results. We have been assigning fixed values to variables, so using prompts will allow the operator to assign values given as a response to a prompt. The **Message box** will allow you to visually see the contents of these variables.

Using message boxes and prompts

Our bot so far has dealt with four types of variables – `String`, `Datetime`, `Boolean`, and `Number`. They have values assigned to them using the assign action or are set as default values. We will now go through and modify our bot. Instead of assigning values using actions, we will replace this with actions from the **Prompt** package. As well as using the **Prompt** package, you will learn how to disable and enable actions for your bot.

In this walk-through, we will be performing the following tasks:

1. Disabling **Assign** actions from the bot

2. Adding **Prompt** actions for capturing `strFirstName` and `strSurname`

3. Outputting results as **Message box**

Let's start this walk-through by performing the following steps:

1. Continuing with the same bot as before, to disable an action, you will notice the three vertical dots at the end of every action line in the development interface. Clicking on this will show the options menus. This gives you a number of editing options for that bot action line.

2. Select the options menu for line **2**:

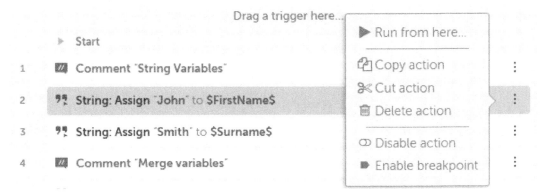

Figure 6.31 – Action line edit options

3. From the options, select **Disable action**.

4. Repeat steps *2* and *3* for line **3**.

5. Values are no longer assigned to the `strFirstName` and `strSurname` variables as these actions have been disabled. To prompt for a value for the `strFirstName` variable, from the **Prompt** package, drag the **For value** action just below line **2**.

6. Set the following properties for the **Prompt: For value** action on line **3**:

    Prompt window caption: `Prompt for String`

    Prompt message: `Enter Firstname:`

    Assign the value to a variable: **strFirstName - String**

    The action properties should look like this:

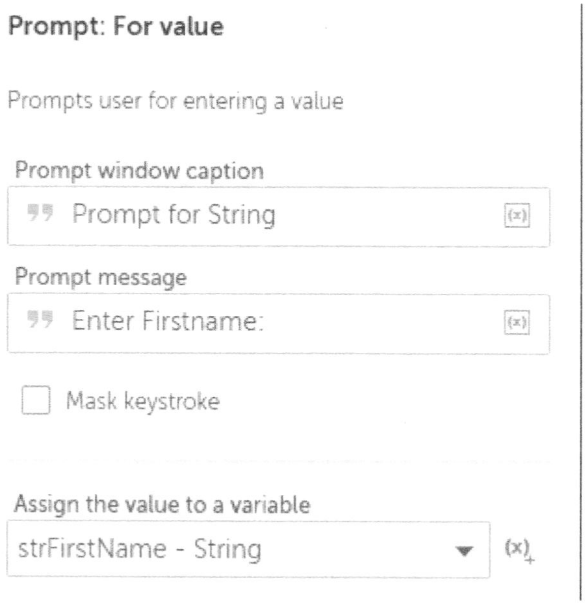

Figure 6.32 – Prompt: For value action properties

7. Click on **Save**.

8. Add another **Prompt: For value** action just below line **4**.

9. Set the following properties for the **String: Assign** action on line **5**:

    Prompt window caption: `Prompt for String`

    Prompt message: `Enter Surname:`

    Assign the value to a variable: **strSurname - String**

10. Click on **Save**.

You have disabled actions and created some prompts to get the name values assigned to our variables. The **Message Box** that's already in place on line **9** will output the merged variable values. The development interface should look something like this:

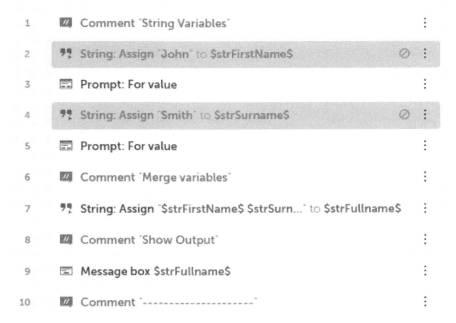

Figure 6.33 – Development interface

A **Message box** can be a very useful action to use as a development tool. Incorporating them as test points throughout your taskbot during development helps ensure your bot is doing what it is supposed to. Once the bot is ready for a production environment, always remember to disable or automatically close any message boxes as they could stop the bot as it awaits a user to click on **OK**.

The other point to remember is, a **Message Box** can only output a `String` data type. If you have a number to output, you will have to convert this using the relevant action. In the next section, we will look at converting variables from one type to another.

Converting data types

As a developer, there is a lot we have to consider when working with data. This applies to software development, and not just RPA. With Automation Anywhere, when data is initially read from a source, it is often assumed to be of the `String` type. If the data item is not a `String`, it will need to be converted to its actual type. Also, the most common output is also a `String` type. If values are outputted to a **Message Box** or log/text files, they need to be a `String`. If they are not, then again, the data item will need to be converted. Luckily, there are a few scenarios in our bot where data conversion will be useful.

The bot we have been building so far already has some great examples of converting the data type. Since the outputs of each walk-through have been as a **Message box**, it is mandatory that the value is of the `String` data type. Message boxes can only show `String` data types.

Let's look at the data conversions performed by the current bot. The first data conversion the bot performs is converting a `Datetime` data type to a `String` data type. Take a look at line **15** from the development interface:

15   🗓 **Datetime: To string** Convert $dteChristmasPlus2Weeks$ and assign result to $strDate$ ⋮

Figure 6.34 – Converting a Datetime data type to String

The next data conversion performed is from a `Boolean` data type to a `String` data type. This is demonstrated on line **24** of the development interface:

24   🏳 **Boolean: To string** $blnLeapYear$ and assign result to a $strLeapYear$ ⋮

Figure 6.35 – Converting a Boolean data type to String

Finally, the bot converts a `Number` data type to a `String` data type. This is on line 33 of the development interface:

33   ♯ **Number: To string** convert $numResult$ to a string datatype and assign output to $strResul...$ ⋮

Figure 6.36 – Converting a Number data type to String

Whenever a data type is converted, two variables are required. The first is the original value that needs to be converted, and the other is the target variable. The target variable should always be the same as target data type.

Go ahead and run your bot. It should have prompts, message boxes, and all the variable conversions and calculations. You have done a great job so far. Being able to create and work with variables of different types is an essential skill for all developers. Your knowledge of not only creating and assigning, but also converting, data types is a great start to building your confidence with Automation Anywhere.

Summary

Great work! Your bot has got some great examples of working with variables. To recap, you have learned how to create different types of variables from numbers, Booleans, and dates. Your knowledge has been expanded by assigning values to these variables as well as performing calculations. We also explored the reasons for using, and how to convert, different data types. Having also created prompts and message boxes, you are well on your way to start learning some more exciting Automation Anywhere packages and actions. This chapter and its walk-throughs are essential to setting a good foundation for all Automation Anywhere developers. All of the skills learned, such as creating and assigning variables, will be used in pretty much every single bot you build. During the development process, you will almost certainly be using message boxes and comments.

In the next chapter, we will expand further on the packages. In particular, you will learn how to launch and navigate around desktop and web applications. We will also explore the use of automation with Excel and email applications.

7
Interacting with Applications

Hopefully, you will be feeling confident about using Automation Anywhere by now. The walk-throughs so far should have given you an opportunity to create and run bots. These may be relatively basic bots, but with each walk-through, we are expanding our knowledge of additional packages. Each Automation Anywhere package and its actions open up more operations that you can automate. Following the walk-throughs gives you hands-on experience, allowing you to add value to your RPA development skills.

There are many tasks that we perform as part of our daily routines at work. These tasks will almost always include working with web-based and desktop applications. Being able to automate tasks that interact with web and desktop applications are key skills that any RPA developer ought to possess.

We have already covered the basics of using Automation Anywhere, so now get ready for some more serious automation. Having a clear understanding of creating and assigning different variable types, we can now start utilizing these skills further to build bots that interact with applications.

This chapter will look at working with web-based and desktop applications. We will be building bots that mimic human interaction. You will learn how to navigate, select, and update applications using keystroke simulation, as well as by clicking and selecting elements within these applications.

In this chapter, we will cover the following topics:

- Automating web applications
- Automating desktop applications
- Simulating keystrokes

By the end of this chapter, you will have the skills needed to build bots that can launch applications, navigate through various application interfaces, interact with buttons and checkboxes, and read and enter data. This chapter will be using the following packages:

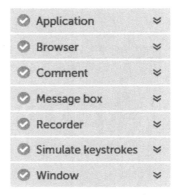

Figure 7.1 – Packages used in this chapter

You will be building two bots in this chapter. The first will be based on web applications, and the second on desktop applications. The walk-throughs will guide you step by step, enabling you to have bots that launch your application and navigate through them just as a human would.

Technical requirements

In order to install the Automation Anywhere Bot agent, the following is required:

- Windows OS version 7 or higher
- A processor with a minimum speed of 3 GHz
- A minimum of 4 GB RAM
- At least 100 MB of hard disk space
- Internet Explorer v10 or higher OR Chrome v49 or higher

- A minimum screen resolution of 1024*768
- An internet connection with a minimum speed of 10 Mb/sec
- Completed registration with Automation Anywhere A2019 Community Edition
- Successful logon to Automation Anywhere A2019 Community Edition
- Successful registration of a local device
- The successful downloading of sample data from GitHub

Automating web applications

During a normal working day, we will use web applications to carry out our daily tasks. These applications may be in the public domain, such as search engines, or intranet-based applications specific to your organization. There is a shift of desktop applications moving to cloud-based web applications. The use of web applications is increasing in business circles.

In the following walk-through, we will be working with a web application. It's a very simple website. We will be navigating to a specific page by looking for a particular tab. The walk-through will then fill a simple online form and conclude by clicking the **Send** button on the form.

In this walk-through, we will be performing the following tasks:

1. Launching the `http://skysoftuk.net` website
2. Clicking on the **CONTACT** tab to navigate to the contact page
3. Completing the **Name**, **Email**, and **Message** fields on the form
4. Clicking the **Send** button

Let's start this walk-through by executing the following steps:

1. Log in to the **Control Room**.
2. Create a new bot and call it `Chapter 7 - Web Apps` in the `\Bot\` folder.
3. As always, we begin by adding some comments to use as a template for our bot, add a new **Comment** action on line **1**, set the value to "`--------------------`", and click on **Save**.
4. Add a new **Comment** action as "`Launch Website`" on line **2** and click on **Save**.

5. Add a new **Comment** action as `"Navigate to Contact Page"` on line **3** and click on **Save**.

6. Add a new **Comment** action as `"Fill on-line form"` on line **4** and click on **Save**.

7. Add a new **Comment** action as `"Click on Send"` on line **5** and click on **Save**.

8. Add a new **Comment** action as `"-------------------"` on line **6** and click on **Save**. Your bot should look like this:

Figure 7.2 – Development interface

9. We can now start to add some functionality. The first thing we want the bot to do is launch the browser and go to our web page. From the **Browser** package, drag the **Launch website** action under line **2**.

10. Set the following properties for the **Browser: Launch website** action on line **3**:

-   **URL**: `http://skysoftuk.net/`

-   **Browser**: **Google Chrome**

    The **Browser: Launch website** action properties should look like this:

Browser: Launch website

This command can be used to open website in browser

URL

🙶 http://skysoftuk.net/   (x)

e.g. http://...

Browser

Google Chrome   ▼

Figure 7.3 – Browser: Launch website properties

11. Click on **Save**.

12. Now it gets really interesting. We will instruct the bot to look for the **CONTACT** tab and then click on it. Currently, the bot will not be able to capture the **CONTACT** tab because the web page isn't actually open. Manually open another session of Chrome and navigate to `http://skysoftuk.net/`. The bot is now ready to capture the **CONTACT** tab.

13. From the **Recorder** package, drag the **Capture** action under line **4**.

    When Automation Anywhere captures an object, the properties are in six sections:

    Object detail – This tells the bot where to look for the object.

    Preview – This is a visual display of what the object looks like.

    Object properties – These list all the attributes for that object; the attributes used to identify the object are checked.

    Action – This tells the bot how to interact with the object.

    Wait for control – This tells the bot to wait for a specific duration for the object. This shows how many seconds to continue looking for the object before moving on to the next line.

    Assign the output to variable – This is always of the `string` type and will assign any value from the control to this variable. It is useful when reading values from an application.

14. Firstly, we need to tell the bot where to look for the object. For our **Browser: Launch website** action on line **5**, set the **Object detail** property to **Window**, and then click the refresh icon, as shown in the following screenshot:

Recorder: Capture
This command can be used to simulate an object's click event.
Object detail
Window
Variable
1
2

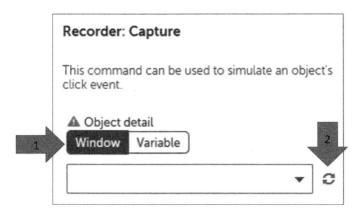

Figure 7.4 – Capturing the Window refresh icon

15. The drop-down list will show all windows that are currently open. Select **Home - Google Chrome**. The **Recorder: Capture** action properties should look like this:

Recorder: Capture
This command can be used to simulate an object's click event.
Object detail
Window
Variable
Home - Google Chrome
Window title
Home - Google Chrome
Use * as a wildcard
Window application path
C:\Program Files (x86)\Google\Chrome\Application\chrome.exe

Figure 7.5 – Recorder: Capture properties window

16. To capture the **CONTACT** tab, click on **Capture object**.

17. The SkySoft web page should appear. Hover your mouse on the web page, and Automation Anywhere will look for all the objects on the page. It highlights what it has found with a red border. Move your mouse until you get the red border around the **CONTACT** tab. The capture screen should look like this:

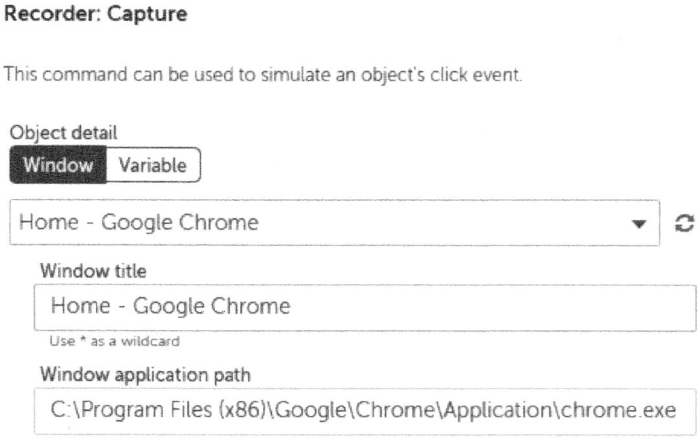

Figure 7.6 – Recorder: Capture – capturing an object

18. Once the correct object has been identified with the red border, click to select it. Once clicked, the bot will capture all the attributes it needs. You will see the selected object in the preview section of the properties. It should look something like this:

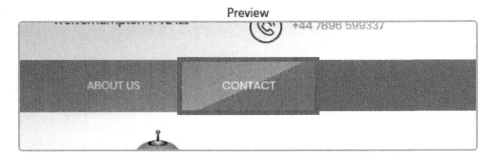

Figure 7.7 – Captured object Preview property

If you didn't manage to capture the correct object, you can always recapture again to try and get it. It can be tricky with some applications and may take a few attempts. It is also a best practice to have your browser zoom set to 100%.

19. The next step is to look at the attributes used to identify the object. If we collapse the **Object properties** list, you will see only the checked attributes used to identify the object. The properties should look like this:

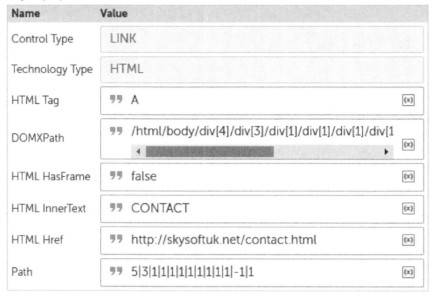

Figure 7.8 – Recorder: Capturing Object properties

These attributes can be modified if needed. Variables can also be used as values. This is useful when you are working with interfaces that are very similar in build with only a few attribute differences.

20. Now that the bot has found the **CONTACT** tab, the next step is to get the bot to click on it. This is where we set the **Action** property. This should be set to **Click**, as shown here:

Figure 7.9 – Recorder: Capturing Action properties

21. Click on **Save**.

22. We have set the first bot interaction with the website. The development interface for this step should look like this:

2	🎞 Comment "Launch Website"	⋮
3	↗ Browser: Launch website "http://skysoftuk.net/"	⋮
4	🎞 Comment "Navigate to Contact Page"	⋮
5	🎥 Recorder: Capture Click on link HTML InnerText "CONTACT" in window "Home - Google Chrome"	⋮

Figure 7.10 – Development interface

At this stage, we are only building the instructions for what we want the bot to perform. As the bot hasn't yet been executed, it hasn't actually done anything. The next step is to fill in the form on the **CONTACT** page. The bot itself hasn't actually clicked on the **CONTACT** tab, so we will do this manually.

23. Manually click on the **CONTACT** tab on the *skysoftuk.net* website. The web page should look like this:

Figure 7.11 – Contacts page

24. There are three items we need to fill in on the form: **Name, Email,** and **Message**. Starting with **Name**, as we did before, add a new **Recorder: Capture** action just below line **6**.

25. For the **Recorder: Capture** action on line **7**, set the **Object detail** properties to **Window**.

26. Refresh the windows drop-down list and select **Contact - Google Chrome**. The action properties should look like this:

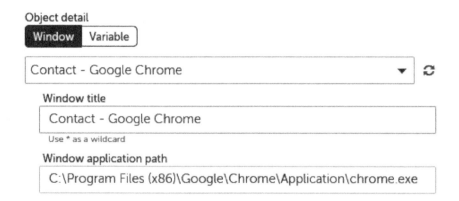

Figure 7.12 – Recorder: Capture properties window

27. To capture the **Name** textbox, click on **Capture object**.

28. When the Contact web page appears, hover the mouse over the **Name** textbox until it has a red border around it, as shown in the following screenshot:

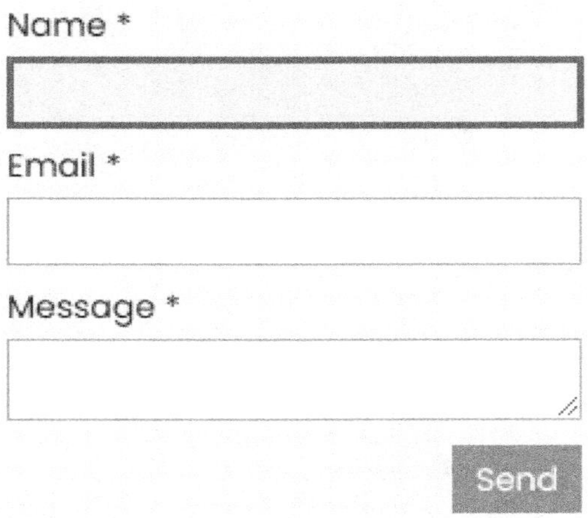

Name *
Email *
Message *
Send

Figure 7.13 – Capturing the Name textbox

29. Click in the red border to capture it. Once captured, check the preview to ensure that the correct object has been captured, as shown in the following screenshot:

Recapture object
Preview
Name *
Email *

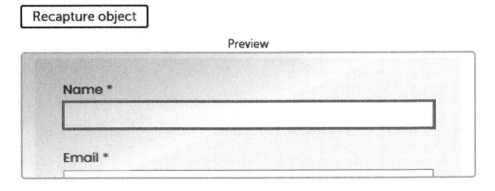

Figure 7.14 – Preview properties

30. This time we want to populate the textbox with your name. Set the following properties for the **Recorder: Capture** action on line **7**:

    Action: **Set text**

    Keystrokes: **Enter keystrokes here or use the on-screen keyboard**

    Value: *(Enter your name)*

The properties should look like the following screenshot:

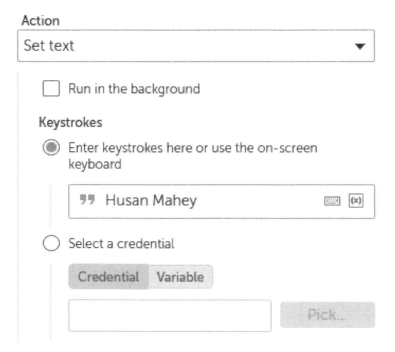

Figure 7.15 – Recorder: Capturing Set text Action properties

31. Click on **Save**.

32. To do the same for the **Email** textbox, add another **Recorder: Capture** action just below line **7**.

33. For the **Recorder: Capture** action on line **8**, set the **Object detail** properties to **Window**.

34. Refresh the windows drop-down list and select **Contact - Google Chrome**.

35. To capture the **Email** textbox, click on **Capture object**.

36. When the Contact web page appears, hover the mouse over the **Email** textbox until it has a red border around it, as shown in the following screenshot:

Figure 7.16 – Capturing the Email textbox

37. Click in the red border to capture it. Once captured, check the preview to ensure the correct object has been captured.

38. This time we want to populate the textbox with your email address. Set the following properties for the **Recorder: Capture** action on line **8**:

Action: **Set text**

Keystrokes: **Enter keystrokes here or use the on-screen keyboard**

Value: *(Enter your email address)*

The properties should look similar to the following screenshot:

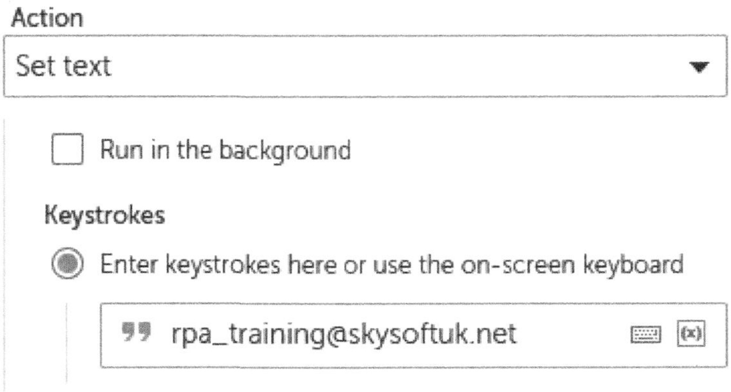

Action

Set text ▼

☐ Run in the background

Keystrokes

◉ Enter keystrokes here or use the on-screen keyboard

💬 rpa_training@skysoftuk.net

Figure 7.17 – Recorder: Capturing Set text Action properties

39. Click on **Save**.

40. To do the same for the **Message** textbox, add another **Recorder: Capture** action just below line **8** and set its **Object detail** properties to **Window**.

41. Refresh the windows drop-down list and select **Contact - Google Chrome**.

42. To capture the **Message** textbox, as before, click on **Capture object**.

43. When the Contact web page appears, hover the mouse over the **Message** textbox until it has a red border around it, as shown in the following screenshot:

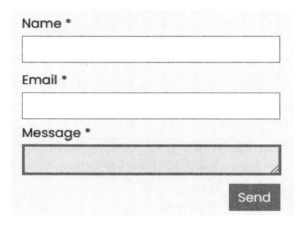

Figure 7.18 – Capturing the Message textbox

44. Click in the red border to capture it. Once captured, check the preview to ensure that the correct object has been captured.

45. This time we want to populate the textbox with your email address. Set the following properties for the **Recorder: Capture** action on line **9**:

Action: Set text

Keystrokes: Enter keystrokes here or use the on-screen keyboard

Value: Having lots of fun learning Automation Anywhere

The properties should look similar to the following screenshot:

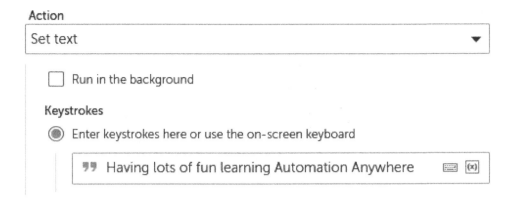

Figure 7.19 – Recorder: Capturing Set text Action properties

46. Click on **Save**. Your development interface for this section should look like this:

Figure 7.20 – Development interface

47. Nearly there! There is just one more object to capture. This time we want the bot to click on the **Send** button. To do this, add another **Recorder: Capture** action just below line **10** and set the **Object details** property to **Window**.

48. Refresh the windows drop-down list and select **Contact - Google Chrome**.

49. To capture the **Send** button, just like before, click on the **Capture** object.

50. When the `Contact` web page appears, hover the mouse over the **Send** button until it has a red border around it, as shown in the following screenshot:

Figure 7.21 – Capturing the Send button

51. Click in the red border to capture it. Once captured, check the preview to ensure that the correct object has been captured.

52. This time we want the bot to click the button. To do this, set the following properties for the **Recorder: Capture** action on line **11**:

Action: **Click**

The properties should look similar to the following screenshot:

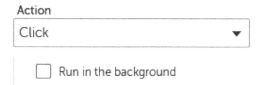

Figure 7.22 – Recorder: Capturing Click Action properties

53. Click on **Save**.

54. We can now close the Google Chrome session with the *skysoftuk.net* website.

55. Finally, a **Message** box action appears just below line **11** to let us know the bot has finished running the task.

56. Set the message to display something like "Bot has sent email successfully".

57. Click on **Save**. The development interface for this section should look like this:

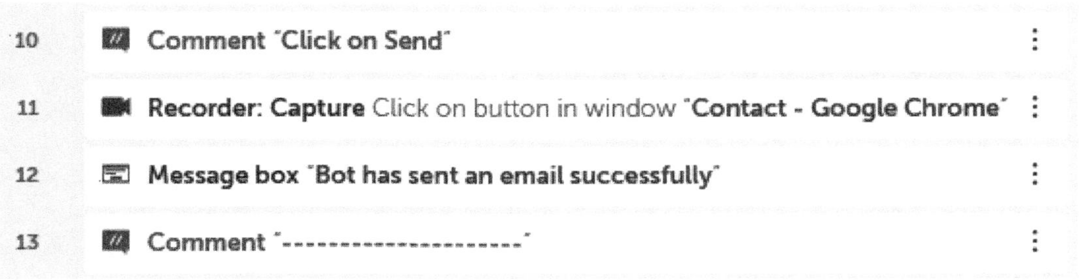

10	🖼 Comment "Click on Send"	⋮
11	🎥 Recorder: Capture Click on button in window "Contact - Google Chrome"	⋮
12	🖾 Message box "Bot has sent an email successfully"	⋮
13	🖼 Comment "---------------------"	⋮

Figure 7.23 – Development interface

Great work! You have completed the walk-through. Feel free to run the bot and test it. It should launch the website, fill in the online form, and click on the send button. Remember to ensure the browser is closed before running your bot.

In the next section, we will expand what we have already learned, moving from automating web applications to working with desktop applications. We will also be learning how to simulate keystrokes to run tasks on desktop applications.

Automating desktop applications

In the previous section, we learned to use Automation Anywhere with browser-based applications. Our tasks are also most likely to include desktop applications. In principle, the automation of desktop applications is the same as web applications. We have already used the **Recorder** package and, in particular, the **Capture** action. The **Capture** action is also used with desktop applications. As with web applications, you have to identify the window, followed by what object to capture, and finally an action to tell the bot what to do with it.

You will be exposed to working with a desktop application, in particular Notepad. I am assuming we all have Notepad on our desktops. We will use the capture action as well as keystroke simulation to perform tasks. These are very useful actions when building an RPA solution as they work in the same way a human interacts with interfaces. Humans interact with interfaces by using keyboards and by clicking or selecting objects on the screen.

In the following walk-through, we will build a bot that will navigate to the SkySoft website and extract some text. The bot will then open a notepad and enter the extracted text. Then we will save the text file using keystrokes and the capture actions.

In this walk-through, we will be performing the following tasks:

1. Launching the `http://skysoftuk.net` website
2. Extracting a paragraph of text and assigning it to a variable
3. Opening the Notepad application
4. Entering the extracted text into Notepad
5. Saving the Notepad text file using keystroke simulation
6. Closing the Notepad application

Let's start this walk-through by executing the following steps:

1. Log in to the **Control Room**.
2. Create a new bot and call it `Chapter 7 - Desktop Apps` in the `\Bot\` folder.
3. As always, we begin by adding some comments to use as a template for our bot. Add a new **Comment** action as line number 1, set the value to "- -", and click on **Save**.
4. Add a new **Comment** action as "`Launch Website`" on line **2** and click on **Save**.
5. Add a new **Comment** action as "`Capture text`" on line **3** and click on **Save**.
6. Add a new **Comment** action as "`Open notepad`" on line **4** and click on **Save**.
7. Add a new **Comment** action as "`Enter text in notepad`" on line **5** and click on **Save**.
8. Add a new **Comment** action as "`Save text file`" on line **6** and click on **Save**.
9. Add a new **Comment** action as "`Close notepad`" on line **7** and click on **Save**.
10. Add a new **Comment** action as "- - - - - - - - - - - - - - - - - - - -" on line **8** and click on **Save**. Your bot should look like this:

Figure 7.24 – Development interface

11. We need to start by launching the website as we did before. Add the **Browser: Launch website** action under line **2**.

12. Set the following properties for the **Browser: Launch website** action on line **3**:

    URL: `http://skysoftuk.net/`

    Browser: **Google Browser**

    The **Browser: Launch website** action properties should look like this:

Figure 7.25 – Browser: Launch website properties

13. Click on **Save**.

14. As before, we need to ensure that the website is available to capture anything. Manually open another session of Chrome and navigate to `http://skysoftuk.net/`.

15. To extract some text from an object, the object needs to be captured. To do this, add a new **Recorder: Capture** action just below line **4**.

16. For the **Recorder: Capture** action on line **5**, set the **Object detail** properties to **Window**.

17. Refresh the windows drop-down list and select **Home - Google Chrome**. The action properties should look like this:

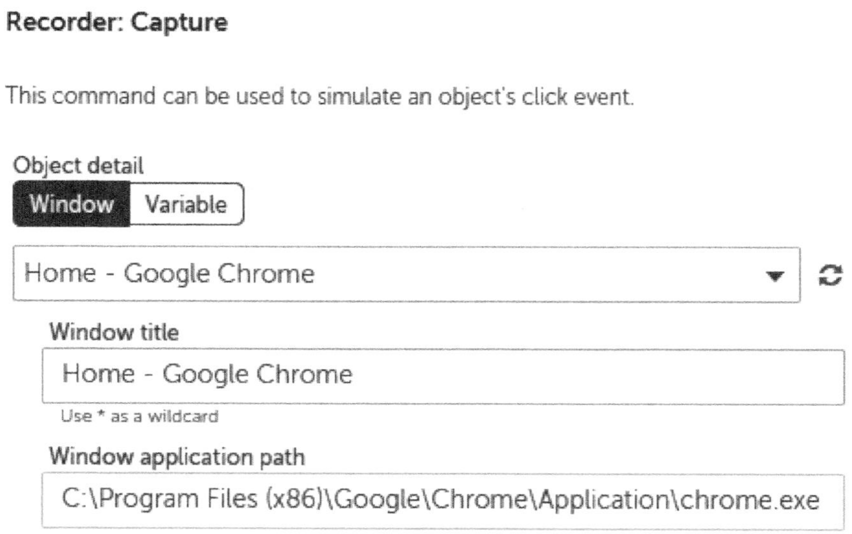

Recorder: Capture

This command can be used to simulate an object's click event.

Object detail

| Window | Variable |

Home - Google Chrome   ▼   ⟳

Window title

Home - Google Chrome

Use * as a wildcard

Window application path

C:\Program Files (x86)\Google\Chrome\Application\chrome.exe

Figure 7.26 – Recorder: Capture properties window

18. To capture the second paragraph on the **HOME** web page, click on the **Capture** object.

19. When the **HOME** web page appears, hover the mouse over the second paragraph until it has a red border around it, as shown in the following screenshot:

Figure 7.27 – Capturing paragraph text

20. Click in the red border to capture it. Once captured, check the preview to ensure that the correct object has been captured.

21. As we want to extract the text, we need to identify which property contains this. If we look through the object properties, we can identify the correct property. Once identified, make a note of it. When I captured this, the text was in the **HTML InnerText** property, as you can see in the following screenshot:

☐ HTML InnerText   　🗣 Commonly known as RPA it enables organisations

Figure 7.28 – HTML InnerText property

22. When you capture the paragraph, you may not necessarily see the text in the same attribute. In some cases, it may be in the **Name** attribute, as shown in the following screenshot:

☐ Name   　🗣 Commonly known as RPA it enables organisations

Figure 7.29 – Paragraph text property name

23. This time we want the bot to extract the text from this object and assign it to the default variable called `prompt-assignment`. To do this, set the following properties for the **Recorder: Capture** action on line **5**:

Action: **Get property**

Property name: `HTML InnerText` (if your property was **Name**, then set as **Name**)

Assign the output to variable: **prompt-assignment - String**

The properties should look similar to the following screenshot:

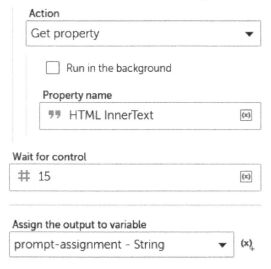

Figure 7.30 – Recorder: Capturing Get property Action properties

24. Click on **Save**. Your development interface should look something like this:

Figure 7.31 – Development interface

The first stage of our bot is now complete. Great work! The bot extracts the text from the second paragraph on the *skysoftuk.net* website. The text is assigned to a variable. Next, our bot will open Notepad and enter the extracted text.

Working with Notepad

As Notepad is available on pretty much all desktops, it makes sense to use it to demonstrate how to automate applications. With any desktop application, we interact by clicking and typing in one way or another.

Clicking controls aspects such as buttons, checkboxes, and drop-down lists. As you have already seen, using the **Recorder: Capture** action is ideal for this type of interaction. It is flexible enough to be applied to all types of applications. We will continue our walk-through as follows:

1. To open Notepad, add the **Application: Open program/file** action just below line **6**.

2. Set the following properties for the **Application: Open program/file** action on line **7**:

    Location of the program/file: C:\Windows\System32\notepad.exe (just using Notepad will also work)

    The properties should look similar to the following screenshot:

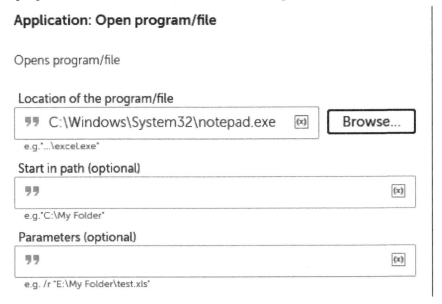

Figure 7.32 – Application: Open program/file action properties

3. Click on **Save**.

4. As before, we are writing the instructions for our bot. It hasn't actually been executed. We now need to enter our text into Notepad. Open Notepad manually so that we can capture the pane for our text.

5. To enter the contents of our variable into Notepad, we need to capture the entry pane. For this, add a new **Recorder: Capture** action just below line **8**.

6. For the **Recorder: Capture** action on line **9**, set the **Object detail** property to **Window**.

7. Refresh the windows drop-down list and select **Untitled - Notepad**. The action properties should look like this:

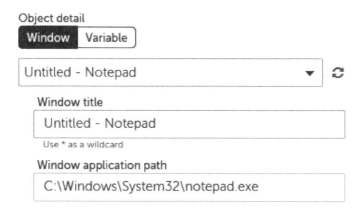

Figure 7.33 – Recorder: Capture properties window

8. To capture the text entry pane, click on **Capture object**.

9. When Notepad appears, hover the mouse over the text entry pane until it has a red border around it, as follows:

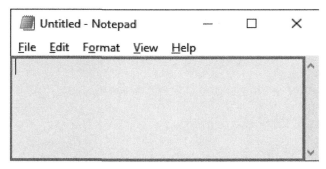

Figure 7.34 – Capturing the Notepad text entry pane

10. Click in the red border to capture it. Once captured, check the preview to ensure that the correct object has been captured.

11. We want to enter the contents of our variable in this pane. Set the following properties for the **Recorder: Capture** action on line **9**:

Action: **Set text**

Keystrokes: $prompt-assignment$

The properties should look similar to the following screenshot:

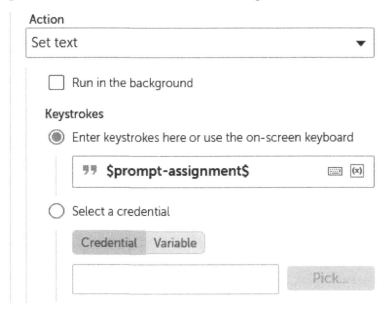

Figure 7.35 – Capturing Object Action properties

12. Click on **Save**. Your development interface should look something like this:

6	🗨 Comment "Open notepad"	⋮
7	⊕ Application: Open program/file "C:\Windows\System32\notepad.exe"	⋮
8	🗨 Comment "Enter text in notepad"	⋮
9	🎥 Recorder: Capture Set text on textbox in window "**Untitled - Notepad**"	⋮

Figure 7.36 – Development interface

You should now be getting pretty good at using the capture action of Automation Anywhere. This is a very useful action. It's what tends to make the difference between traditional programming languages and RPA development, allowing the ability to quickly and easily interact with any web or desktop objects.

In the next stage, we will introduce keystroke simulation. Again, we can automate tasks by replicating keystrokes to perform a task. This can be useful when capturing objects may be difficult or this option may not be available.

Simulating keystrokes

We have our text in Notepad now and it is ready to be saved as a file. We can use the recorder package to capture the menu items and save the file. To demonstrate how to simulate keystrokes, you will not be using the capture action to save the file. We will continue with our walk-through, demonstrating how to achieve this by using the **Simulate Keystrokes** action instead. As before, the bot hasn't actually executed any actions yet; we need to replicate this manually. So let's copy and paste the text from the second paragraph into Notepad. Notepad should look like this:

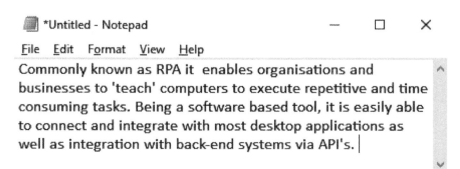

Figure 7.37 – Notepad window

If we wanted to save the file in Notepad using just keystrokes, we would need to identify the keystroke sequence. By inspecting the menu options, we can identify that the sequence to bring up the **Save As** dialog is *Ctrl + Shift + S* or *Alt* then *F* then *A*.

We have now established the keystroke sequence needed for our bot to trigger the **Save As** dialog. Observe the following walk-through to implement this:

1. Add the **Simulate Keystrokes** action under line **10**.

2. For the **Simulate Keystrokes** action on line **11**, set the **Select window** property to **Window**.

3. Refresh the windows drop-down list and select ***Untitled - Notepad**. The action properties should look like this:

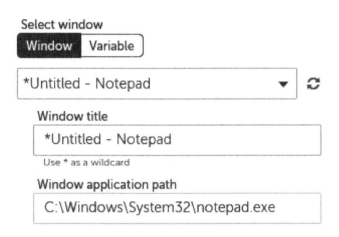

Figure 7.38 – Simulate keystrokes properties

4. Click on **Save**.

5. To assign the keystroke sequence of *Alt + F + A*, set the **Keystrokes** property to **Enter keystrokes here or use the on-screen keyboard**.

6. Click on the keyboard icon, as shown in the following screenshot:

Figure 7.39 – The Insert Keystroke icon

7. The keyboard will appear with all the special keys. Any alphanumeric keys can just be typed in the desired case. Select the sequence *Alt + F + A*. This property should look like this:

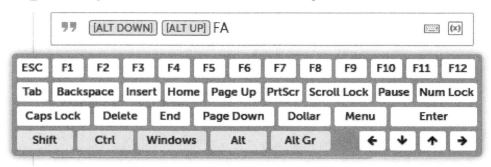

Figure 7.40 – Inserting keystrokes via the keyboard (Alt + F + A)

8. Click on **Save**.

9. Manually select **Save As** from Notepad to launch the **Save As** dialog. Here we want to enter the file path and click on the **Save** button. As we are doing this using keystrokes, we can see that the keystroke sequence to navigate to the file path textbox is *Alt + n*, and for the **Save** button it's *Alt + S*. *Alt* can be entered using the action keystrokes keyboard and *n* and *S* just by using your workstation keyboard. We can see the required shortcuts in the following screenshot:

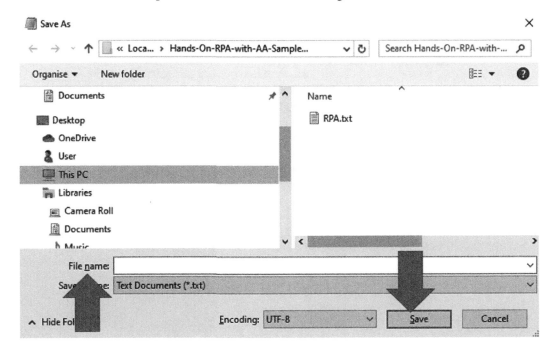

Figure 7.41 – The Save As dialog from Notepad

10. To navigate to the **File name** textbox, add another **Simulate Keystrokes** action just below line **11**.

11. For the **Simulate Keystrokes** action on line **12**, set the **Select window** property to **Window**.

12. Refresh the windows drop-down list and select **Save As**. The action properties should look like this:

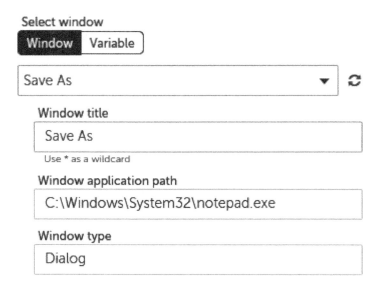

Figure 7.42 – Simulate keystrokes properties

13. Click on **Save**.

14. To assign the keystroke sequence of *Alt* + *n*, set the **Keystrokes** property to **Enter keystrokes here or use the on-screen keyboard**.

15. Once the keyboard appears, select the sequence *Alt* + *n*. This property should look like this:

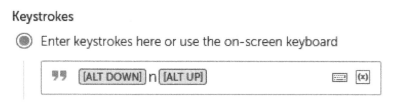

Figure 7.43 – Inserting keystrokes

16. Click on **Save**.

17. To enter the file path of C:\Hands-On-RPA-with-AA-Sample-Data\
    Chapter07.txt, add another **Simulate Keystrokes** action just below line **12**.

18. For the **Simulate Keystrokes** action on line **13**, set the **Select window** property to
    Window.

19. Refresh the windows drop-down list and select **Save As**.

20. Click on **Save**.

21. To assign the file path, set the **Keystrokes** property to **Enter keystrokes here or use
    the on-screen keyboard**.

22. Once the keyboard appears, enter C:\Hands-On-RPA-with-AA-Sample-
    Data\Chapter07.txt, as shown in the following screenshot:

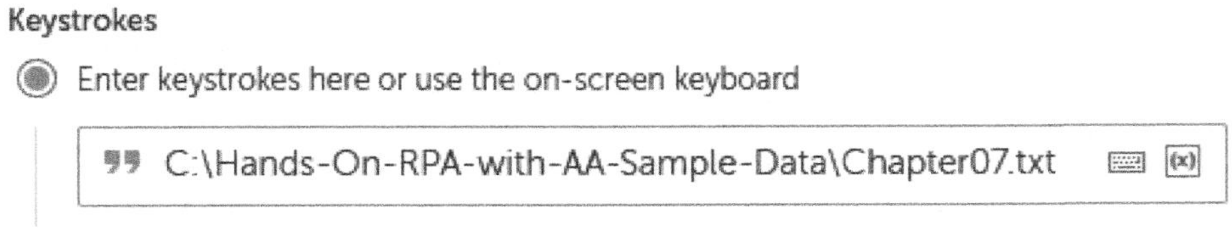

Keystrokes

⊙ Enter keystrokes here or use the on-screen keyboard

> 🮥🮥 C:\Hands-On-RPA-with-AA-Sample-Data\Chapter07.txt   ⌨ ⓧ

Figure 7.44 – Inserting keystrokes

23. Click on **Save**.

24. To initiate the **Save** button using *Alt* + *S*, add another **Simulate Keystrokes** action
    just below line **13**.

25. For the **Simulate Keystrokes** action on line **14**, set the **Select window** property to
    Window.

26. Refresh the windows drop-down list and select **Save As**.

27. Click on **Save**.

28. To assign the keystroke sequence of *Alt* + *S*, set the **Keystrokes** property to **Enter
    keystrokes here or use the on-screen keyboard**.

29. Once the keyboard appears, select the sequence *Alt + S*. This property should look like this:

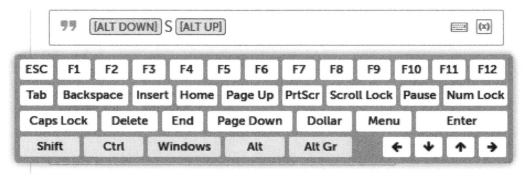

Figure 7.45 – Clicking on the save button in the dialog box

30. Click on **Save**. Your development interface for this section should look something like this:

Figure 7.46 – Development interface

31. Manually save the Notepad file, as it would have been saved at this point if the bot was processing the task.

32. All that's left now is to close Notepad. To do this, add the **Window: Close** action so that it's just below line **15**.

33. For the **Window: Close** action on line **16**, set the **Select window** property to **Window**.

34. Refresh the windows drop-down list and select Chapter07.txt - Notepad. The properties should look like this:

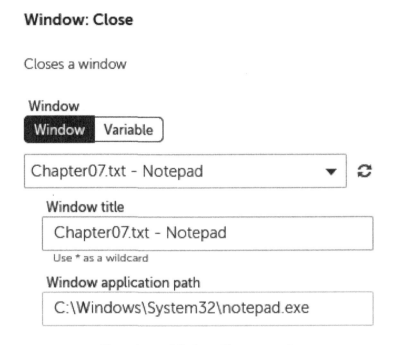

Figure 7.47 – Window: Close properties

35. Click on **Save**.

The bot is now complete. Close all websites apart from the **Control Room** and also close Notepad. Your complete development interface should look like this:

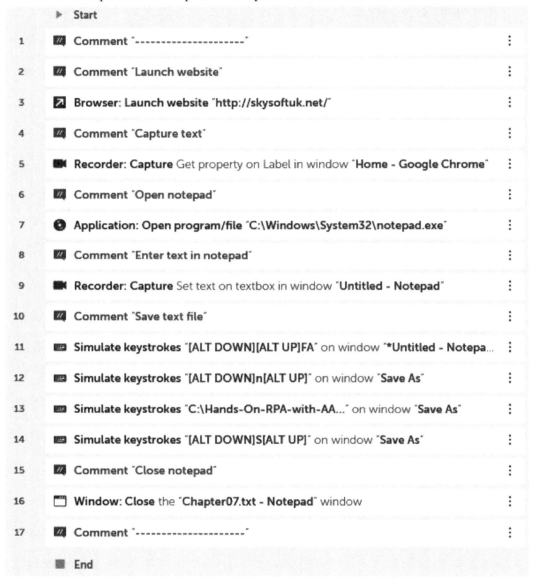

	▶ Start	
1	◰ Comment "---------------------"	⋮
2	◰ Comment "Launch website"	⋮
3	◿ Browser: Launch website "http://skysoftuk.net/"	⋮
4	◰ Comment "Capture text"	⋮
5	▦ Recorder: Capture Get property on Label in window "**Home - Google Chrome**"	⋮
6	◰ Comment "Open notepad"	⋮
7	◉ Application: Open program/file "C:\Windows\System32\notepad.exe"	⋮
8	◰ Comment "Enter text in notepad"	⋮
9	▦ Recorder: Capture Set text on textbox in window "**Untitled - Notepad**"	⋮
10	◰ Comment "Save text file"	⋮
11	▤ Simulate keystrokes "[ALT DOWN][ALT UP]FA" on window "*Untitled - Notepa...	⋮
12	▤ Simulate keystrokes "[ALT DOWN]n[ALT UP]" on window "Save As"	⋮
13	▤ Simulate keystrokes "C:\Hands-On-RPA-with-AA..." on window "Save As"	⋮
14	▤ Simulate keystrokes "[ALT DOWN]S[ALT UP]" on window "Save As"	⋮
15	◰ Comment "Close notepad"	⋮
16	▭ Window: Close the "Chapter07.txt - Notepad" window	⋮
17	◰ Comment "---------------------"	⋮
	▪ End	

Figure 7.48 – Development interface

The time has come to test your bot. Before you do, remember to delete the `Chapter07.txt` file as the bot will create this. It should launch the website, extract the text, and then create and save a text file using Notepad. You have learned a lot of valuable skills in this walk-through. Recorder and keystrokes are vital actions used in most automation tasks.

Summary

This chapter has covered some key elements of implementing RPA in relation to your daily tasks. Understanding how to interact with web and desktop applications is what we humans do. All the tasks that we perform while sitting in front of a computer involve interacting with an application of some sort. This interaction may involve selecting or clicking on objects as well as entering inputs using the keyboard.

The walk-throughs in this chapter have given you the practical knowledge to enable you to create bots that navigate through applications, as well as read and enter text. You will be confident with capturing objects such as textboxes and drop-down lists, as well as tabs and buttons. Your journey to becoming an RPA developer is truly underway.

You are doing great work and will continue building on this in the next chapter, where we will explore how to perform string manipulation. This includes creating and looping through `List` type variables when working with strings. There will be a number of different data transformation and parsing actions that we will look at – include, replace, substrings, extract, and trim, and we will use regular expressions to find string patterns.

8
String Manipulation and List Variables

As you progress in this book, you will gain experience with more actions at each stage. Each action you learn will build upon your existing knowledge. This will all contribute to making you a more confident RPA developer.

In this chapter, we will be covering the different actions available for string manipulation. This is a common task needed when your bot is working with data. Typically, your data format and layout needs to be transformed and parsed so that it meets system requirements. When transferring data from one source to another, there may be slight differences in the required formats. String manipulation routines are needed to transform your data so that it meets the desired requirements.

In order to fully understand how to work with data, this chapter will also cover List type variables. We use these when we need to iterate through a single string by splitting it with a specific delimiter. By the end of this chapter, you will have the skills to confidently handle various formats of strings and be able to manipulate them so that they meet any system requirement. You will also be able to create List variables and loop through the data for any manipulation that may be needed. Another skill that you will learn is how to apply some simple logical conditions using variables.

In this chapter, we will cover the following topics:

- Manipulating strings
- Creating and looping through List variables
- Applying simple conditional logic

In this chapter, you will be guided by a walk-through so that you can build a fully functional bot. This will be a bit intensive, but you will gain some valuable experience in implementing a number of useful actions. We will be working with a number of Automation Anywhere packages, some of which you have already used in this book. We will be using the following packages:

Figure 8.1 – Packages that will be used in this chapter

You will be building a single bot to solve a specific problem. As we progress, we will cover different aspects of manipulating strings. By the end, you will have a fully functional bot that performs a specific task. This task will be pretty generic and easy to understand, giving you further ideas on where you may be able to use RPA to help automate your current routine tasks.

Technical requirements

You will need the following in order to install the Automation Anywhere Bot agent:

- Windows operating system version 7 or higher
- Processor with a minimum speed of 3 GHz
- Minimum of 4 GB RAM
- At least 100 MB hard disk space
- Internet Explorer v10 or higher OR Chrome v49 or higher
- A minimum screen resolution of 1024*768
- An internet connection with a minimum speed of 10 Mb/sec

- Completed registration with Automation Anywhere A2019 Community Edition
- Logged on successfully to Automation Anywhere A2019 Community Edition
- A successfully registered local device
- Successfully downloaded sample data from GitHub

Manipulating strings

When dealing with data, it isn't always in the format we need it to be in. Developers will often write routines to manipulate data so that it suits its purpose. A number of actions are available to help us manipulate data. This walk-through will give you the skills you need to build effective data manipulation routines. In the example, you will read a single string that consists of a few names. This is the format the data is initially available in. The bot is tasked with manipulating it to produce a CSV file. This file will have separated all the names into two columns. The first column will contain the surname in capitals, while the second column will contain the forename and any initials. The forename will be in *Proper* case, while the initials will be in uppercase.

While working through this walk-through, we will look at the following string manipulation actions:

- **Replace**
- **Find**
- **Substring**
- **Split**
- **Trim**
- **Uppercase**
- **Lowercase**

We will also learn how to use regular expressions to find patterns within a string. We have already looked at variables, but in this walk-through, you will be introduced to a new type of variable. We will be also using the List variable to help the bot complete its task. Here, we will build a simple loop to iterate through our lists. There will also be an opportunity to introduce a simple conditional logic statement. There is a lot to cover in this chapter, all of which will give you a wealth of experience with further Automation Anywhere actions.

This walk-through will cover performing the following tasks:

1. Reading a single string of names from a text file to a `String` variable.

2. Splitting this string into individual names and placing them in a `List` variable.

3. Looping through the list.

4. Identifying name counterparts; that is, `Surname` and `Forename`.

5. Formatting the name as (case-sensitive) `Surname, Forename`.

6. Checking if there are any middle names and if so, assigning them to a `List` type variable.

7. Looping through the middle names and formatting them so that only the initial is capitalized.

8. Saving the results as a CSV file.

We will break this walk-through into six sections to make it easier to follow:

- Section 1 – Initializing lists and loops

- Section 2 – Getting full names

- Section 3 – Getting forenames

- Section 4 – Getting surnames

- Section 5 – Getting middle names

- Section 6 – Outputting the results

As always, we will start by adding some comments that will help guide us. We will begin with just the basic skeleton and add further levels of detail as we progress.

Let's start this walk-through by executing the following steps:

1. Log into **Control Room**.

2. Create a new bot and call it `Chapter 8 - String Manipulation`. Do this inside the `\Bot\` folder.

3. As always, we'll begin by adding some comments that will be used as a template for our bot. Add a new **Comment** action on line **1**, set the value to `"-------------------------"`, and click on **Save**.

4. Add a new **Comment** action of `"------- Section 1 - Initialize List and Loop"` on line **2** and click on **Save**.

5. Add a new **Comment** action of "`------- Section 2 - Get Full name`" on line **3** and click on **Save**.

6. Add a new **Comment** action of "`------- Section 3 - Get Forename`" on line **4** and click on **Save**.

7. Add a new **Comment** action of "`------- Section 4 - Get Surname`" on line **5** and click on **Save**.

8. Add a new **Comment** action of "`------- Section 5 - Get Middle Names`" on line **6** and click on **Save**.

9. Add a new **Comment** action of "`------- Section 6 - Output Results`" on line **7** and click on **Save**.

10. Add a new **Comment** action of "`---------------------`" on line **8** and click on **Save**. Now, your bot should look like this:

Figure 8.2 – Development interface

We are now ready to start on our six sections. We will start with *Section 1 – Initializing lists and loops*. This will involve assigning the initial string to all the names. Once this is done, you will get some experience with using the **Split** action and creating a simple loop.

Section 1 – Initializing lists and loops

First, we need to create our variables; we will need a `Table` data type variable to read the source text file and a `List` type variable to assign the table variable values to. Once in the list, we will also need a `String` type variable so that we can store each full name from the list. Let's get started:

1. Create a `Table` type variable called `tblSourceText`. The **Create variable** dialog should look like this:

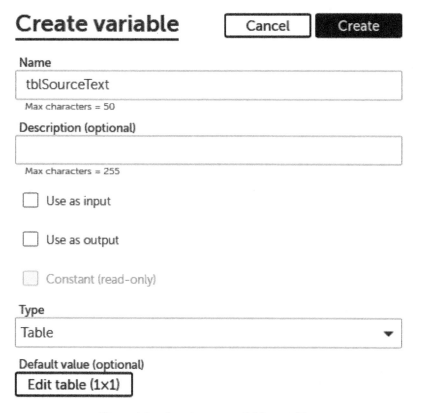

Figure 8.3 – Creating a new Table variable

2. This variable will need to be split into a `List` type variable. Create a `List` type variable called `lstSourceList`. The new variable dialog should look like this:

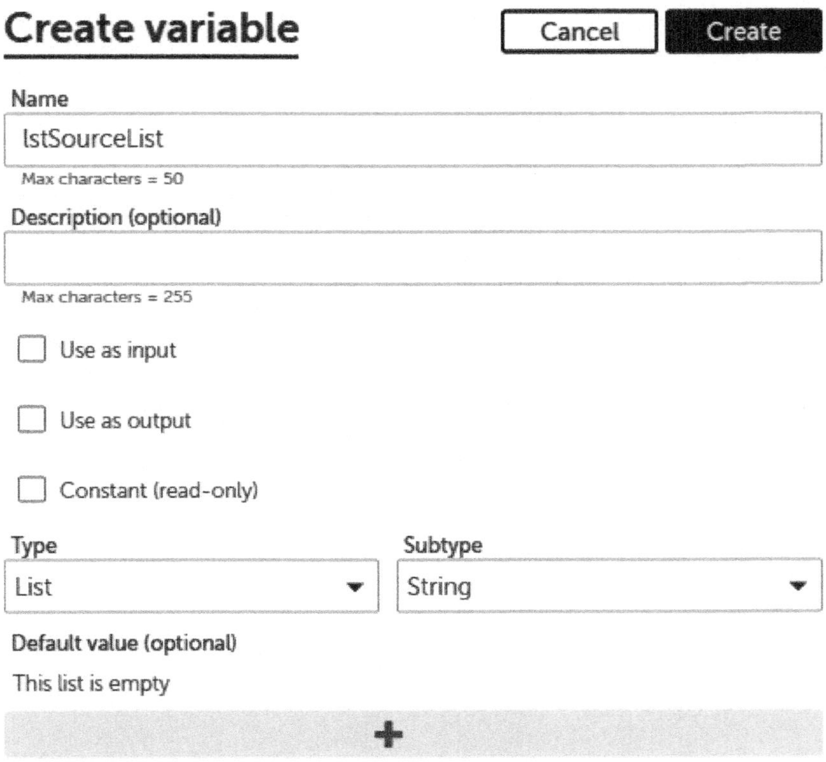

Create variable

Cancel   Create

Name

lstSourceList

Max characters = 50

Description (optional)

Max characters = 255

☐ Use as input

☐ Use as output

☐ Constant (read-only)

Type   **Subtype**

List   ▼   String   ▼

Default value (optional)

This list is empty

✚

Figure 8.4 – Creating a new List variable

3. To store each full name from the list, create a String type variable called strFullName. The initial variable list should look like this:

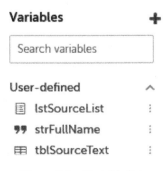

Variables   ✚

Search variables

User-defined   ︿

　📋 lstSourceList   ⋮

　❞ strFullName   ⋮

　▦ tblSourceText   ⋮

Figure 8.5 – Variable list

4. The source list of names that we will be using is stored in the `Chapter08_InputData.txt` file in our root folder, which can be found at `C:\Hands-On-RPA-with-AA-Sample-Data`. The content of this file is a single string containing the following data:

```
"husan lal mahey, priya mahey, sonam mahey, ravinder raj
lal mahey, sunita kumari mahey, manisha Mahey"
```

The contents of a text file can be read into a `Table` type variable, but first, we must open the text file. To do this, add the **CSV/TXT: Open** action just below line **2**.

5. Set the following properties for the **CSV/TXT: Open** action on line **3**:

Session name: txt_Source

File path: Desktop file – `C:\Hands-On-RPA-with-AA-Sample-Data\Chapter08_InputData.txt`

Contains header: *Unchecked*

Delimiter: **Newline**

The properties should look like this:

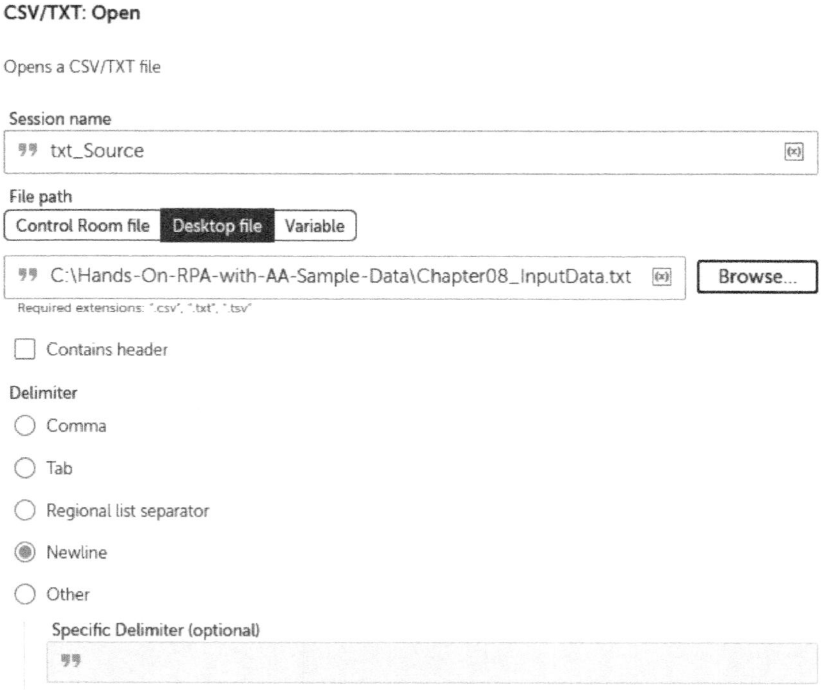

CSV/TXT: Open

Opens a CSV/TXT file

Session name

    〟 txt_Source   [x]

File path

| Control Room file | **Desktop file** | Variable |

    〟 C:\Hands-On-RPA-with-AA-Sample-Data\Chapter08_InputData.txt [x] | Browse... |
    Required extensions: ".csv", ".txt", ".tsv"

☐ Contains header

Delimiter

○ Comma

○ Tab

○ Regional list separator

◉ Newline

○ Other

    Specific Delimiter (optional)
    〟

Figure 8.6 – CSV/TXT: Open properties

6. Click on **Save**.

7. To read the contents to a table, add the **CSV/TXT: Read** action just below line **3**.

8. Set the following properties for the **CSV/TXT: Read** action on line **4**:

    Session name: txt_Source

    Assign value to the variable: tblSourceText - Table

    The properties should look like this:

    ### CSV/TXT: Read

    Reads the entire content of a CSV file

    Session name

    " txt_Source

    Assign value to the variable

    tblSourceText - Table   ▾   (x)₊

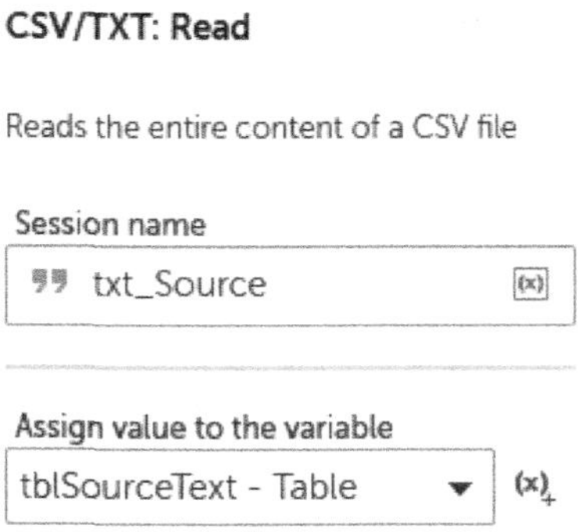

    Figure 8.7 – CSV/TXT: Read properties

9. Click on **Save**.

10. Finally, we need to close the CSV file session. To do this, add the **CSV/TXT: Close** action just below line **4**.

11. Set the following properties for the **CSV/TXT: Close** action on line **5**:

    Session name: txt_Source

    The properties should look like this:

    ### CSV/TXT: Close

    Closes CSV/TXT session

    Session name

    " txt_Source

    Figure 8.8 – CSV/TXT: Close properties

12. Click on **Save**.

With that, we have our source data assigned. It gets more interesting now as we start using some of the string manipulation actions. We'll start with the **Split** action. This action is used to split a variable by a defined delimiter and assign the results to a `List` type variable. This is very useful when working with different grouped data. An example of this would be if a variable contained a full postal address and you needed to break this down into subsections such as street, city, and so on. The **Split** action would be ideal in this scenario.

Applying the Split action

When a string needs to be separated into a `List` variable, we can apply the **Split** action. We have already created our `List` type variable; that is, `lstSourceList`. To split a variable, it is essential we know what character to use for the split. Let's take a look at our source string:

```
husan lal mahey, priya mahey, sonam mahey, ravinder raj lal
mahey, sunita kumari mahey, manisha mahey
```

Here, we can clearly see that the separator is a comma. We will use this to identify each item in the list. Let's continue with the walk-through and apply the **Split** action:

1. To split by a comma and assign to a list, drag the **String: Split** action to just below line **5**.

2. Set the following properties for the **String: Split** action on line **6**:

    Source string: `$tblSourceText[0][0]$`

    Delimiter: ,

    Delimiter is: **Not case sensitive**

    Split into substrings: **All possible**

    Assign the output to list variable: **lstSourceList – List of Strings**

    The properties should look like this:

String: Split

Splits the source string into multiple strings using a delimiter.

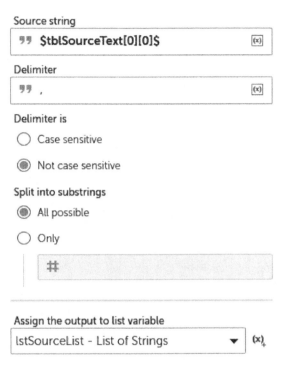

Figure 8.9 – String: Split properties dialog

3.   Click on **Save**. Your development interface for this section should look like this:

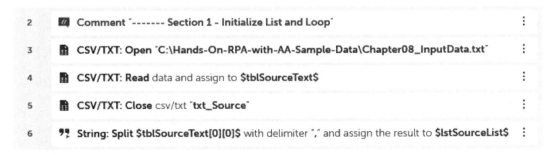

Figure 8.10 – Development interface

With that, you have successfully applied the **Spilt** action to split a variable and assign the results to a List variable. This will allow the bot to work with each name individually within the list. In order to work through the list, we have to implement a loop. In the next section, we will introduce you to loops—in particular, looping through lists. This list is a collection of individual names. We want to process each individual, and a loop allows you to do this. It effectively loops through each individual from a list until it reaches the end of the list.

Looping through lists

In this section, we will be looping through the lstSourceList list variable. As we go through the list, a variable will be needed to store the current name within the list. You created a variable for this earlier called strFullName.

To loop through a list, we must use the **Loop** action. Let's continue with the walk-through and apply the **Loop** action:

1. Drag the **Loop** action from the **Loop** package just below line **6**.

2. Set the following properties for the **Loop** action on line **7**:

    Loop Type: Iterator

    Iterator: **For each item in the list**

    list: **lstSourceList - List**

    For: **All items in the list**

    Assign the current value to variable: **strFullName - String**

    The properties should look like this:

Loop

Repeats the actions in a loop until a break

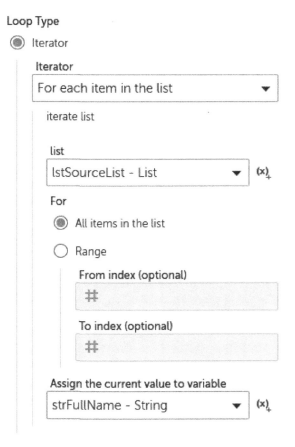

Figure 8.11 – Loop properties dialog

3. Click on **Save**.

4. All the actions that need to be performed within the loop are represented by being indented within the **Loop** action. Let's align our comments (lines **8** to **12**) so that they are within the loop. This can be done by selecting lines **8** to **12**, then dragging and dropping these lines just below line **7**, ensuring they are inside the loop on line **7**.

5. Click on **Save**.

6. Now would be a good idea to check the progress of our bot at each section. We can add a message box to show us what has been done so far. This is best placed at the output stage. So, add a **Message box** action just below line **12** while keeping it within the loop on line **7**.

7. Since we have now split the source text into the `strFullName` variable, we can add this value inside our **Message box**. Set the following properties for the **Loop** action on line **7**:

    Enter the message box window title: `String Manipulation`

    Enter the message to display: `Full name:  |$strFullName$|` *(note the bars before and after the variable. This is so we can clearly identify any white characters, such as spaces.)*

    The properties should look like this:

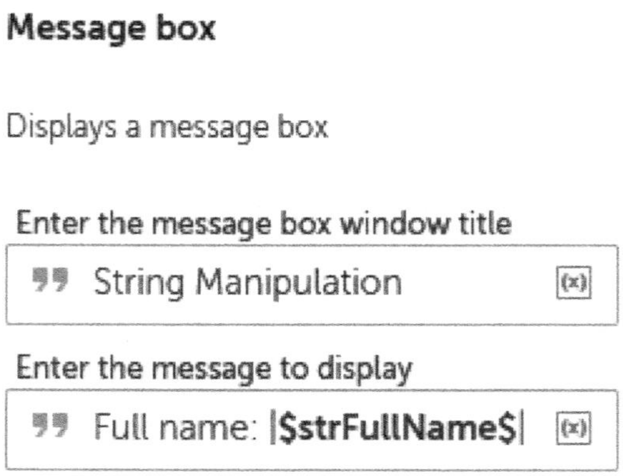

    ### Message box

    Displays a message box

    Enter the message box window title

    > 💬 String Manipulation [x]

    Enter the message to display

    > 💬 Full name: **|$strFullName$|** [x]

    Figure 8.12 – Message box properties

8. Click on **Save**. Your development window for this section should look like this:

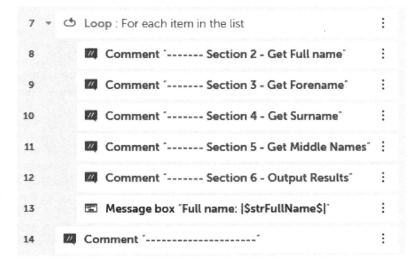

Figure 8.13 – Development interface

Great! We are now in a position to run the bot and test what progress we've made so far. The bot should split each individual name from the initial string and show it in the message box. With that, you have successfully created a List type variable and built a loop to iterate through the split list. You can go ahead and run the bot to test it.

In the next section, we will start working with each name by manipulating and formatting them as required.

Section 2 – Getting full names

We already have the full name of each individual that's been assigned to the strFullName variable. However, this isn't how we want this to work. During testing, we can tell there are spaces in some of the names by looking at the start and end of the string. These will need to be trimmed. Also, we cannot be sure what case the string is initially in. Since we need to set its case, it would be good to set it all as *uppercase* to start with. This way, we'll know for sure what case to work with. We already have our strFullName variable so that we can store the full name, so a variable won't be required.

Using the Trim action

There is a little bit of formatting we need to do with the full name, just to ensure our results are as required. The first action we will assign is the **Trim** action. This action will remove spaces before and after any string type variable. When using the **Trim** action, you can specify whether you wish to trim preceding or trailing spaces or both. Follow this walk-through to learn how to trim our variable:

1. Add the **String: Trim** action just below line **8**.

2. Set the following properties for the **String: Trim** action on line **9**:

    Source String: $strFullName$

    Trim from the beginning: *Checked*

    Trim from the end: *Checked*

    Assign the output to variable: **strFullName - String**

    The properties should look like this:

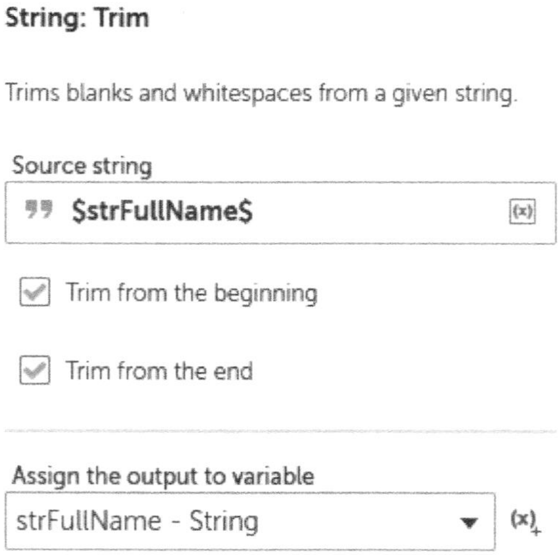

    String: Trim

    Trims blanks and whitespaces from a given string.

    Source string

    > $strFullName$ (x)

    ☑ Trim from the beginning

    ☑ Trim from the end

    Assign the output to variable

    strFullName - String   ▼   (x).

    Figure 8.14 – String: Trim properties

3. Click on **Save**.

We now know that there won't be any spaces before and after the full name. In this instance, this is very important because we can now confidently identify any forenames, middle names, and surnames using the space between each name. If we left the spaces in, this may have caused errors.

The next thing we need to do is convert the full name into uppercase.

Applying uppercase to a string

When we break the name down into its counterparts, the required case is specified; for example, **Surname** needs to be in uppercase and **Forename** in proper case. We do not know what case we initially get the data in, so it is always a good idea to initialize this by setting everything to a fixed standard. You then know what format you are working with. Here, we will convert everything into uppercase. Execute the following steps to convert the case:

1. To convert the case, we will use the **String: Uppercase** action by dragging it just below line **9**.

2. Set the following properties for the **String: Uppercase** action on line **10**:

   Source String: $strFullName$

   Assign the output to variable: **strFullName - String**

   The properties should look like this:

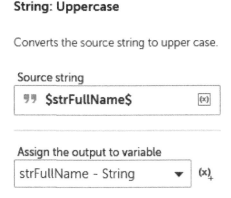

Figure 8.15 – String: Uppercase properties

3. Click on **Save**. Your development interface for this section should look like this:

Figure 8.16 – Development interface

Great work! With that, the first two sections are now complete. Since we already have the message box, go ahead and run the bot. The bot should now loop through each name, showing it formatted without any leading or trailing spaces, as well as it being all in uppercase.

In the next section, we will continue with more data manipulation by learning how to extract a forename from a full name. To do this, you will need to learn how to use the **Extract** and **Substring** actions.

Section 3 – Getting forenames

The requirement for the forename is to format it as proper case. This is where the first letter is capitalized and the rest are in lowercase. To achieve this, we will need to create two new variables. The `strForename` variable will be used to store the resulting forename, while the `strInitial` variable will be used to store the first letter of the forename. The following steps will show you how to get the forename:

1. Create two `String` type variables called `strForename` and `strInitial`.

2. It would be a good idea to add these variables to our message box to help us with progress testing. Edit the message display property of the message box on line **15** to the following:

Figure 8.17 – Message box properties

3. Click on **Save**.

To get the forename from the full name, we can use the **Extract** action. This action allows you to extract part of a string by indicating its start and end characters. You can also specify which occurrence of a character to use.

Using the Extract action

In this section, we will use the **Extract** action to extract everything up until the first space from the `strFullName` variable. This will capitalize the forename for us. You will notice that there are a lot of options available when using this action. For instance, it also trims the output, as shown in the following steps:

1. To extract the forename, add the **String: Extract** action just below line **11**.

2. Set the following properties for the **String: Extract** action on line **12**:

    Source String: $strFullName$

    Get characters: After

    (After) End before text: *(enter a space)*

    (After) Occurrence: 1

    If no match found, return: Empty (null) String

    Number of characters to get: All

    Trim the extracted text: *Checked*

    Remove Enter from the Extracted text: *Checked*

    Assign the output to variable: strForename - String

The properties should look like this:

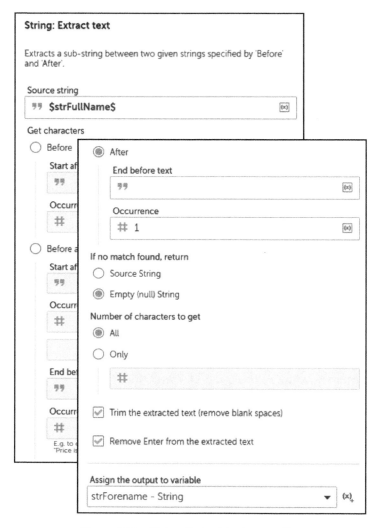

Figure 8.18 – String: Extract text properties

3.   Click on **Save**.

Now that we have updated our message box, you can run the bot to test it. You should get the full name and the forename, all in uppercase. We will now work with the forename and format it as proper case. We'll achieve this by taking the first letter from the forename; this will leave the part of the name that needs to be converted into lowercase. To split the name in such a way, we will use the **Substring** action.

Using the Substring action

The **Substring** action allows you to extract a substring from a given string variable by character location. This is ideal for our requirement as we know we need the first letter for the `strInitial` variable. For the rest of the name, we know we need all the characters starting from the second. Follow these steps to add the **Substring** action:

1. To get the first character from the `strForename` variable, drag the **String: Substring** action just below line 12.

2. Set the following properties for the **String: Substring** action on line **13**:

   Source String: `$strForename$`

   Start from: `1`

   Length: `1`

   Assign the output to variable: `strInitial - String`

   The properties should look like this:

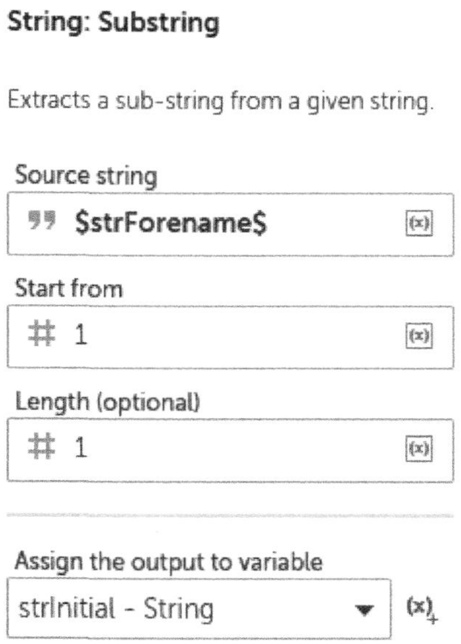

   ### String: Substring

   Extracts a sub-string from a given string.

   Source string

   `"" $strForename$`   (x)

   Start from

   `# 1`   (x)

   Length (optional)

   `# 1`   (x)

   Assign the output to variable

   strInitial - String   ▼   (x)

   Figure 8.19 – String: Substring properties

3. Click on **Save**.

4. To get the rest of the forename (without the first letter), add another **String: Substring** action just below line **13**.

5. Set the following properties for the **String: Substring** action on line **14**:

    Source String: $strForename$

    Start from: 2

    Assign the output to variable: strForename - String

    The properties should look like this:

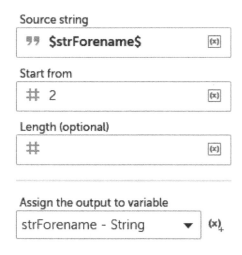

Figure 8.20 – String: Substring properties

6. Click on **Save**.

    With that, we have split the name. Next, we need to convert the forename into lowercase. To do this, we will use the **String: Lowercase** action and drag it just below line **14**.

7. Set the following properties for the **String: Lowercase** action on line **15**:

    Source String: $strForename$

    Assign the output to variable: strForename - String

    The properties should look like this:

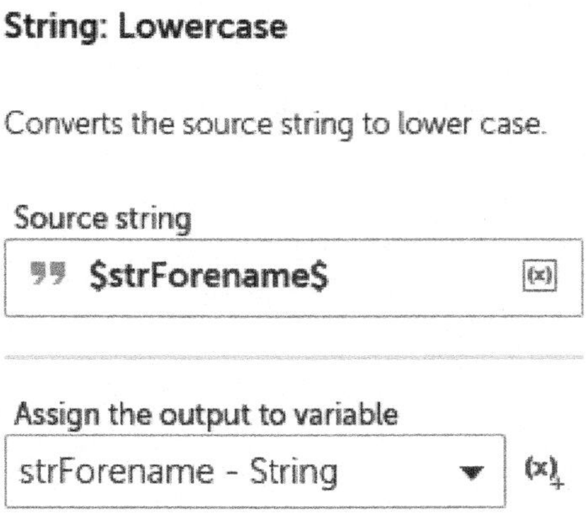

String: Lowercase

Converts the source string to lower case.

Source string

> 99 **$strForename$**   (x)

Assign the output to variable

strForename - String   ▼   (x)

Figure 8.21 – String: Lowercase properties

8. Click on **Save**.

9. Now that we have both parts of the forename, we just need to concatenate them. We can do this by adding the **String: Assign** action just below line **15**.

10. Set the following properties for the **String: Assign** action on line **16**:

    Select the source string variable: $strInitial$$strForename$

    Select the destination string variable: strForename - String

    The properties should look like this:

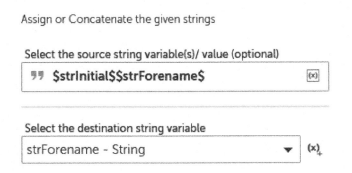

String: Assign

Assign or Concatenate the given strings

Select the source string variable(s)/ value (optional)

> 99 **$strInitial$$strForename$**   (x)

Select the destination string variable

strForename - String   ▼   (x)

Figure 8.22 – Concatenating two strings

11. Click on **Save**.

You are doing great! That's *Section 3 – Getting forenames* complete. You can run the bot to test it. You will see that the forename is now correctly formatted as proper case. The development interface for this section should look this:

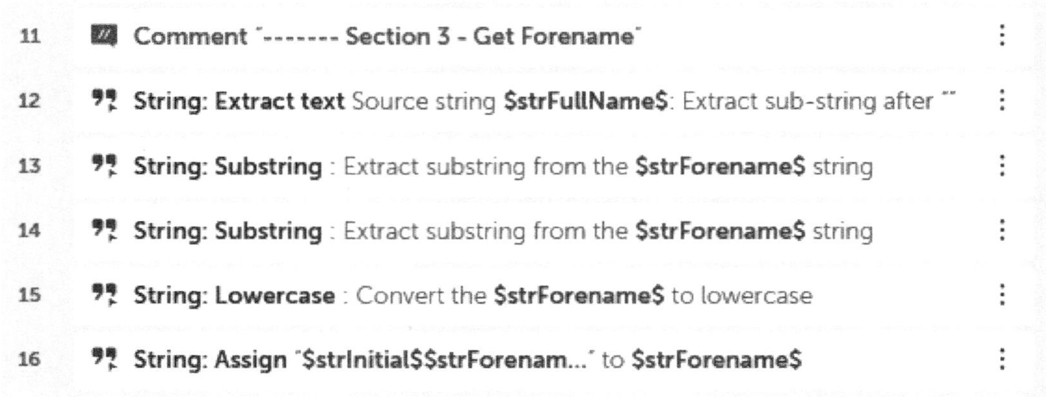

11	▨	Comment "------- Section 3 - Get Forename"	⋮
12	🔤	**String: Extract text** Source string **$strFullName$**: Extract sub-string after ""	⋮
13	🔤	**String: Substring** : Extract substring from the **$strForename$** string	⋮
14	🔤	**String: Substring** : Extract substring from the **$strForename$** string	⋮
15	🔤	**String: Lowercase** : Convert the **$strForename$** to lowercase	⋮
16	🔤	**String: Assign** "$strInitial$$strForenam..." to **$strForename$**	⋮

Figure 8.23 – Development interface

In the next section, we'll get the surname and format it in uppercase. We will get this from our *full name* variable. This is already in uppercase, so formatting shouldn't be a problem. By now, you will have discovered that there are many different ways to manipulate strings. In the next section, we will use the **Find** action to apply regular expressions.

Section 4 – Getting surnames

For the surname, we need the last word from our full name string. There are many ways to do this. One way would be to reverse the string using the **Reverse** action and then get the first word. This would be the surname since the variable has been reversed. Since Automation Anywhere also allows you to use regular expressions to find patterns, in this instance, we will be using this method.

Using the Find action and regular expressions

Automation Anywhere also allows you to apply regular expressions to find a substring. A regular expression can be very useful when working with data. It is essentially a sequence of characters used to find patterns in a string. To find the character where the last word starts in a string, we would use `(\w+)$` as the regular expression. In this section, we will use the **Find** action and apply this regular expression to get the surname. The only issue is the $ character in our regular expression as this is a reserved character for representing variables. In Automation Anywhere, you should replace this with $$ to represent a single US dollar character. The **String: Find** action will return a numeric value that represents the location of where the surname starts.

We will need two further variables to get the surname: the Number variable for the location and the String variable to store the surname. The following walk-through will help you perform this task:

1. Create a new Number variable called numLoc for the surname location.

2. Create a new String variable called strSurname for the surname.

3. Add the **String: Find** action just below line **17**.

4. Set the following properties for the **String: Find** action on line **18**:

   Source string variable: $strFullName$

   Find string: (\w+)$$

   When finding: Do not match case

   The "find string" is: A regular expression

   Start from: 1

   Assign the output to variable: numLoc - Number

   The properties should look like this:

   String: Find

   Locates a given string within the source string.

   Source string
   `" $strFullName$` (x)

   Find string
   `" (\w+)$$` (x)

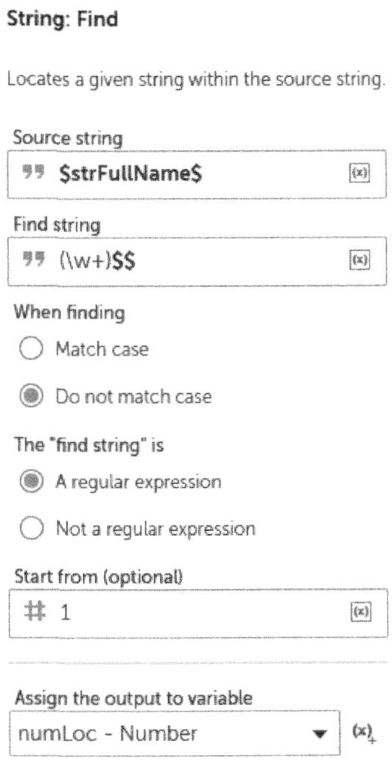

   When finding
   ○ Match case
   ● Do not match case

   The "find string" is
   ● A regular expression
   ○ Not a regular expression

   Start from (optional)
   `# 1` (x)

   Assign the output to variable
   `numLoc - Number` ▼ (x)

   Figure 8.24 – String: Find action using a regular expression

5. Click on **Save**.

6. We now have the location of where the surname starts from. To get the surname, add the **String: Substring** action just below line **18**.

7. Set the following properties for the **String: Substring** action on line **19**:

   Source String: $strFullName$

   Start from: $numLoc$

   Assign the output to variable: **strSurname - String**

   The properties should look like this:

String: Substring

Extracts a sub-string from a given string.

Source string

    " $strFullName$ (x)

Start from

    # $numLoc$ (x)

Length (optional)

    #   (x)

Assign the output to variable

    strSurname - String   ▼   (x),

Figure 8.25 – String: Substring properties

8. Click on **Save**.

9. Now that the surname has been extracted, add it to the final message box on line **22**. Edit the message display property of the message box so that it includes the following:

Message box

Displays a message box

Enter the message box window title

> " String Manipulation   (x)

Enter the message to display

> " Full name: |$strFullName$|
> Initial: |$strInitial$|
> Forename:|$strForename$|
> Surname: |$strSurname$| (x)

Figure 8.26 – Message box properties

10. Click on **Save**.

Great progress! That's *Section 4 – Getting surnames* complete. Run the bot to test it. We now have the forename and the surname in the correct format. The development interface for this section should look like this:

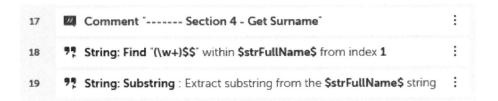

17	Comment "------- Section 4 - Get Surname"	⋮
18	String: Find "(\w+)$$" within $strFullName$ from index 1	⋮
19	String: Substring : Extract substring from the $strFullName$ string	⋮

Figure 8.27 – Development interface

In the next section, we'll gather the middle names. The requirement is to get the initial of each middle name for every individual. Here, you will learn how to use the **Replace** action, as well as how to use the **Split** and **Loop** actions to make a nested loop.

Section 5 – Getting middle names

We have a challenge with the middle names. Any individual may have none, one, or many middle names. We just don't know! At least with the surname and forename we know that everyone has one of each. The first stage will be to extract all the middle names as a string. A new variable will be needed to store all the middle names. Since we already know the surname and forename, the easiest method would be to replace these with blanks, thus leaving us with only the middle names. We can use the **String: Replace** action to achieve this.

Using the Replace action

Initially, we had the full name, replaced the forename of the full name with spaces, and then did the same with the surname. By applying the **Trim** action, we will get only the middle names. Follow these steps to apply the **Replace** action:

1. Create a new **String** variable called `strMiddleNames` for storing the middle names.

2. Add the **String: Replace** action just below line **20**.

3. Set the following properties for the **String: Replace** action on line **21**:

   Source String: `$strFullName$`

   Find string: `$strForename$`

   When finding: **Do not match case**

   The "find string" is: **Not a regular expression**

   Start from: `1`

   Replace with: *(enter space)*

   Assign the output to variable: **strMiddleNames - String**

   The properties should look like this:

String: Replace

Replaces specified part of a 'Source string' with a 'Replacement string'

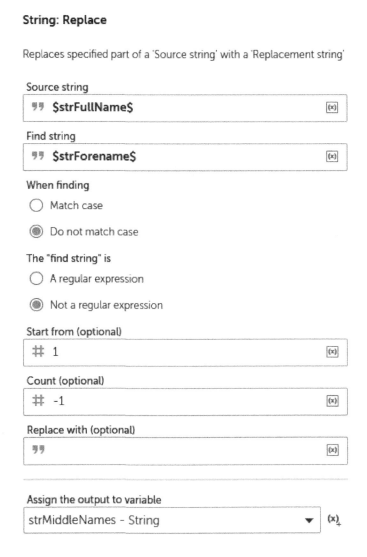

Source string

💬 **$strFullName$**

Find string

💬 **$strForename$**

When finding

○ Match case

◉ Do not match case

The "find string" is

○ A regular expression

◉ Not a regular expression

Start from (optional)

1

Count (optional)

-1

Replace with (optional)

💬

Assign the output to variable

strMiddleNames – String ▼

Figure 8.28 – String: Replace action properties

4. Click on **Save**.

5. That's the forename removed. To remove the surname, add another **String: Replace** action just below line **21**.

6. Set the following properties for the **String: Replace** action on line **22**:

Source String: $strMiddleNames$

Find string: $strSurname$

When finding: **Do not match case**

The "find string" is: **Not a regular expression**

Start from: 1

Replace with: *(enter space)*

Assign the output to variable: **strMiddleNames - String**

The properties should look like this:

Figure 8.29 – String: Replace action properties

7. Click on **Save**.

8. Having replaced the forename and surname with spaces, we now need to remove these spaces. The best way to do this is to use the **String: Trim** action. Add the **String: Trim** action just below line **22**.

9. Set the following properties for the **String: Trim** action on line **23**:

   Source String: $strMiddleNames$

   Trim from the beginning: *Checked*

   Trim from the end: *Checked*

   Assign the output to variable: strMiddleNames - String

   The properties should look like this:

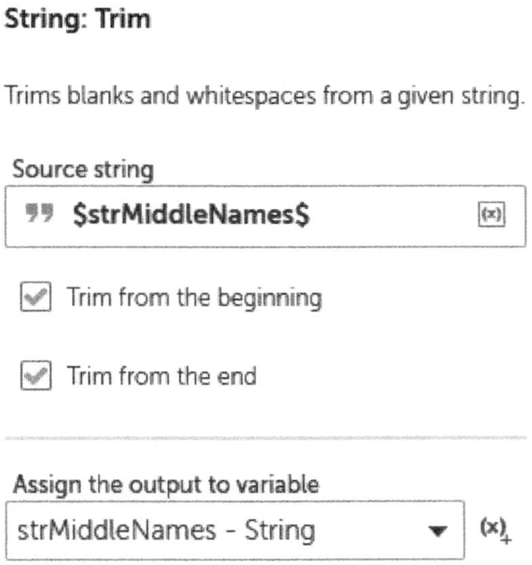

   String: Trim

   Trims blanks and whitespaces from a given string.

   Source string

   99 **$strMiddleNames$**   (x)

   ☑ Trim from the beginning

   ☑ Trim from the end

   Assign the output to variable

   strMiddleNames - String   ▼   (x)

   Figure 8.30 – String: Trim action properties

10. Click on **Save**.

11. The middle names have now been extracted to a variable. Let's add this variable to the final message box on line **25**. Edit the message display property of the **Message box** so that it includes this:

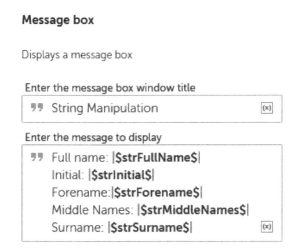

Message box

Displays a message box

Enter the message box window title

> 99 String Manipulation

Enter the message to display

> 99 Full name: |$strFullName$|
> Initial: |$strInitial$|
> Forename:|$strForename$|
> Middle Names: |$strMiddleNames$|
> Surname: |$strSurname$|

Figure 8.31 – Message box properties

12. Click on **Save**.

Go ahead and run the bot to check its progress. We will now be getting all the middle names too, but they are placed together as one variable. Our goal is to get the initial of each middle name. The plan is to append any initials to the strInitial variable, so we will need to ensure it is blank before we process each individual.

Assigning a null value to a string

The bot reads each individual's middle names into a single variable, but we don't know how many middle names anyone may have. All the initials for the middle names need to be collated and assigned to a variable. The best way to do this is to loop through each middle name and append the initial at each iteration. To remove the risk of any middle name initials being bought forward from any previous individual, we should initialize it to null before it gets these initials. We can use the strInitial variable for this as it's already there and we are not using it for anything else. The following instructions will take you through the steps to achieve this:

1. To assign a null value to the strInitial variable, drag the **String: Assign** action just below line **23**.

2. Set the following properties for the **String: Assign** action on line **24**:

    Select the source string variable: *(leave empty)*

    Select the destination string variable: **strInitial - String**

    The properties should look like this:

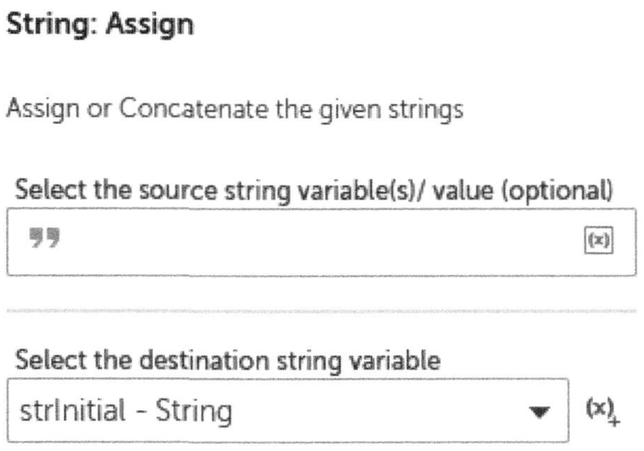

String: Assign

Assign or Concatenate the given strings

Select the source string variable(s)/ value (optional)

> **??**   (x)

Select the destination string variable

> strInitial – String   ▼   (x)₊

Figure 8.32 – String: Assign null value to a string

3. Click on **Save**.

You are doing a great job so far. Moving forward, the bot has to get the initial of each middle name. What we have to be careful about is that in some cases, there may be no middle names at all. In order to cope with this, we can use a simple logic condition to check the contents of our `strMiddleNames` variable.

In the next section, we will learn how to apply a simple **If** statement as our logical condition. Applying this condition will allow the bot to get middle names where they exist. If this is not applied, it may cause our bot to fail when looking for individuals without any middle names.

Applying a simple logical condition

A condition needs to be added to check that the `strMiddleNames` variable is not empty. There is no point in trying to get the middle name initials if there are no middle names. The following instructions will take you through the steps to achieve this:

1. To assign a simple logical condition, drag the **If** action just below line **24**.

2. Set the following properties for the **If** action on line **25**:

   Condition: String condition

   Source value: `$strMiddleNames$`

   Operator: Not equal to

   Target value: *(leave blank)*

   The properties should look like this:

Figure 8.33 – If statement properties

3. Click on **Save**.

All the actions that we want the bot to perform need to be placed indented within the *If* condition statement, similar to placing actions for loops. It gets more interesting now: within our middle names' variable, there may be one or more middle names. We just don't know this. Since we need to get the initial of each middle name, the best way to achieve this is to split this variable by using spaces. This will create a list of every individual middle name. We can then extract the initial and append it to our `strInitial` variable.

The bot is already processing within a loop, so creating another list to loop through will give you some great experience in how to implement a nested loop, which is a loop within another loop.

Implementing a nested loop

We will be splitting the `strMiddleNames` variable by any spaces to create a list. For this to work, we will create a few additional variables. Since the bot loops through the list, we will need to store the current middle name and the current initial of that name. We will also need a `List` type variable to store the list of middle names once it's been split. The following instructions will take you through the steps to achieve this:

1. Create a `List` type variable called `lstMiddleNames`.

2. Create two `String` type variables called `strCurrentMiddleName` and `strCurrentMiddleNameInitial`. Your variables list should now look similar to this:

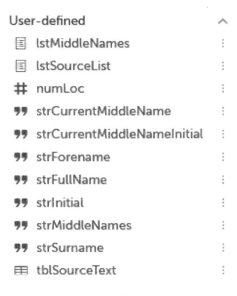

Figure 8.34 – Variables list

3. To split the `strMiddleNames` variable into a list, add the **String: Split** action just below line **25**, ensuring it is within the **If** action on line **25**.

4. Set the following properties for the **String: Split** action on line **26**:

Source string: $strMiddleNames$

Delimiter: *(enter a space)*

Delimiter is: **Not case sensitive**

Split into substrings: **All possible**

Assign the output to list variable: **lstMiddleNames - List of Strings**

The properties should look like this:

Figure 8.35 – String: Split properties dialog

5. Click on **Save**.

6. Now, we have the middle names in a list. To loop through this list, add a **Loop** action just below line **26**, ensuring it remains within the **If** statement on line **25**.

7. Set the following properties for the **Loop** action on line **27**:

    Loop Type: Iterator

    Iterator: For each item in the list

    List: lstMiddleNames -List

    For: All items in the list

    Assign the current value to variable: strCurrentMiddleName - String

    The properties should look like this:

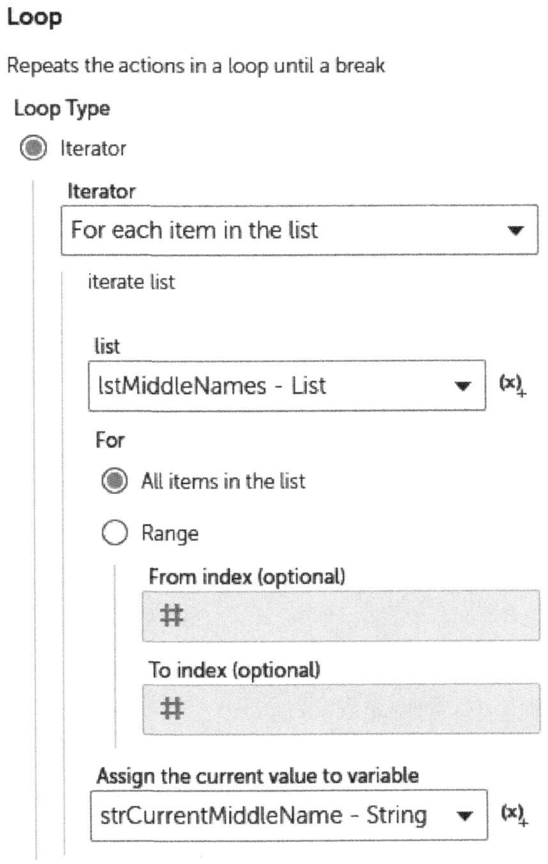

Loop

Repeats the actions in a loop until a break

Loop Type

◉ Iterator

Iterator

| For each item in the list ▼ |

iterate list

list

| lstMiddleNames - List ▼ | (x)₊

For

◉ All items in the list

○ Range

From index (optional)

| # |

To index (optional)

| # |

Assign the current value to variable

| strCurrentMiddleName - String ▼ | (x)₊

Figure 8.36 – Loop properties dialog

8. Click on **Save**.

We can now manipulate each middle name. This job has been assigned to the `strCurrentMiddleName` variable. The requirement is to get the first initial of each middle name. As we did previously, we will use the **String: Substring** action for this. Once we have this, we can concatenate it to our initials so far. Let's get started:

1. To get the first letter of each middle name, add the **String: Substring** action just below line **27**, ensuring it is indented within the **Loop** action on line **27**.

2. Set the following properties for the **String: Substring** action on line **28**:

   Source String: `$strCurrentMiddleName$`

   Start from: `1`

   Length: `1`

   Assign the output to variable: strCurrentMiddleNameInitial - String

   The properties should look like this:

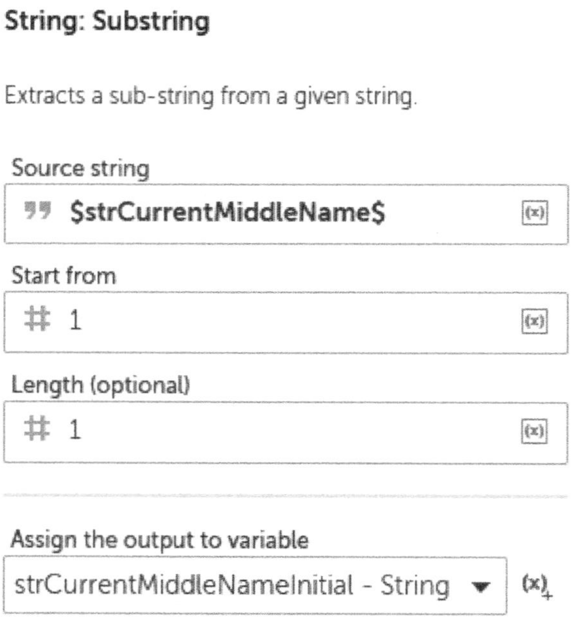

String: Substring

Extracts a sub-string from a given string.

Source string

> `" $strCurrentMiddleName$`   (x)

Start from

> `# 1`   (x)

Length (optional)

> `# 1`   (x)

Assign the output to variable

> `strCurrentMiddleNameInitial - String` ▼   (x)

Figure 8.37 – String: Substring action properties

3. Click on **Save**.

4. To append this to our middle name initials, add the **String: Assign** action just below line **28**, ensuring it remains indented within the **Loop** action on line **27**.

5. Set the following properties for the **String: Assign** action on line **29**:

   Select the source string variable(s)/ value (optional):
   `$strInitial$$strCurrentMiddleNameInitial$`

   Select the destination string variable: strInitial - String

   The properties should look like this:

   ## String: Assign

   Assign or Concatenate the given strings

   Select the source string variable(s)/ value (optional)

   `" " $strInitial$$strCurrentMiddleNameInitial$` (x)

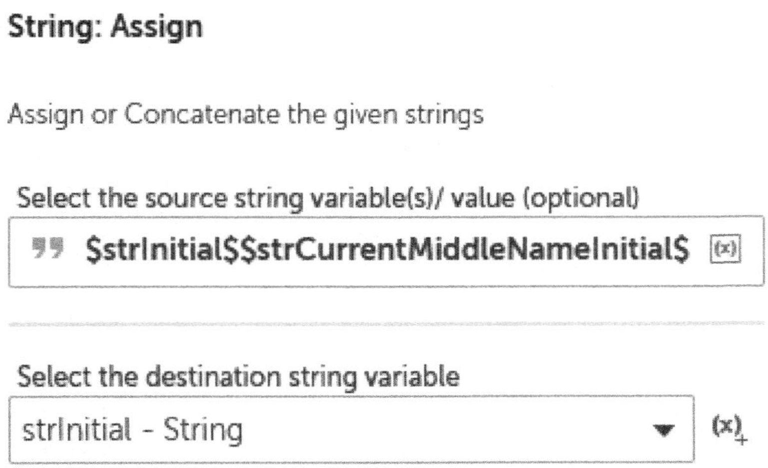

   Select the destination string variable

   strInitial - String ▼   (x)

   Figure 8.38 – Concatenating two strings

6. Click on **Save**.

With that, another section is complete. There's only one more to go! Now, you can run your bot. You should now have all the name items as required; that is, the forename in proper case, the surname in uppercase, and the middle name initials all together. The development interface for this section should look like this:

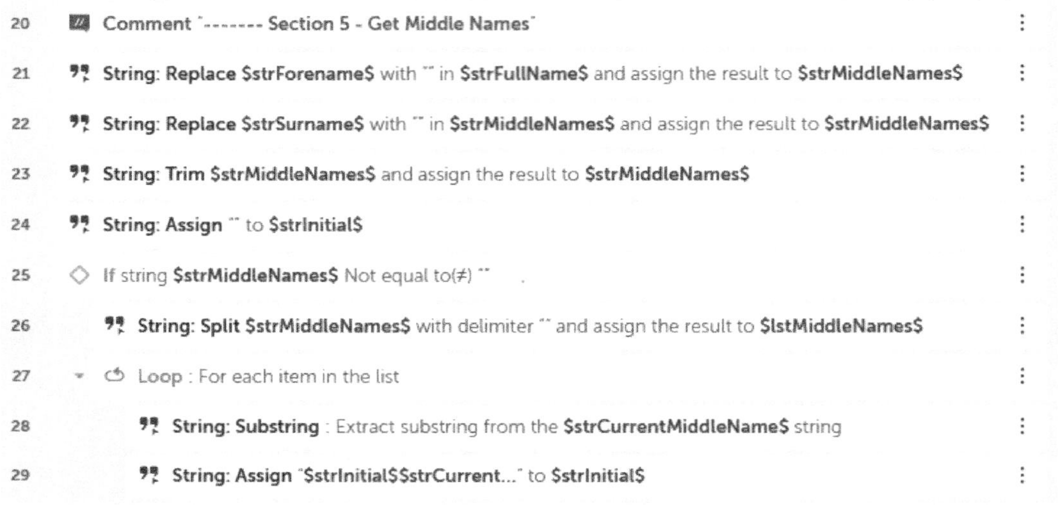

20	🔲 Comment `------- Section 5 - Get Middle Names`	⋮
21	🟨 **String: Replace** $strForename$ with "" in $strFullName$ and assign the result to **$strMiddleNames$**	⋮
22	🟨 **String: Replace** $strSurname$ with "" in $strMiddleNames$ and assign the result to **$strMiddleNames$**	⋮
23	🟨 **String: Trim** $strMiddleNames$ and assign the result to **$strMiddleNames$**	⋮
24	🟨 **String: Assign** "" to $strInitial$	⋮
25	◇ If string **$strMiddleNames$** Not equal to(≠) "" .	⋮
26	🟨 **String: Split** $strMiddleNames$ with delimiter "" and assign the result to **$lstMiddleNames$**	⋮
27	▾ ↻ Loop : For each item in the list	⋮
28	🟨 **String: Substring** : Extract substring from the **$strCurrentMiddleName$** string	⋮
29	🟨 **String: Assign** "$strInitial$$strCurrent..." to $strInitial$	⋮

Figure 8.39 – Development interface

In the next and last section, we will output our results to a CSV file. We will be appending a new line of names for each individual to our CSV file. This is best placed to replace our message box. However, we do need to create the file at the beginning, along with the required headers. We will be using the **Log to file** action to do this.

Section 6 – Outputting the results

A CSV file with headers will need to be created just before the primary loop as we only want this to be created once. The record should be added while we're within the primary loop so that it's created once per individual. Once we've done this, we will need to identify the sequence of our name items as required. The output should be in the following format:

```
Surname in uppercase, Forename in Proper case, Middle name
initials in uppercase
```

So, for the first record, it would look like this: MAHEY, Husan L.

Let's get started:

1. To create the CSV file with headers, add the **Log to file** action just below line **2**. This will make this the first action the bot performs.

2. Set the following properties for the **Log to file** action on line **3**:

   File path: `C:\Hands-On-RPA-with-AA-Sample-Data\Chapter08_Output.csv`

   Enter text to log: `Surname, Forename/Initials`

   When logging: **Overwrite existing log file**

   The properties should look like this:

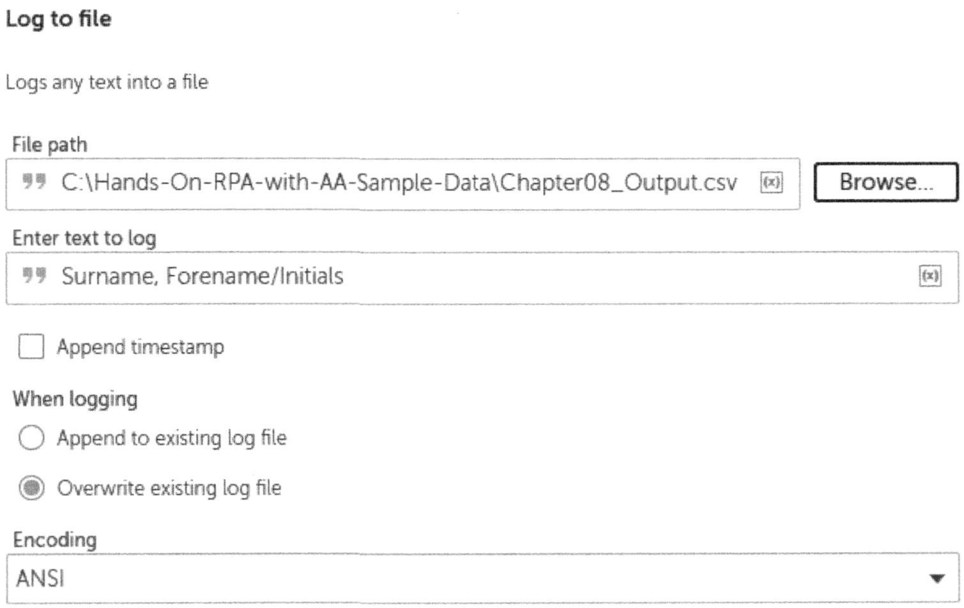

Log to file

Logs any text into a file

File path

> C:\Hands-On-RPA-with-AA-Sample-Data\Chapter08_Output.csv [x]   Browse...

Enter text to log

> Surname, Forename/Initials   [x]

☐ Append timestamp

When logging

◯ Append to existing log file

◉ Overwrite existing log file

Encoding

ANSI   ▼

Figure 8.40 – Log to file properties

3. Click on **Save**.

4. To add each individual to our file, add the **Log to file** action just below line **31**.

5. Set the following properties for the **Log to file** action on line **32**:

File path: `C:\Hands-On-RPA-with-AA-Sample-Data\Chapter08_ Output.csv`

Enter text to log: `$strSurname$, $strForename$ $strInitial$`

When logging: **Append existing log file**

The properties should look like this:

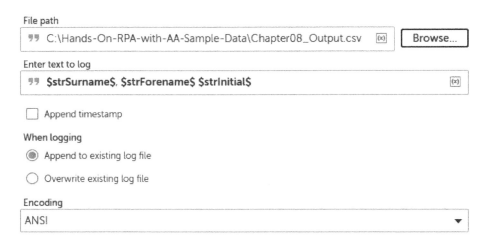

Figure 8.41 – Log to file properties

6. Click on **Save**.

7. Finally, delete the **Message box** action on line **33** and click on **Save**.

Congratulations – you have completed your bot! The development interface for this final section should look like this:

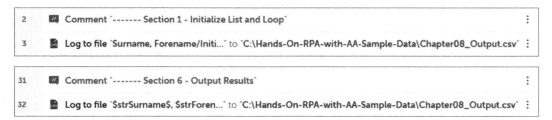

Figure 8.42 – Development interface

Now, it's time to test the bot. When it's executed, you will get the `Chapter08_Output.csv` file at `C:\Hands-On-RPA-with-AA-Sample-Data\Chapter08_Output.csv`.

The contents should look like this:

	A	B
1	Surname	Forename/Initials
2	MAHEY	Husan L
3	MAHEY	Priya
4	MAHEY	Sonam
5	MAHEY	Ravinder RL
6	MAHEY	Sunita K
7	MAHEY	Manisha

Figure 8.43 – Output file

This has been quite an intensive walk-through; we have gone through some of the most common string manipulation actions. However, you will have noticed that there are still more actions for you to discover.

Hopefully, you feel a lot more confident with using Automation Anywhere to automate your routine tasks.

Summary

Having gone through this walk-through, you have not only gained experience with how to use string manipulation actions but now also have an idea of what sort of scenarios they could be best applied to. To recap, we have covered a number of useful actions, including extracting a specific substring from a string via locations, extracting a substring from a string via specific text, finding a specific substring within a string, replacing parts of a string, converting strings into upper or lowercase, trimming leading/trailing spaces from strings, using regular expressions to find string patterns, splitting strings with a specific delimiter, concatenating strings, creating list variables, looping through list variables, and finally, understanding simple logical conditions.

You are now becoming more experienced with building more complex bots. In the next chapter, we will continue to build on this progress by looking at working with the filesystem. This will include how to move, delete, and rename files and folders. We will also look at conditional logic and loops in more detail.

9
Working with Conditional Logic, Loops, and the Filesystem

In the previous chapter, you discovered how to manage string manipulation in a number of ways. We examined the **Strings** package and went through actions such as **Split**, **Substring**, **Assign**, and **Find**, to name a few. All of these are very useful actions. We also applied a simple **If** statement, as well as a loop.

In this chapter, we will continue expanding our knowledge of Automation Anywhere packages and actions. We will look deeper into building loops and the different types of looping Automation Anywhere offers. We will also look at the functionality of the filesystem, which includes moving, deleting, and renaming files and folders. This chapter will also look at the different types of logical conditions available and how to apply these.

In this chapter, we will cover the following topics:

- Applying different types of loops
- Applying logical conditions
- Working with the filesystem

Like the previous chapter, this chapter will also take the form a building a bot, but in this case, you will be building two bots. Both will be by taking you through a walk-through. This will be a bit intensive, but you will gain some valuable experience in terms of how to implement a number of useful actions. This method also puts these actions into context as they are all working toward a complete task. We will use the following packages:

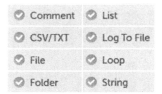

Figure 9.1 – Packages that will be used in this chapter

For this chapter, the two bots we'll be building will be automating a human process. The first process involves reading each record in a CSV file and then sorting these records into a file management subfolder system. The second bot will collate files from subfolders, and then rename and delete files and folders. Progressing through the walk-throughs will enable you to build your confidence and understanding of loops, condition statements, and working with the filesystem. By the end of this chapter, you will be able to add rule-based decisions for your bot, manage files and folders, and build repeating processes by using loops.

Technical requirements

You will need the following in order to install Automation Anywhere Bot agent:

- Windows operating system version 7 or higher
- Processor with a minimum speed of 3 GHz
- Minimum of 4 GB RAM
- At least 100 MB hard disk space
- Internet Explorer v10 or higher OR Chrome v49 or higher
- A minimum screen resolution of 1024*768

- An internet connection with a minimum speed of 10 Mb/sec
- Completed registration with Automation Anywhere A2019 Community Edition
- Logged on successfully to Automation Anywhere A2019 Community Edition
- A successfully registered local device
- Successfully downloaded the sample data from GitHub

Applying different types of loops

The majority of business applications work with data in some capacity or another. The obvious ones are applications that have a database in the backend. This could include sales ledgers, customer details, and product data. This data can be large in volume. Developers often design routines to process large datasets. This involves processing each individual record from these datasets. To build this sort of functionality, we use loops.

Being able to build loops is probably a function that's included with all development platforms. Looping is basically having the ability to repeat an action or actions. Loops can be applied in a number of ways; the number of times a process is repeated can be fixed, based on a variable or a number of other conditions. There are many scenarios where loops are deployed, some of which are as follows:

- For every email in a particular folder of a mailbox
- For every row in a table
- For every file in a folder
- For each row in a CSV/TXT file
- For each row in an Excel worksheet
- Condition-based; that is, loop until a file is created/updated

We have already built bots that loop through CSV files and lists. This will be explored further when you are introduced to the `Record` variable type. This is a useful variable type for storing all the fields for a single record. Our walk-through will involve looping through the records of a CSV file and also looping through a list. The bot we'll build will be automating a manual process that involves extracting each record from a daily CSV file and filing it as an alphabetically grouped file.

In the upcoming walk-through, we will be automating the following manual task:

1. The operator receives a daily `.csv` customer file.
2. Each record from the customer file needs to be appended to a corresponding file.

3. The corresponding file is located in an alphabetically grouped naming system.

4.   The groups are made up of the following subfolders: ABCD, EFGH, IJKL, MNOP, QRST, UVWX, and YZ.

5. Use the surname initial to identify which subfolder relates to the record.

6. Check if the subfolder exists – create it if it doesn't.

7. Check if a corresponding file exists and if not, create a file with headers.

8. Append the customer details to this file.

9. Move to the next record in the file until all the records have been processed.

We will break this walk-through into six sections to make it easier to follow:

- Section 1 – Opening the source file
- Section 2 – Looping through each row
- Section 3 – Getting the surname initial and identifying the group
- Section 4 – Checking or creating a subfolder

    Section 4a – Creating a subfolder and output file if it doesn't exist

- Section 5 – Updating the output file
- Section 6 – Closing the the source file

As always, we will start by adding some comments to guide us. We will begin with just the basic skeleton and add further levels of detail as we progress.

Let's start this walk-through by executing the following steps:

1. Log into **Control Room**.

2. Create a new bot and call it Chapter 9 - Loops & Conditions. Place it in the \Bot\ folder.

3. As always, we'll begin by adding some comments to use as templates for our bot. Add a new **Comment** action called "- - - - - - - - - - - - - - - - - - - -" on line **1** and click on **Save**.

4. Add a new **Comment** action called "- - - - - - - - Section 1 - Open the Source file" on line **2** and click on **Save**.

5. Add a new **Comment** action called "- - - - - - - Section 2 - Loop through each row" on line 3 and click on Save.

6. Add a new **Comment** action called "`------- Section 3 - Get Surname initial & identify group`" on line **4** and click on **Save**.

7. Add a new **Comment** action called "`------- Section 4 - Check if sub folder exists`" on line **5** and click on **Save**.

8. Add a new **Comment** action called "`------- Section 4a - Create sub folder & output file if it doesn't exist`" on line **6** and click on **Save**.

9. Add a new **Comment** action called "`------- Section 5 - Update output file`" on line **7** and click on **Save**.

10. Add a new **Comment** action called "`------- Section 6 - Close the Source file`" on line **8** and click on **Save**.

11. Add a new **Comment** action called "`----------------------`" on line **9** and click on **Save**. Our initial development interface should look like this:

1	Comment `----------------------`	⋮
2	Comment `------- Section 1 - Open the Source file`	⋮
3	Comment `------- Section 2 - Loop through each row`	⋮
4	Comment `------- Section 3 - Get Surname initial & identify group`	⋮
5	Comment `------- Section 4 - Check if sub folder exists`	⋮
6	Comment `------- Section 4a - Create sub folder & output file if it doesn't exist`	⋮
7	Comment `------- Section 5 - Update output file`	⋮
8	Comment `------- Section 6 - Close the Source file`	⋮
9	Comment `----------------------`	⋮

Figure 9.2 – Development interface

We are now ready to start on our six sections. We will start with *Section 1 – Opening the source file*. This file is available in this book's GitHub repository.

Section 1 – Opening the source file

To instruct your bot to open the `Chapter09_InputData.csv` source file, please execute the following steps:

1. Drag the **CSV/TXT: Open** action just below line **2**.

2. Set the following properties for the **CSV/TXT: Open** action on line **3**:

    Session name: Data

    File path: **Desktop file** – C:\Hands-On-RPA-with-AA-Sample-Data\ Chapter09_InputData.csv

    Contains header: *Checked*

    Delimiter: **Comma**

    Trim leading spaces: *Checked*

    Trim trailing spaces: *Checked*

    The properties window should look like this:

Figure 9.3 – CSV/TXT: Open properties

3. Click on **Save**. The development window for this section should look like this:

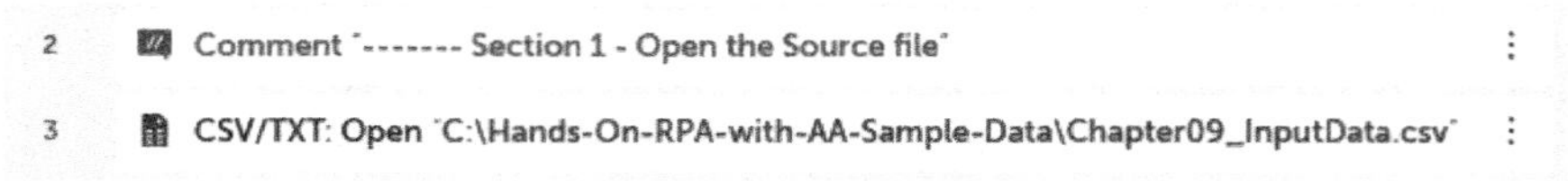

| 2 | Comment `------- Section 1 - Open the Source file` | ⋮ |
| 3 | CSV/TXT: Open `C:\Hands-On-RPA-with-AA-Sample-Data\Chapter09_InputData.csv` | ⋮ |

Figure 9.4 – Development interface

With that, we have instructed our bot to open the source file. Next, we will create a **Loop**. This loop will go through the whole file, processing each record. When opening a file, it creates a session, which is like a connection. This is set as Data. We need to remember this because when we create the loop, we will need to specify the session. This way, the bot will know what source it needs to iterate from. There may be scenarios where multiple sources are open at the same time; having a unique session name for each individual source stops any sources getting mixed up.

Section 2 – Looping through each row

As we will be looping through each record, we will use the Record variable type to store the working record. Follow these steps to create the variable and the loop:

1. Create a new variable named recSource as a Record type. The **Create variable** dialog should look like this:

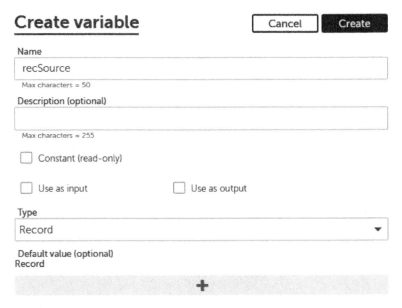

Figure 9.5 – Creating a Record type variable

2. Drag the **Loop** action just below line **4**.

3. Set the following properties for the **Loop** action on line **5**:

    Loop Type: Iterator

    Iterator: For each row in CSV/TXT

Session name: `Data`

Assign the current row to this variable: recSource - Record

The properties window should look like this:

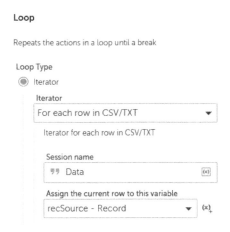

Figure 9.6 – Loop properties

4. Click on **Save**.

5. The steps *3* to *5* will be performed with the loop. Move the comments by dragging and dropping lines **6** to **9** so that they are within the **Loop** element on line **5**. We're doing this so the bot knows which actions are to be repeated.

6. Click on **Save**. The completed development window should look like this:

Figure 9.7 – Development interface

That completes *Section 2 – Looping through each row*! You seem to be whizzing through this. So far, our bot will connect to the source file and loop through each record, assigning it to our `recSource` variable. Once it has gone through the whole file, it will close it. Next, we have to get the surname initial and identify which group the record belongs to. For example, the surname for the first record is BOWMAN. By taking the initial of B, we need to identify the subfolder group. The ABCD subfolder group contains the initial B. This identification process needs to be done for each record.

Section 3 – Getting the surname initial and identifying the group

To identify the subfolder group, we need the surname initial. When data is assigned to a `Record` type variable, fields can be accessed via the index number. The index is 0-based, so the first field is index 0 and so forth. From looking at the source file at `C:\Hands-On-RPA-with-AA-Sample-Data\Chapter09_InputData.csv`, we can see that the surname is the second field. This would give it an index of 1. For this section, we will need a variable to store the surname initial. As it's the reference value that will be used to identify the subfolder group, let's call this `strRefInitial`. Let's get started:

1. Create a `String` type variable named `strRefInitial`.

2. We know the surname is the second field, so it will be indexed at 1. Drag the **String: Substring** action just below line **6**, ensuring it is within the **Loop** element on line **5**.

3. Set the following properties for the **String: Substring** action on line **7**:

    Source String name: $recSource[1]$

    Start from: 1

    Length: 1

    Assign the output to variable: strRefInitial - String

The properties window should look like this:

Figure 9.8 – String: Substring properties

4.   Click on **Save**.

We now have our surname initial. Next, we need to identify which subfolder group this initial belongs to. There are seven sub folders: ABCD, EFGH, IJKL, MNOP, QRST, UVWX, and YZ. Our bot needs to make a decision here. Since this is a rule-based decision, it's ideal for RPA. We will now look at how to apply conditions in order to make statements using Automation Anywhere A2019. These conditions will be used to decide which subfolder group the surname initial belongs to.

Applying logical conditions

Using logical conditions is a way to apply decision-making for your bots. Bots can make rule-based decisions, and these rules can be based on a number of scenarios. Automation Anywhere offers a plethora of options to base decisions on. The following is a breakdown of all the scenarios that conditions can be based on:

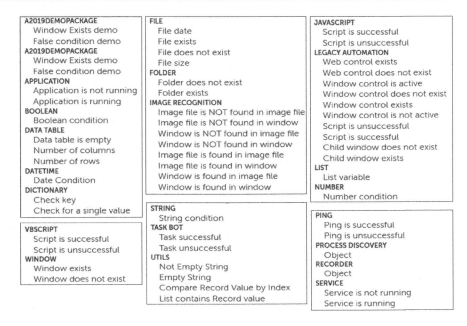

A2019DEMOPACKAGE	FILE	JAVASCRIPT
Window Exists demo	File date	Script is successful
False condition demo	File exists	Script is unsuccessful
A2019DEMOPACKAGE	File does not exist	LEGACY AUTOMATION
Window Exists demo	File size	Web control exists
False condition demo	FOLDER	Web control does not exist
APPLICATION	Folder does not exist	Window control is active
Application is not running	Folder exists	Window control does not exist
Application is running	IMAGE RECOGNITION	Window control exists
BOOLEAN	Image file is NOT found in image file	Window control is not active
Boolean condition	Image file is NOT found in window	Script is unsuccessful
DATA TABLE	Window is NOT found in image file	Script is successful
Data table is empty	Window is NOT found in window	Child window does not exist
Number of columns	Image file is found in image file	Child window exists
Number of rows	Image file is found in window	LIST
DATETIME	Window is found in image file	List variable
Date Condition	Window is found in window	NUMBER
DICTIONARY		Number condition
Check key	STRING	
Check for a single value	String condition	PING
	TASK BOT	Ping is successful
VBSCRIPT	Task successful	Ping is unsuccessful
Script is successful	Task unsuccessful	PROCESS DISCOVERY
Script is unsuccessful	UTILS	Object
WINDOW	Not Empty String	RECORDER
Window exists	Empty String	Object
Window does not exist	Compare Record Value by Index	SERVICE
	List contains Record value	Service is not running
		Service is running

Figure 9.9 – If statement scenarios

As you can see, the opportunities for applying automation decisions are wide and varied. Getting back to our walk-through, we need to identify the subfolder for our surname initial. Our approach will be to create a list of all the subfolders and to loop through this list while checking if it's the correct folder. We will need a few variables for this process: an initial `String` variable for storing the list of subfolders, a `List` variable for assigning the folders to a list, and a `String` variable for storing the allocated folder for our surname initial.

Let's continue with our walk-through and add our condition:

1. Create a `String` type variable named `strSubFoldersList` for storing our subfolders.

2. Create a `List` type variable, set as a `String` subtype named `lstSubFoldersList`, for looping through our subfolders.

3. Create a `String` type variable named `strSubFolder` for storing the allocated subfolder.

The variables list should look like this:

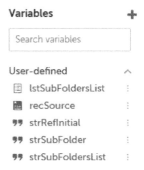

Figure 9.10 – Variables list

4. To assign our subfolder groups to the `strSubFoldersList` variable, drag the **String: Assign** action just below line **7**, ensuring it is within the **Loop** element on line **5**.

5. Set the following properties for the **String: Assign** action on line **8**:

    Select the source string variable/value:
    `ABCD,EFGH,IJKL,MNOP,QRST,UVWX,YZ`

    Select the destination string variable: **strSubFoldersList - String**

    The properties window should look like this:

Figure 9.11 – String: Assign properties

6. Click on **Save**.

7. Next, we need to split this variable into our `List` variable so that we can loop through it. Drag the **String: Split** action just below line **8**, ensuring it is within the **Loop** element on line **5**.

8. Set the following properties for the **String: Assign** action on line **9**:

Source string: $strSubFoldersList$

Delimiter: ,

Assign the output to list variable: lstSubFoldersList - List of Strings

The properties window should look like this:

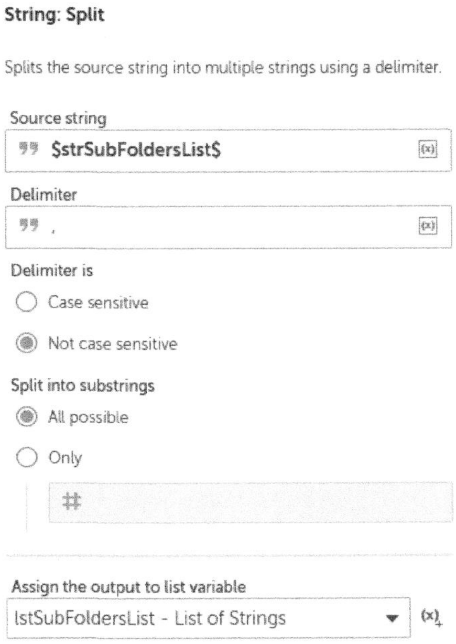

String: Split

Splits the source string into multiple strings using a delimiter.

Source string

99 $strSubFoldersList$ [x]

Delimiter

99 ,   [x]

Delimiter is

◯ Case sensitive

⦿ Not case sensitive

Split into substrings

⦿ All possible

◯ Only

#

Assign the output to list variable

lstSubFoldersList - List of Strings   ▼ (x)

Figure 9.12 – String: Split properties

9. Click on **Save**.

10. We now have a list of our seven subfolder groups and have our surname initial. Next, we will create a loop that will iterate through the list of subfolder groups. Add the **Loop** action just below line **9**, ensuring it is within the **Loop** element on line **5**.

11. Set the following properties for the **Loop** action on line **10**:

Loop Type: Iterator

Iterator: For each item in the list

List: lstSubFoldersList - List

For: All items in the list

Assign the current value to variable: strSubFoldersList - String

The properties window should look like this:

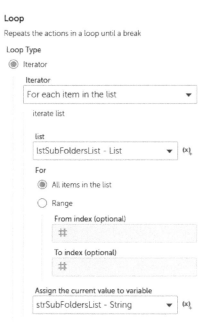

Figure 9.13 – Loop properties

12. Click on **Save**.

13. Next, we will add a condition statement that checks whether our surname initial is contained in the current subfolder group. Drag the **If** action just below line **10**, ensuring it is within the **Loop** element on line **10**.

14. Set the following properties for the **If** action on line **11**:

    Condition: **String condition**

    Source value: `strSubFoldersList`

    Operator: **Includes**

    Target value: `$strRefInitial$`

    The properties window should look like this:

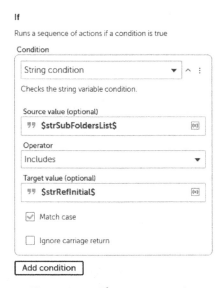

Figure 9.14 – If action properties

15. Click on **Save**.

16. We can assign the allocated subfolder group to our variable if this condition is met. Drag the **String: Assign** action just below line **11**, ensuring it is within the **If** statement on line **11**.

17. Set the following properties for the **String: Assign** action on line **12**:

    Select the source string variable(s)/value (optional): $strSubFoldersList$

    Select the destination string variable: strSubFolder - String

    The properties window should look like this:

Figure 9.15 – String: Assign properties

18. Click on **Save**.

The bot is at a stage now where it has identified the subfolder group for the working record using the surname initial. This brings *Section 3 – Getting the surname initial and identifying the group*, to an end. The development interface for this section should look like this:

6	📝 **Comment** "------- Section 3 - Get Surname initial & identify group"	⋮
7	🔢 **String: Substring** : Extract substring from the **$recSource[1]$** string	⋮
8	🔢 **String: Assign** "ABCD,EFGH,IJKL,MNOP,QRS..." to **$strSubFoldersList$**	⋮
9	🔢 **String: Split** **$strSubFoldersList$** with delimiter "," and assign the result to **$lstSubFold**...	⋮
10	▾ 🔁 **Loop** : For each item in the list	⋮
11	▾ ◇ **If** string **$strSubFoldersList$** Includes **$strRefInitial$**	⋮
12	🔢 **String: Assign** **$strSubFoldersList$** to **$strSubFolder$**	⋮

Figure 9.16 – Development interface

Our next task is to append our working record to an output file. This output file is within the subfolder that has been identified. This output folder and file may not exist, so the bot should create the file/folder in this case. The name of the file should be `Output.csv`.

Section 4 – Checking or creating a subfolder

The output subfolders should be created in the `C:\Hands-On-RPA-with-AA-Sample-Data\Chapter09_Output\` folder path if they don't exist. Currently, this folder is empty; a subfolder will need to be created whenever a customer record is added to the subfolder group. Let's get started:

1. We know that the output subfolder has been assigned to the `strSubFolder` variable, so we need to check that it exists. Drag the **If** action just below line **13**, ensuring it is within the **Loop** element on line 5.

2. Set the following properties for the **If** action on line **14**:

    Condition: **Folder does not exist**

    Folder path: `C:\Hands-On-RPA-with-AA-Sample-Data\Chapter09_Output\$strSubFolder$`

The properties window should look like this:

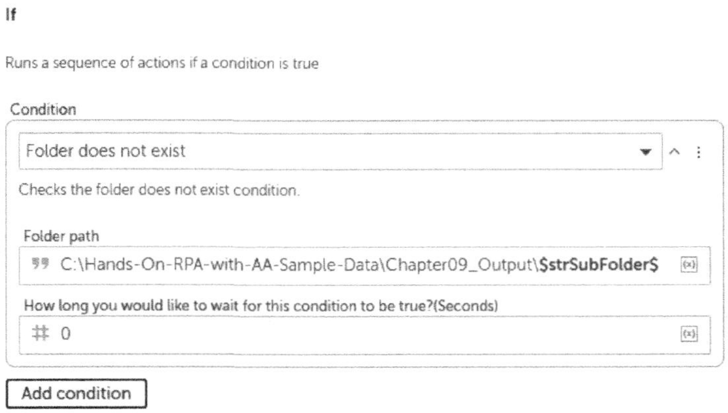

If

Runs a sequence of actions if a condition is true

Condition

| Folder does not exist | ▾ | ∧ ⋮ |

Checks the folder does not exist condition.

Folder path

❞ C:\Hands-On-RPA-with-AA-Sample-Data\Chapter09_Output\$strSubFolder$

How long you would like to wait for this condition to be true?(Seconds)

0

[Add condition]

Figure 9.17 – If action properties

3. Click on **Save**.

All the actions within the **If** action on line **14** will only be performed if the output folder doesn't exist. The bot will need to create this folder and the output file containing headers only. We'll look at creating this in the next section.

Section 4a – Creating a subfolder and output file

Before we create the folder and file, it would make sense to move the **Comment** on line **15** so that it's within the **If** action on line **14**. This will make the bot more readable and logically accurate. The output file we're creating should be identical to the source file in terms of structure. This field structure is Ref, Surname, FirstName, Amount.

Let's continue with the walk-through and move the **Comment** before creating the output subfolder and file:

1. Drag the **Comment** on line **15** so that it's within the **If** action on line **14**. The **Comment** line should remain as line **15**.

2. To create the subfolder, drag the **Folder: Create** action just below line **15**, ensuring it remains within the **If** action on line **14**.

3. Set the **Folder** property for the **Folder: Create** action on line **16** to C:\Hands-On-RPA-with-AA-Sample-Data\Chapter09_Output\$strSubFolder$.

4.   The properties window should look like this:

Folder: Create

Creates a folder

Folder

C:\Hands-On-RPA-with-AA-Sample-Data\Chapter09_Output**$strSubFolder$**

e.g. C:\MyDoc\MyNewFolder

☐ Overwrite an existing folder

Figure 9.18 – Folder: Create properties

5.   Click on **Save**.

6.   To create the output file with headers, add the **Log to file** action just below line **16**.

7.   Set the following properties for the **Log to file** action on line 17:

File path: `C:\Hands-On-RPA-with-AA-Sample-Data\Chapter09_Output\$strSubFolder$\Output.csv`

Enter text to log: `Ref,Surname,FirstName,Amount`

When logging: Overwrite existing log file

The properties window should look like this:

Log to file

Logs any text into a file

File path

C:\Hands-On-RPA-with-AA-Sample-Data\Chapter09_Output**$strSubFolder$**\Output.csv   Browse...

Enter text to log

Ref,Surname,FirstName,Amount

☐ Append timestamp

When logging

○ Append to existing log file

◉ Overwrite existing log file

Encoding

ANSI

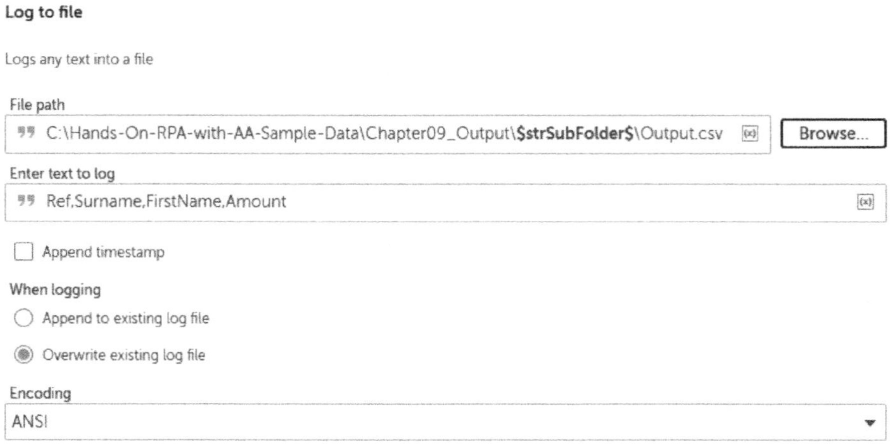

Figure 9.19 – Log to file properties

8.   Click on **Save**.

Great work – that's *Section 4 – Checking or creating a subfolder*, complete! Our bot will create the necessary subfolder and file if needed. The development window for this section should look like this:

13	🖼 Comment "------- Section 4 - Check if sub folder exists"	⋮
14	◇ If folder does not exist at "C:\Hands-On-RPA-with-AA-Sample-Data\Chapter09_Output\$strSubFolder$"	⋮
15	🖼 Comment "------- Section 4a - Create sub folder & output file if it doesn't exist"	⋮
16	☐ Folder: Create "C:\Hands-On-RPA-with-AA-Sample-Data\Chapter09_Output\$strSubFolder$"	⋮
17	📄 Log to file "Ref,Surname,FirstName,A..." to "C:\Hands-On-RPA-with-AA-Sample-Data\Chapter09_...	⋮

Figure 9.20 – Development interface

In the next section, we will append the working record to our output file. This goes for every record in the source file. At this stage of the process, the output will be present with headers, even if it contains no records.

Section 5 – Updating the output file

It's time to append our record to the output file. The result will be one file in each subfolder. This file will contain one or more records. Since we have assigned the record to a `Record` type variable, we will use the field index to get the values. We know that there are four fields in each record, so we'll have an index from 0 to 3 (as it's a zero-based index). Let's get started:

1. To append the record to our output file, add the **Log to file** action just below line **18**, ensuring it is within the **Loop** element on line 5.

2. Set the following properties for the **Log to file** action on line **19**:

    File path: `C:\Hands-On-RPA-with-AA-Sample-Data\Chapter09_Output\$sSubFolder$\Output.csv`

    Enter text to log: `$recSource[0]$,$recSource[1]$,$recSource[2]$,$recSource[3]$`

    When logging: Append existing log file

The properties window should look like this:

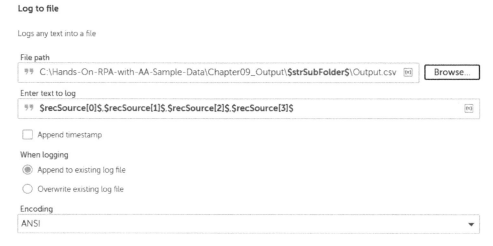

Figure 9.21 – Log to file properties

3.   Click on **Save**.

And that's it – great work! Our bot is now complete. The development interface for this section should look like this:

Figure 9.22 – Development interface

The bot will now append the customer record to the correct output file in the correct location. In the next section, we will be closing the source file since all the records will have been processed by now.

Section 6 – Closing the source file

Remember when we created the file session in *Section 1 – Opening the source file*? Well, that session needs to be closed. It is best practice to add the **Close** action at the same time you create a session. Follow these steps to close the session:

1.   Add the **CSV/TXT: Close** action just below line **20**.

2. Set the following properties for the **CSV/TXT: Close** action on line **21**:

Session name: `Data`

The properties window should look like this:

Figure 9.23 – CSV/TXT: Close properties

3. Click on **Save**.

And that's it – great work! Our bot is now complete. The development interface for this section should look like this:

Figure 9.24 – Development interface

Go ahead and run the bot to test it. It should create the necessary subfolders. Each subfolder should have an output file. The bot will process each record by appending it to the correct output file.

Here, you have had some good practice creating loops and applying certain condition statements. In the next section, we will explore files and folders further. So far, we have been working on a CSV file at a fixed location. However, there may be cases where you will have to move, rename, copy, and delete files and folders. Due to this, understanding how to work with files and folders is a very useful skill to have.

Working with the filesystem

There may be instances where we must create, delete, move, or rename files and folders. Automation Anywhere has two packages: one for files and one for folders. In the following screenshot, you can see the actions that are available for managing the filesystem in Automation Anywhere:

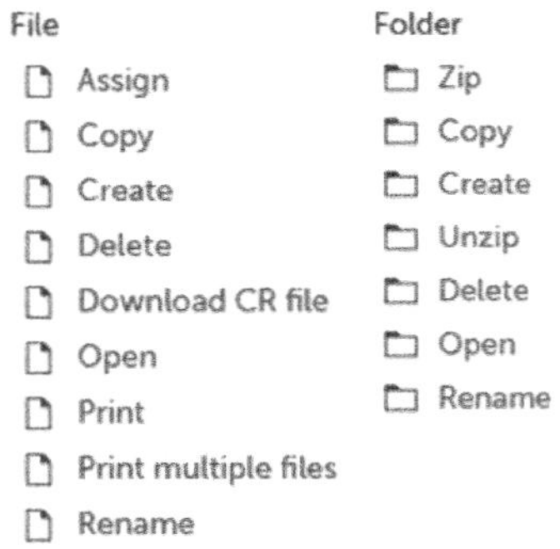

File

- Assign
- Copy
- Create
- Delete
- Download CR file
- Open
- Print
- Print multiple files
- Rename

Folder

- Zip
- Copy
- Create
- Unzip
- Delete
- Open
- Rename

Figure 9.25 – File/Folder package and its actions

Our current bot creates seven subfolders, with each folder containing a CSV file called output.csv. To get some hands-on experience with files and folders, we are going to automate the following process:

1. Rename every output.csv file to its subfolder name.
2. Move the renamed file(s) to C:\Hands-On-RPA-with-AA-Sample-Data\ Chapter09_Output.
3. Delete the empty subfolder(s).

You may have noticed that there isn't a file move action. In order to achieve this, we will perform a copy and delete. We will break this walk-through into five sections to make it easier to follow:

- Section 1 – Looping through subfolders
- Section 2 – Renaming the output file
- Section 3 – Copying the output file
- Section 4 – Deleting the output file
- Section 5 – Deleting the subfolder

As always, we will start by adding some comments to guide us. We will begin with just the basic skeleton and add further levels of detail as we progress.

Let's start this walk-through by executing the following steps:

1. Log into the **Control Room** section.

2. Create a new bot and call it `Chapter 9 - Files & Folders`. Place it in the `\Bot\` folder.

3. As always, we'll begin by adding some comments that will be used as templates for our bot. Add a new **Comment** action on line **1**, set the value to " - ", and click on **Save**.

4. Add a new **Comment** action called " - - - - - - - Section 1 - Loop through Sub Folders" on line **2** and click on **Save**.

5. Add a new **Comment** action called " - - - - - - - Section 2 - Rename output file" on line **3** and click on **Save**.

6. Add a new **Comment** action called " - - - - - - Section 3 - Copy output file" on line **4** and click on **Save**.

7. Add a new **Comment** action called " - - - - - - - Section 4 - Delete file" on line **5** and click on **Save**.

8. Add a new **Comment** action called " - - - - - - - Section 5 - Delete Sub Folder" on line **6** and click on **Save**.

9. Add a new **Comment** action called " - " on line **7** and click on **Save**. Your bot should look like this:

Figure 9.26 – Development interface

With that, we can proceed with this walk-through as we know what our bot will be performing. Since this bot works with the files that were generated in the previous walk-through, it is key to build it once the previous bot has been built and tested.

Section 1 – Looping through subfolders

To loop through all the subfolders that were created, follow these steps:

1. We will need a variable to store the subfolder name. For this, create a `String` type variable called `strSubFolder`.

2. To loop through all the subfolders, add the **Loop** action just below line **2**.

3. Set the following properties for the **Loop** action on line **3**:

   Loop Type: For each folder in folder

   Folder path: `C:\Hands-On-RPA-with-AA-Sample-Data\Chapter09_Output`

   Assign folder name to this variable: strSubFolder - String

   The properties window should look like this:

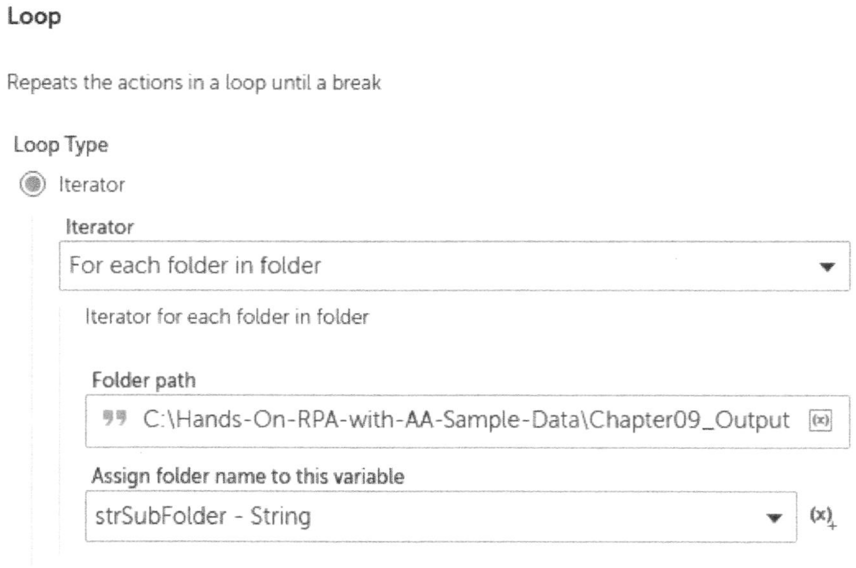

   Loop

   Repeats the actions in a loop until a break

   Loop Type

   ⦿ Iterator

   Iterator

   | For each folder in folder   ▼ |

   Iterator for each folder in folder

   Folder path

   | 〞 C:\Hands-On-RPA-with-AA-Sample-Data\Chapter09_Output ⒳ |

   Assign folder name to this variable

   | strSubFolder - String   ▼ | (x)

Figure 9.27 – Loop properties

4. Click on **Save**.

5. Since all the other sections will be completed within this **Loop**, drag **Comment** lines **4** to **7** so that they are within the **Loop** element on line **3**. The development interface should look like this:

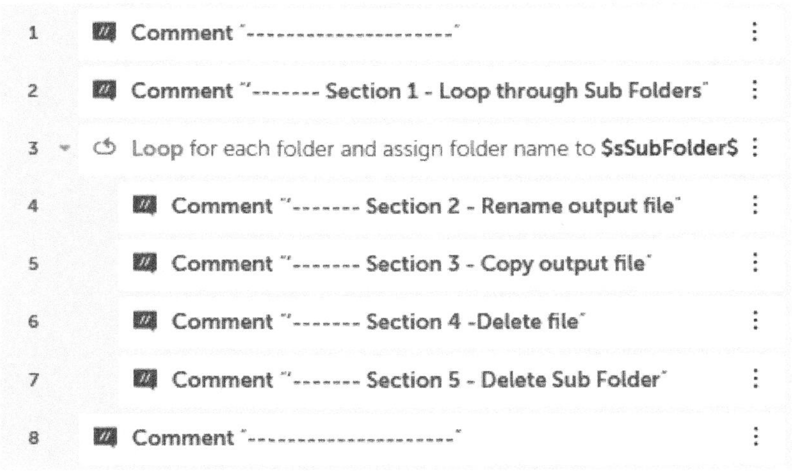

1	📝 Comment "----------------------"	⋮
2	📝 Comment "------- Section 1 - Loop through Sub Folders"	⋮
3 ▾	↻ Loop for each folder and assign folder name to **$sSubFolder$**	⋮
4	📝 Comment "------- Section 2 - Rename output file"	⋮
5	📝 Comment "------- Section 3 - Copy output file"	⋮
6	📝 Comment "------- Section 4 -Delete file"	⋮
7	📝 Comment "------- Section 5 - Delete Sub Folder"	⋮
8	📝 Comment "----------------------"	⋮

Figure 9.28 – Development interface

The initial loop has now been created. This will instruct the bot to iterate through every subfolder within C:\Hands-On-RPA-with-AA-Sample-Data\Chapter09_ Output\. The remaining actions will also be repeated for each subfolder. In the next section, we will rename our output.csv file so that its name is the same as the subfolders'.

Section 2 – Renaming the output file

Here, we will use the variable holding the current subfolder, strSubFolder, in order to rename the file. We already know that the original name will be output.csv. Let's get started:

1. To rename a file, drag the **File: Rename** action just below line **4**.

2. Set the following properties for the **File: Rename** action on line **5**:

   File: C:\Hands-On-RPA-with-AA-Sample-Data\Chapter09_ Output\$strSubFolder$\output.csv

   New file name: $strSubFolder$.csv

The properties window should look like this:

Figure 9.29 – File: Rename properties

3.   Click on **Save**.

That's *Section 2 – Renaming the output file*, completed. We have not only automated the process of renaming of a file, but have also used variables to identify the file and folder names. Next, we have to move this file, but since a move action isn't available, we will copy and delete instead.

Section 3 – Copying the output file

The **Copy** action for files duplicates a file. We could have used this function to perform the rename and move process in one action, but I decided against this as I wanted to demonstrate how to use the rename action. Let's get started:

1.   To copy a file, drag the **File: Copy** action just below line **6**.

2.   Set the following properties for the **File: Copy** action on line **7**:

      Source file: `C:\Hands-On-RPA-with-AA-Sample-Data\Chapter09_Output\$sSubFolder$\$strSubFolder$.csv`

      Destination file/folder: `C:\Hands-On-RPA-with-AA-Sample-Data\Chapter09_Output\$strSubFolder$.csv`

The properties window should look like this:

File: Copy

Copies a file

Source file

C:\Hands-On-RPA-with-AA-Sample-Data\Chapter09_Output**$strSubFolder$\$strSubFolder$**.csv   [x]   Browse...

e.g. C:\MyDoc*.doc

Destination file/folder

C:\Hands-On-RPA-with-AA-Sample-Data\Chapter09_Output**$strSubFolder$**.csv   [x]

e.g. C:\Backup\ , C:\Backup*.doc

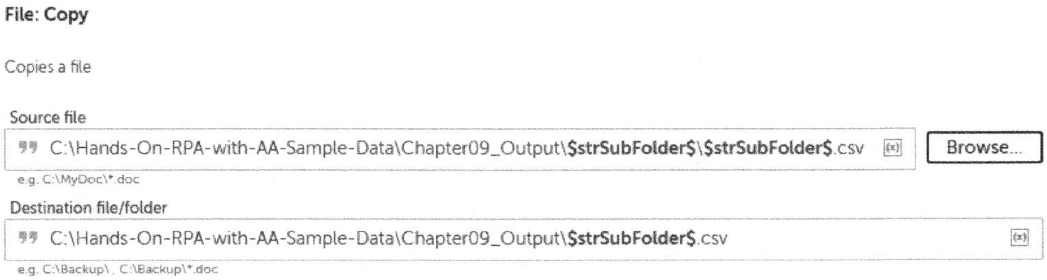

Figure 9.30 – File: Copy properties

3.   Click on **Save**.

With that, *Section 3 – Copying the output file*, has been completed; the file has been copied to our target destination. Now, we need to delete the original source file.

Section 4 – Deleting the output file

You will have noticed how similar the file and folder actions are. As with the previous file actions, we will now delete the file from our subfolder. Let's get started:

1.   To delete the source file, drag the **File: Delete** action just below line **8**.

2.   Set the following properties for the **File: Delete** action on line **9**:

File: C:\Hands-On-RPA-with-AA-Sample-Data\Chapter09_
Output\$strSubFolder$\$strSubFolder$.csv

The properties window should look like this:

File: Delete

Deletes a file

File

C:\Hands-On-RPA-with-AA-Sample-Data\Chapter09_Output**$strSubFolder$\$strSubFolder$**.csv   [x]   Browse...

e.g. C:\MyDoc*.doc

Figure 9.31 – File: Delete properties

3.   Click on **Save**.

We are fast approaching the end of this process. We have one last action to perform, deleting the subfolder.

Section 5 – Deleting the subfolder

Now that we have an empty folder that is obsolete, it needs to be deleted. Deleting a folder is very similar to deleting a file: it can be done with just one parameter. Let's get started:

1. To delete the subfolder, drag the **Folder: Delete** action just below line **10**.

2. Set the following properties for the **Folder: Delete** action on line **11**:

    Folder: `C:\Hands-On-RPA-with-AA-Sample-Data\Chapter09_Output\$strSubFolder$`

    The properties window should look like this:

Figure 9.32 – Folder: Delete properties

3. Click on **Save**.

Now that the bot is complete, you can go ahead and run it. The development interface should look like this:

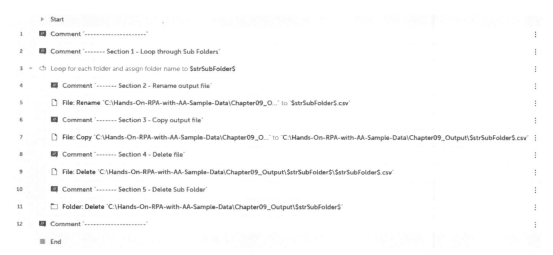

Figure 9.33 – Development interface

This bot should collate and rename all the files that were generated by the first bot in this chapter. It will also delete all the subfolders that were created. I've made you work hard in this chapter by building two bots. Hopefully, you have had some great insight into the types of tasks that can be automated using RPA.

Summary

I know this has been a pretty full-on chapter, but you have persevered through it, so I think a big congratulations is in order. In this chapter, we went through two separate walk-throughs and built two separate bots. We have covered a lot of packages. Just to recap once more, first, we built some nested loops that went through lists, records, and folders. We also discovered a new `Record` data type variable. You were then given some exposure to all the other types of looping available, all of which we will cover in later chapters. The walk-throughs also included building some rule-based decisions with conditional statements, using variables, and checking if files exist.

Hopefully, you have had a great confidence boost in your RPA skills, but there is still more to come. In the next chapter, we will be delving into how to automate XML files. For this, I have a great walk-through for you. It will involve working with nodes within XML files, which will include updating, creating, and deleting node values, as well as reading multiple nodes.

10

Working with XML Files

The previous chapter covered some of the most common actions that you will use to build automated solutions. Knowing how to apply loops and conditions is key for pretty much all types of software development. Just to recap, the previous walk-throughs also included working with files and folders, as well as introducing you to the Record type variable.

Now that you have a better understanding of the functionalities Automation Anywhere provides, in this chapter, we will examine XML files. By the end of this chapter, you will know how to read, update, create, and delete nodes in XML files. We will also introduce you to the **Step** action. This action doesn't really serve much use but is helpful in organizing our bot's structure. Previously, we used the **Comment** action to show us the skeleton of our bot. Instead of doing this, we can use the **Step** action to group a collection of steps. From a visualization perspective, this allows us to collapse and expand all the actions within each step.

To change things up a little, we will not be building a single bot to demonstrate XML actions. Instead, we will go through the individual actions within the XML package. Each walk-through will provide a step-by-step guide that shows you how to use each action. We will be using the following packages:

Figure 10.1 – Packages that will be used in this chapter

For this chapter, we will go through several separate walk-throughs. Each one has been designed to demonstrate specific XML actions. We will start by creating XML sessions so that we can work with an XML data stream. Following this, we will look at reading data from XML files. This will include reading a single node, as well as multiple nodes. To do this, we will need to build a loop that will iterate through all the records in an XML data stream. In the next walk-through, we will look at updating, creating, and deleting nodes within an XML data stream. By the end of this chapter, you will be fully confident with all the different aspects of XML data streams, including reading, updating, creating, and deleting nodes.

In this chapter, we will cover the following topics:

- Starting, validating, and ending XML sessions
- Reading and updating XML nodes
- Inserting and deleting XML nodes
- Executing XPath functions
- Let's get started!

Technical requirements

You will need the following to install Automation Anywhere Bot agent:

- Windows operating system version 7 or higher
- Processor with a minimum speed of 3 GHz
- Minimum of 4 GB RAM
- At least 100 MB hard disk space
- Internet Explorer v10 or higher OR Chrome v49 or higher
- A minimum screen resolution of 1024*768
- An internet connection with a minimum speed of 10 Mb/sec
- Completed registration with Automation Anywhere A2019 Community Edition
- Logged on successfully to Automation Anywhere A2019 Community Edition
- Successfully registered a local device
- Successfully downloaded the sample data from GitHub

Starting, validating, and ending XML sessions

Whenever we use an external data source, regardless of its type, a connection needs to be established. Once we have consumed this data, the connection needs to be closed. Not only does this apply to Automation Anywhere but to most development platforms. How we make this connection is where things differ. Automation Anywhere refers to this connection as a **session**. We will create various types of sessions as we progress through this book. We created some sessions previously in this book, when we connected to CSV files. In the coming chapters, you will come across more sessions as we start working with databases, emails, and spreadsheets.

Since an XML file is an external data source, whether it be for input or output, a session needs to be established before we can do anything else with the data. Another benefit of having a specific session for each data source is that this allows you to work with multiple data sources simultaneously. Since each session has a unique name, this removes any confusion that may arise with having multiple simultaneous connections. This is why it is always a good idea to give your sessions a suitable, clear-cut name.

For the first exercise, you'll learn how to start and end an XML session. The XML data stream can be stored as a `String` variable or read from an XML file. We will be using the sample XML file that's available as part of this book's GitHub repository. If you copied this book's GitHub repository to your `C:\` drive, the file we will be using can be found at `C:\ Hands-On-RPA-with-AA-Sample-Data\Chapter10_SampleFile.xml`. The following screenshot shows a partial view of this file:

```
 1     <?xml version="1.0"?>
 2   <catalog>
 3       <book id="bk101">
 4           <author>Gambardella, Matthew</author>
 5           <title>XML Developer's Guide</title>
 6           <genre>Computer</genre>
 7           <price>44.95</price>
 8           <publish_date>2000-10-01</publish_date>
 9           <description>An in-depth look at creating applications
10           with XML.</description>
11       </book>
12       <book id="bk102">
13           <author>Ralls, Kim</author>
14           <title>Midnight Rain</title>
15           <genre>Fantasy</genre>
16           <price>5.95</price>
17           <publish_date>2000-12-16</publish_date>
18           <description>A former architect battles corporate zombies,
19           an evil sorceress, and her own childhood to become queen
20           of the world.</description>
21       </book>
```

Figure 10.2 – Sample XML file

For this first walk-through, we will perform the following tasks:

1. Create a new XML session for the sample XML file.

2. Validate the XML file.

3. End the newly created session and close the XML file.

As always, we will start by adding some comments to guide us. Since we are just looking at creating a session, we don't need to add a lot of comments.

Let's start this walk-through by executing the following steps:

1. Log into **Control Room**.

2. Create a new bot and call it `Chapter 10 - XML`. Place it in the `\Bot\` folder.

3. As always, we'll begin by adding some comments that will be used as templates for our bot. Add a new **Comment** action called " - " on line **1** and click on **Save**.

4. Add another **Comment** action called " - - - - - - - `Create XML Session`" on line **2** and click on **Save**.

5. Add another **Comment** action called "`Validate XML data`" on line **3** and click on **Save**.

6. Add another **Comment** action called "`End XML Session`" on line **4** and click on **Save**.

7. Add another **Comment** action called " - " on line **5** and click on **Save**. Our initial development interface should look like this:

Figure 10.3 – Development interface

8. To create our XML session, go to the **XML** package and drag the **Start session** action just below line **2**.

9. Set the following properties for the **XML: Start session** action on line **3**:

Session name: xml_data

Data Source: **File**

Desktop file: C:\Hands-On-RPA-with-AA-Sample-Data\Chapter10_ SampleFile.xml

The properties window should look like this:

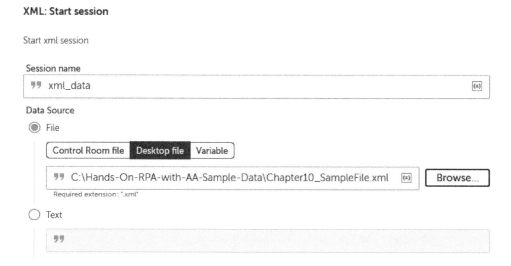

Figure 10.4 – XML: Start session properties

10. Click on **Save**.

When a new XML session is created, we should check that the XML data format is valid. To check the format, we can use the **Validate XML document** action. This action returns a string with a value of either `Valid` or `Invalid`. To store this result, we will create a `String` type variable called `sValidXML`:

1. Now that the XML session has been created, we can validate it. To validate our XML session, drag the **XML: Validate XML document** action just below line **4**.

2. Set the following properties for the **XML: Validate XML document** action on line **5**:

   Session name: `xml_data`

   Select validation type: **Well formed**

   Assign the output to variable: **sValidXML - String**

The properties window should look like this:

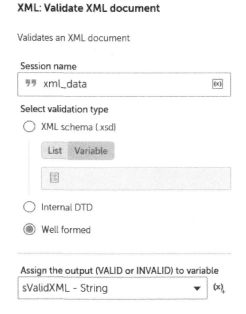

Figure 10.5 – XML: Validate XML document properties

3. Click on **Save**.

4. We now have our validation result assigned to the sValidXML variable. However, we only want to proceed if the XML data stream is valid. We can ensure this happens by adding a condition statement. To add this, drag the **If** action just below line **5**.

5. Set the following properties for the **If** action on line **6**:

    Condition: **String condition**

    Source value: $sValidXML$

    Operator: **Equals to (=)**

    Target value: VALID

    Match case: *Checked*

The properties window should look like this:

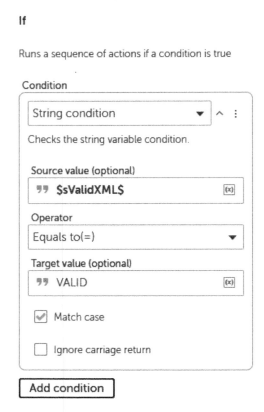

Figure 10.6 – If action properties

6. Click on **Save**.

7. So that we know what the validation result is, we will add a message box for each outcome. To add a message for a valid XML file, drag the **Message box** action just below line **6**.

8. Set the **Message box** action properties on line **7** to the following:

    Enter the message box window title: XML - Validation Check

    Enter the message to display: Result: $sValidXML$ - Bot will continue...

The properties window should look like this:

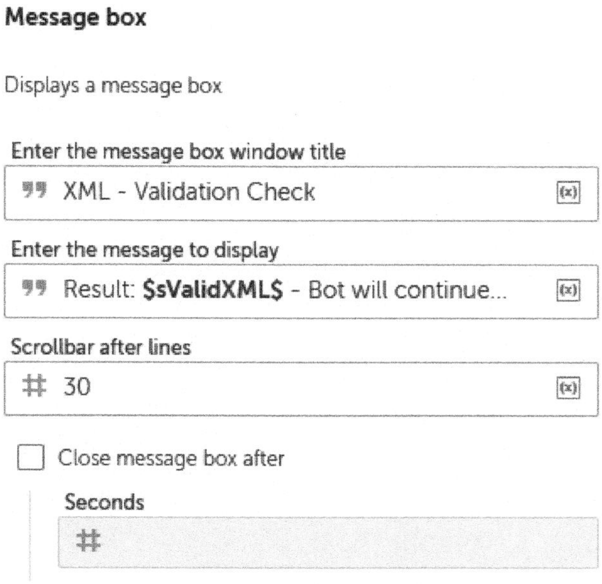

Message box

Displays a message box

Enter the message box window title

> 99   XML - Validation Check   [(x)]

Enter the message to display

> 99   Result: **$sValidXML$** - Bot will continue...   [(x)]

Scrollbar after lines

> #   30   [(x)]

[ ] Close message box after

    Seconds

    #

Figure 10.7 – Message box properties

9. Click on **Save**.

10. To add a message box in case the XML file is invalid, we will add an **Else** action to our condition. Drag the **Else** action from the **If** package just below line **7**. No properties need to be set for this.

11. Click on **Save**.

12. Add the message box for the invalid case by dragging the **Message box** action just below line **8**.

13. Set the **Message box** action properties on line **9** to the following:

Enter the message box window title: XML - Validation Check

Enter the message to display: Result: $sValidXML$ - Bot will Stop!

The properties window should look like this:

Figure 10.8 – Message box properties

14. Click on **Save**.

15. Now that we have completed our XML session, we need to close it. Always refer to the session name whenever you're working with any type of connection to a data source. Remember that there may be instances where you may have multiple data sources open; you wouldn't want to use the wrong one. To end our XML session, drag the **XML: End session** action just below line **10**.

16. Set the following properties for the **XML: End session** action on line **11**:

Session name: xml_data

The properties window should look like this:

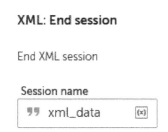

Figure 10.9 – XML: End session properties

17. Click on **Save**. Your development interface should look like this:

	▶ Start	
1	Comment "--------------------"	⋮
2	Comment "------- Create XML Session"	⋮
3	XML: **Start session** using File "C:\Hands-On-RPA-with-AA-Sample-Data\Chapter10_SampleFile.xml"	⋮
4	Comment "------- Validate XML data"	⋮
5	XML: **Validate XML document** Well formed in session "**xml_data**" and assign to variable **$sValidXML$**	⋮
6	◇ If string **$sValidXML$** Equals to(=) "**VALID**"	⋮
7	Message box "Result: $sValidXML$ - Bot will continue..."	⋮
8	◇ If: Else	⋮
9	Message box "Result: $sValidXML$ - Bot will stop!"	⋮
10	Comment "------- End XML Session"	⋮
11	XML: **End session** End XML session "xml_data"	⋮
12	Comment "--------------------"	⋮
	■ End	

Figure 10.10 – Development interface

That wasn't too difficult. Now that we know how to establish an XML session, we are ready to start working with the XML data. Go ahead and run your bot to check your progress so far. It should tell you whether the XML file is valid or not. You can try testing this out by modifying the file. Remember to save it back to its original format afterward.

In the next section, we will continue learning how to read XML nodes before introducing you to the **Step** action, which allows you to group a set of actions together as a single step.

Reading XML nodes

As we progress through this chapter, we will be learning the different ways we can work with XML data. To organize the workflow, we will start by using the Step action. The Step action is like creating a block of actions that perform a complete step or task within your taskbot. Each step can be collapsed or expanded, which makes it easier for you to read and understand your actions. As with the *If* statements and loops, all the actions related to a step must be indented within the step they belon to.

There may be many instances where you need to look up a single value from your XML data stream, especially when the XML data is being used for reference purposes. We will continue to build on our walk-through by providing you with steps on how to read a specific single node, as well as multiple nodes, from our XML file.

Reading a single node

Our sample XML file contains five records of books. To read a single node, we must specify which record we wish to read. For this example, we will get our bot to read the book title for the second record.

Let's start this walk-through by executing the following steps:

1. We will need a variable that will store our book title value. For this, create a `String` type variable called `sTitle`.

2. Next, we'll add our first step so that we can start reading a single node group. Drag the **Step** action just below line **7**, ensuring it is indented within the **If** action on line **6**.

3. Set the **Title** property of the **Step** action on line **8** to `Reading a Single Node`. The properties window should look like this:

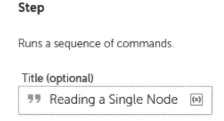

Figure 10.11 – Step action property settings

4. Click on **Save**.

5. To read the title for the second record, drag the **Get single node** action from the **XML** package to just below line **8**, ensuring it is indented within the **Step** action we just created.

6. Set the following properties for the **XML: Get single node** action on line **9**:

Session name: `xml_data`

XPath expression: `book[2]/title`

Assign the output to variable: sTitle - String

The properties window should look like this:

XML: Get single node

Fetch value of a specific node from the xml

Session name

　　🔊 xml_data   (x)

XPath expression

　　🔊 book[2]/title   (x)
　　　e.g. /bookstore/book/title

Attribute (optional)

　　🔊   (x)

Assign the output to variable

sTitle - String   ▼   (x)₊

Figure 10.12 – XML: Get single node properties

7. Click on **Save**.

8. Let's add a message box so that we can see the book title the bot has read from the XML file. We can do this by dragging the **Message box** action just below line **9**, ensuring it remains within our **Step** action.

9. Set the **Message box** action properties on line **10** to the following:

    Enter the message box window title: Reading a Single Node

    Enter the message to display: Book Title: |$sTitle$|

    The properties window should look like this:

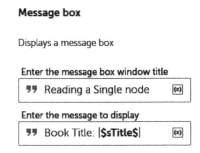

Message box

Displays a message box

Enter the message box window title

　🔊 Reading a Single node   (x)

Enter the message to display

　🔊 Book Title: |$sTitle$| (x)

Figure 10.13 – Message box properties

10. Click on **Save**.

Great work – you have just created your first complete **Step**! This **Step** has been tasked with reading a single node. In this example, we specified the second record and the node name. Remember that you can always replace these hard values with variables if needed. Your **Step** action in the development interface should look like this:

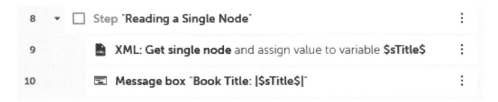

Figure 10.14 – Step action in the development interface

To make your development interface more readable and understandable, the **Step** action can be expanded and collapsed using the arrow icon on line **8**. Go ahead and run the bot; it should display two message boxes. The first will show the validity check result, while the second will show the book title. Now that we have tested the bot and know that the **Step** action works, collapse it – we don't really need to visit this again.

In the next section, we will learn how to read the title nodes for each record in our XML data stream. In our sample data, we have five book titles. We will build upon our bot so that it loops through each title.

Reading multiple nodes

In this section, we will still read the book title but for every record in our file. This will involve building a loop. There is a specific loop available just for working with XML files. We won't need a new variable as we already have sTitle from the previous section.

Let's start this walk-through by executing the following steps:

1. Add a new **Step** action on line **11**, ensuring it is aligned with the previous **Step** action on line **8**.

2. Set the **Title** property of this new **Step** action on line **11** to Reading Multiple Nodes. Your development interface for this section should look like this:

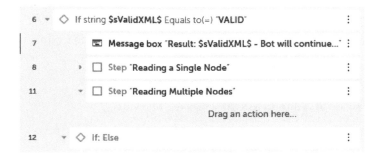

Figure 10.15 – Development interface

3. Click on **Save**.

4. To loop through our XML dataset, we need to identify which node we will be reading. To do this, drag the **Get multiple nodes** action from the **XML** package to just below line **11**, ensuring it is indented within the **Step** action on line **11**.

5. Set the following properties for the **XML: Get multiple nodes** action on line **12**:

    Session name: xml_data

    XPath expression: book/title

    Get each node: **Text value**

    The properties window should look like this:

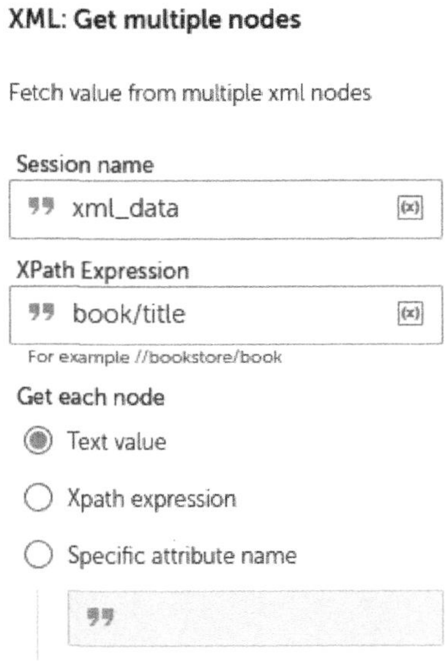

XML: Get multiple nodes

Fetch value from multiple xml nodes

Session name

    ⁇ xml_data   [(x)]

XPath Expression

    ⁇ book/title   [(x)]

For example //bookstore/book

Get each node

◉ Text value

○ Xpath expression

○ Specific attribute name

    ⁇

Figure 10.16 – XML: Get multiple nodes properties

6. Click on **Save**.

7. Next, we will add the loop for our XML file by dragging the **Loop** action to just below line **12**, ensuring it is indented within the **Step** action on line **11**.

8. Set the following properties for the **Loop** action on line **13**:

    Iterator: **For each Node in a XML Dataset**

    Session name: xml_data

    Assign the current row to this variable: **sTitle - String**

    The properties window should look like this:

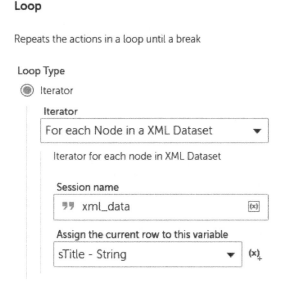

Figure 10.17 – Loop properties for XML dataset

9. Click on **Save**.

10. Like we did previously, add a message box that shows the title by dragging the **Message box** action just below line **13**, ensuring it remains within the **Loop** action on line **13**.

11. Set the following properties for the **Message Box** action on line **14**:

Enter the message box window title: `Reading Multiple Nodes`

Enter the message to display: `Book Title: |$sTitle$|`

The properties window should look like this:

Figure 10.18 – Message box properties

12. Click on **Save**. Your development window should look like this:

Figure 10.19 – New Step action in the development interface

Now, you can run your bot. It should loop through all the book titles, displaying the titles as it iterates through the XML dataset. Once you have tested the bot, you can collapse the steps. Your bot's development interface should look like this:

	▶ Start	
1	🗏 Comment "-------------------"	⋮
2	🗏 Comment "------- Create XML Session"	⋮
3	📄 XML: Start session using File "C:\Hands-On-RPA-with-AA-Sample-Data\Chapter10_SampleFile.xml"	⋮
4	🗏 Comment "------- Validate XML data"	⋮
5	📄 XML: Validate XML document Well formed in session "xml_data" and assign to variable $sValidXML$	⋮
6 ▾	◇ If string $sValidXML$ Equals to(=) "VALID"	⋮
7	▣ Message box "Result: $sValidXML$ - Bot will continue..."	⋮
8	▸ ☐ Step "Reading a Single Node"	⋮
11	▸ ☐ Step "Reading Multiple Nodes"	⋮
15 ▾	◇ If: Else	⋮
16	▣ Message box "Result: $sValidXML$ - Bot will stop!"	⋮
17	🗏 Comment "------- End XML Session"	⋮
18	📄 XML: End session End XML session "xml_data"	⋮
19	🗏 Comment "-------------------"	⋮
	⬛ End	

Figure 10.20 – New Step action in the development interface

In the next section, we will continue building our bot by learning how to update nodes in an XML dataset. Our approach will be to create additional steps that demonstrate each action from the XML package.

Updating XML nodes

At this point, you should be confident with reading data from XML files. In this section, we will be looking at updating nodes. We will start by updating a single node value. As we did previously, we will need to know the specific record we wish to update. Once we have learned how to update a single node, we will learn how to update multiple nodes. Again, a loop will be needed to perform this task.

Updating a single node

From our sample XML file, we will be updating the genre for the first record. It is currently set to Computer. We will update this to Computer - Software. We know that the record number is 1, and we also know the node is genre. In our XML file, this record currently looks like this:

```
<book id="bk101">
    <author>Gambardella, Matthew</author>
    <title>XML Developer's Guide</title>
    <genre>Computer</genre>
    <price>44.95</price>
    <publish_date>2000-10-01</publish_date>
    <description>An in-depth look at creating applications
    with XML.</description>
</book>
```

Figure 10.21 – Current XML record

To apply an update, a two-step process must be performed. Here, you need to make the update and then save the change back to your XML file. You'll need a string variable to save the change back to your file.

Let's start this walk-through by executing the following steps:

1. Create a String type variable called sXML_DataStream for saving any updates back to our file.

2. Add a new **Step** action on line **15**, ensuring it is aligned with the previous **Step** action on line **11**.

3. Set the **Title** property of the **Step** action on line **15** to Updating a Single Node. Your development interface should look like this:

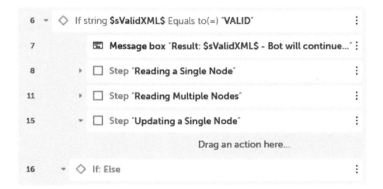

Figure 10.22 – Development interface

4. Click on **Save**.

5. To update the genre property of the first record, drag the **XML: Update node** action from the **XML** package just below line **15**, ensuring it is indented with the **Step** action we have just created.

6. Set the following properties for the **XML: Update node** action on line **16**:

Session name: xml_data

XPath expression: book[1]/genre

New value: Computer - Software

The properties window should look like this:

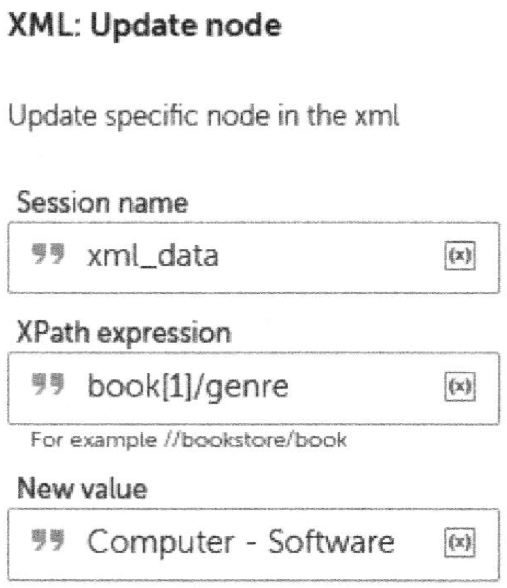

XML: Update node

Update specific node in the xml

Session name

    ⁇⁇ xml_data   [⋈]

XPath expression

    ⁇⁇ book[1]/genre   [⋈]

For example //bookstore/book

New value

    ⁇⁇ Computer - Software   [⋈]

Figure 10.23 – XML: Update node properties

7. Click on **Save**.

8. To save this update back to our sample file, drag the **Save session data** action from the **XML** package just below line **16**, ensuring it remains indented with the **Step** action on line **15**.

9. Set the following properties for the **XML: Save session data** action on line **17**:

Session name: xml_data

Write XML data: *Checked*

File path: C:\Hands-On-RPA-with-AA-Sample-Data\Chapter10_SampleFile.xml

Overwrite: *Checked*

Assign the output to variable: **sXML_DataStream - String**

The properties window should look like this:

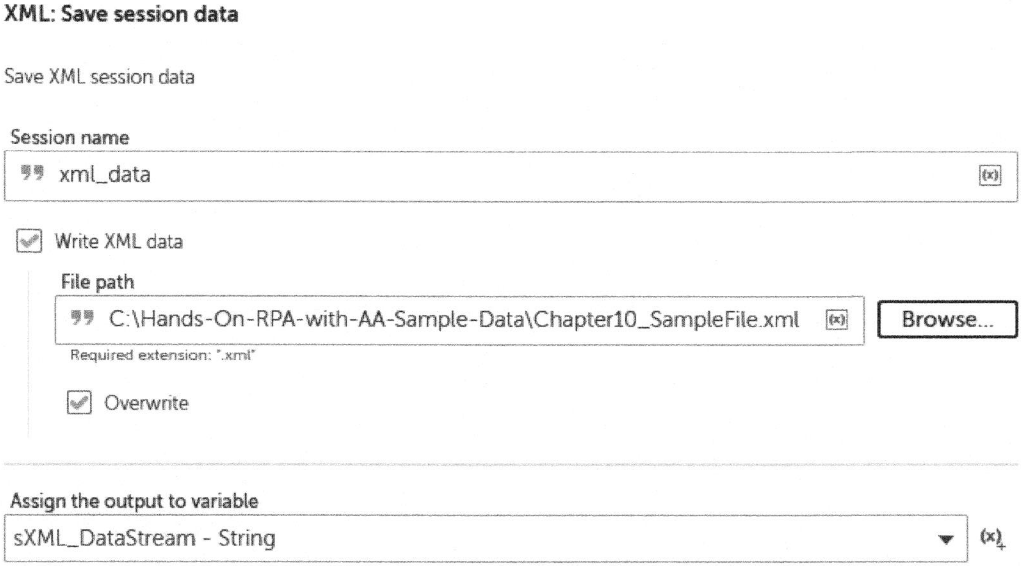

XML: Save session data

Save XML session data

Session name

> 〞 xml_data   (x)

☑ Write XML data

> File path
>
> 〞 C:\Hands-On-RPA-with-AA-Sample-Data\Chapter10_SampleFile.xml   (x) | Browse... |
>
> Required extension: ".xml"
>
> ☑ Overwrite

Assign the output to variable

sXML_DataStream - String   ▼   (x)

Figure 10.24 – XML: Save session data properties

10. Click on **Save**.

11. As with all the previous steps, we must add a message box so that we can see what the bot is doing. Add a **Message box** action just below line **17**, ensuring it remains within the **Step** action on line **15**.

12. Set the following properties for the **Message box** action on line **18**:

Enter the message box window title: Updating a Single Node

Enter the message to display: Record Number: 1

                    Previous Genre: Computer

                    New Genre: Computer Programming

The properties window should look like this:

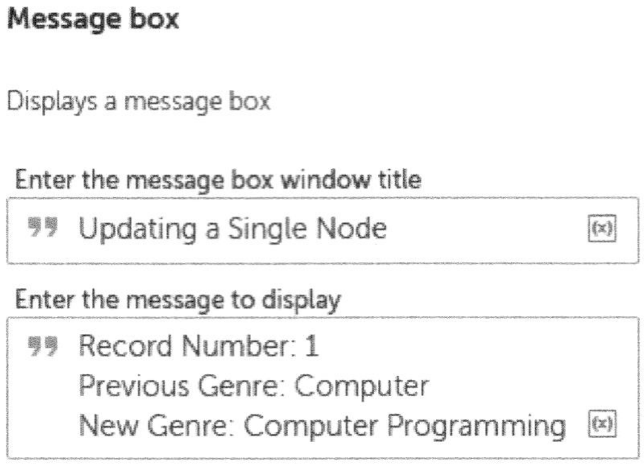

Message box

Displays a message box

Enter the message box window title

> 🔹 Updating a Single Node   (x)

Enter the message to display

> 🔹 Record Number: 1
> Previous Genre: Computer
> New Genre: Computer Programming   (x)

Figure 10.25 – Message box properties

13. Click on **Save**.

That wasn't too difficult! With that, you have learned how to update a single node, as long as you know which record it is for. Your **Step** action should look like this in the development interface:

Figure 10.26 – Step action in the development interface

You should be getting the hang of this by now. Once you have run the bot, have a look at your XML file; the first record should have been updated. It should look as follows:

```
<book id="bk101">
  <author>Gambardella, Matthew</author>
  <title>XML Developer's Guide</title>
  <genre>Computer - Software</genre>
  <price>44.95</price>
  <publish_date>2000-10-01</publish_date>
  <description>An in-depth look at creating applications
  with XML.</description>
</book>
```

Figure 10.27 – Updated XML record

In the next section, we will move on to updating multiple nodes in our XML file.

Updating multiple nodes

In this section, we will try and create a realistic user case for updating multiple nodes in our XML file. Here, we will apply a 10% price increase to all the books in our XML data stream. This will involve performing the following steps:

1. Building a loop to iterate through all the records.

2. Reading the current price.

3. Calculating the new price with a 10% increase.

4. Updating the XML file with the new prices.

Every node that is read from an XML file is returned as a String type. Since we want to calculate the price, we will need to convert this String into a Number. The same applies to updating a node: all the updated values need to be of the String data type. This means that once we have calculated the new price, we will need to assign this to a String type variable. To perform these updates on multiple nodes, we will need three variables for storing the old price, the new price, and the record number, respectively. A Number type and a String type will be required for each of these. This means that an additional six variables will need to be created.

Let's start this walk-through by executing the following steps:

1. Create three String type variables called sRecordNum, sOldPrice, and sNewPrice.

2. Create three Number type variables called nRecordNum, nOldPrice, and nNewPrice.

   Your variable list should look like this:

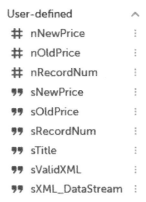

Figure 10.28 – Variables list

3. Add a **Step** action on line **19**, ensuring it is aligned with the previous **Step** action on line **15**.

4. Set the **Title** property of this new **Step** action on line **19** to Updating Multiple Nodes. Your development interface should look like this:

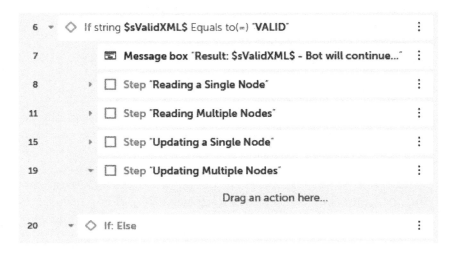

Figure 10.29 – Development interface

5. Click on **Save**.

6. To read the price nodes for all the records, drag the **Get multiple nodes** action from the **XML** package to just below line **19**, ensuring it is indented within the **Step** action on line **19**.

7. Set the following properties for the **XML: Get multiple nodes** action on line **20**:

Session name: xml_data

XPath expression: book/price

Get each node: **Text value**

The properties window should look like this:

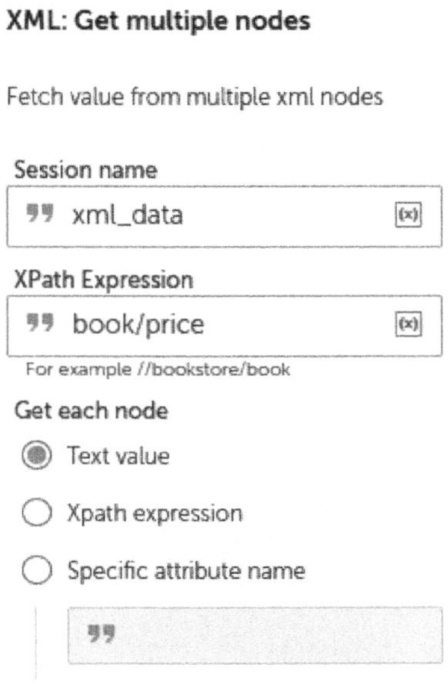

XML: Get multiple nodes

Fetch value from multiple xml nodes

Session name

> 💬 xml_data   (x)

XPath Expression

> 💬 book/price   (x)

For example //bookstore/book

Get each node

◉ Text value

○ Xpath expression

○ Specific attribute name

| 💬 |

Figure 10.30 – XML: Get multiple nodes properties

8. Click on **Save**.

9. Now, we can add our loop so that we can iterate through the price property of each record. Add the **Loop** action just below line **20**, ensuring it is within the **Step** action on line **19**.

10. Set the following properties for the **Loop** action on line **21**:

Iterator: For each Node in a XML Dataset

Session name: xml_data

Assign the current row to this variable: sOldPrice - String

The properties window should look like this:

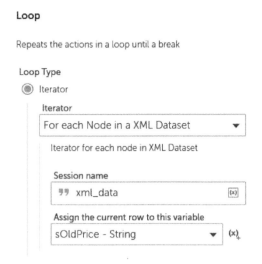

Figure 10.31 – Loop properties for our XML dataset

11. Click on **Save**.

12. The default number that's assigned to our nRecordNum variable is 0. We need to increment this value for each record. We can do this by adding the **Assign** action from the **Number** package just below line **21**, ensuring it is within the **Loop** action on line **21**.

13. Set the following properties for the **Number: Assign** action on line **22**:

    Select the source string variable/ value: $nRecordNum$ + 1

    Select the destination number variable: nRecordNum – Number

    The properties window should look like this:

Figure 10.32 – Number: Assign properties

14. Click on **Save**.

15. Since we will be passing the record number as a parameter when applying the update, we need convert this into a **String**. To do this, drag the **To string** action from the **Number** package just below line **22**, ensuring it is within the **Loop** action on line **21**.

16. Set the following properties for the **Number: To string** action on line **23**:

    Enter a number: $nRecordNum$

    Enter the number of digits after decimal: 0

    Assign the output to variable: **sRecordNum - String**

    The properties window should look like this:

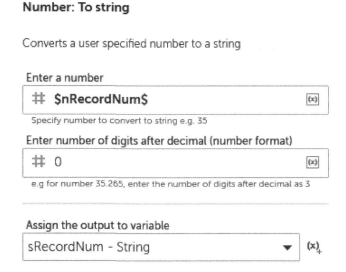

Figure 10.33 – Number: To string properties

17. Click on **Save**.

18. To calculate the old price, we need to convert this value into a **Number** type variable. To do this, drag the **To number** action from the **String** package just below line **23**, ensuring it is within the **Loop** action on line **21**.

19. Set the following properties for the **String: To number** action on line **24**:

Enter the string: $sOldPrice$

Assign the output to variable: nOldPrice - Number

The properties window should look like this:

String: To number

Converts a string to a number

Enter the string

    ⁹⁹ **$sOldPrice$**   (x)

String entered must be a valid number

Assign the output to variable

nOldPrice - Number   ▼   (x)

Figure 10.34 – String: To number properties

20. Click on **Save**.

21. To add a 10% price increase, we will multiply the old price by 1.1 and assign this to the new price **Number** variable. We can do this by dragging the **Calc** action from the **NumberUtils** package just below line **24**, ensuring it is within the **Loop** action on line **21**.

22. Set the following properties for the **NumberUtils: Calc** action on line **25**:

Expression to be calculated: $nOldPrice$ * 1.1

Calculated Expression: nNewPrice - Number

The properties window should look like this:

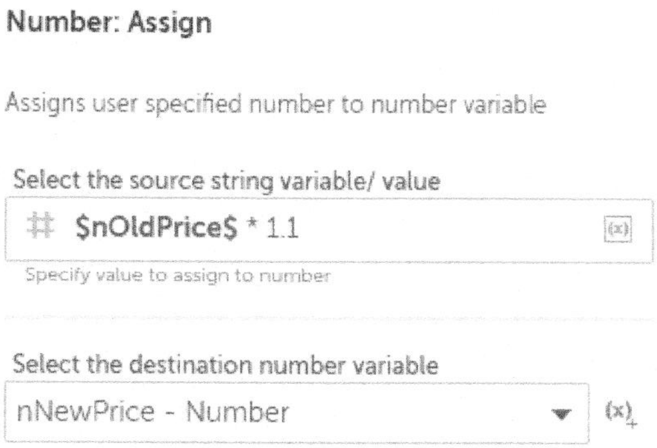

Number: Assign

Assigns user specified number to number variable

Select the source string variable/ value

> ⌗ **$nOldPrice$** * 1.1   (x)

Specify value to assign to number

Select the destination number variable

> nNewPrice - Number   ▼   (x)

Figure 10.35 – NumberUtils: Calc properties

23. Click on **Save**.

24. Since we will be updating our XML file, the new price needs to be converted into a **String**. You can do this by dragging the **To string** action from the **Number** package just below line **25**, ensuring it is within the **Loop** action on line **21**.

25. Set the following properties for the **Number: To string** action on line **26**:

   Enter a number: $nNewPrice$

   Enter number of digits after decimal: 2

   Assign the output to variable: nNewPrice – String

   The properties window should look like this:

Number: To string

Converts a user specified number to a string

Enter a number

> ⌗ **$nNewPrice$**   (x)

Specify number to convert to string e.g. 35

Enter number of digits after decimal (number format)

> ⌗ 2   (x)

e.g for number 35.265, enter the number of digits after decimal as 3

Assign the output to variable

> sNewPrice - String   ▼   (x)

Figure 10.36 – Number: To string properties

26. Click on **Save**.

27. We are now ready to update our node. We do this in exactly the same way we update a single node. We have our record number saved to a **String** variable, as well as the updated price. Apply the update by dragging the **Update node** action from the **XML** package just below line **26**, ensuring it is within the **Loop** action on line **21**.

28. Set the following properties for the **XML: Update node** action on line **27**:

    Session name: XML_data

    XPath expression: book[$sRecordNum$]/price

    New value: $sNewPrice$

    The properties window should look like this:

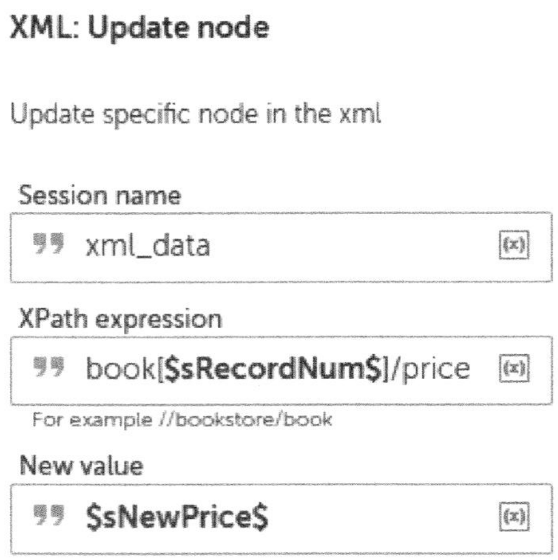

    XML: Update node

    Update specific node in the xml

    Session name

    `" xml_data` `(x)`

    XPath expression

    `" book[$sRecordNum$]/price` `(x)`

    For example //bookstore/book

    New value

    `" $sNewPrice$` `(x)`

    Figure 10.37 – XML: Update node properties

29. Click on **Save**.

30. Next, we'll add a message box, as we did previously, but this time we will set a close timer so that the message box will close itself once a certain amount of time has passed. This will mean you won't have to click on the **Close** button to continue. To add a **Message box** action, drag this action just below line **27**, ensuring it remains within the **Loop** action on line **21**.

31. Set the following properties for the **Message Box** action on line **28**:

   Enter the message box window title: Updating Multiple Nodes

   Enter the message to display: Record Number: $sRecordNum$

   Old Price: $sOldPrice$

   New Price: $sNewPrice$

   Close message box after: *Checked*

   Seconds: 5

   The properties window should look like this:

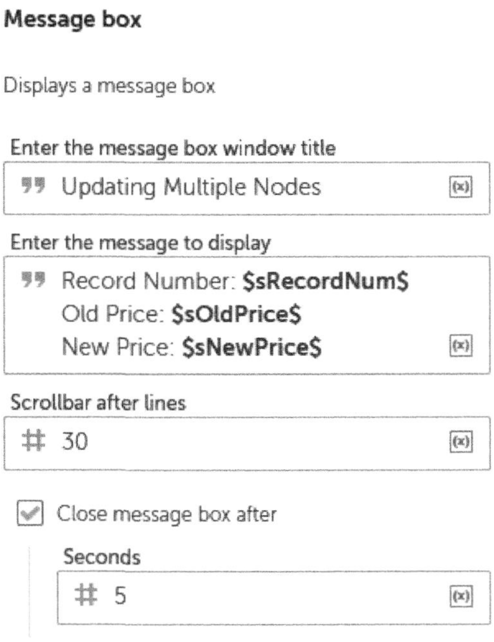

   Message box

   Displays a message box

   Enter the message box window title

   | 🗩 Updating Multiple Nodes | (x) |

   Enter the message to display

   🗩 Record Number: **$sRecordNum$**
   Old Price: **$sOldPrice$**
   New Price: **$sNewPrice$**   (x)

   Scrollbar after lines

   # 30   (x)

   ✔ Close message box after

   Seconds

   # 5   (x)

   Figure 10.38 – Message box properties

32. Click on **Save**.

33. Now that we've completed the loop, all we have to do is save the updates back to our sample file. This only needs to be done once all the prices have been updated so that this can take place outside the loop. To save all the updates, drag the **Save session data** action from the **XML** package just below line **28**, ensuring it remains within the **Step** action on line **19** but also outside the **Loop** action on line **21** (it may help to collapse the **Loop** action by using the collapse arrow on the **Loop** action on line **21**).

34. Set the following properties for the **XML: Save session data** action on line **29**:

Session name: `xml_data`

Write XML data: *Checked*

File path: `C:\Hands-On-RPA-with-AA-Sample-Data\Chapter10_SampleFile.xml`

Overwrite: *Checked*

Assign the output to variable: **sXML_DataStream**

The properties window should look like this:

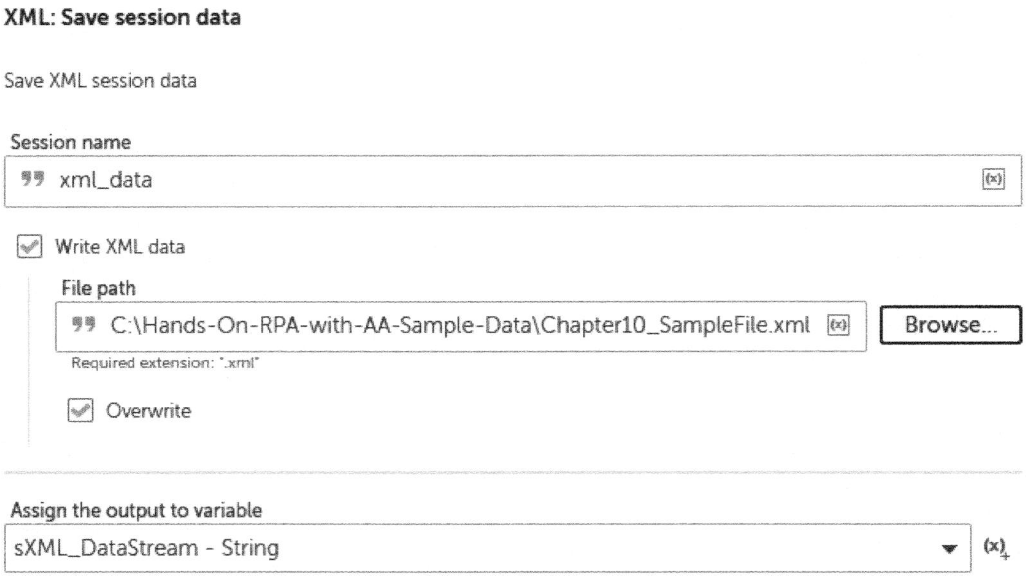

XML: Save session data

Save XML session data

Session name

> 🔤 xml_data   [x]

☑ Write XML data

> File path
>
> 🔤 C:\Hands-On-RPA-with-AA-Sample-Data\Chapter10_SampleFile.xml [x]   Browse...
>
> Required extension: ".xml"
>
> ☑ Overwrite

Assign the output to variable

sXML_DataStream - String   ▼   (x)₊

Figure 10.39 – XML: Save session data properties

35. Click on **Save**.

Great job! With that, you have learned how to update multiple nodes within an XML data stream and save the results back to an XML file. Your **Step** action should look like this in the development interface:

19	▾ ☐ Step "Updating Multiple Nodes"	⋮
20	📄 XML: Get multiple nodes Text value from xpath localtion "book/price" session "xml_data"	⋮
21	▾ ↻ Loop Each node In a XML Dataset "xml_data"	⋮
22	# Number: Assign "$nRecordNum$ + 1" to $nRecordNum$	⋮
23	# Number: To string convert $nRecordNum$ to a string datatype and assign output to $sRecordNum$	⋮
24	🔢 String: To number Convert string $sOldPrice$ to a number and assign it to number variable $nOldPrice$	⋮
25	# Number: Assign "$nOldPrice$ * 1.1" to $nNewPrice$	⋮
26	# Number: To string convert $nNewPrice$ to a string datatype and assign output to $sNewPrice$	⋮
27	📄 XML: Update node Update node value $sNewPrice$ at xpath location "book[$sRecordNum$]/price" in session "xml_data"	⋮
28	🖵 Message box "Record Number: $sRecordNum$ Old Price: $sOldPrice$ New Price: $sNewPrice$"	⋮
29	📄 XML: Save session data assigned to variable $sXML_DataStream$ write session data into file "C:\Hands-On-RPA-with-AA-Sa...	⋮

Figure 10.40 – Step action in the development interface

Go ahead and run your bot. Once you've done this, check your prices – they should have all had a 10% price increase. Now, you can collapse the last **Step** action we created on line **19**. Your development interface for the complete bot should look like this:

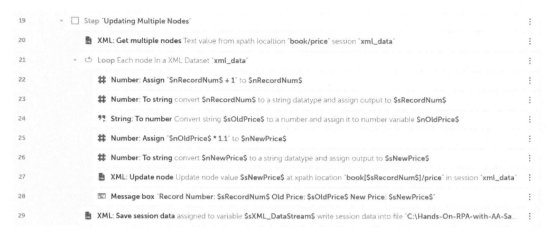

1	🗎 Comment "---------------------"	⋮
2	🗎 Comment "------- Create XML Session"	⋮
3	📄 XML: Start session using File "C:\Hands-On-RPA-with-AA-Sample-Data\Chapter10_SampleFile.xml"	⋮
4	🗎 Comment "------- Validate XML data"	⋮
5	📄 XML: Validate XML document Well formed in session "xml_data" and assign to variable $sValidXML$	⋮
6	▾ ◇ If string $sValidXML$ Equals to(=) "VALID"	⋮
7	🖵 Message box "Result: $sValidXML$ - Bot will continue..."	⋮
8	▸ ☐ Step "Reading a Single Node"	⋮
11	▸ ☐ Step "Reading Multiple Nodes"	⋮
15	▸ ☐ Step "Updating a Single Node"	⋮
19	▸ ☐ Step "Updating Multiple Nodes"	⋮
30	▾ ◇ If: Else	⋮
31	🖵 Message box "Result: $sValidXML$ - Bot will stop!"	⋮
32	🗎 Comment "------- End XML Session"	⋮
33	📄 XML: End session End XML session "xml_data"	⋮
34	🗎 Comment "---------------------"	⋮

Figure 10.41 – Development interface

You're making great progress! Let's keep this pace going. Since XML data streams are data sources, we may need to add additional nodes or fields, especially if we are dynamically building the XML data steam. In the next section, you will learn how to insert nodes into our sample XML file.

Inserting XML nodes

In some cases, we may need insert additional nodes into our XML file. In this section, we will explore how to achieve this with Automation Anywhere. Now that you're more familiar with the **XML** package, you've probably guessed that to perform any XML action, you need to specify the session, **Node**, and **Action**. When inserting a node, the same principle applies. In this walk-through, we will be creating a new node for all the records in our sample XML file. The node we'll be inserting will be named format and will be assigned the Paperback value. We will start by created a new **Step** action, as we did previously.

Let's start this walk-through by executing the following steps:

1. Add a **Step** action to line **30**, ensuring it is aligned with the previous **Step** action on line **19**.

2. Set the **Title** property of this **Step** action on line **30** to Inserting a Node. Your development interface should look like this:

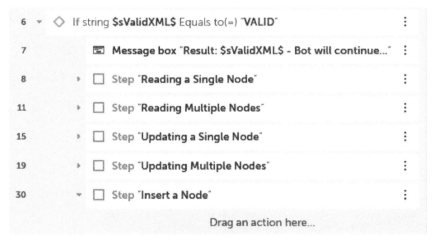

Figure 10.42 – Development interface

3. Click on **Save**.

4. To insert a new node called `format` and assign it a value of `Paperback`, drag the **Insert node** action from the **XML** package just below line **30**, ensuring it is within the **Step** action we have just created.

5. Set the following properties for the **XML: Insert node** action on line **31**:

    Session name: `xml_data`

    XPath Expression: `book`

    Node name: `format`

    Node value: `Paperback`

    If node name is present then: **Insert it anyways**

    Insert node location: **End of child nodes**

    The properties window should look like this:

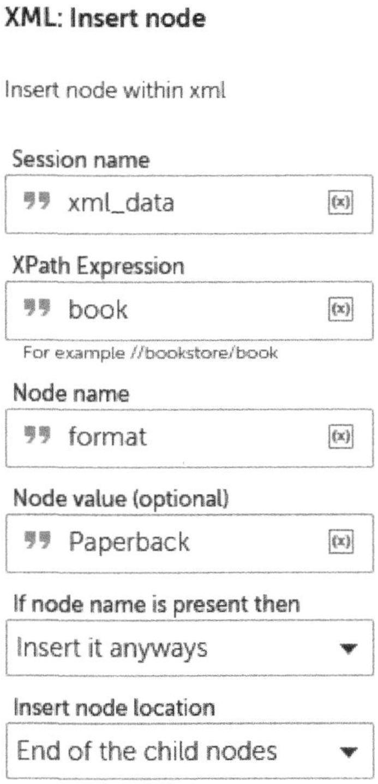

XML: Insert node

Insert node within xml

Session name

> ``` xml_data                    (x)

XPath Expression

> ``` book                        (x)

For example //bookstore/book

Node name

> ``` format                      (x)

Node value (optional)

> ``` Paperback                   (x)

If node name is present then

Insert it anyways   ▼

Insert node location

End of the child nodes   ▼

Figure 10.43 – XML: Insert node for all records

There may be instances where you may want to just insert a node for a specific record. To do this, simply specify the record number when setting the **XPath Expression** property, as follows:

Figure 10.44 – XML: Insert node for a specific record

6. Click on **Save**.

7. As we've done previously, we need to save this insert in our sample file. Drag the **Save session data** action from the **XML** package just below line **31**, ensuring it is within the **Step** action on line **30**.

8. Set the following properties for the **XML: Save session data** action on line **32**:

Session name: xml_data

Write XML data: *Checked*

File path: C:\Hands-On-RPA-with-AA-Sample-Data\Chapter10_ SampleFile.xml

Overwrite: *Checked*

Assign the output to variable: sXML_DataStream - String

The properties window should look like this:

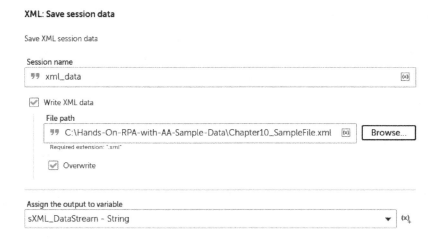

Figure 10.45 – XML: Save session data properties

9. Click on **Save**.

10. Also like we did previously, we must add a message box so that we can see what the bot is doing. Add a **Message box** action just below line **32**, ensuring it remains within the **Step** action on line **30**.

11. Set the following properties for the **Message Box** action on line **32**:

    Enter the message box window title: Inserting a Node

    Enter the message to display: Node Inserted: format, value Paperback

    The properties window should look like this:

    Message box

    Displays a message box

    Enter the message box window title

    > Inserting a Node   (x)

    Enter the message to display

    > Node Inserted: format, value Paperback   (x)

Figure 10.46 – Message Box properties

12. Click on **Save**.

Your **Step** action should look like this in the development interface:

30	▾	☐ Step `Insert a Node`	⋮
31		📄 **XML: Insert node** Insert node with name `format` and value `Paperback` at xpath location `book` in session `xml_data`	⋮
32		📄 **XML: Save session data** assigned to variable $sXML_DataStream$ write session data into file `C:\Hands-On-RPA-with-AA-Sample...`	⋮
33		🖾 **Message box** `Node Inserted: format, value Paperback`	⋮

Figure 10.47 – Step action in the development interface

Now, run the bot; you may want to disable all the previous steps for this. Once the bot has completed the task at hand, have a look at the sample XML file. It should now have a new node format for each record. This node should have the Paperback value assigned to it. Now that you have learned how to insert nodes into an XML file, in the next section, we will learn how to delete format nodes from XML files.

Deleting XML nodes

Now that we've learned how to insert nodes, it is only fair that we have a walk-through on how to delete nodes. We inserted the `format` node in the previous section. Just for fun, we will be deleting it in this section. Since we will be deleting it for all records, we will only be specifying the node as `book/format`. If we wanted to delete the node for a specific record only, we would specify this as `book[2]/format`.

Let's start this walk-through by executing the following steps:

1. Add a **Step** action on line **34**, ensuring it is aligned with the previous **Step** action on line **30**.

2. Set the **Title** property of the **Step** action on line **34** to `Delete a Node`. Your development interface should look like this:

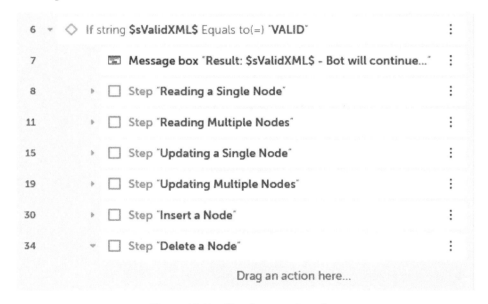

Figure 10.48 – Development interface

3. Click on **Save**.

4. To delete the `format` node, drag the **Delete node** action from the **XML** package just below line **34**, ensuring it is within the **Step** action on line **34**.

5. Set the following properties for the **XML: Delete node** action on line **35**:

    Session name: `xml_data`

    XPath Expression: `book/format`

The properties window should look like this:

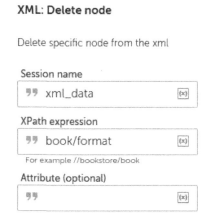

Figure 10.49 – XML: Delete node for all records

In cases where you need to delete a node for a specific record, just specify the record number when setting the **XPath Expression** property, as shown in the following screenshot:

Figure 10.50 – XML: Delete node for a specific record

6. Click on **Save**.

7. As you may have guessed, we need to save the XML file. So, drag the **Save session data** action from the **XML** package just below line **35**, ensuring it remains within the **Step** action on line **34**.

8. Set the following properties for the **XML: Save session data** action on line **36**:

    Session name: xml_data

    Write XML data: *Checked*

    File path: C:\Hands-On-RPA-with-AA-Sample-Data\Chapter10_ SampleFile.xml

    Overwrite: *Checked*

    Assign the output to variable: **sXML_DataStream - String**

The properties window should look like this:

XML: Save session data

Save XML session data

Session name

> 🥢 xml_data   (x)

☑ Write XML data

> File path
>
> 🥢 C:\Hands-On-RPA-with-AA-Sample-Data\Chapter10_SampleFile.xml (x)   [Browse...]
>
> Required extension: ".xml"
>
> ☑ Overwrite

Assign the output to variable

sXML_DataStream - String   ▼   (x)

Figure 10.51 – XML: Save session data properties

9. Click on **Save**.

10. To add a message box so that we can check the file at this point, add a **Message box** action just below line **36**, ensuring it remains within the **Step** action on line **34**.

11. Set the following properties for the **Message box** action on line **37**:

Enter the message box window title: Deleting a Node

Enter the message to display: Node Deleted: format, value Paperback

The properties window should look like this:

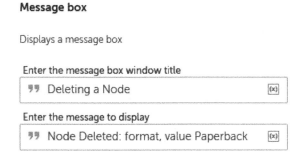

Message box

Displays a message box

Enter the message box window title

> 🥢 Deleting a Node   (x)

Enter the message to display

> 🥢 Node Deleted: format, value Paperback   (x)

Figure 10.52 – Message box properties

12. Click on **Save**.

Your **Step** action should look like this in the development interface:

34	▾ ☐ Step "Delete a Node"	⋮
35	📄 **XML: Delete node** Delete node attribute "" at xpath location **"book/format"** in session **"xml_data"**	⋮
36	📄 **XML: Save session data** assigned to variable **$sXML_DataStream$** write session data into file "C:\Hands-On-RPA-...	⋮
37	🗔 **Message box** "Node Deleted: format, value Paperback"	⋮

Figure 10.53 – Step action in the development interface

Now, collapse all these steps and run the bot. It should successfully delete the format node. You will need to check the XML file while the bot is waiting for a message box response. With that, we have covered pretty much all the actions we can use when working with the data within an XML file.

For those of you who use XPath functions to query XML data streams, in the next section, we will look at how to execute XPath functions.

Executing XPath functions

For those of you who use XPath functions, we will be running a simple XPath function in this walk-through. We want to know how many records are in our sample XML file. To get this information, we can run the count(//book) XPath function. We will also need a variable to assign the results of our function. All the results that are returned from an XPath function are saved as a string. In this walk-through, you will learn how easy it is to run XPath functions using Automation Anywhere.

Let's start this walk-through by executing the following steps:

1. To save the results of our XPath function, create a String type variable called sBookCount.

2. Add a **Step** action on line **38**, ensuring it is aligned with the previous **Step** action on line **34**.

3. Set the **Title** property of this **Step** action on line **38** to Execute XPath Function.

Your development interface should look like this:

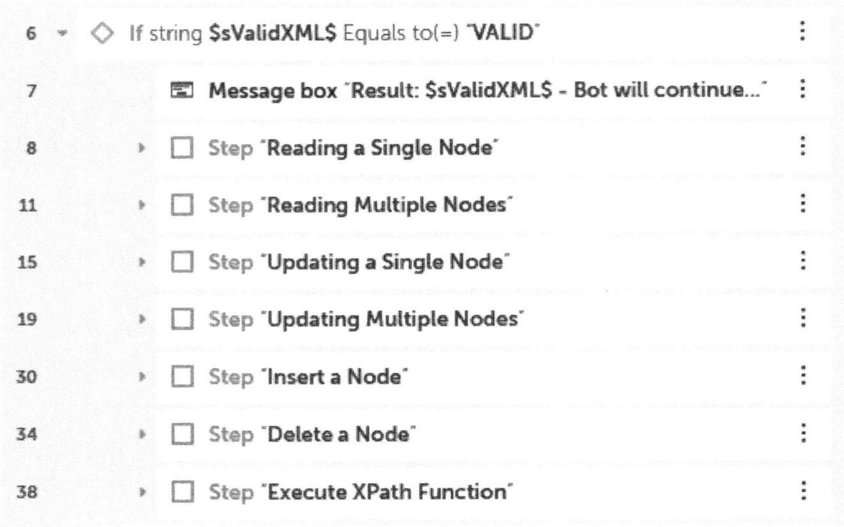

6 ▼	◇	If string **$sValidXML$** Equals to(=) **"VALID"**	⋮
7		🖃 **Message box** "Result: $sValidXML$ - Bot will continue..."	⋮
8	▸ ☐	Step **"Reading a Single Node"**	⋮
11	▸ ☐	Step **"Reading Multiple Nodes"**	⋮
15	▸ ☐	Step **"Updating a Single Node"**	⋮
19	▸ ☐	Step **"Updating Multiple Nodes"**	⋮
30	▸ ☐	Step **"Insert a Node"**	⋮
34	▸ ☐	Step **"Delete a Node"**	⋮
38	▸ ☐	Step **"Execute XPath Function"**	⋮

Figure 10.54 – Development interface

4. Click on **Save**.

5. To execute our XPath function, drag the **Execute XPath function** action from the **XML** package just below line **38**, ensuring it is within the **Step** action on line **38**.

6. Set the following properties for the **XML: Execute XPath function** action on line **39**:

    Session name: `xml_data`

    XPath Expression: `count(//book)`

    Assign the output to variable: sBookCount - String

The properties window should look like this:

XML: Execute XPath function

Executes the XPath function on the XML

Session name

> xml_data   (x)

XPath expression

> count(//book)   (x)

e.g. /bookstore/book/title

Assign the output to variable

sBookCount - String   ▼   (x)₊

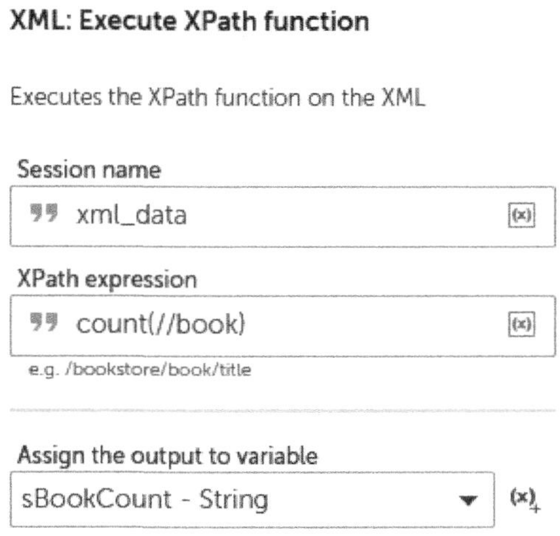

Figure 10.55 – XML: Execute XPath function properties

7. Click on **Save**.

8. Now, we need to add a message box so that we can view the results of our XPath function. Add a **Message box** action just below line **39**, ensuring it remains within the **Step** action on line **38**.

9. Set the following properties for the **Message Box** action on line **40**:

    Enter the message box window title: Execute XPath Function

    Enter the message to display: Number of Books: $sBookCount$

    The properties window should look like this:

Message box

Displays a message box

Enter the message box window title

> Execute XPath Function   (x)

Enter the message to display

> Number of Books: **$sBookCount$**   (x)

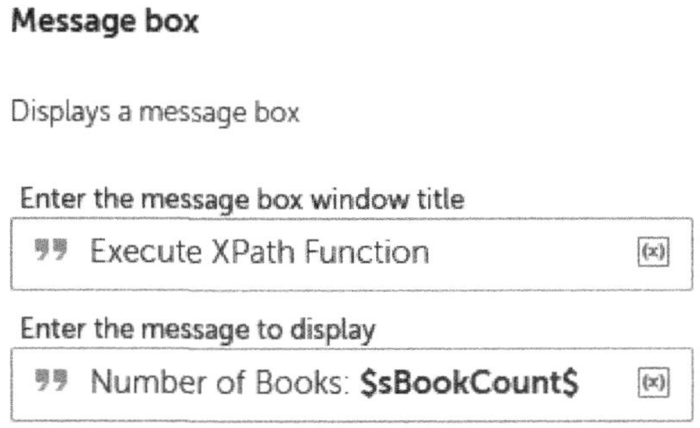

Figure 10.56 – Message box properties

10. Click on **Save**.

Your **Step** action should look like this in the development interface:

38	▾ ☐ Step "Execute XPath Function"	⋮
39	📄 XML: Execute XPath function and assign value to variable $sBookCount$	⋮
40	▣ Message box "Number of Books: $sBookCount$"	⋮

Figure 10.57 – Step action in the development interface

Now, for the final time, run the bot. You should get a result of 5. There are five book records in our sample XML file. Collapse all the steps; your development interface should look like this:

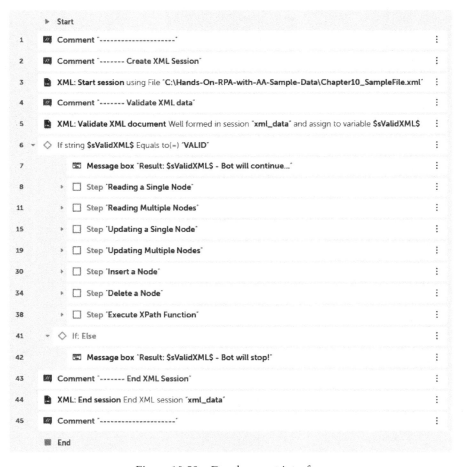

	▷ Start	
1	📝 Comment "--------------------"	⋮
2	📝 Comment "------- Create XML Session"	⋮
3	📄 XML: Start session using File "C:\Hands-On-RPA-with-AA-Sample-Data\Chapter10_SampleFile.xml"	⋮
4	📝 Comment "------- Validate XML data"	⋮
5	📄 XML: Validate XML document Well formed in session "xml_data" and assign to variable $sValidXML$	⋮
6	▾ ◇ If string $sValidXML$ Equals to(=) "VALID"	⋮
7	▣ Message box "Result: $sValidXML$ - Bot will continue..."	⋮
8	▸ ☐ Step "Reading a Single Node"	⋮
11	▸ ☐ Step "Reading Multiple Nodes"	⋮
15	▸ ☐ Step "Updating a Single Node"	⋮
19	▸ ☐ Step "Updating Multiple Nodes"	⋮
30	▸ ☐ Step "Insert a Node"	⋮
34	▸ ☐ Step "Delete a Node"	⋮
38	▸ ☐ Step "Execute XPath Function"	⋮
41	▾ ◇ If: Else	⋮
42	▣ Message box "Result: $sValidXML$ - Bot will stop!"	⋮
43	📝 Comment "------- End XML Session"	⋮
44	📄 XML: End session End XML session "xml_data"	⋮
45	📝 Comment "--------------------"	⋮
	■ End	

Figure 10.58 – Development interface

That is fantastic work! This bot demonstrates all the different actions that are available for XML data streams. Hopefully, you are now confident with dealing with XML data streams in whatever scenario comes your way. You should also be able to appreciate the relevance and importance of using **Step** actions. We have broken our bot down into multiple stages to help you understand the logical workflow of the different tasks being implemented.

Summary

This has been another hands-on chapter. We have covered every action that is available in the XML package and learned some great skills. This chapter's walk-throughs have taken you through a multitude of exercises, including reading single and multiple nodes from XML data streams. You also learned how to update single and multiple nodes within XML files. Furthermore, you've learned how to insert and delete nodes and values from XML files. Apart from this, we built our bot so that it executes XPath functions that return results. Since many applications typically utilize the XML format, understanding how to work with these files can help us discover many of the automation opportunities that are available to us. Creating your own XML files can also be a good way to store metadata for your bots.

In the next chapter, we will learn how to apply RPA to Excel tasks. We will cover the basics of opening, closing, and saving workbooks. We will also be reading and updating data in Excel worksheets. We will also cover reading and setting formulas, as well as how to run macros in our macro-enabled workbooks.

11
Automating Excel

You must be feeling like an XML automation guru now. In the previous chapter, we covered all the actions available in the XML package, giving hands-on experience with reading and updating XML files as well as running XPath functions against your XML datasets.

In this chapter, we will be looking into using automation with Microsoft Excel. We will go through several walk-throughs, looking at how we can build bots to automate Excel workbooks and worksheets. Automation Anywhere 2019 has two packages offering loads of Excel actions. These packages are Excel basic and Excel advanced. Starting with the basics will enable you to feel confident with opening, closing, and saving workbooks. You will also learn how to read datasets from Excel as well as write to worksheets. This will include creating loops to iterate through rows of data. As we move onto the advanced package, we will look at manipulating worksheets by doing things such as inserting columns, adding formulas, and sorting tables. You will also learn how to run macros from a macro-enabled workbook.

In this chapter, we will cover the following:

- Opening, closing, and saving Excel workbooks
- Reading and writing data within Excel worksheets
- Working with data in Excel
- Running macros

We will be taking the same approach as the previous chapter, with a number of walk-throughs exploring the different Excel actions. As before, we will be building our bots with multiple steps to help us keep things structured. We will be using the following packages:

Figure 11.1 – Packages used in this chapter

The basic Excel package works with files with the `.xlsx` extension only, whereas the advanced package works with Excel files with extensions of `.xlsx`, `.xls`, `.xlsm`, `.xlsb`, and `.csv`. As we progress through this chapter, we will be using both packages, and you will learn about the different actions available from each one. We will start by creating a bot that opens, saves, and closes an Excel workbook. For this, we will be using the Excel basic package and the sample file that is part of the GitHub repository that was downloaded previously.

Technical requirements

In order to install the Automation Anywhere Bot agent, the following requirements are necessary:

- Windows operating system version 7 or higher
- A processor with a minimum speed of 3 GHz

- A minimum of 4 GB RAM

- At least 100 MB hard disk space

- Web browser: Internet Explorer v10 or higher or Chrome v49 or higher

- A minimum screen resolution of 1024*768

- An internet connection with a minimum speed of 10 Mbps

- You must have completed registration for Automation Anywhere A2019 Community Edition

- You must have logged on successfully to Automation Anywhere A2019 Community Edition

- A successfully registered local device

- Successfully downloaded sample data from GitHub

Opening, closing, and saving Excel workbooks

Whenever we use an external data source, no matter what type this may be, a connection needs to be established. Once we have consumed the data, the connection needs to be closed. Not only does this apply to Automation Anywhere but to most development platforms. How we make this connection is where it differs. Automation Anywhere refers to this connection as a **session**. We will create various types of sessions as we progress through this book. We have already created sessions when connecting with CSV files.

The first thing we need to learn about Excel is how to open, close, and save workbooks. So, we'll start off with a simple walk-through. You will open an Excel workbook, save it, and close it. For this walk-through, we will use the sample workbook `Chapter11_Catalog.xlsx` from the GitHub repository.

Let's start this walk-through by executing the following steps:

1. Log into **Control Room**.

2. Create a new bot and call it `Chapter 11 - Excel Basic` in the folder `\Bot\`.

3. As always, we begin by adding some comments to use as a template for our bot. Add a new **Comment** action as `"--------------------"` on line **1** and click on **Save**.

4. Add a new **Comment** action as `"------- Open Excel Worksheet"` on line **2** and click on **Save**.

5. Add a new **Comment** action as "`------- Save Excel Worksheet`" on line **3** and click on **Save**.

6. Add a new **Comment** action as "`------- Close Excel Worksheet`" on line **4** and click on **Save**.

7. Add a new **Comment** action as "`--------------------`" on line **5** and click on **Save**. Our initial development interface should look like this:

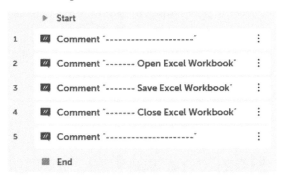

Figure 11.2 – Development interface

8. To open the workbook, drag the **Excel basic: Open** action just below line **2**.

9. Set the following properties for the **Excel basic: Open** action on line **3**:

Session name: xl_data

File path: **Desktop file** - C:\Hands-On-RPA-with-AA-Sample-Data\Chapter11_Catalog.xlsx

Specific sheet name: *Checked* - Catalog

Open in: **Read-write mode**

Sheet contains a header: *Checked*

The properties should look like this:

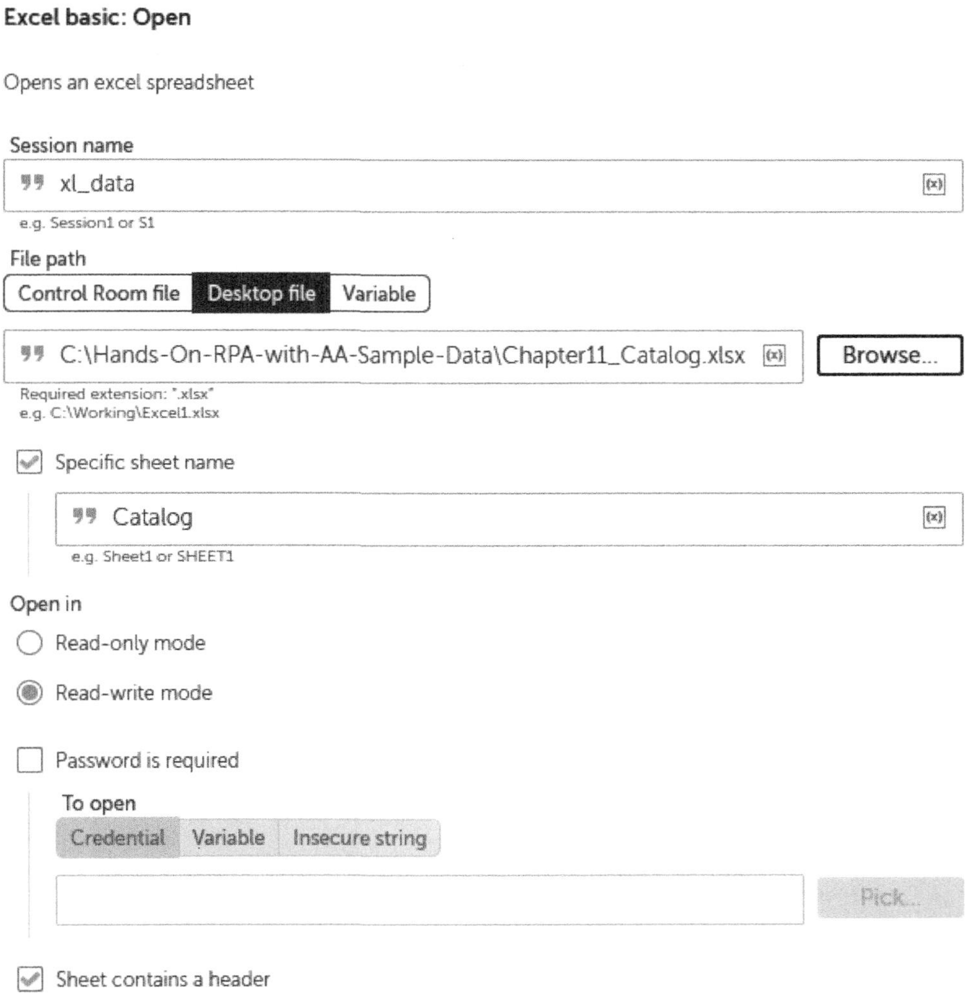

Excel basic: Open

Opens an excel spreadsheet

Session name

> " xl_data   (x)

e.g. Session1 or S1

File path

| Control Room file | **Desktop file** | Variable |

> " C:\Hands-On-RPA-with-AA-Sample-Data\Chapter11_Catalog.xlsx (x)   Browse...

Required extension: ".xlsx"
e.g. C:\Working\Excel1.xlsx

[✓] Specific sheet name

> " Catalog   (x)

e.g. Sheet1 or SHEET1

Open in

◯ Read-only mode

◉ Read-write mode

☐ Password is required

To open

| Credential | Variable | Insecure string |

[   ]   Pick...

[✓] Sheet contains a header

Figure 11.3 – Excel basic: Open properties

10. Click on **Save**.

11. To save the workbook, drag the **Excel basic: Save workbook** action just below line **4**.

12. Set the following properties for the **Excel basic: Save workbook** action on line **5**:

Session name: xl_data

The properties should look like this:

Excel basic: Save workbook

Saves an excel spreadsheet

Session name

e.g. Session1 or S1

Figure 11.4 – Excel basic: Save workbook properties

13. Click on **Save**.

14. To close the workbook, drag the **Excel basic: Close** action just below line **6**.

15. Set the following properties for the **Excel basic: Close** action on line **7**:

Session name: xl_data

Save changes when closing file: *Unchecked*

The properties should look like this:

Excel basic: Close

Closes an excel spreadsheet

Session name

```
99  xl_data                               (x)
```

e.g. Session1 or S1

☐ Save changes when closing file

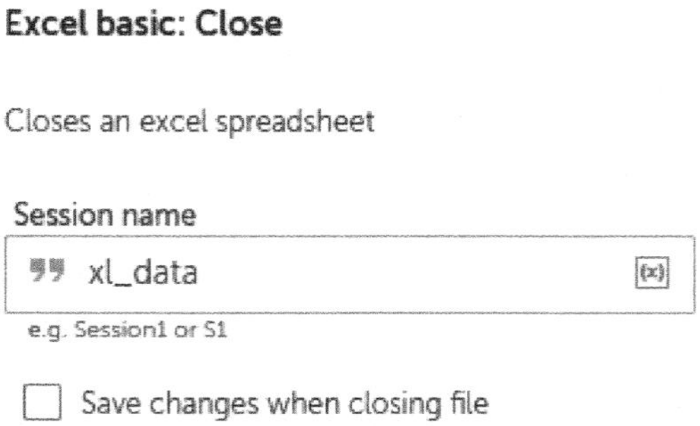

Figure 11.5 – Excel basic: Close properties

16. Click on **Save**.

You could choose to save the workbook when closing it by checking the **Save changes when closing file** box. In some cases, you may need to save your workbook intermittently without closing. In these instances, the **Excel basic: Save workbook** action should be used.

We have looked at the basics—opening, saving, and closing an Excel workbook. Your development window should look like this:

Figure 11.6 – Development interface

Now that we can open a workbook, the next stage is to learn how to read data from an Excel worksheet.

Reading and writing data within Excel worksheets

Working with data using Excel is a key part of most business roles. Having the ability to automate tasks using Excel can free substantial time from our daily routine. The following walk-throughs will look at reading datasets from Excel followed by writing data to Excel. Like the previous chapter, we will be adding new steps at each stage to make our bot more structured.

Reading from Excel worksheets

Data in Excel is usually presented as a table, which means it consists of a fixed set of columns with each row as a record or transaction. The sample data file has a worksheet named `Catalog`. The dataset looks like this:

◢	A	B	C	D	E	F
1	ID	Author	Title	Genre	Price	Publish Date
2	bk101	Gambardella, Matthew	XML Developer's Guide	Computer - Software	44.95	01/10/2000
3	bk102	Ralls, Kim	Midnight Rain	Fantasy	5.95	16/12/2000
4	bk103	Corets, Eva	Maeve Ascendant	Fantasy	5.95	17/11/2000
5	bk104	Corets, Eva	Oberon's Legacy	Fantasy	5.95	10/03/2001
6	bk105	Corets, Eva	The Sundered Grail	Fantasy	5.95	10/09/2001

Catalog   Sheet2   ⊕

Figure 11.7 – Excel Catalog worksheet dataset

In this walk-through, we want our bot to read each record and show the `Title` and `Price` in a message box. To read the record, we need a `Record` type variable, which will be named `recBook`. Once a record is assigned to a `Record` type variable, it is accessed using an index. The index is zero-based so the first column is identified as index `0`. In this case, the `Title` is the third column, giving it an index of `2`, and the `Price` is the fifth column, making it have an index value of `4`. We will continue to build on our bot that we have already created.

Let's start this walk-through by executing the following steps:

1. Create a `Record` type variable called `recBook`.

2. Add a **Step** action just below line **3**.

3. Set the **Title** property of the **Step** on line **4** as Read Worksheet Records.

4. Click on **Save**.

   Your development interface should look like this:

Figure 11.8 – Development interface

5. The `Catalog` worksheet has already been specified when we opened the workbook. To loop through each row from the dataset, add a **Loop** action just below line number **4** ensuring it remains within the **Step** on line **4**.

6. Set the following properties for the **Loop** action on line **5**:

    Loop Type*: For each row in worksheet

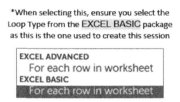

    Figure 11.9 – Selecting Loop Type

    Session name: `xl_data`

    Loop through: All rows

    Assign the current value to this variable: recBook - Record

    The properties should look like this:

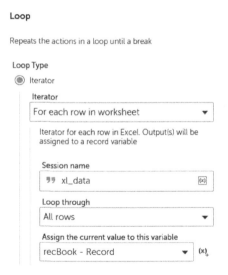

    Figure 11.10 – Loop properties

7. Click on **Save**.

8. That's all there is to it. All that's left is to create a message box to display the book `Title` and `Price`. Add a **Message box** action just below line **5**, ensuring it remains within the **Loop** on line **5**.

9. Set the following properties for the **Message box** action on line **6**:

Enter the message box window title: `Reading Excel Worksheet`

Enter the message to display: `$recBook[2]$ - Price: $recBook[4]$`

Close message box after: *Checked*

Seconds: 4

The properties should look like this:

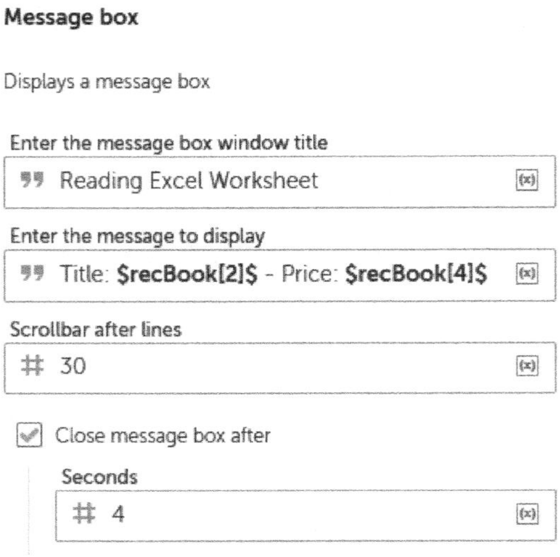

Message box

Displays a message box

Enter the message box window title

    🔊 Reading Excel Worksheet   (x)

Enter the message to display

    🔊 Title: **$recBook[2]$** - Price: **$recBook[4]$**   (x)

Scrollbar after lines

    # 30   (x)

☑ Close message box after

    Seconds

        # 4   (x)

Figure 11.11 – Message box properties

10. Click on **Save**, the development interface for this section should look like this:

4	▾ ☐ Step "Read Worksheet Records"	⋮
5	▾ ↻ Loop : For each row in worksheet and assign to **$recBook$**	⋮
6	▣ Message box "Title: **$recBook[2]$** - Price: **$recBook[4]$**"	⋮

Figure 11.12 – Development interface

You are now ready to test your bot. Go ahead and run it. It should read each record from the `Catalog` worksheet, displaying the `Title` and `Price`. Now that we can read from an Excel worksheet, naturally, we also need to know how to write data back to a spreadsheet. In the next section, we will learn how to insert values into our Excel worksheet. As inserting values into Excel can be a common task we do manually, knowing how to automate this can be a valuable skill to have.

Writing to Excel worksheets

In this walk-through, you will learn how to write to Excel. We will continue building on our current bot. We know our dataset consists of a list of books. The task of our bot is to write the total number of books at the bottom of the list. To achieve this, we will need two Number type variables: one to store the number of records, and another to store the row to write the results to. As there is a header row in our dataset, the first available blank row will be number of records + 2. For each Number type variable, a String will also be needed as output can only be a string variable. As we are looping through the dataset, we will add an **Increment** action to get the number of records.

Let's start this walk-through by executing the following steps:

1. Create two Number type variables called numRecCount and numResultRow.

2. Create two String type variables called strRecCount and strResultRow.

3. To use an increment to get the number of records, add the **Number: Increment** action just below line **5**, ensuring it remains within the **Loop** on line **5**.

4. Set the following properties for the **Number: Increment** action on line **6**:

   Enter number: $numRecCount$

   Enter increment value: 1

   Assign the output to variable: numRecCount - Number

   The properties should look like this:

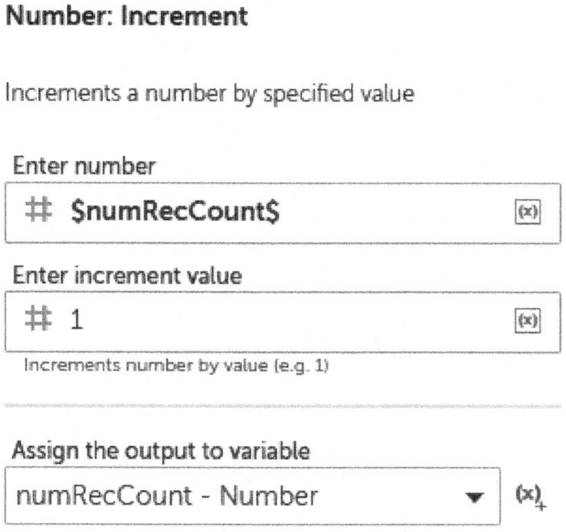

Figure 11.13 – Number: Increment properties

5. Click on **Save**. The development interface for the **Loop** should look like this:

Figure 11.14 – Development interface

6. Add a **Step** action just below line **7**, ensuring it is not indented within the **Loop** on line **5**.

7. Set the **Title** property of this **Step** on line **8** as Write to Excel.

   Click on **Save** and collapse the **Step** on line **4**.

   Your development interface should look like this:

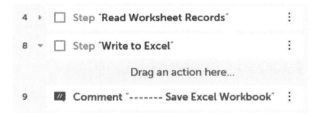

Figure 11.15 – Development interface

8. To get the output row, we know it's number of records + 2; add the **Number: Assign** action just below line **8**, ensuring it remains within the **Step** on line **8**.

9. Set the following properties for the **Number: Assign** action on line **9**:

   Select the source string variable/ value: $numRecCount$ + 2

   Select the destination number variable: **numResultRow - Number**

   The properties should look like this:

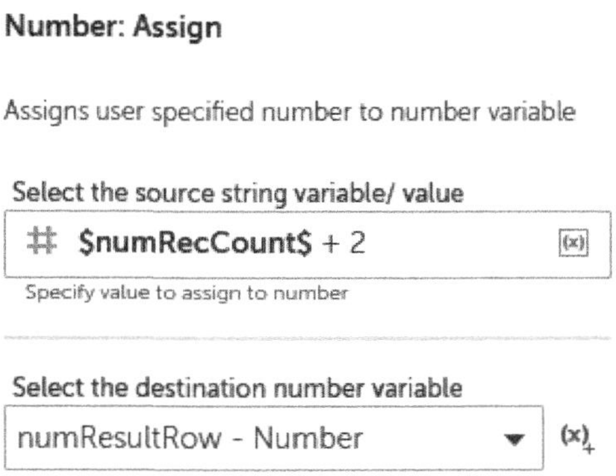

Number: Assign

Assigns user specified number to number variable

Select the source string variable/ value

$numRecCount$ + 2

Specify value to assign to number

Select the destination number variable

numResultRow - Number

Figure 11.16 – Number: Assign properties

10. Click on **Save**.

11. Now we have the output row and the records count, they both need to be converted to a String variable type. Add the **Number: To string** action just below line **9**, ensuring it remains within the **Step** on line **8**.

12. Set the following properties for the **Number: To string** action on line **10**:

Enter a number: $numRecCount$

Enter number of digits after decimal: 0

Assign the output to variable: strRecCount - String

The properties should look like this:

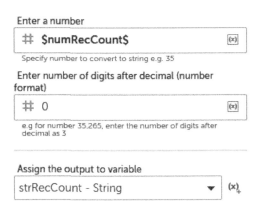

Number: To string

Converts a user specified number to a string

Enter a number

$numRecCount$

Specify number to convert to string e.g. 35

Enter number of digits after decimal (number format)

0

e.g for number 35.265, enter the number of digits after decimal as 3

Assign the output to variable

strRecCount - String

Figure 11.17 – Number: To string properties

13. Click on **Save**.

14. Do the same for the output row by adding another **Number: To string** action just below line **10**, ensuring it remains within the **Step** on line **8**.

15. Set the following properties for the **Number: To string** action on line **11**:

    Enter a number: $numResultRow$

    Enter number of digits after decimal: 0

    Assign the output to variable: strResultRow - String

    The properties should look like this:

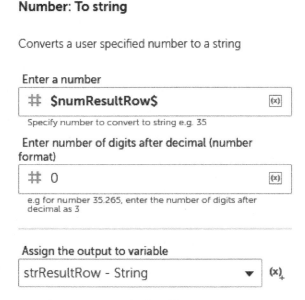

Number: To string

Converts a user specified number to a string

Enter a number

| ♯ **$numResultRow$** | (x) |

Specify number to convert to string e.g. 35

Enter number of digits after decimal (number format)

| ♯ 0 | (x) |

e.g for number 35.265, enter the number of digits after decimal as 3

Assign the output to variable

| strResultRow - String ▼ | (x) |

Figure 11.18 – Number: To string properties

16. Click on **Save**.

17. To write this back to our worksheet, let's put the text Total: in column A at the end of our list. Add the **Excel basic: Set cell** action just below line **11**, ensuring it remains within the **Step** on line **8**.

18. Set the following properties for the **Excel basic: Set cell** action on line **12**:

Session name: `xl_data`

Use: Specific cell – `A$strResultRow$`

Value to set: `Total:`

The properties should look like this:

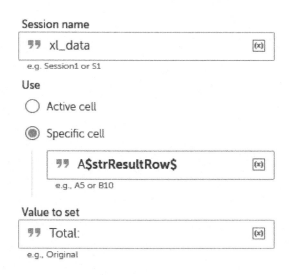

Excel basic: Set cell

Sets a value in a given cell of an excel spreadsheet

Session name

🔊 xl_data   (x)

e.g. Session1 or S1

Use

○ Active cell

◉ Specific cell

🔊 A$strResultRow$ (x)

e.g., A5 or B10

Value to set

🔊 Total: (x)

e.g., Original

Figure 11.19 – Excel basic: Set cell properties

19. Click on **Save**.

20. Finally, to write the record count to our worksheet in column B, add the **Excel basic: Set cell** action just below line **12**, ensuring it remains within the **Step** on line **8**.

21. Set the following properties for the **Excel basic: Set cell** action on line **13**:

Session name: `xl_data`

Use: Specific cell – `B$strResultRow$`

Value to set: `$strRecCount$`

The properties should look like this:

Excel basic: Set cell

Sets a value in a given cell of an excel spreadsheet

Session name

    ⁹⁹ xl_data   (x)

e.g. Session1 or S1

Use

○ Active cell

◉ Specific cell

        ⁹⁹ B$strResultRow$ (x)

        e.g., A5 or B10

Value to set

    ⁹⁹ $strRecCount$ (x)

e.g., Original

Figure 11.20 – Excel basic: Set cell properties

22. Click on **Save**. The development interface should look like this:

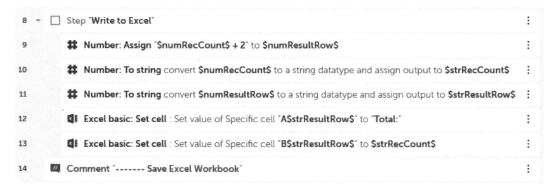

8 ▾	☐ Step "Write to Excel"	⋮
9	**#** **Number: Assign** "$numRecCount$ + 2" to $numResultRow$	⋮
10	**#** **Number: To string** convert $numRecCount$ to a string datatype and assign output to **$strRecCount$**	⋮
11	**#** **Number: To string** convert $numResultRow$ to a string datatype and assign output to **$strResultRow$**	⋮
12	▣ **Excel basic: Set cell** : Set value of Specific cell "A$strResultRow$" to "Total:"	⋮
13	▣ **Excel basic: Set cell** : Set value of Specific cell "B$strResultRow$" to $strRecCount$	⋮
14	▨ Comment "------- Save Excel Workbook"	⋮

Figure 11.21 – Development interface

All done, which is great. You can go ahead and run your bot. Your bot should display the book title and price for every record. Once the bot has completed, open the sample workbook. It should now also contain a total count, as shown in the following screenshot:

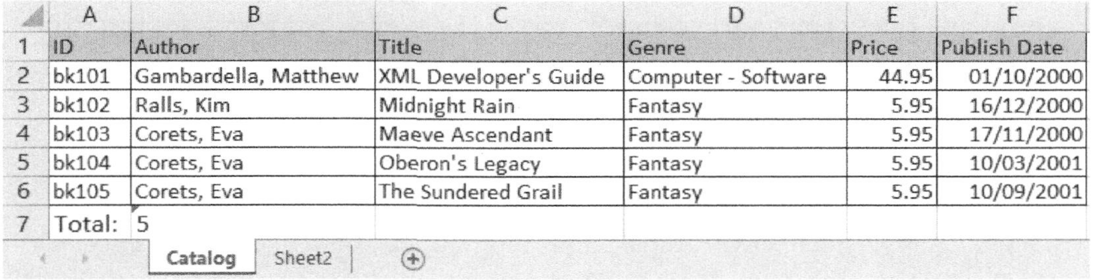

	A	B	C	D	E	F
1	ID	Author	Title	Genre	Price	Publish Date
2	bk101	Gambardella, Matthew	XML Developer's Guide	Computer - Software	44.95	01/10/2000
3	bk102	Ralls, Kim	Midnight Rain	Fantasy	5.95	16/12/2000
4	bk103	Corets, Eva	Maeve Ascendant	Fantasy	5.95	17/11/2000
5	bk104	Corets, Eva	Oberon's Legacy	Fantasy	5.95	10/03/2001
6	bk105	Corets, Eva	The Sundered Grail	Fantasy	5.95	10/09/2001
7	Total:	5				

Catalog   Sheet2   ⊕

Figure 11.22 – Updated Excel worksheet

You should now be comfortable with reading and writing to Excel. This is just the start of how you can automate Excel using Automation Anywhere. As mentioned earlier, there are two Excel packages available with Automation Anywhere. We have so far been looking at the Excel basic package. In the next section, we'll move onto the Excel advanced package and discover what other Excel tasks can be automated. We'll start by looking at manipulating data within worksheets, such as by inserting columns and formulas as well as sorting data.

Working with data in Excel

In the previous section, we looked at the basics of Excel automation, such as opening, reading, writing, saving, and closing Excel workbooks. In this section, we will explore the Automation Anywhere Excel advanced package. The walk-through will involve building a bot that performs a specific role. The bot will replace a manual task that involves updating an Excel spreadsheet. The file used is available as part of the GitHub repository Chapter11_SampleData.xlsm:

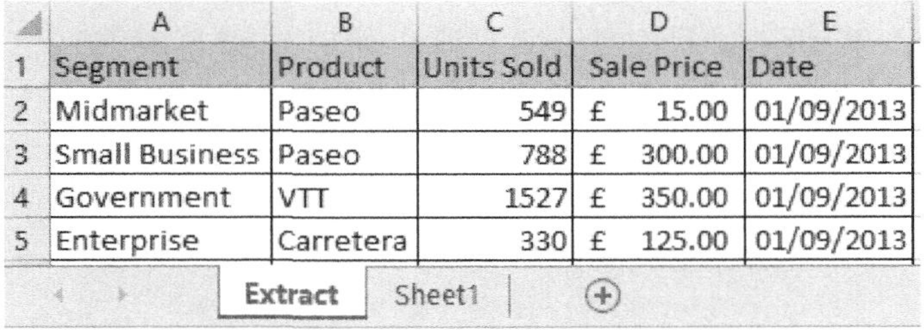

	A	B	C	D	E
1	Segment	Product	Units Sold	Sale Price	Date
2	Midmarket	Paseo	549	£ 15.00	01/09/2013
3	Small Business	Paseo	788	£ 300.00	01/09/2013
4	Government	VTT	1527	£ 350.00	01/09/2013
5	Enterprise	Carretera	330	£ 125.00	01/09/2013

Extract   Sheet1   ⊕

Figure 11.23 – Snapshot of the Chapter11_SampleData.xlsm file

This file contains a data table of sales achieved by a fictitious organization. In order to automate the file, we perform the following steps:

1. Open the Excel file `Chapter11_SampleData.xlsm`.

2. Insert a new column after column 4 and call it `Amount` on the worksheet `Extract`.

3. Add a formula in the new column to calculate the sales amount (`Units Sold * Sale Price`).

4. Sort the data table by the `Segment` column in ascending order.

5. In the last row, add an `Amount` column and sum the `total value` of orders.

6. Save and close the workbook.

Let's start this walk-through by executing the following steps:

1. Log into **Control Room**.

2. Create a new bot and call it `Chapter 11 - Excel Advanced` in the `\Bot\` folder.

3. Starting with the comments, add a new **Comment** action as "`- - - - - - - - - - - - - - - - - - - - -`" on line **1** and click on **Save**.

4. Add a new **Comment** action as "`- - - - - - - Open Excel Worksheet`" on line **2** and click on **Save**.

5. Add a new **Comment** action as "`- - - - - - - Inserting a Column`" on line **3** and click on **Save**.

6. Add a new **Comment** action as "`- - - - - - - Setting Cell Formula`" on line **4** and click on **Save**.

7. Add a new **Comment** action as "`- - - - - - - Sorting Data`" on line **5** and click on **Save**.

8. Add a new **Comment** action as "`- - - - - - - Finding Empty Cell`" on line **6** and click on **Save**.

9. Add a new **Comment** action as "`- - - - - - - Save & Close Excel`" on line **7** and click on **Save**.

10. Add a new **Comment** action as "`- - - - - - - - - - - - - - - - - - - - -`" on line **8** and click on **Save**. Our development interface should look like this:

Figure 11.24 – Development interface

11. To open the workbook, drag the **Excel advanced: Open** action just below line **2**.

12. Set the following properties for **Excel advanced: Open** action on line **3**:

Session name: xl_data

File path: **Desktop file** - C:\Hands-On-RPA-with-AA-Sample-Data\Chapter11_SampleData.xlsm

Specific sheet name: *Checked* - Extract

Open in: **Read-write mode**

Sheet contains a header: *Checked*

The properties should look like this:

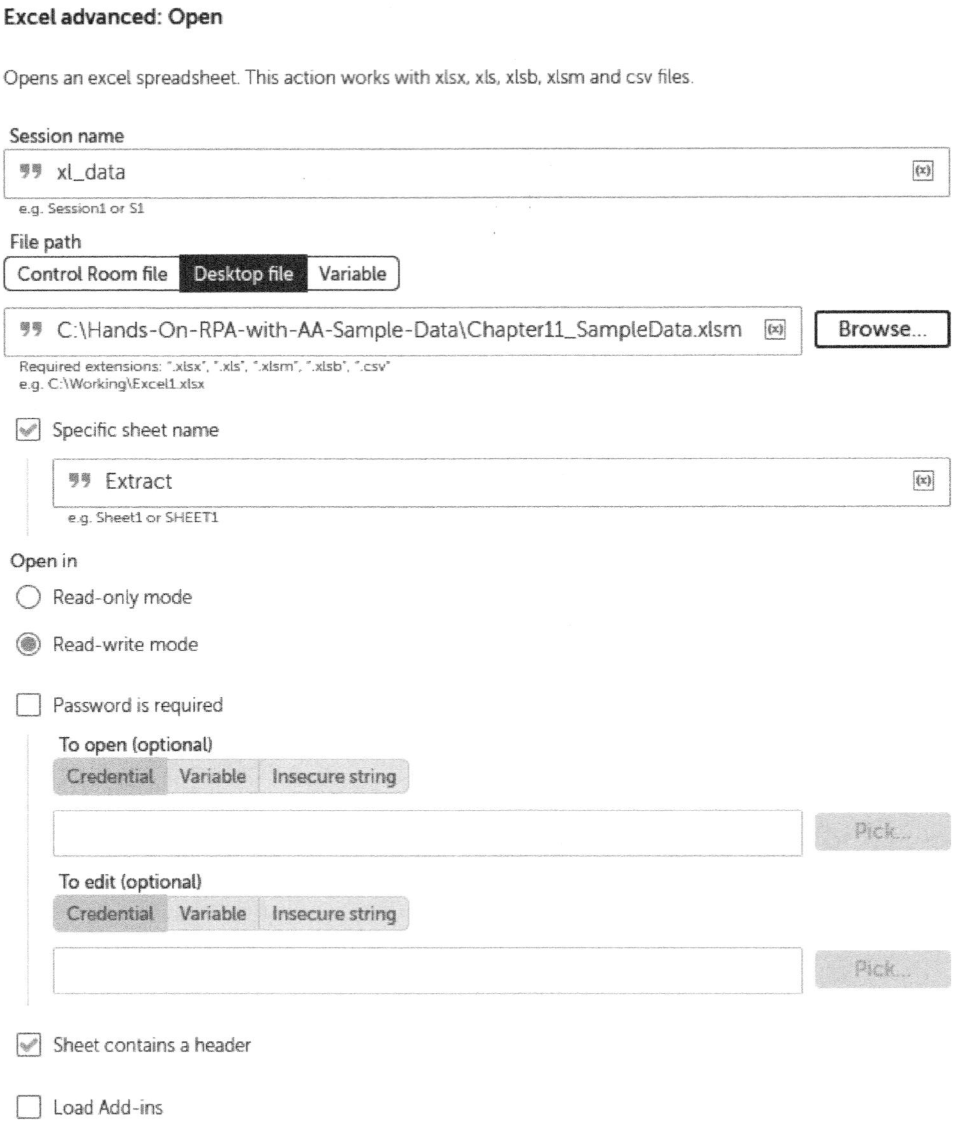

Excel advanced: Open

Opens an excel spreadsheet. This action works with xlsx, xls, xlsb, xlsm and csv files.

Session name

> 🔢 xl_data   (x)

e.g. Session1 or S1

File path

[Control Room file | **Desktop file** | Variable]

> 🔢 C:\Hands-On-RPA-with-AA-Sample-Data\Chapter11_SampleData.xlsm (x)   [Browse...]

Required extensions: ".xlsx", ".xls", ".xlsm", ".xlsb", ".csv"
e.g. C:\Working\Excel1.xlsx

☑ Specific sheet name

> 🔢 Extract   (x)

e.g. Sheet1 or SHEET1

Open in

◯ Read-only mode

◉ Read-write mode

☐ Password is required

To open (optional)

[Credential | Variable | Insecure string]

[   ]   [Pick...]

To edit (optional)

[Credential | Variable | Insecure string]

[   ]   [Pick...]

☑ Sheet contains a header

☐ Load Add-ins

Figure 11.25 – Excel advanced: Open properties

13. Click on **Save**.

The bot will now have the file open, ready to start processing. The first task is to insert a column.

Inserting a column

We need to add a new column and call it `Amount`. This will be column `E`, which is the sixth column in our data table. The data table in the sample worksheet is named `Data`:

1. To insert a new column as column 5 called `Amount`, drag the **Excel advanced: Insert table column** action just below line **4**.

2. Set the following properties for the **Excel advanced: Insert table column** action on line **5**:

   Session name: `xl_data`

   Table name: `Data`

   Column name: `Amount`

   Column position: 5

   The properties should look like this:

Excel advanced: Insert table column

Inserts a table column in a spreadsheet. This action works with xlsx, xls, xlsb and xlsm files.

Session name

    ⁇ xl_data   (x)

e.g. Session1 or S1

Table name

    ⁇ Data   (x)

e.g. Table1

Column name (optional)

    ⁇ Amount   (x)

Column position (at)

    # 5   (x)

Figure 11.26 – Excel advanced: Insert table column properties

3. Click on **Save**.

The instruction to add the new column is now complete. We'll move on to the next task – setting a formula in the new column.

Setting a cell formula

Now that there is a column called Amount (column E), it needs to be populated. The value of this column is to be set as Units Sold * Sale Price. We know the first row with data is 2, making the initial cell E2:

1. To set the formula in cell E2, add the **Excel advanced: Set cell formula** action just below line **6**.

2. Set the following properties for the **Excel advanced: Set cell formula** action on line **7**:

   Session name: xl_data

   Set cell formula for: **Specific cell** – E2

   Enter formula for specific cell: =[@[Units Sold]]*[@[Sale Price]]

   The properties should look like this:

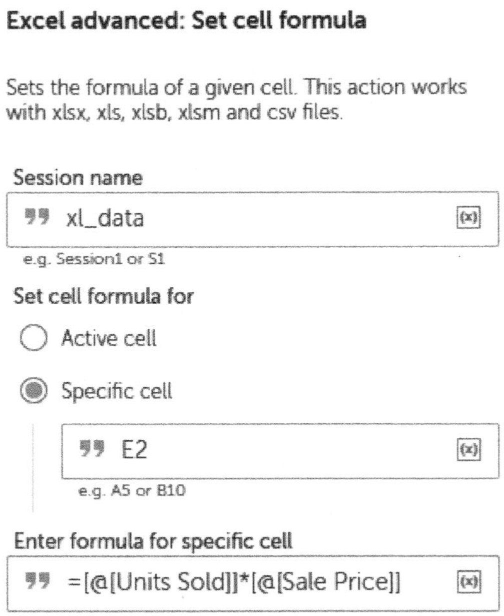

Excel advanced: Set cell formula

Sets the formula of a given cell. This action works with xlsx, xls, xlsb, xlsm and csv files.

Session name

| 〃 xl_data | (x) |

e.g. Session1 or S1

Set cell formula for

○ Active cell

◉ Specific cell

| 〃 E2 | (x) |

e.g. A5 or B10

Enter formula for specific cell

| 〃 =[@[Units Sold]]*[@[Sale Price]] | (x) |

Figure 11.27 – Excel advanced: Set cell formula properties

3. Click on **Save**.

This formula will populate itself for each record within the data table. As we are automating a specific manual task, the next step in our criteria is to sort the data table.

Sorting data

A part of the requirement is to sort the data table by the `Segment` column (column `A`). This should be sorted in ascending order:

1. To sort the data table, add the **Excel advanced: Sort table** action just below line **8**.

2. Set the following properties for the **Excel advanced: Sort table** action on line **9**:

    Session name: `xl_data`

    Table name: `Data`

    Sort for: **Column name** - `Segment`

    Sort order: **Text** - **A-to-Z**

    The properties should look like this:

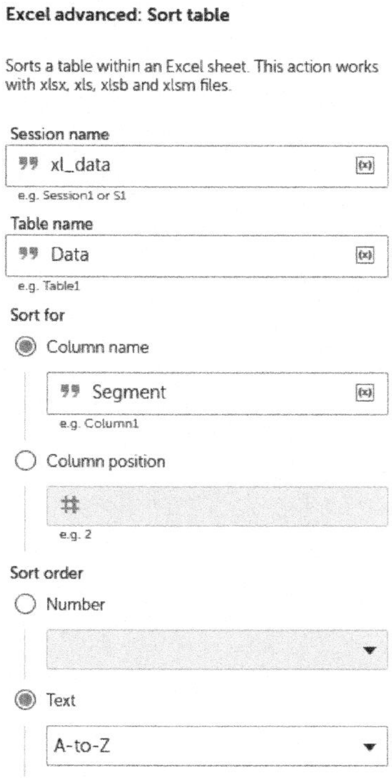

Excel advanced: Sort table

Sorts a table within an Excel sheet. This action works with xlsx, xls, xlsb and xlsm files.

Session name

  xl_data

e.g. Session1 or S1

Table name

  Data

e.g. Table1

Sort for

◉ Column name

    Segment

    e.g. Column1

○ Column position

    #

    e.g. 2

Sort order

○ Number

    ▼

◉ Text

    A-to-Z ▼

Figure 11.28 – Excel advanced: Sort table properties

3. Click on **Save**.

The data table should now be sorted as required. The next step is to add the total sum of sales at the end of the data table.

Finding empty cells

To add the sum of the Amount column, we need to identify which cell to enter this sum formula into. We can get this by identifying the first empty row, which would be the target row for our sum. We already know the column is E as we created this earlier. A String type variable will be needed to store the cell address:

1. Create a String type variable and call it strTotalCell.

2. To get the first empty cell in column E, add the **Excel advanced: Find next empty cell** action just below line **10**.

3. Set the following properties for the **Excel advanced: Find next empty cell** action on line **11**:

   Session name: xl_data

   Transverse by: **column**

   Start from: **specific cell**

   Cell address: E1

   Assign the output to variable: **strTotalCell - String**

   The properties should look like this:

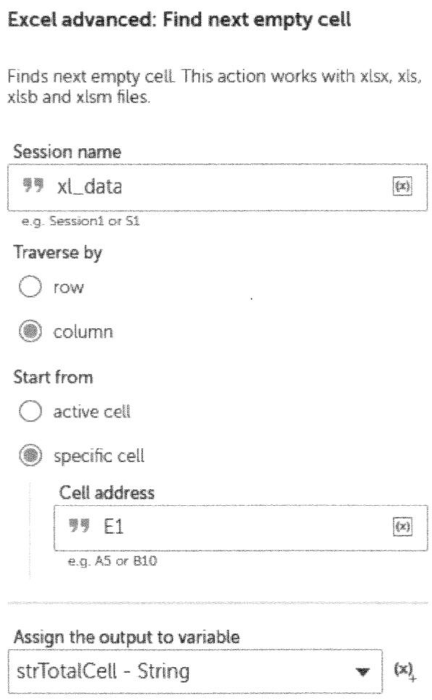

Figure 11.29 – Excel advanced: Find next empty cell properties

4. Click on **Save**.

5. Now we have the cell address for the total sales amount, we can add the sum formula by dragging the **Excel advanced: Set cell formula** action just below line **11**.

6. Set the following properties for the **Excel advanced: Set cell formula** action on line **12**:

   Session name: xl_data

   Set cell formula for: **Specific cell** – $strTotalCell$

   Enter formula for specific cell: =SUM(Data[Amount])

   The properties should look like this:

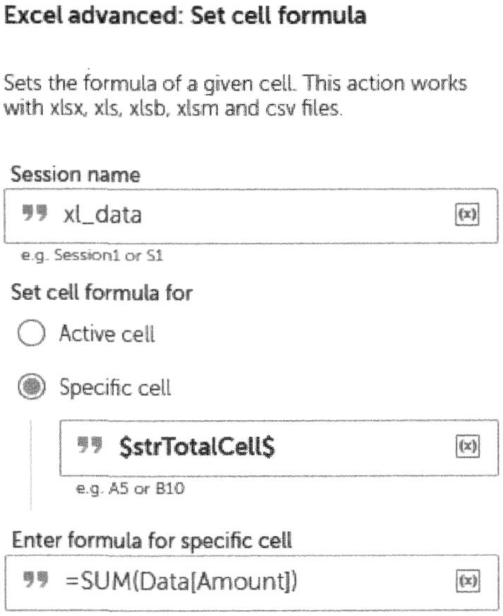

   Excel advanced: Set cell formula

   Sets the formula of a given cell. This action works with xlsx, xls, xlsb, xlsm and csv files.

   Session name

   | 🍮 xl_data | (x) |

   e.g. Session1 or S1

   Set cell formula for

   ◯ Active cell

   ⦿ Specific cell

   | 🍮 **$strTotalCell$** | (x) |

   e.g. A5 or B10

   Enter formula for specific cell

   | 🍮 =SUM(Data[Amount]) | (x) |

   Figure 11.30 – Excel advanced: Set cell formula properties

7. Click on **Save**.

Great – you have now instructed your bot to calculate the total sum of sales and to set this value in the last row of the data table. All that is left to do is to close our workbook.

Saving and closing the workbook

The last task for the bot to perform is to save and close our worksheet. As the workbook was opened using the **Excel Advanced** package, it needs to be closed with it too:

1. To save and close the workbook, drag the **Excel advanced: Close** action just below line **13**.

2. Set the following properties for the **Excel advanced: Close** action on line **14**:

    Session name: xl_data

    Save changes when closing file: *Checked*

    The properties should look like this:

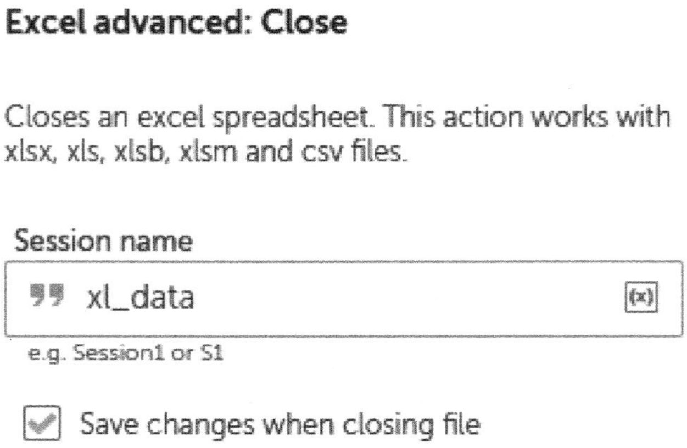

Excel advanced: Close

Closes an excel spreadsheet. This action works with xlsx, xls, xlsb, xlsm and csv files.

Session name

> ❞❞ xl_data   (x)

e.g. Session1 or S1

☑ Save changes when closing file

Figure 11.31 – Excel advanced: Close properties

3. Click on **Save**.

Our bot is now complete and should be good to go and perform our task to completion. We have looked at some of the more advanced actions available for Excel. This has included actions such as inserting columns and setting formulas. Your development window should look like this:

1   Comment "----------------------"

2   Comment "------- Open Excel Worksheet"

3   Excel advanced: Open "C:\Hands-On-RPA-with-AA-Sample-Data\Chapter11_SampleData.xlsm"

4   Comment "------- Inserting a Column"

5   Excel advanced: Insert table column "Amount" to table "Data" into current worksheet

6   Comment "------- Setting Cell Formula"

7   Excel advanced: Set cell formula "=[@[Units Sold]]*[@[Sal..." into Specific cell "E2"

8   Comment "------- Sorting Data"

9   Excel advanced: Sort table "Data" for column "Segment" with sort order A-to-Z

10 Comment "------- Finding Empty Cell"

11 Excel advanced: Find next empty cell in column from specific cell from "E1" and store value to $strTotalCell$

12 Excel advanced: Set cell formula "=SUM(Data[Amount])" into Specific cell $strTotalCell$

13 Comment "------- Save & Close Excel"

14 Excel advanced: Close

15 Comment "----------------------"

Figure 11.32 – Development interface

That's all done; time to run your bot. Your bot should perform all the tasks seamlessly and edit the sample file by inserting a new column and populating it with a formula. It should also add the sum at the bottom of the data table. Once you have executed the bot, open the sample file. It should look like this:

	A	B	C	D	E	F
1	Segment	Product	Units Sold	Sale Price	Amount	Date
82	Small Business	VTT	2151	£ 300.00	£ 645,300.00	01/09/2014
83	Small Business	VTT	986	£ 300.00	£ 295,800.00	01/09/2014
84	Small Business	Paseo	2905	£ 300.00	£ 871,500.00	01/11/2014
85					£ 15,445,109.00	

Figure 11.33 – Snapshot of the final data table

Hopefully, you will now be confident with performing numerous Excel tasks using Automation Anywhere. A key feature of Excel is having the ability to create and run macros. As macros are used widely in business, Automation Anywhere can also be used to trigger Excel macros. In the next section, you will learn how to run macros. This will be ideal if you are automating a manual process that involves running Excel macros.

Running macros

In this section, we will learn about running Excel macros. The sample file has a macro called procFilterSegment. This macro will filter the Segment column by the given argument. In the following walk-through, the bot will open the sample workbook in read-only mode and run this macro. We will send an Enterprise argument to the macro. This should result in the bot applying a filter of Enterprise to the Segment column.

Let's start this walk-through by executing the following steps:

1. Log into **Control Room**.

2. Create a new bot and call it Chapter11 - Excel Macro in the \Bot\ folder.

3. Starting with the comments, add a new **Comment** action as " - " on line **1** and click on **Save**.

4. Add a new **Comment** action as " - - - - - - - Open Excel Worksheet" on line **2** and click on **Save**.

5. Add a new **Comment** action as " - - - - - - - Run Macro" on line **3** and click on **Save**.

6. Add a new **Comment** action as " - " on line **4** and click on **Save**. Our development interface should look like this:

Figure 11.34 – Development interface

7. To open the workbook, drag the **Excel advanced: Open** action just below line number **2**.

8. Set the following properties for the **Excel advanced: Open** action on line **3**:

    Session name: xl_data

    File path: Desktop file - C:\Hands-On-RPA-with-AA-Sample-Data\ Chapter11_SampleData.xlsm

    Specific sheet name: *Checked* – Extract

Open in: Read-only mode

Sheet contains a header: *Checked*

The properties should look like this:

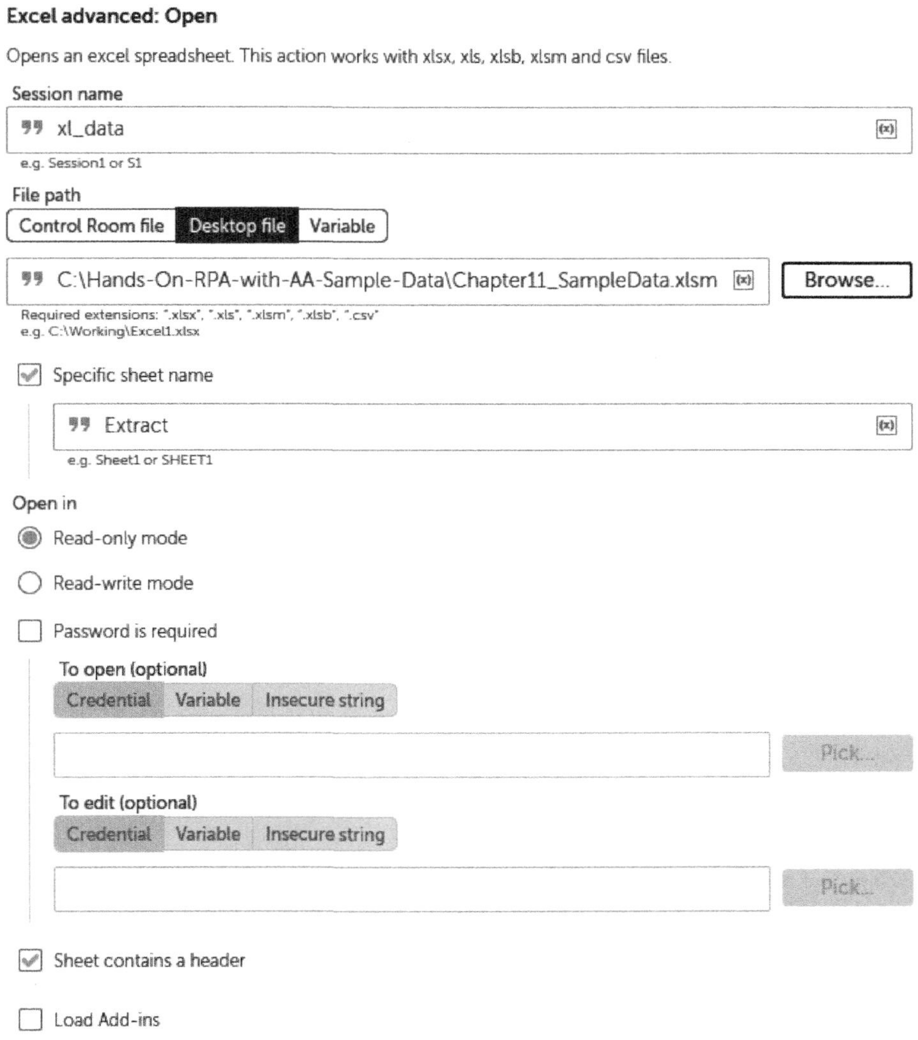

Excel advanced: Open

Opens an excel spreadsheet. This action works with xlsx, xls, xlsb, xlsm and csv files.

Session name

| 🔊 xl_data | {x} |

e.g. Session1 or S1

File path

| Control Room file | **Desktop file** | Variable |

| 🔊 C:\Hands-On-RPA-with-AA-Sample-Data\Chapter11_SampleData.xlsm {x} | Browse... |

Required extensions: ".xlsx", ".xls", ".xlsm", ".xlsb", ".csv"
e.g. C:\Working\Excel1.xlsx

☑ Specific sheet name

| 🔊 Extract | {x} |

e.g. Sheet1 or SHEET1

Open in

◉ Read-only mode

◯ Read-write mode

☐ Password is required

　To open (optional)

| Credential | Variable | Insecure string |

| | Pick... |

　To edit (optional)

| Credential | Variable | Insecure string |

| | Pick... |

☑ Sheet contains a header

☐ Load Add-ins

Figure 11.35 – Excel advanced: Open properties

9.　Click on **Save**.

10.　To run the macro `procFilterSegment` and pass an argument with it, drag the **Excel advanced: Run macro** action just below line **4**.

11. Set the following properties for the **Excel advanced: Run macro** action on line **5**:

    Session name: `xl_data`

    Macro name: `procFilterSegment`

    Macro arguments: `Enterprise`

    The properties should look like this:

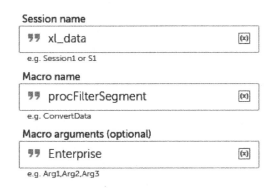

Figure 11.36 – Excel advanced: Run macro properties

12. Click on **Save**. The development interface should look like this:

Figure 11.37 – Development interface

It's testing time again; try running your bot. You will find it passes the argument through to the macro that applies the filter to the Segment column. Now you should be confident with using Automation Anywhere to automate your Excel-based manual tasks.

Summary

A wide selection of actions from both the Excel basic and advanced package has been covered in this chapter. The walk-throughs will have given you the opportunity to build three individual bots all performing different tasks. You should be confident with opening, closing, and saving Excel documents, as well as reading and writing to them. The skills gained should also include working with data within Excel documents, such as sorting, inserting columns, adding formulas, as well as running macros.

The next chapter continues with Microsoft applications. In this case, we will be looking at Microsoft Word. You will learn how to create and edit documents. You will build a role-based bot that will include working with Excel to generate Word documents.

12
Automation Using Word

In the previous chapter, we looked at Excel and what can be automated. You learned about the two packages available and how Automation Anywhere bots work with Excel. Our walk-through included looping through datasets, inserting columns, sorting data, and adding formulas. We will be applying what you have already learned about Excel in this chapter.

In this chapter, we will continue working with applications as we learn about how tasks with Word can be automated. This chapter will take a different approach: we will build a bot that performs a complete user role. This role involves automation with Excel and Word working together. The walk-through is designed to mimic a real-life business role scenario. We will be using the following packages:

✓ Comment	✓ List	✓ Step
✓ Datetime	✓ Loop	✓ String
✓ Excel advanced	✓ MS Word	✓ System
✓ File	✓ Number	

Figure 12.1 – Packages used in this chapter

This chapter will take you through a fictitious user role. The role is based in a finance company within the loans approval department. The walk-through will allow you to understand how to apply Excel and Word automation in a real-life scenario. We will build a bot that performs the current manual process end to end.

In this chapter, we will cover the following topics:

- Understanding the manual process
- Creating new Word documents
- Inserting text in Word documents
- Inserting paragraphs in Word documents
- Replacing text in Word documents

Technical requirements

In order to install the Automation Anywhere Bot agent, the following requirements are necessary:

- Windows OS version 7 or higher
- A processor with a minimum speed of 3 GHz
- A minimum of 4 GB RAM
- At least 100 MB hard disk space
- Internet Explorer v10 or higher or Chrome v49 or higher
- A minimum screen resolution of 1024*768
- An internet connection with a minimum speed of 10 Mbps
- Completed registration with Automation Anywhere A2019 Community Edition
- Successful login to Automation Anywhere A2019 Community Edition
- A successfully registered local device
- Successfully downloaded sample data from GitHub

Understanding the manual process

As this walk-through will take you through a business role, it is essential that we understand the manual process that needs to be automated. The current manual process for the user is as follows:

1. An administrator receives an Excel workbook on a daily basis. This document contains a list of clients whose loans have been approved.

2. The administrator is tasked with creating a confirmation letter using Word for each client on the Excel worksheet and saving the document with the client's reference number as the filename.

3. A Word document is provided as a template, but two additional paragraphs have to be inserted: one has the company telephone number and the other is the signatory.

4. The administrator also has to date the letter with the system date.

5. The administrator also inserts the loan details at specific placeholders in the Word document.

The files used for this walk-through are available in the GitHub repository. The Word template file is `Chapter12_Template.docx`, and the Excel source data file is `Chapter12_LoanData.xlsx`. The column names in the Excel worksheet are also the names of the placeholders in the Word template document. To automate this task, we'll map the process for our bot.

From this role specification, the process for our bot is shown in the following figure:

1. Understanding the manual process.

2. Reading source data.

    1. Opening Excel workbook.

    2. Reading and assigning column names to a list variable.

    3. Looping through each Excel record.

        1. Creating the output letter.

            1. Creating a new Word document from the template.

        2. Updating the output letter.

            1. Inserting the system date in the Word document.

            2. Adding additional paragraphs in the Word documents.

            3. Looping through each column from the list.

                1. Replacing placeholder in Word with the value from Excel.

3. Closing Excel data source.

Figure 12.2 – Process map for our bot

Now that we know what our bot needs to perform, we can start building it. We will start by adding the comments by breaking the process down into three sections: *reading the source data*, *creating the output letter*, and finally, *updating the output letter*. We will also use the **Step** action to further break the process down into subsections.

Let's start this walk-through by executing the following steps:

1. Log in to **Control Room**.

2. Create a new bot and call it Chapter 12 - Word Automation in the \Bot\ folder.

3. Add a new **Comment** action as "--------------------" on line **1** and click on **Save**.

4. Add a new **Comment** action as "------- Read source data" on line **2** and click on **Save**.

5. Add a new **Comment** action as "------- Create output letter" on line **3** and click on **Save**.

6. Add a new **Comment** action as "------- Update output letter" on line **4** and click on **Save**.

7. Add a new **Comment** action as "--------------------" on line 5 and click on **Save**. Your initial development interface should look like this:

Figure 12.3 – Development interface

8. To replicate the process map, add a step just below line **2** and set the **Title** property to Open Excel Workbook, and click on **Save**.

9. Add a step just below line **3**, ensuring it is aligned with the previous step, set the **Title** property to Get Column Names, and click on **Save**.

10. Add a step just below line **4**, ensuring it is aligned with the previous step, set the **Title** property to `Read each loan record`, and click on **Save**.

11. Drag the **Comment** actions on lines **6** and **7** so that they are indented within the step on line **5** and click on **Save**.

12. Add a step just below line **6**, ensuring it is aligned with the **Comment** action on line **6**, set the **Title** property to `Create new word document`, and click on **Save**.

13. Add a step just below line **8**, ensuring it is aligned with the **Comment** action on line **7**, set the **Title** property to `Insert Date`, and click on **Save**.

14. Add a step just below line **9**, ensuring it is aligned with the previous step, set the **Title** property to `Add Paragraphs`, and click on **Save**.

15. Add a step just below line **10**, ensuring it is aligned with the previous step, set the **Title** property to `Replace placeholders with values`, and click on **Save**.

16. Add a step just below line **11**, ensuring it is aligned with the step on line **5**, set the **Title** property to `Close Excel Workbook`, and click on **Save**. The development interface should look like this:

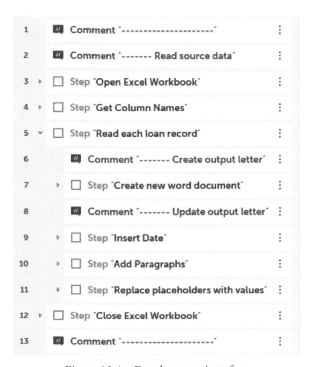

Figure 12.4 – Development interface

Looking good, we now have our bot design built. There are a number of steps that need to be built for this bot, so having a skeleton design ensures the bot aligns with the specification throughout the build process.

In the next section, we can start with the first task of the bot, which is to start reading the source data.

Reading the source data

The source data is stored in the `Chapter12_LoanData.xlsx` file, which has a worksheet called `Approved`. The data looks as shown in the following screenshot:

	A	B	C	D	E	F	G	H	I	J	K	L	M
1	[Ref]	[Title]	[Forename]	[Surname]	[Address]	[City]	[County]	[Postcode]	[Amount]	[Term]	[Interest]	[Payable]	[Monthly]
2	Q298	Mr	John	Pince	21 Hobart St	Parkham	Devon	EX39 5DJ	£5,000.00	24	3.40%	£5,176.08	£ 215.67
3	Q299	Mrs	Vannessa	Casper	45 Bradfield St	Newquay	Cornwall	TR7 1LS	£3,500.00	12	8.50%	£3,657.12	£ 304.76
4	Q300	Miss	Sarah	Mchughes	73 Parkfield Rd	Parwich	Derbyshire	DE6 1QN	£7,500.00	48	3.00%	£7,961.76	£ 165.87
5	Q301	Dr	David	Hawkin	30 Aughton St	Norton Canes	Staffordshire	WS11 9RH	£8,000.00	60	3.00%	£8,616.00	£ 143.60
6	Q302	Mr	Roger	Day	7 Richmond St	Hilton	Aberdeenshire	AB24 2RR	£4,000.00	36	8.50%	£4,524.48	£ 125.68

Approved

Figure 12.5 – Snapshot of source data

You will notice the column names are within square brackets. The reason for this is that they also act as the placeholder text within the Word template file. This ensures that only the specified placeholders are updated in the output Word letter. This is achieved using a **Replace** action; the column name text in the letter is replaced by the values derived from the Excel worksheet. In the next section, we will start by opening the source data worksheet.

Opening the workbook

As we have already covered Excel worksheets, this should be pretty easy. In this instance, we will be using the Excel advanced package, as we will need actions such as **Read row**, which is only available in this package.

Let's continue the walk-through to build our bot by executing the given steps:

1. To open the source data workbook, add the **Excel advanced: Open** action just below line **3**, ensuring it is within the step on line **3**.

2. Set the following properties for the **Excel advanced: Open** action on line **4**:

   Session name: `xl_data`

   File path: **Desktop file** – `C:\Hands-On-RPA-with-AA-Sample-Data\Chapter12_LoanData.xlsx`

Specific sheet name: *Checked* – Approved

Open in: **Read-only mode**

Sheet contains a header: *Checked*

The properties should look like this:

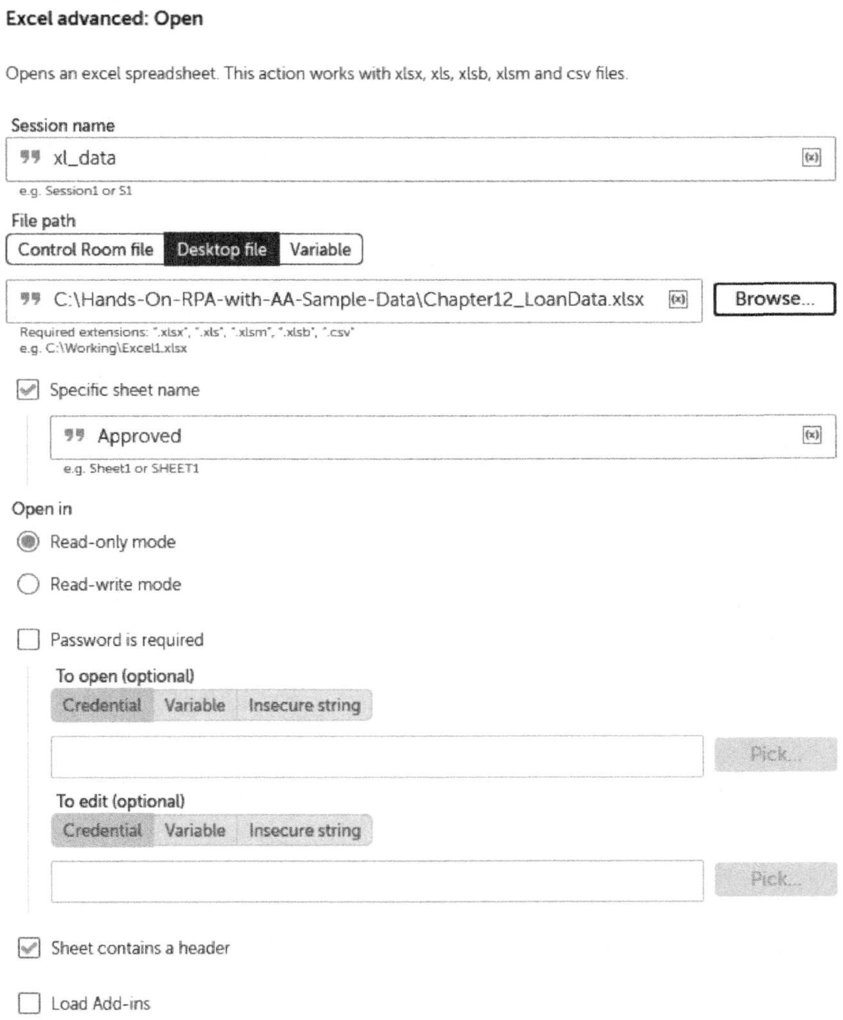

Excel advanced: Open

Opens an excel spreadsheet. This action works with xlsx, xls, xlsb, xlsm and csv files.

Session name

💬 xl_data   (x)

e.g. Session1 or S1

File path

| Control Room file | Desktop file | Variable |

💬 C:\Hands-On-RPA-with-AA-Sample-Data\Chapter12_LoanData.xlsx   (x) | Browse... |

Required extensions: ".xlsx", ".xls", ".xlsm", ".xlsb", ".csv"
e.g. C:\Working\Excel1.xlsx

☑ Specific sheet name

💬 Approved   (x)

e.g. Sheet1 or SHEET1

Open in

⦿ Read-only mode

◯ Read-write mode

☐ Password is required

To open (optional)

| Credential | Variable | Insecure string |

| | Pick... |

To edit (optional)

| Credential | Variable | Insecure string |

| | Pick... |

☑ Sheet contains a header

☐ Load Add-ins

Figure 12.6 – Excel advanced: Open properties

3. Click on **Save**.

You should be a dab hand at opening Excel documents as you've done it a few times now.

As the column headers are also the placeholder names, we will need to save them to a variable. This takes us to the next section, where we will read all the column names and assign them to a variable.

Getting column names

The column names are all in the first row of the `Approved` worksheet. The ideal data type to use to store a range is a `List` type variable. To get the column names, we will create a `List` type variable and assign the first row to it. Each value from the `List` type variable can then be accessed via the index number. The action to read a complete row is only available in the Excel advanced package, which is why this was used to open our worksheet:

1. Create a `List` type variable to store our column names and name it `lstColumns`.

2. To read the entire first row to our `List` type variable, add the **Excel advanced: Read row** action just below line **5**, ensuring it is within the step on line **5**.

3. Set the following properties for the **Excel advanced: Read row** action on line **6**:

   Session name: `xl_data`

   Cell option: **From specific cell**

   Cell address: `A1`

   Read full row: *Checked*

   Read option: **Read cell value**

   Assign the output to variable: lstColumns – List of Strings

   The properties should look like this:

Excel advanced: Read row

Reads values from a row. This action works with xlsx, xls, xlsb and xlsm files.

Figure 12.7 – Excel advanced: Read row properties

4.   Click on **Save**. The development interface for this section should look like this:

Figure 12.8 – Excel advanced: Read row properties

The bot is set to open the source worksheet. Once it is open, it needs to read the data. The data should be read one record at a time. For each record, the bot will process the loan approval by creating the Word letter, before moving on to the next record.

Reading the loan records

To read each row from our worksheet, a **Loop** action needs to be added. A `Record` type variable will also be required to store the row values. Just like with the `List` type variable, the values can be accessed via an index number:

1. Create a `Record` type variable to store our Excel loan record and name it `recLoan`.

2. To read each row, we use a loop by adding the **Loop** action just below line **7**, ensuring it is within the step on line **7**.

3. Set the following properties for the **Loop** action on line **8**:

   Iterator: **For each row in worksheet** (*Excel advanced*)

   Session name: `xl_data`

   Loop through: **All rows**

   Read option: **Read cell value**

   Assign the current value to this variable: **recLoan - Record**

The properties should look like this:

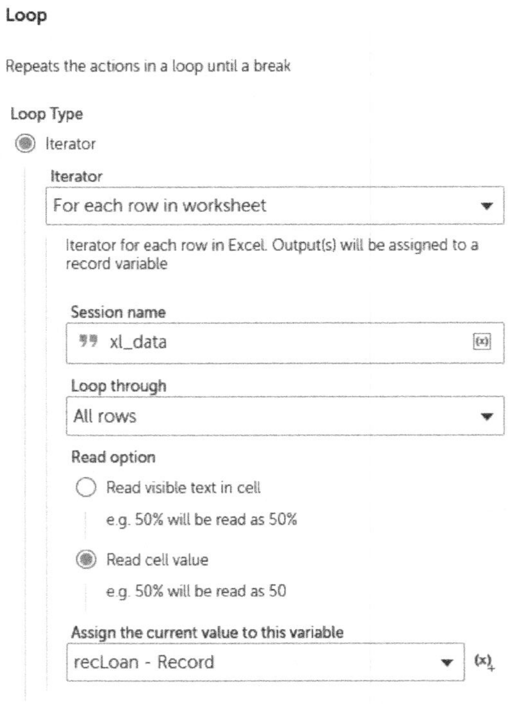

Loop

Repeats the actions in a loop until a break

Loop Type

◉ Iterator

Iterator

| For each row in worksheet ▼ |

Iterator for each row in Excel. Output(s) will be assigned to a record variable

Session name

| ⁷⁷ xl_data [x] |

Loop through

| All rows ▼ |

Read option

○ Read visible text in cell

  e.g. 50% will be read as 50%

◉ Read cell value

  e.g. 50% will be read as 50

Assign the current value to this variable

| recLoan - Record ▼ | (x)₊ |

Figure 12.9 – Loop properties

4. Click on **Save**.

5. Creating and updating the Word document needs to be performed for each row in Excel. To achieve this, drag lines **9** to **14** so that they are within the **Loop** action just created on line **8**.

6. Click on **Save**. The development interface for this section should look like this:

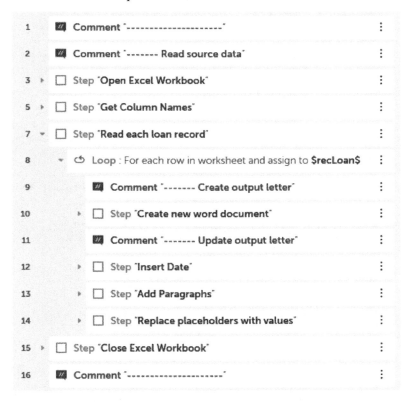

Figure 12.10 – Development interface

The interaction with Excel is now complete. The bot reads the column names and loops through each data row. The column names are assigned to a `List` variable and the data row to a `Record` type variable.

The next section is to start working with Word. The first task is to create our Word document from the given template. As we have this template, our approach is to just copy this file and name it `Reference number` from our Excel worksheet.

Creating an output letter

We have a Word document named `Chapter12_Template.docx` to use as a template. The document looks as shown in the following figure:

[Title] [Forename] [Surname]
[Address]
[City]
[County]
[Postcode]

Our Ref: [Ref]

Dear [Forename],

Congratulations! Based on the information provided by you, we are pleased to inform you that you have been pre-approved for your recent loan application.

Loan Details

Amount:	[Amount]
Term:	[Term] months
Interest Rate (APR):	[Interest]
Total Payable:	[Payable]
Monthly Payment:	[Monthly]

Figure 12.11 – Word template document

The placeholders are clearly identified as they are wrapped within square brackets. These match the related column names from the Excel worksheet. The bot needs to create a new Word document using the template file and save it as `Reference number`, which is the first column in the Excel data. As the data has a zero-based index, the first column will be identified with an index of `0`. As we will be making further updates to the new Word document, it makes sense to store the file path and name to a variable; a `String` type will be needed for this.

Let's continue with creating our Word document by following the given steps:

1. Create a `String` type variable to store the file path and name of the new Word letter. Name it `strLoanLetter`.

2. To assign the new filename as the reference for our record, add the **String: Assign** action just below line **10**, ensuring it is within the step on line **10**.

3. Set the following properties for the **String: Assign** action on line **11**:

    Select the source string variable(s)/value: C:\Hands-On-RPA-with-AA-Sample-Data\Chapter12_$recLoan[0]$.docx

    Select the destination string variable: strLoanLetter - String

    The properties should look like this:

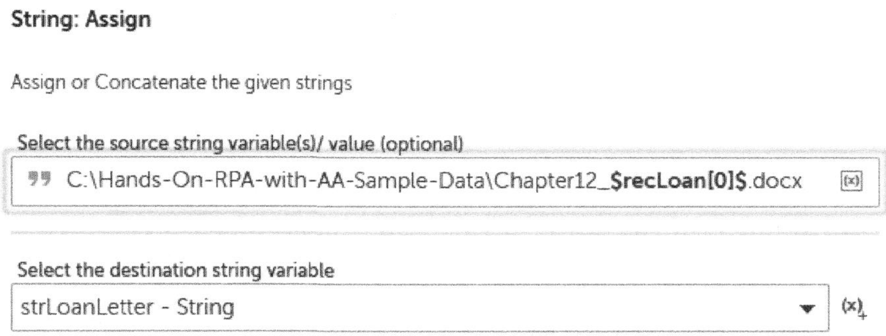

    String: Assign

    Assign or Concatenate the given strings

    Select the source string variable(s)/ value (optional)

    ❞ C:\Hands-On-RPA-with-AA-Sample-Data\Chapter12_**$recLoan[0]$**.docx   [⋈]

    Select the destination string variable

    strLoanLetter - String   ▼ (x)₊

Figure 12.12 – String: Assign properties

4. Click on **Save**.

5. The best way to create the new file is to make a copy of the template file. We do this by adding the **File: Copy** action just below line **11**, ensuring it is within the step on line **10**.

6. Set the following properties for the **File: Copy** action on line **12**:

    Source file: C:\Hands-On-RPA-with-AA-Sample-Data\Chapter12_Template.docx

    Destination file/folder: $strLoanLetter$

    Overwrite existing files: *Checked*

The properties should look like this:

File: Copy

Copies a file

Source file

    " C:\Hands-On-RPA-with-AA-Sample-Data\Chapter12_Template.docx   (x) | Browse... |

    e.g. C:\MyDoc*.doc

Destination file/folder

    " $strLoanLetter$ (x)

    e.g. C:\Backup\ , C:\Backup*.doc

    ☑ Overwrite existing files

Figure 12.13 – File: Copy properties

7. Click on **Save**.

    A new Word document should now be created and named as the reference number
    for each specific record. The development interface for this section should look
    like this:

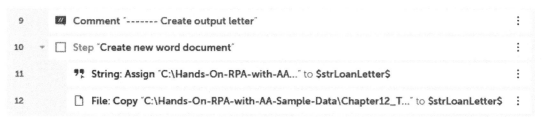

9	🖉 Comment "------- Create output letter"	⋮
10	▾ ☐ Step "Create new word document"	⋮
11	" String: Assign "C:\Hands-On-RPA-with-AA..." to $strLoanLetter$	⋮
12	🗋 File: Copy "C:\Hands-On-RPA-with-AA-Sample-Data\Chapter12_T..." to $strLoanLetter$	⋮

Figure 12.14 – Development interface

Great progress! We are now ready to move on to the next section. We have a new Word
letter; it now needs to be edited and updated. The first update is to add the system date to
the letter.

Updating the output letter

Updating the letter includes adding the date. There is a bookmark called bmDate for the
date's location in the Word letter. After inserting the date, the bot is tasked with adding a
couple of paragraphs. One has the contact telephone and office opening times. The other
is the signatory footer for the letter. In the next section, we start by inserting the date.

Inserting text

The system date can be retrieved from the system variable called `Date`. This variable is in `Datetime` format, so it will need to be converted into a `String` type in order for us to insert it. For this, a `String` type variable will be needed. Let's continue building our bot further and insert the date by following the given steps:

1. Create a `String` type variable to store the system date. Name this variable `strDate`.

2. To assign the system date to our variable, add the **Datetime: To string** action just below line **14**, ensuring it is within the step on line **14**.

3. Set the following properties for the **Datetime: To string** action on line **15**:

   Source date and time variable: **System:Date - Datetime**

   Select date time format: **Custom format – d MMM YYYY**

   Assign the output to a variable: **strDate - String**

   The properties should look like this:

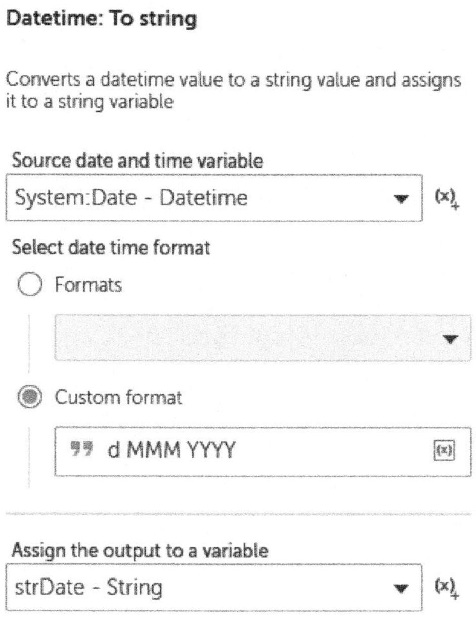

Figure 12.15 – Datetime: To string properties

4. Click on **Save**.

5. We now have our system date assigned to a variable. To insert this into the bmDate bookmark in the Word letter, add the **MS Word: Insert Text** action just below line **15**, ensuring it is within the step on line **14**.

6. Set the following properties for the **MS Word: Insert Text** action on line **16**:

Select the Word document: Desktop file – $strLoanLetter$

Enter Bookmark Name: bmDate

Enter Text to be Inserted at Bookmark position: $strDate$

The properties should look like this:

Figure 12.16 – MS Word: Insert Text properties

7. Click on **Save**. The development interface for this section should look like this:

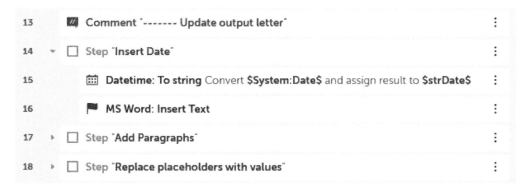

Figure 12.17 – Development interface

The bot will now insert the system date at the correct location. The walk-through will now continue with updating the Word letter. In the next section, we will look at adding the contact details and signatory paragraphs to our Word letter.

Adding paragraphs

We have just inserted the date in the previous section. To insert text, a predefined bookmark needs to be present within the target document. Now, we will move on to adding paragraphs. The paragraphs are appended to the target document, so no location information is needed. Only the content of the paragraph and the target file are needed. In our scenario, the office opening times and number and the signatory details need to be added as paragraphs. The paragraphs that need to be added to our loan approval letter are as follows:

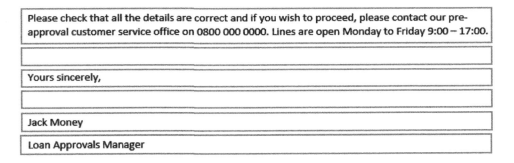

Figure 12.18 – Paragraphs to be added

There are six paragraphs that need to be inserted into the loan approval letter. Each red block contains the contents of each paragraph. A blank paragraph will result in a carriage return in our letter.

Let's continue with adding paragraphs to our bot by following these steps:

1. To add the first paragraph, add the **MS Word: Add Paragraph** action just below line **17**, ensuring it is within the step on line **17**.

2. Set the following properties for the **MS Word: Add Paragraph** action on line **18**:

   Select the Word document: Desktop file – $strLoanLetter$

   Please write paragraph or select variable: Please check that all the details are correct and if you wish to proceed, please contact our pre-approval customer service office on 0800 000 0000. Lines are open Monday to Friday 9:00 - 17:00.

The properties should look like this:

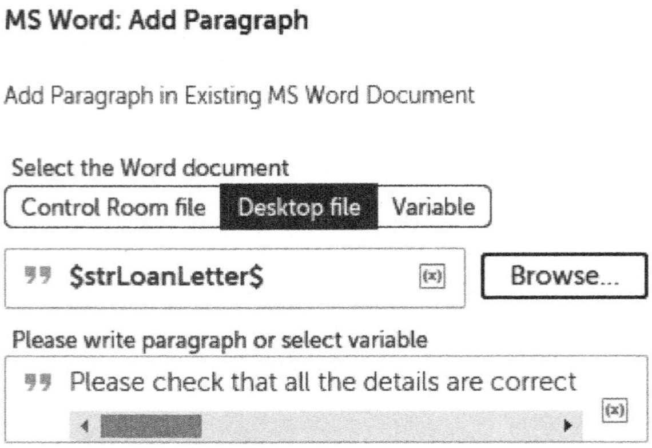

MS Word: Add Paragraph

Add Paragraph in Existing MS Word Document

Select the Word document

| Control Room file | Desktop file | Variable |

᠉᠉ $strLoanLetter$ (x)   Browse...

Please write paragraph or select variable

᠉᠉ Please check that all the details are correct   (x)

Figure 12.19 – MS Word: Add Paragraph properties

3. Click on **Save**.

4. Adding the second paragraph works pretty much the same as the first. Add the **MS Word: Add Paragraph** action just below line **18**, ensuring it is within the step on line **17**.

5. Set the following properties for the **MS Word: Add Paragraph** action on line **19**:

   Select the Word document: **Desktop file** – $strLoanLetter$

   Please write paragraph or select variable: (*add a few spaces only*)

6. Click on **Save**.

7. Add the third paragraph by adding another **MS Word: Add Paragraph** action just below line **19**, ensuring it is within the step on line **17**.

8. Set the following properties for the **MS Word: Add Paragraph** action on line **20**:

   Select the Word document: **Desktop file** – $strLoanLetter$

   Please write paragraph or select variable: Yours sincerely,

9. Click on **Save**.

10. Add the fourth paragraph by adding another **MS Word: Add Paragraph** action just below line **20**, ensuring it is within the step on line **17**.

11. Set the following properties for the **MS Word: Add Paragraph** action on line **21**:

    Select the Word document: **Desktop file** – $strLoanLetter$

    Please write paragraph or select variable: (*add a few spaces only*)

12. Click on **Save**.

13. Add the fifth paragraph by adding another **MS Word: Add Paragraph** action just below line **21**, ensuring it is within the step on line **17**.

14. Set the following properties for the **MS Word: Add Paragraph** action on line **22**:

    Select the Word document: Desktop file – $strLoanLetter$

    Please write paragraph or select variable: Jack Money

15. Click on **Save**.

16. Add the last paragraph by adding another **MS Word: Add Paragraph** action just below line **22**, ensuring it is within the step on line **17**.

17. Set the following properties for the **MS Word: Add Paragraph** action on line **23**:

    Select the Word document: Desktop file – $strLoanLetter$

    Please write paragraph or select variable: Loans Approval Manager

18. Click on **Save**. Your development interface for this section should look like this:

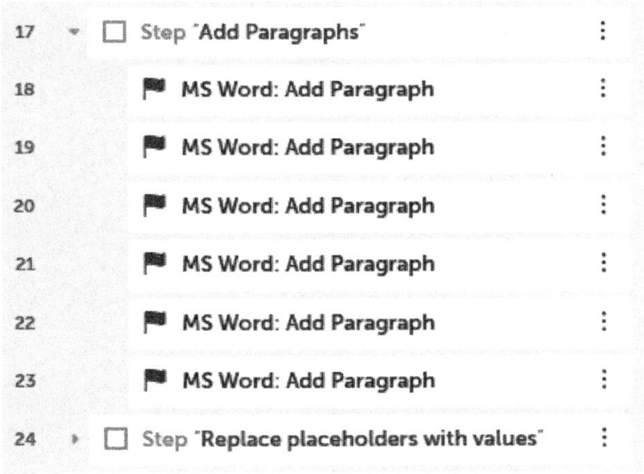

Figure 12.20 – Development interface

All the paragraphs are added – great work. There is one more Word action that we will look at; this is replacing text. The final and most crucial update we need to make to our loan's approval letter is to put the actual client and loan details in. In the next section, we will learn how to apply the **Replace Text** action using Automation Anywhere. This would have been a pretty time-consuming and tedious task to perform manually, so automating this will definitely help the administrator perform their role more effectively.

Replacing text

All the placeholders within the loan approvals letter need to be replaced with data from our source worksheet. The column names that are stored in our `lstColumns List` variable will be used as our placeholder text. The actual value to replace the placeholder is assigned to our `recLoan Record` type variable. A **Loop** action will be needed to iterate through the list of column names. In order to iterate through the loop, we will need a `Number` type variable to be deployed as the index. Two further `String` type variables will be needed for storing the current column name and current value.

Let's continue building our bot to replace the placeholder text with actual values from the data worksheet:

1. Create a `Number` type variable called `numColumnIndex` to be used as our index.

2. Create two `String` type variables for the value and placeholder text. Call them `strPlaceHolder` and `strValue`.

3. Before we add our loop, we will have to initialize our index to `-1` so that we can increment it as it loops through each column. Do this by adding the **Number: Assign** action just below line **24**, ensuring it is within the step on line **24**.

4. Set the following properties for the **Number: Assign** action on line **25**:

   Select the source string variable/ value: `-1`

   Select the destination number variable: numColumnIndex - Number

   The properties should look like this:

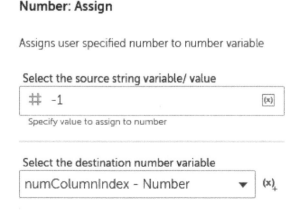

Number: Assign

Assigns user specified number to number variable

Select the source string variable/ value

    # -1   (x)

Specify value to assign to number

Select the destination number variable

    numColumnIndex - Number   ▼   (x)₊

Figure 12.21 – Number: Assign properties

5. Click on **Save**.

6. To loop through each item in the record and assign it to the `strValue` variable, add the **Loop** action just below line **25**, ensuring it is within the step on line **24**.

7. Set the following properties for the **Loop** action on line **26**:

   Iterator: **For each value in record**

   Record variable: **recLoan - Record**

   Assign the current value to this variable: **strValue - String**

   The properties should look like this:

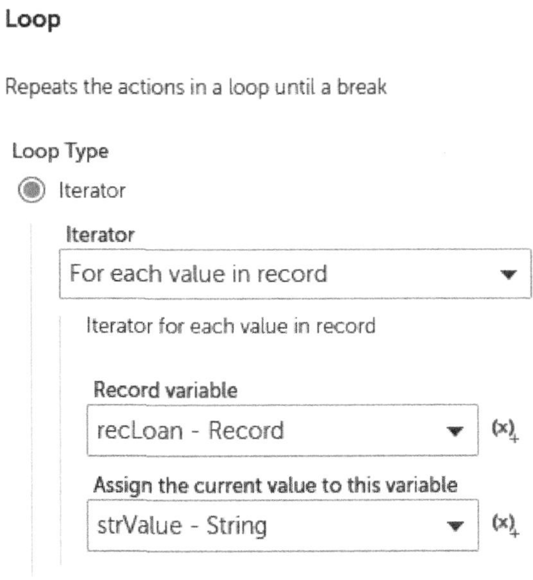

   Loop

   Repeats the actions in a loop until a break

   Loop Type

   ◉ Iterator

   Iterator

   [For each value in record   ▼]

   Iterator for each value in record

   Record variable

   [recLoan - Record   ▼] (x)₊

   Assign the current value to this variable

   [strValue - String   ▼] (x)₊

   Figure 12.22 – Loop properties

8. Click on **Save**.

9. Now, to start processing each value, we need to increment the index by 1. Let's do this by adding the **Number: Increment** action just below line **26**, ensuring it is within the **Loop** action on line **26**.

10. Set the following properties for the **Number: Increment** action on line **26**:

    Enter number: $numColumnIndex$

    Enter increment value: 1

    Assign the output to variable: **numColumnIndex - Number**

The properties should look like this:

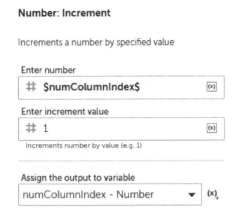

Number: Increment

Increments a number by specified value

Enter number

\# **$numColumnIndex$**

Enter increment value

\# 1

Increments number by value (e.g. 1)

Assign the output to variable

numColumnIndex - Number

Figure 12.23 – Number: Increment properties

11. Click on **Save**.

12. To assign our placeholder variable with the current column name from our List variable, add the **List: Get item** action just below line **27**, ensuring it is within the **Loop** action on line **26**.

13. Set the following properties for the **List: Get item** action on line **28**:

List variable: **lstColumns - List**

Index number: $numColumnIndex$

Assign the output to variable: **strPlaceHolder - String**

The properties should look like this:

List: Get item

Gets an item from the List from a given index position

List variable

lstColumns - List

Index number

\# **$numColumnIndex$**

Assign the output to variable

strPlaceHolder - String

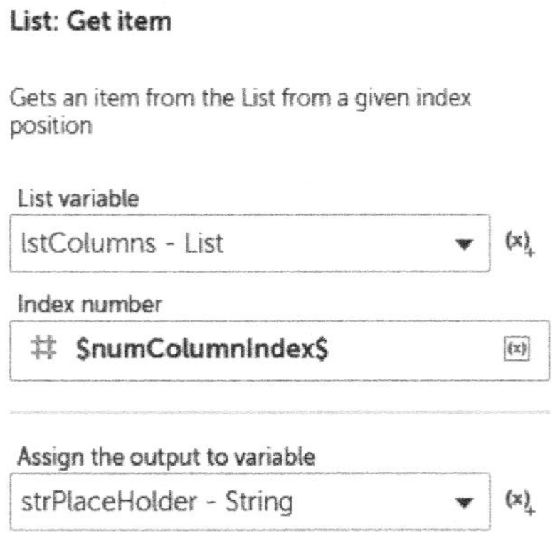

Figure 12.24 – List: Get item properties

14. Click on **Save**.

15. The actual replacing of the placeholder text with the `strValue` variable is done by adding the **MS Word: Replace Text** action just below line **28**, ensuring it is within the **Loop** action on line number **26**.

16. Set the following properties for the **MS Word: Replace Text** action on line **29**:

    Select the Word document: Desktop file – `$strLoanLetter$`

    Enter Text to be replaced: `$strPlaceHolder$`

    Enter new Text: `$strValue$`

    The properties should look like this:

    MS Word: Replace Text

    Replace Existing text in MS Word Document

    Select the Word document
    | Control Room file | Desktop file | Variable |

    `55` **$strLoanLetter$** `(x)`   Browse...

    Enter Text to be replaced
    `55` **$strPlaceHolder$** `(x)`

    Enter new Text
    `55` **$strValue$** `(x)`

    Figure 12.25 – MS Word: Replace Text properties

17. Click on **Save**.

18. The final task is to close the session that we opened at the start. Add the **Excel advanced: Close** action just below line **30**, ensuring it is within the step on line **30**.

19. Set the following properties for the **Excel advanced: Close** action on line **31**:

    Session name: `xl_data`

    Save changes when closing file: *Unchecked*

The properties should look like this:

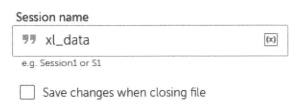

Excel advanced: Close

Closes an excel spreadsheet. This action works with xlsx, xls, xlsb, xlsm and csv files.

Session name

💬 xl_data   (x)

e.g. Session1 or S1

☐ Save changes when closing file

Figure 12.26 – Excel advanced: Close properties

20. Click on **Save**.

That's it, you can relax now, as it's all done. Your bot is now complete. The development interface for the last section should look like this:

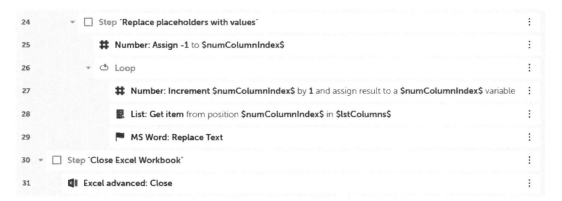

24	▾ ☐ Step "Replace placeholders with values"	⋮
25	✻ **Number: Assign -1 to $numColumnIndex$**	⋮
26	▾ ↻ Loop	⋮
27	✻ **Number: Increment $numColumnIndex$** by **1** and assign result to a **$numColumnIndex$** variable	⋮
28	▤ **List: Get item** from position **$numColumnIndex$** in **$lstColumns$**	⋮
29	▣ **MS Word: Replace Text**	⋮
30	▾ ☐ Step "Close Excel Workbook"	⋮
31	▦ **Excel advanced: Close**	⋮

Figure 12.27 – Development interface

You must be itching to test your bot. When you run the bot, it will create five Word documents in the repository folder. Each file will be a letter in Word with client and loan details from the loan data worksheet.

Summary

In this chapter, we learned how Automation Anywhere can be used to automate tasks using Word. We learned how to add paragraphs, insert text using bookmarks, and replace text. The bot that we built in this chapter has also shown us how Excel and Word can be used together to fully automate a business role end to end. All this automation provides a more effective way to perform the same task without the risk of errors and also increases efficiency as it reduces the manual effort involved.

We will continue working with automating applications in the next chapter. We will be learning all about using email. You will learn how to connect to mailboxes, read emails, and reply to emails, as well as how to create and send emails. This is not all; you will also learn how to work with email folders and attachments.

13
Working with Emails

We just explored how to automate tasks using Word in *Chapter 12, Automation Using Word*. Hopefully, the bot you built has given you the confidence to edit and update Word documents using Automation Anywhere A2019. You have learned how to insert text into defined bookmarks, replaced selected text, and added new paragraphs. All these skills and practical experience will build your confidence and help you become a competent RPA Automation Anywhere developer. In this chapter, we will be using the following packages:

Figure 13.1 – Packages used in this chapter

This chapter will explore automating tasks that use **email**. We will be looking at the **Email** package in Automation Anywhere. We will look at how to connect to different types of email accounts, such as **Exchange Web Services (EWS)**, IMAP, and POP3. You will also learn about sending and receiving emails, as well as looping through different email folders. The walk-throughs will include working with attachments. This chapter will also introduce the `Dictionary` variable type. A `Dictionary` variable type is used to store key-value pairs. Each item in the dictionary has a key and a value. The key is used as a mapping reference to the value. A system dictionary already exists for using emails in Automation Anywhere. We will learn how to use this system dictionary variable type.

In this chapter, we will cover the following:

- Connecting to mailboxes
- Reading emails and attachments
- Sending emails and attachments

Technical requirements

In order to install Automation Anywhere Bot agent, the following requirements are necessary:

- Windows OS version 7 or higher
- A processor with a minimum speed of 3 GHz
- A minimum of 4 GB RAM
- At least 100 MB hard disk space
- Internet Explorer v10 or higher OR Chrome v49 or higher
- A minimum screen resolution of 1024*768
- An internet connection with a minimum speed of 10 Mb/sec
- Completed registration with Automation Anywhere A2019 Community Edition
- Successful log-on to Automation Anywhere A2019 Community Edition
- A successfully registered local device
- Successfully downloaded sample data from GitHub

Connecting to mailboxes

A big part of our daily routine involves working with email. This can be receiving attachments, such as invoices, as well as replying to emails with document attachments. There are different types of email accounts, such as **Exchange Web Services (EWS)**, **POP3**, and **IMAP**. Each type of mailbox will have its own account, which is hosted on a mail server. These accounts will require credentials and mail server details in order to access them. In the majority of cases, applications such as Outlook are used to access and manage emails. Automation Anywhere can work with these different types of mailboxes. Account details are needed to connect, except when you are using Outlook. As Outlook is already connected to your mailbox, no credentials are needed. However, Automation Anywhere only supports Outlook when there is only one mailbox connected. It does not support multiple mailboxes in Outlook.

Also, note that there are two different types of connections – one for incoming email and one for outgoing email. The incoming type is required for reading and searching emails. The outgoing type is needed for sending, replying to, and forwarding emails.

The **Email: Connect** action is used to create an email session. As with all sessions, they need to be closed once they are no longer required. With email, a session is closed using the **Email: Disconnect** action. A session with the incoming server details is needed whenever you need to access a mailbox for reading or searching emails. You will need the outgoing server details for sending, replying to, and forwarding any emails. For all these actions, a session is not needed, as a server connection to the outgoing mailbox is established within the action properties itself.

In the first walk-through, you will learn how to create a new session by connecting to the following:

- An Outlook mailbox
- An POP3/IMAP mailbox
- An EWS mailbox

The practical approach for this chapter will be to demonstrate the different actions from the **Email** package. We will be using comments and steps to help structure all the actions. As the first section will look at how we can connect to different types of mailboxes, we can begin by building the initial skeleton using comments and steps.

Let's start this walk-through by executing the following steps:

1. Log in to **Control Room**.
2. Create a new bot in the `\Bot\` folder and call it `Chapter 13 - Email Automation`.

3. Add a new **Comment** action on line **1** as "- -" and click on **Save**.

4. Add a **Step** just below line **1**, set the **Title** property as `"Connecting to mailboxes"`, and click on **Save**.

5. Add another **Step** just below line **2**, ensuring it is within the previous **Step** on line **2**, set the **Title** property as `"Connecting to Outlook"`, and click on **Save**.

6. Add another **Step** just below line **3**, ensuring it is aligned to the **Step** on line **3**, set the **Title** property as `"Connecting to POP3/IMAP"`, and click on **Save**.

7. Add another **Step** just below line **4**, ensuring it is aligned to the **Step** on line **4**, set the **Title** property as `"Connecting to EWS"`, and click on **Save**.

8. Add a new **Comment** action on line **6** as "- -" and click on **Save**. Your initial development interface should look like this:

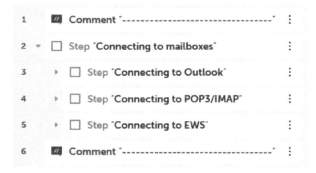

Figure 13.2 – Development interface

That's great, we now have a structure for our walk-through. The first connection we will look at is Microsoft Outlook.

Connecting to Outlook

Outlook already has your mailbox configured, whether it is POP3, IMAP, Gmail, or Exchange. Because of this, no details or credentials are needed. Something to remember is that Automation Anywhere does not support multiple mailboxes on Outlook. If you do have more than one mailbox connected to Outlook, your bot will use the default mailbox.

Let's start this walk-through by executing the following steps:

1. Expand the **Step** on line **3** titled `"Connecting to Outlook"`.

2. To create an Outlook session, add the **Email: Connect** action just below line **3**, ensuring it is within the **Step** on line **3**.

3. Set the following properties for the **Email: Connect** action on line **4**:

Session name: `EmailOutlook`

Connect to: **Outlook**

The properties should look like this:

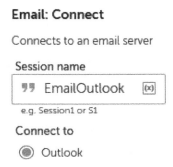

Figure 13.3 – Email: Connect – Outlook properties

4. Click on **Save**.

5. The session is now created. Once you have finished, you will need to disconnect from the mailbox. To do this, add the **Email: Disconnect** action just below line **4**, ensuring it is within the step on line **3**.

6. Set the following property for the **Email: Disconnect** action on line **5**:

Session name: `EmailOutlook`

The property should look like this:

Figure 13.4 – Email: Disconnect property

7. Click on **Save** and your development interface for this section should look like this:

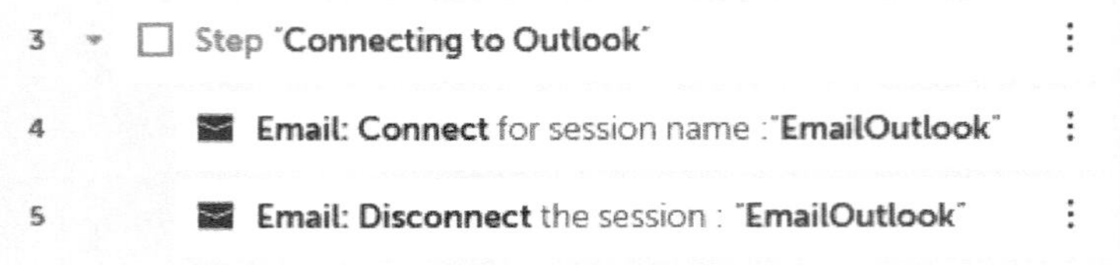

3	▼ ☐ Step 'Connecting to Outlook'	⋮
4	✉ Email: **Connect** for session name : 'EmailOutlook'	⋮
5	✉ Email: **Disconnect** the session : 'EmailOutlook'	⋮

Figure 13.5 – Development interface

That's all there is to it; once a session has been established, the bot can start working with the mailbox. This could be tasks such as reading, searching, and moving emails. In the next section, we will look at how to establish a connection with a POP3 and IMAP mailbox to create a session.

Connecting to a POP3/IMAP mailbox

When connecting to a POP3 or IMAP mailbox, you will need the mailbox and credential details. This information would be needed whenever you want to connect to your mailbox using any email application. The following information is needed to establish a connection and read emails:

- Incoming mail server name
- Whether SSL is required
- Port number
- Email address/username
- Password

To give an example of this information, if you were connecting to a Gmail account, the details would be as shown in the following figure:

POP3 Settings	
Incoming Mail Server:	pop.gmail.com
Requires SSL:	Yes
Port:	995
Email address	*****@gmail.com
Password	**********

IMAP Settings	
Incoming Mail Server:	imap.gmail.com
Requires SSL:	Yes
Port:	993
Email address	*****@gmail.com
Password	**********

Figure 13.6 – Gmail incoming server settings

For our walk-through, we will be connecting to a Gmail account using IMAP, but you can use any mailbox as long as you have the required information.

> **Connecting to a Gmail account using IMAP**
>
> When connecting to a Gmail account using IMAP, you will need to ensure that the session secure app access is set to *on*. If it is set as *off*, Automation Anywhere will not be able to connect to your Gmail account. This setting is not required when connecting using POP.
>
> Further details on how to configure this setting can be found at `https://support.google.com/accounts/answer/6010255?hl=en`.

We will enter our email address/password as an insecure string, in this case, but alternatively, you can use a variable.

Let's start this walk-through by executing the following steps:

1. Expand the step on line **6** titled `"Connecting to POP3/IMAP"`.

2. To create the **IMAP** session, add the **Email: Connect** action just below line **6**, ensuring it is within the step on line **6**.

3. Set the following properties for the **Email: Connect** action on line **7**:

   Session name: `EmailSession`

   Connect to: **Email server**

   Host: `imap.gmail.com`

   Port: `993`

   Username: **Insecure string** – `******@gmail.com` (*enter your email address*)

   Password: **Insecure string** – `*********` (*enter your email password*)

   Use secure connection(SSL/TLS): *Checked*

   Protocol: **IMAP** (*Select POP3 for a POP3 mailbox connection*)

The properties should look like this:

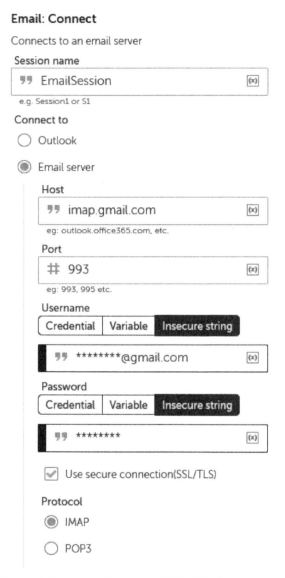

Figure 13.7 – Email: Connect – POP3/IMAP properties

4. Click on **Save**.

5. To disconnect from the mailbox, just add the **Email: Disconnect** action below line **7**, ensuring it is aligned to the action on line **7**.

6. Set the following property for the **Email: Disconnect** action on line **5**:

Session name: EmailSession

The property should look like this:

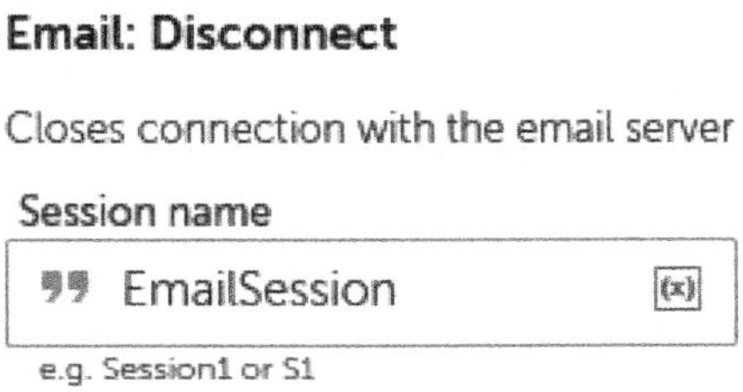

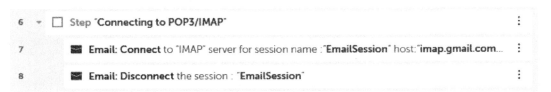

Email: Disconnect

Closes connection with the email server

Session name

> EmailSession   (x)

e.g. Session1 or S1

Figure 13.8 – Email: Disconnect property

7. Click on **Save**. Your development interface for this section should look like this:

6	▾ ☐ Step "Connecting to POP3/IMAP"	⋮
7	Email: **Connect** to "IMAP" server for session name :"**EmailSession**" host:"imap.gmail.com...	⋮
8	Email: **Disconnect** the session : "**EmailSession**"	⋮

Figure 13.9 – Development interface

That's another connection established. You should now be comfortable with connecting to mailboxes using the POP3 or IMAP protocol. Another popular type of mailbox is **Exchange Server**. We will learn how to connect to an Exchange mailbox in the next section.

Connecting to an EWS mailbox

When connecting to an Exchange mail server, only a few pieces of information are needed. The following information would be required whenever you want to connect to your mailbox using any email application to read emails:

- Username or email address
- Password
- Domain name (optional)
- Exchange server version

To give an example of this information, if you were connecting to an Outlook Exchange account, the details would be as shown in the following figure:

Exchange Server Settings	
Email:	******@outlook.com
Password:	********
Server:	outlook.com
Version:	Exchange 2010

Figure 13.10 – Outlook Exchange Server settings

For our walk-through, we will be connecting to an Outlook Exchange Server account, but you can use any Exchange mailbox as long as you have the required information. As we did in the *Connecting to a POP3/IMAP mailbox* section previously, we will enter the email address/password as an insecure string.

Let's start this walk-through by executing the following steps:

1. Expand the **Step** on line **9** titled "Connecting to EWS".

2. To create the Exchange session, add the **Email: Connect** action just below line **9**, ensuring it is within the step on line **9**.

3. Set the following properties for the **Email: Connect** action on line **10**:

    Session name: EmailSessionEWS

    Connect to: EWS server

    Username: **Insecure string** – ******@outlook.com (*enter your email address*)

    Password: **Insecure string** – ********* (*enter your email password*)

    Enter Domain name (optional): outlook.com

    Exchange Version: Exchange2010

    The properties should look like this:

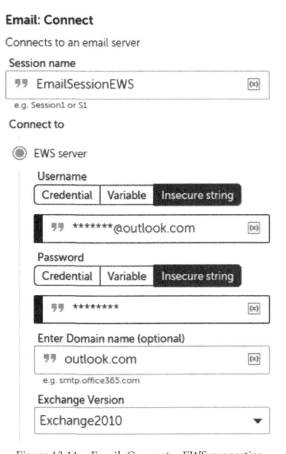

Figure 13.11 – Email: Connect – EWS properties

4. Click on **Save**.

5. To disconnect from the mailbox, just add the **Email: Disconnect** action below line **10**, ensuring it is aligned to the action on line **10**.

6. Set the following property for the **Email: Disconnect** action on line **11**:

    Session name: `EmailSessionEWS`

The property should look like this:

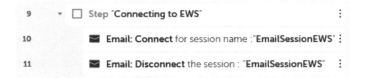

Figure 13.12 – Email: Disconnect property

7. Click on **Save** and your development interface for this section should look like this:

Figure 13.13 – Development interface

Great job! In this section, you've learned how to connect to the different types of mailboxes. The complete development interface for all the mailbox connections should look like this:

Figure 13.14 – Development interface

If you run the bot, it will look as if it hasn't done much, but your bot has connected to each mailbox and disconnected. As long as the mailbox and the credentials are correct, the bot will complete the task without raising any errors.

Before we move on to the next section, let's ensure that our bot is neat and tidy. You can collapse the step on line **2** and then disable this step by clicking on the three dots on line **2** and selecting **Disable action**. As you are disabling the step, all the actions and the sub-steps within this step will be disabled:

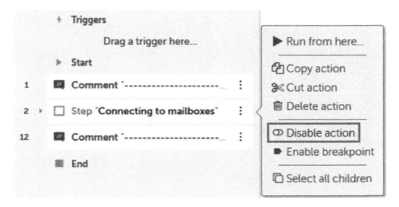

Figure 13.15 – Disable step action

Our bot is now nice and tidy and we are ready to move on to the next section. In the next section, we will learn how to read emails from your mailbox and save attachments.

Reading emails and attachments

Once connected to our mailbox, we want our bot to process emails in one form or another. More than likely, our manual task would involve working with specific emails, such as emails sent from a particular sender. It could also include saving any attachments from our emails. In this section, you will learn how to create a loop to iterate through the inbox and only read unread emails from a specific sender. The bot will then change the email status to read and save any attachments.

You will also be introduced to the `Dictionary` type variable; Automation Anywhere already has a pre-built dictionary for emails. A `Dictionary` type variable stores a value for a given key value. Together, these are known as a **key-value pair**. For each email that your bot reads, the `Dictionary` variable will store the following information:

Key	Value
emailSubject	Email Subject
emailFrom	Senders Email
emailTo	Who the Email is addressed to
emailCc	Any Email CC's
emailBcc	Any Email Bcc's
emailMessage	Email Message
emailReceivedTime	Time Email received
emailReceivedDate	Date Email received

Figure 13.16 – Email dictionary

For this walk-through, we will use Outlook as our mailbox. You can, however, apply a different type of connection if you wish. As we have disabled the previous actions from our bot, we can continue using the same task bot. Before we add any actions for the bot to perform, we will begin by building the skeleton structure with comments and steps. You will build a bot that performs the following tasks:

1. Loops through emails in the inbox

2. Applies filters and specifies folders

3. Updates email status

4. Saves attachments

Let's start this walk-through by executing the following steps:

1. Add a step just below line **12**, set the **Title** property as `"Reading Emails"`, and click on **Save**.

2. Add a new **Comment** action as `"------- Connect to Mailbox"` on line **14**, ensuring it is within the **Step** on line **13**, and click on **Save**.

3. Add a new **Comment** action as `"------- Loop through Inbox"` on line **15**, ensuring it is within the **Step** on line **13**, and click on **Save**.

4. Add a new **Comment** action as `"------- Update Status"` on line **16**, ensuring it is within the **Step** on line **13**, and click on **Save**.

5. Add a new **Comment** action as `"------- Save Attachments"` on line **17**, ensuring it is within the **Step** on line **13**, and click on **Save**.

6. Add a new **Comment** action as `"------- Disconnect Mailbox"` on line **18**, ensuring it is within the **Step** on line **13**, and click on **Save**.

7. Add a new **Comment** action as `"------------------------------"` on line **19** and click on **Save**. Your initial development interface should look like this:

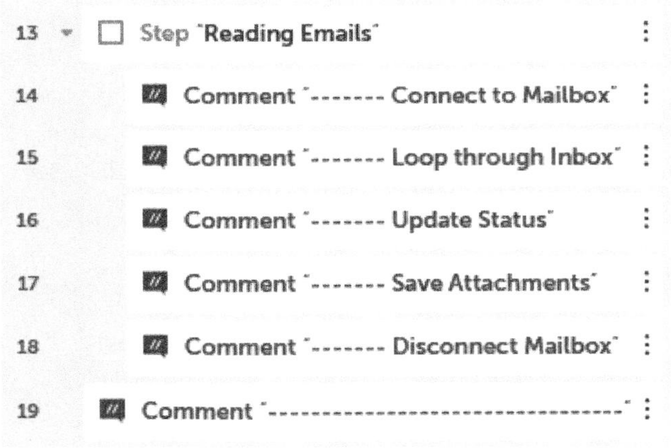

Figure 13.17 – Development interface

That's great! We now have a structure for our walk-through. As we did in the previous section, *Connecting to mailboxes*, we will begin by creating our connection to Outlook:

1. To create the Outlook session, add the **Email: Connect** action just below line **14**, ensuring it is within the step on line **13**.

2. Set the following properties for the **Email: Connect** action on line **15**:

Session name: EmailSession

Connect to: Outlook

The properties should look like this:

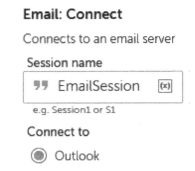

Figure 13.18 – Email: Connect - Outlook properties

3. Click on **Save**.

4. Let's also add the disconnect action by adding **Email: Disconnect** just below line **19**, ensuring it is aligned to the **Comment** action on line **19**.

5. Set the following property for the **Email: Disconnect** action on line **20**:

    Session name: EmailSession

    The property should look like this:

Figure 13.19 – Email: Disconnect property

6. Click on **Save** and your development interface for this section should look like the following:

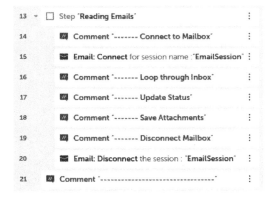

Figure 13.20 – Development interface

We have now established the connection to the mailbox. In the next section, you will learn how to add a **Loop** action so that the bot can read email messages from the inbox.

Looping through emails from a folder

Once we have the loop in place, we will need a variable to store details of each individual email. For an email message, we will use the Dictionary variable type. Follow the given walk-through to guide you on how to build the loop and store each email:

1. For our Dictionary variable type, create a new variable called dctEmail and set **Type** to **Dictionary** and **Subtype** to **String**, as follows:

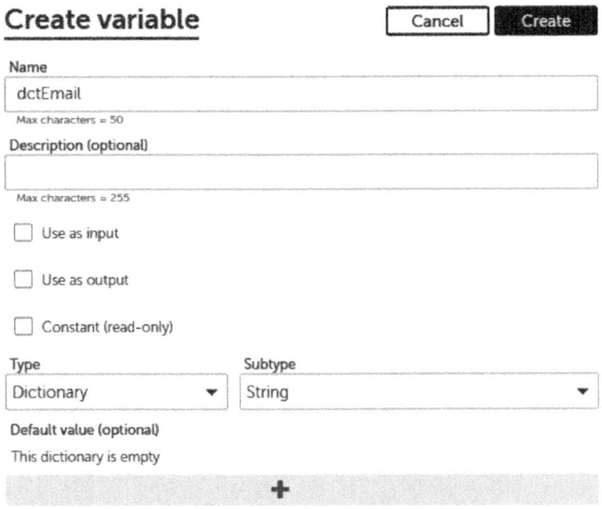

Figure 13.21 – Creating a Dictionary variable type

2. To add our loop to read all emails, drag the **Loop** action just below line **16**, ensuring it is aligned to the **Comment** action on line **16**.

3. Set the following properties for the **Loop** action on line **17**:

Loop Type: Iterator

Iterator: For each mail in mail box

Session name: EmailSession

Type of email to get: **ALL**

Message format: **PLAINTEXT**

Assign the current value to variable: dctEmail – Dictionary of Strings

The properties should look like this:

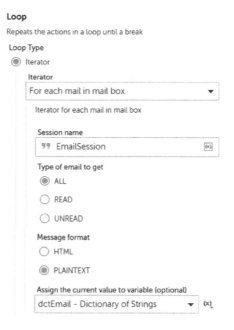

Figure 13.22 – Email loop properties

4. Click on **Save**.

That's great! You have learned how to add a **Loop** action so that your bot can read each email from your mailbox. In the next section, you will learn how to add filters and specify folders to read.

Applying filters and specifying folders

The bot will read all emails from the connected mailbox, but to perform specific tasks, we often need to work with specific emails. To allow our bot to only look for emails that meet certain criteria, we can apply filters within our loop. These filters include the following:

- Specifying the email status
- Specifying the mailbox folders
- Specifying the email subject line text
- Specifying the email sender
- Specifying the date and time of the received email

For this walk-through, we want our bot to only look for emails in the inbox that are unread. To configure our bot to only loop through these specific emails, execute the following steps:

1. Update the loop properties for the **Loop** action on line **17**:

    Type of email to get: **UNREAD**

    From a specific folder (optional): Inbox

    The properties should look like this:

Figure 13.23 – Email loop – filter properties

2. Click on **Save**.

As you can see, all the filters are configured on the **Loop** action. In the following subsections, we will outline all the other filters that can be applied.

Specifying the email status

You have just updated the email status filter, but you can see, as per the following screenshot, that you have an option to select either **ALL**, **READ**, or **UNREAD** emails only:

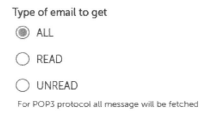

Figure 13.24 – Email loop – status filter

Specifying the mailbox folders

You can set a specific folder here. Wildcard characters can also be used as part of the folder name. Nested subfolders can be specified using the Inbox/SubFolder1 format. If needed, variables can also be used to enter this value. The following screenshot shows how to set Inbox as the specified folder:

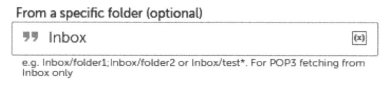

Figure 13.25 – Email loop – folder filter

Specifying the email subject line text

To set a particular text in the subject line, you can do so here. If needed, **String** type variables can also be used to enter this value:

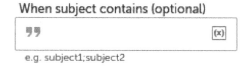

Figure 13.26 – Email loop – subject filter

Specifying the email sender

Here, you can look at emails from a specific sender. Enter the sender's email address (you can also enter multiple email addresses separated by a semicolon). If needed, String type variables can also be used to enter this value:

Figure 13.27 – Email loop – sender filter

Specifying the date and time of the received email

You can also set a date/time filter. Again, variables can be used here, but they need to be of the `Datetime` type:

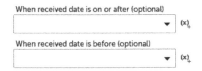

Figure 13.28 – Email loop – date/time filter

Hopefully, this has given you an overview of how you would configure your bot to apply the different types of filters to your **Loop** action. As we continue with our walk-through, we have already added our loop. All our actions for each email need to be moved to within our loop.

Let's continue with our bot by moving our comments so that they are inside our loop:

1. Drag the **Comment** actions to lines **18** and **19** so that they are within the loop on line **17**.

2. Click on **Save** and your development window should be looking like this:

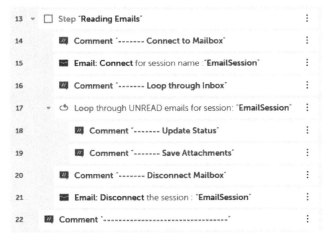

Figure 13.29 – Development interface

All looking good so far; the bot will now loop through all unread emails in the inbox. In the next section, we will look at how to update the email status.

Updating the email status

As our bot will only be processing unread emails, we do not want it to duplicate the process multiple times for the same email. If we update the email status to **READ**, it will ensure that the same email is not picked up by the bot again.

Let's start this walk-through by executing the following steps:

1. To update the status, add the **Email: Change status** action just below line **18**, ensuring it is aligned to the **Comment** action on line **18**.

2. Set the following properties for the **Email: Change status** action on line **19**:

    Session name: EmailSession

    Change status to: Read

    The properties should look like this:

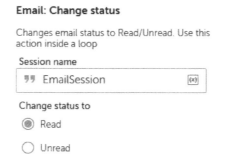

Figure 13.30 – Email: Change status properties

3. Click on **Save**.

Great progress! Your bot will now update the status of each unread email to read, ensuring any processing is not duplicated. Quite often, we work with attachments in our emails. In the next section, you will learn how to save email attachments.

Saving attachments

When automating tasks that involve email, we tend to perform tasks with attached documents. We will continue with our walk-through and further build the bot. Here, you will learn about managing attached documents. We will instruct our bot to save any attachments to a specific folder.

To ensure the bot is robust, we will check whether the target folder exists and create it if it doesn't. We will configure our bot to save any attachments to the folder at C:\Hands-On-RPA-with-AA-Sample-Data\Chapter13_Emails.

Let's start this walk-through by executing the following steps:

1. To check whether our target folder exists, add the **If** action just below line **20**, ensuring it is aligned to the **Comment** action on line **20**.

2. Set the following properties for the **If** action on line **21**:

   Condition: Folder does not exist

   Folder path: C:\Hands-On-RPA-with-AA-Sample-Data\Chapter13_Emails

   How long you would like to wait for this condition to be true?(Seconds): 0

   The properties should look like this:

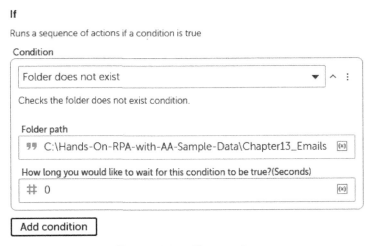

Figure 13.31 – If properties

3. Click on **Save**.

4. To create the folder if it doesn't exist, add the **Folder: Create** action just below line **21**, ensuring it is within the **If** action on line **21**.

5. Set the following properties for the **Folder: Create** action on line **22**:

   Folder: C:\Hands-On-RPA-with-AA-Sample-Data\Chapter13_Emails

   Overwrite an existing folder: *Unchecked*

The properties should look like this:

Folder: Create

Creates a folder

Folder

» C:\Hands-On-RPA-with-AA-Sample-Data\Chapter13_Emails [x]

e.g. C:\MyDoc\MyNewFolder

☐ Overwrite an existing folder

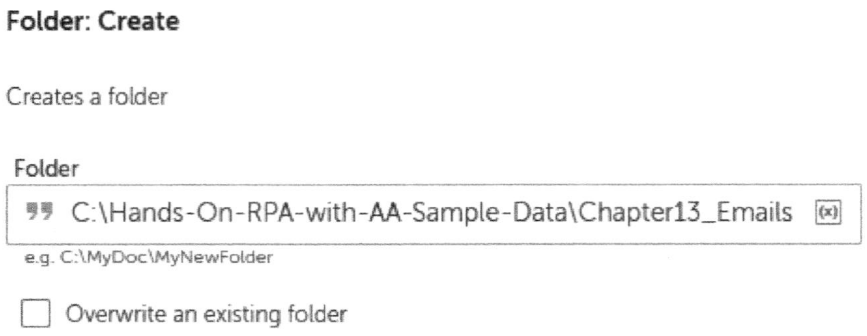

Figure 13.32 – Folder: Create properties

6. Click on **Save**.

7. We are now ready to add the action to save any email attachments. Add the **Email: Save attachments** action just below line **22**, ensuring it is within the **Loop** action on line **17** but not within the **If** condition on line **21**. We will set the **Overwrite files** property to True, as we may test the bot multiple times and we do not want it to fail while trying to save an attachment that already exists.

8. Set the following properties for the **Email: Save attachments** action on line **23**:

    Save attachments to folder: C:\Hands-On-RPA-with-AA-Sample-Data\ Chapter13_Emails

    Overwrite file(s): *Checked*

The properties should look like this:

Email: Save attachments

Saves all attachments of a single email. Use this action inside a loop.

Save attachments to folder

» C:\Hands-On-RPA-with-AA-Sample-Data\Chapter13_Emails [x]

D:/Emails

☑ Overwrite file(s)

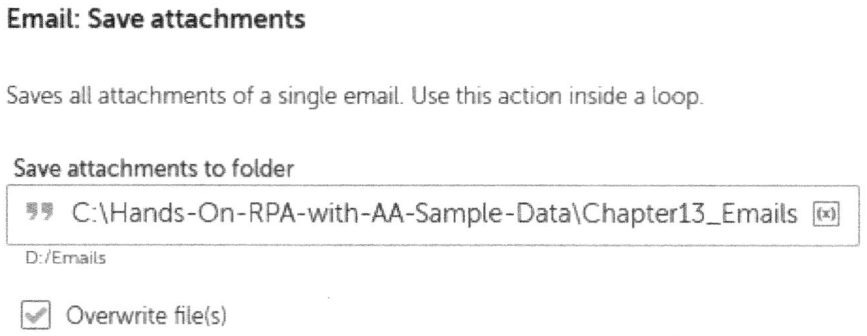

Figure 13.33 – Email: Save attachments properties

9. Click on **Save**.

10. Just one final action left. Let's add a message box so that we can see the contents of each email the bot reads. For this, we will use the `Dictionary` variable we created. Add the **Message box** action just below line **23**, ensuring it is within the **Loop** action on line **17** but not within the **If** condition on line **21**.

11. Set the following properties for the **Message box** action on line **24**:

Enter the message box window title: `Reading Emails`

Enter the message to display:

`subject: |$dctEmail{emailSubject}$|`

`From: |$dctEmail{emailFrom}$|`

`Message: |$dctEmail{emailMessage}$|`

Scrollbar after lines: `30`

Close message box after: *Checked*

Seconds: `5`

The properties should look like this:

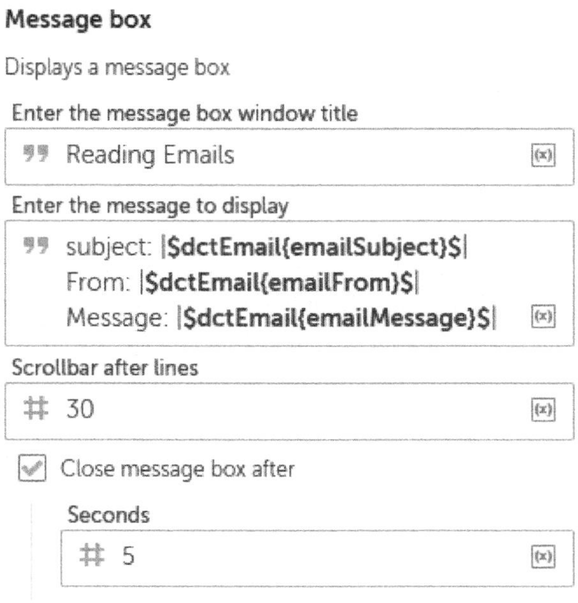

Message box

Displays a message box

Enter the message box window title

> 🔱 Reading Emails   (x)

Enter the message to display

> 🔱 subject: |$dctEmail{emailSubject}$|
> From: |$dctEmail{emailFrom}$|
> Message: |$dctEmail{emailMessage}$| (x)

Scrollbar after lines

> ♯ 30   (x)

☑ Close message box after

> Seconds
>
> ♯ 5   (x)

Figure 13.34 – Message box properties

12. Click on **Save**. The development window for the **Reading Emails** section should look like this:

12	Comment "--------------------------------"	
13	Step "Reading Emails"	
14	Comment "------- Connect to Mailbox"	
15	Email: **Connect** for session name : "EmailSession"	
16	Comment "------- Loop through Inbox"	
17	Loop through UNREAD emails for session: "EmailSession"	
18	Comment "------- Update Status"	
19	Email: **Change status** to "Read"	
20	Comment "------- Save Attachments"	
21	If folder does not exist at "C:\Hands-On-RPA-with-AA-Sample-Data\Chapter13_...	
22	Folder: **Create** "C:\Hands-On-RPA-with-AA-Sample-Data\Chapter13_Emails"	
23	Email: **Save attachments** from an email in "C:\Hands-On-RPA-with-AA-Sample-D...	
24	Message box "subject: |$dctEmail(emailSubject)$| From: |$dctEmail(emailFrom)...	
25	Comment "------- Disconnect Mailbox"	
26	Email: **Disconnect** the session : "EmailSession"	
27	Comment "--------------------------------"	

Figure 13.35 – Development interface

You can send yourself some emails and test your bot. Ensure you have the correct incoming server details if you are not using Outlook. The bot will read the new emails, save all attachments, and update the status. Good work. We will next look at sending emails.

Sending emails and attachments

We have looked at connecting with incoming mail servers to read emails. We will now move on to the next section, where we will be exploring how to send emails. Emails are always sent in one of the following three ways – either a simple independent email, a forwarded message, or a reply. For all three, you will need to know the outgoing mailbox details. As it is the same with reading emails, you can send an email via Outlook, POP3/IMAP, or Exchange. The information needed for the outgoing server is as follows:

- Outgoing mail server name
- Whether SSL/TLS/authentication is required

- SSL/TLS port number
- Email address/username
- Password

To give an example of this information, if you were connecting to a Gmail account, the outgoing server IMAP details would be as shown in the following figure:

Gmail IMAP Settings	
Outgoing Mail Server:	smtp.gmail.com
Requires SSL:	Yes
Requires Authentication:	Yes
Port for SSL:	465
Port for TLS/STARTTLS:	587
Email address:	*****@gmail.com
Password:	*********

Figure 13.36 – Gmail IMAP outgoing server settings

For our walk-through, we will be demonstrating how to perform the following actions:

- Sending an email
- Forwarding an email
- Replying to an email

When forwarding or replying to an email, a source email is needed. For instance, you need an initial email in order to reply to it and you need an initial email in order to forward it. This is why both the **Reply** and **Forward** actions need to be performed within an email session. This ensures they have a source email to work with. When just sending an email by itself, a session is not needed as it's not dependent on a source email.

For this walk-through, we will demonstrate all three methods of sending an email. As always, we will start by creating the skeleton using comments and steps.

Let's start this walk-through by executing the following steps:

1. Add a step just below line **27**, set the **Title** property as "Sending Emails", and click on **Save**.

2. Add a new **Comment** action as "------- Sending an Email" on line **29**, ensuring it is within the **Step** on line **28**, and click on **Save**.

3. Add a new **Comment** action as "------- Forwarding an Email" on line **30**, ensuring it is within the **Step** on line **28**, and click on **Save**.

4. Add a new **Comment** action as "`------- Replying to an Email`" on line **31**, ensuring it is within the **Step** on line **28**, and click on **Save**.

5. Add a new **Comment** action as "`--------------------`" on line **32**, and click on **Save**. Your development interface should look as in the following screenshot:

| 28 | ▾ ☐ Step "Sending Emails" | ⋮ |

| 29 | 🔳 Comment "------- Sending an Email" | ⋮ |

| 30 | 🔳 Comment "------- Forwarding a Email" | ⋮ |

| 31 | 🔳 Comment "------- Replying to a email" | ⋮ |

| 32 | 🔳 Comment "----------------------------------" | ⋮ |

Figure 13.37 – Development interface

That's good, we now have a structure for our demonstration. In the next section, we will start by looking at sending a simple email and then one that includes an attached document.

Sending an email

For this walk-through, we will use a Gmail account to send our email. We know what the SMTP outgoing server settings need to be for this. You will need to know your email account credentials for testing.

> **Connecting to a Gmail account using IMAP**
>
> When connecting to a Gmail account using IMAP, you will need to ensure that the less secure app access is set to *on*. If it is set as *off*, Automation Anywhere will not be able to connect to your Gmail account. This setting is not required when connecting using POP.
>
> Further details on how to configure this setting can be found at `https://support.google.com/accounts/answer/6010255?hl=en`.

Let's begin by executing the following steps:

1. To send our email, add the **Email: Send** action just below line **29**, ensuring it is within the step on line **28**.

2. There are a number of properties to set for the **Email: Send** action. Starting with the recipient and subject details, set the following properties for the **Email: Send** action on line **30**:

    To address: ＊＊＊＊＊＊@gmail.com (*the email address you are sending to*)

    Subject: RPA - Sending Emails

    These property settings should look like this:

Figure 13.38 – Email: Send – recipient/subject properties

3. Continue with configuring the **Email: Send** action on line **30** by adding the following settings to configure the message contents:

Send email as: **Plain text**

Message: This is message sent from your RPA Bot

These property settings should look like this:

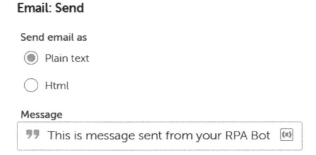

Figure 13.39 – Email: Send – email body properties

4. Finally, to configure the outgoing server connection details, add the following settings for the **Email: Send** action on line **30**:

Send email via: **Email server**

From address: ******@gmail.com (*email address you are sending from*)

Email server host: smtp.gmail.com

Email server port: 587

Use secure connection (SSL/TLS): **True**

My server requires authentication: **True**

Username (optional): **Insecure string** – ******@gmail.com (*enter your email address*)

Password (optional): **Insecure string** – ********* (*enter your email password*)

These properties should look like this:

Figure 13.40 – Email: Send – connection properties

5. Click on **Save**.

All set to send an email, great work! As long as you have the correct mail server settings, it should all be good to go. We will continue by adding an attachment to this email in the following section.

Attaching a document to an email

Here, we will further build on our bot and add an attachment to our email. This is all done within the **Email: Send** action. Follow the given steps to add a document to the email:

1. To add an attachment, update the following property for the **Email: Send** action on line **30**:

    Attachment (optional): Desktop file – C:\Hands-On-RPA-with-AA-Sample-Data\Chapter05_InputData.csv

The property should look like this:

Attachment (optional)

[Control Room file] **Desktop file** [Variable]

❝❝ C:\Hands-On-RPA-with-AA-Sample-Data\Chapter05_InputData.csv (x) | Browse... |

☐ Validate if attachment is missing

Figure 13.41 – Email: Send – attach document property

2.   Click on **Save**.

Your bot can now send an email. To do this, you don't need an email session; all the required information is contained within the **Email: Send** action. In the next section, we will look at forwarding an email.

Forwarding an email

You can only perform an **Email: Forward** action from within an email session and loop. There needs to be a source email that you are actually forwarding, but apart from that, all that's needed is the forwarding email address, a message (optional), and your outgoing server mailbox details.

In this example, we will use Outlook as our outgoing mailbox. Let's assume you have already built your email session and loop to read your emails from your incoming mailbox. To configure your bot to forward an email, just follow these steps:

1.   Add the **Email: Forward** action just below line **31**, ensuring it is within the step on line **28**.

2.   Set the following properties for the **Email: Forward** action on line **32**:

To address: `******`@gmail.com (*the email address you are forwarding the message to*)

Send email as: **Plain text**

Message (optional): `This email is forwarded by your RPA Bot`

Send email via: **Outlook**

The properties should look like this:

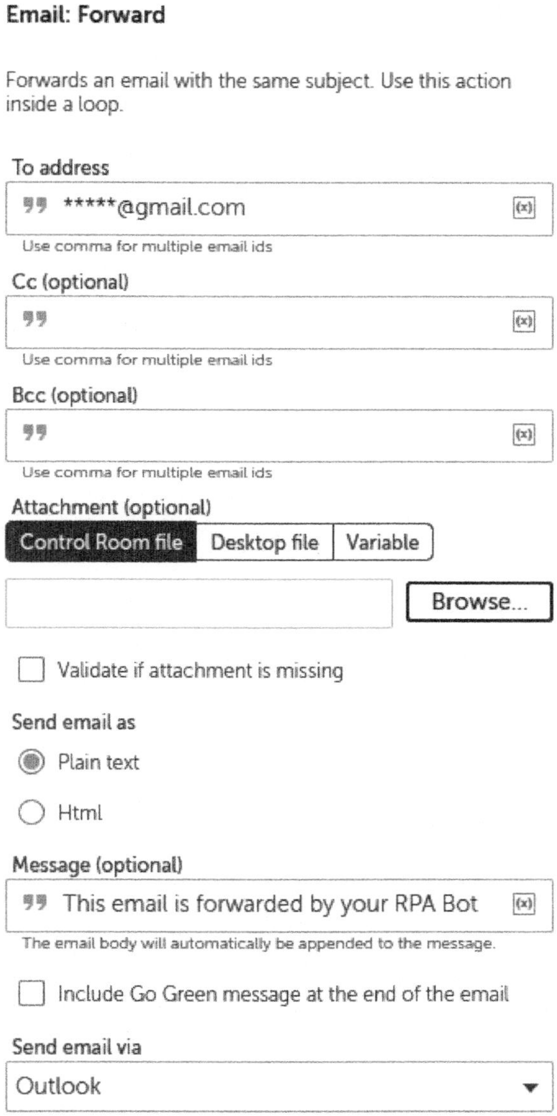

Email: Forward

Forwards an email with the same subject. Use this action inside a loop.

To address

> ***** @gmail.com

Use comma for multiple email ids

Cc (optional)

>

Use comma for multiple email ids

Bcc (optional)

>

Use comma for multiple email ids

Attachment (optional)

| Control Room file | Desktop file | Variable |

[   ] Browse...

☐ Validate if attachment is missing

Send email as

⦿ Plain text

◯ Html

Message (optional)

> This email is forwarded by your RPA Bot

The email body will automatically be appended to the message.

☐ Include Go Green message at the end of the email

Send email via

Outlook ▼

Figure 13.42 – Email: Forward – Outlook properties

3. Click on **Save**.

It's as simple as that; attachments can be added in the same way as you would when sending a standard email. Only one more type of email sending to go – that is, replying to an email, which we will look at next.

Replying to an email

Just like forwarding an email, you can only perform an **Email: Reply** action from within an email session and loop. In this example, we will again use Outlook as our outgoing mailbox and once again assume you have already built your email session and loop to read your emails from your incoming mailbox. To configure your bot to reply to an email, just follow the given steps:

1. Add the **Email: Reply** action just below line **33**, ensuring it is within the step on line **28**.

2. Set the following properties for the **Email: Reply** action on line **34**:

    Send email as: **Plain text**

    Message (optional): `This email is a reply by your RPA Bot`

    Send email via: **Outlook**

    The properties should look like this:

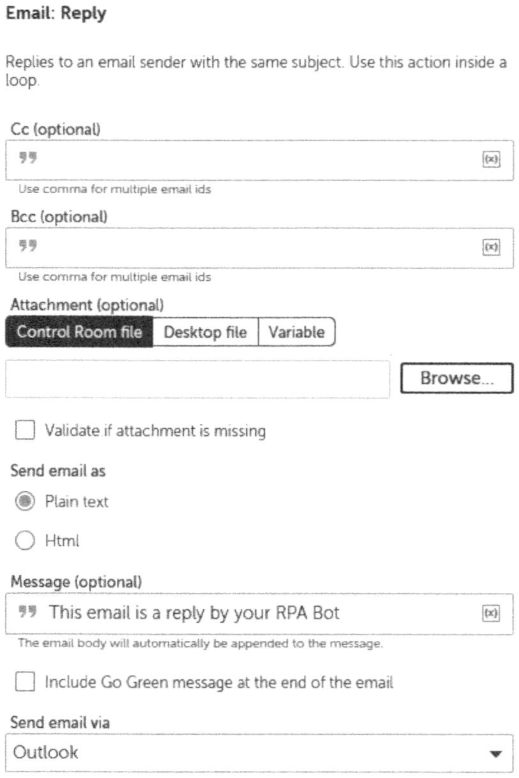

Figure 13.43 – Email: Reply – Outlook properties

3. Click on **Save**. The development window for the **Reading Emails** section should look like this:

29	Comment "------- Sending an Email"	⋮
30	**Email: Send** an email to "******@gmail.com" with subject : "RPA - Sending Emails"	⋮
31	Comment "------- Forwarding a Email"	⋮
32	**Email: Forward** an email in current session with Plain text	⋮
33	Comment "------- Replying to a email"	⋮
34	**Email: Reply** to an email in current session with Plain text	⋮
35	Comment "---------------------------------"	⋮

Figure 13.44 – Development interface

You have done absolutely great! All three types of outgoing emails are completed. Again, attaching files works the same in all three. Your bot is ready for any email-related automation you need.

Summary

This chapter has been about everything related to email. The walk-throughs have demonstrated how to connect to the different types of mail servers, as well as using Outlook. You learned how to read from any email folder using specified criteria, such as a certain sender or a particular value in the subject line. You further built your knowledge of learning how to send emails, including replying and forwarding emails. That's not all; we also included how to save and add attachments to our emails.

In the next chapter, we will move on to using automation with PDF files. PDF files are very popular and are commonly used. There are many uses – one being invoices. You will learn how to use a bot to read PDF files, including extracting text and images. You will also learn how to split and merge documents and decrypt and encrypt PDF files.

14
Working with PDF Files

To recall what we learned in the last chapter, we worked with automating emails. This included reading and looping through specified mailbox folders, as well as applying filters, such as filtering by subject-line text or the sender's email address. The walk-through also demonstrated how to save attachments from received emails. We also walked through how to use RPA to send emails, as well as replying to and forwarding them.

Progressing onward, in this chapter, we will be exploring PDF files. PDF files are used extensively within businesses. They can take many forms, such as business flow documents, design plans, or invoices. This chapter will teach you how to extract text from a PDF file, as well as saving a document as an image. Other actions that you will learn include manipulating PDF files by merging and splitting PDF documents. Finally, you will also get to encrypt a PDF file, as well as decrypt it. This is an essential part of adding additional security to your PDF files.

In this chapter, we will be using the following packages:

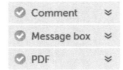

Figure 14.1 – Packages used in this chapter

Just as we discovered the `Dictionary` variable type for email in the preceding chapter, Automation Anywhere also has a built-in dictionary for PDF files. You will also learn how to use this dictionary in order to get document properties, such as the *author* and the *filename*. All the files used for the walk-throughs are available in the GitHub repository.

In this chapter, we will cover the following topics:

- Extracting text and images
- Splitting and merging documents
- Encrypting and decrypting documents
- Using the PDF dictionary

Technical requirements

In order to install Automation Anywhere Bot agent, the following requirements are necessary:

- Windows OS version 7 or higher
- A processor with a minimum speed of 3 GHz
- A minimum of 4 GB RAM
- At least 100 MB hard disk space
- Internet Explorer v10 or higher OR Chrome v49 or higher
- A minimum screen resolution of 1024*768
- An internet connection with a minimum speed of 10 Mb/sec
- Completed registration with Automation Anywhere A2019 Community Edition
- Successful log-on to Automation Anywhere A2019 Community Edition
- A successfully registered local device
- Successfully downloaded sample data from GitHub

Extracting text and images

In this section, we will look at how to extract any text from a PDF file and save it to a text file. The walk-through will also show how a PDF can be saved as an image file.

Extracting text from a PDF file

When working with PDF files, we often have to read the text contained within them in order to process the text. A good example would be extracting the text from an invoice in PDF format. This text includes product information, including a description, the quantity, and the costs. As part of a business role, you may then validate the information before posting it to a purchase ledger. In the following walk-through, you will extract the text from the `Chapter14_Letter.pdf` sample PDF file. You may remember this file; it's one of the sample loan letters used in *Chapter 12, Automation Using Word*. You will begin by adding the comments as usual.

Let's start this walk-through by executing the following steps:

1. Log in to **Control Room**.

2. Create a new bot in the `\Bot\` folder and call it `Chapter14 - PDF Files`.

3. Add a new **Comment** action as "`--------------------`" on line **1**, and click on **Save**.

4. Add a new **Comment** action as "`------- Extract Text`" on line **2**, and click on **Save**.

5. Add a new **Comment** action as "`--------------------`" on line **3**, and click on **Save**. Your initial development interface should look as in the following screenshot:

1	Comment `--------------------` ⋮
2	Comment `------- Extract Text` ⋮
3	Comment `--------------------` ⋮

Figure 14.2 – Development interface

6. To extract all the text from our PDF file, add the **PDF: Extract text** action just below line **2** so that you can start to set the properties.

7. Firstly, we need to specify the PDF file that will be used. To do this, set the following property for the **PDF: Extract text** action on line **3**:

   PDF path: Desktop file – `C:\Hands-On-RPA-with-AA-Sample-Data\Chapter14_Letter.pdf`

   As this file is not password-protected, no credentials are needed. If it was, then you would also need to enter the password.

   The property should look as in the following screenshot:

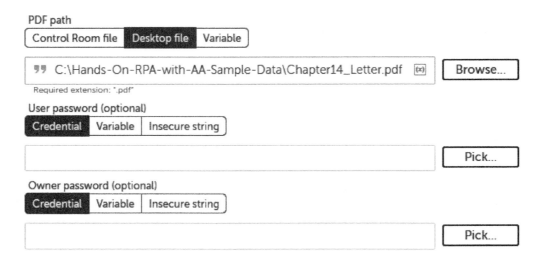

Figure 14.3 – PDF: Extract text – file property

8. Click on **Save**.

9. Continue setting the properties. Next, specify the page range and format of the text required. To do this, set the following properties for the **PDF: Extract text** action on line **3**:

   Text type: Plain text (*Structured text would keep the layout – that is, tabs and spaces*)

   Page range: All pages

The properties should look as in the following screenshot:

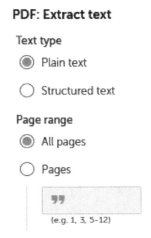

Figure 14.4 – PDF: Extract text – output format properties

10. Click on **Save**.

11. The final property to set is to specify the output text file. To do this, set the following properties for the **PDF: Extract text** action on line **3**:

    Export data to text file: C:\Hands-On-RPA-with-AA-Sample-Data\ Chapter14_Letter.txt

    Overwrite files with the same name: *Checked*

    The properties should look as in the following screenshot:

Figure 14.5 – PDF: Extract text – output file properties

12. Click on **Save**. The development interface for this section should look as in the following screenshot:

1   📝 Comment `---------------------`   ⋮

2   📝 Comment `------- Extract Text`   ⋮

3   📄 **PDF: Extract text** from `C:\Hands-On-RPA-with-AA-Sample-Data\Chapter14_L...` to `...` ⋮

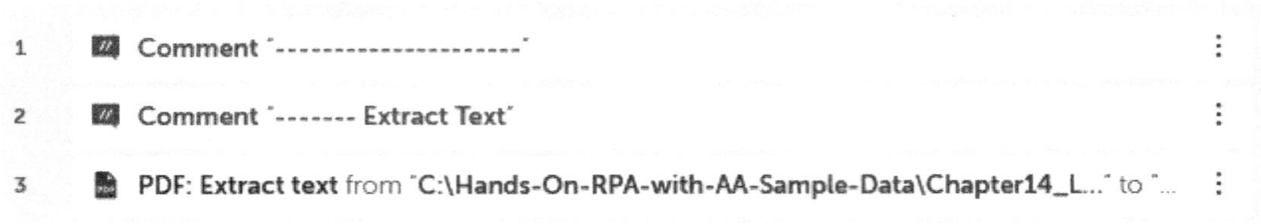

Figure 14.6 – Development interface

That's all there is to it. You can run the bot to test it. Once it has completed processing, a text file called Chapter14_Letter.txt will be generated, containing all the text from the PDF file. The output file should look as in the following screenshot:

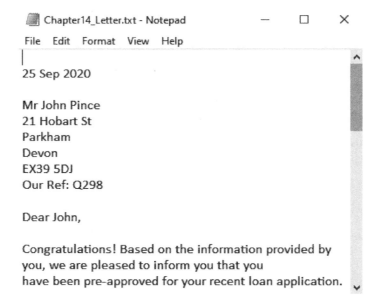

Figure 14.7 – Output text file

Now you know how to extract the text from a PDF file. The output file is now ready to start any processing using the string manipulation actions. We will continue with our bot and start to look at how to extract an image from a PDF file.

Extracting an image from a PDF file

In this section, you will learn how to extract an image from a PDF file. This action will export the specific page(s) as an image file. For this example, we will be using the `Chapter14_Chart.pdf` file. The example PDF file consists of a flowchart, which will be exported as a JPEG file. Like always, let's begin by adding our comments:

1. Add a new **Comment** action just below line **3**, "`-------  Extract Image`", and click on **Save**.

2. To extract the PDF file as an image, add the **PDF: Extract image** action just below line **4** so that you can start to set the properties.

3. Firstly, we need to specify the PDF file that will be used. To do this, set the following property for the **PDF: Extract image** action on line **5**:

   PDF path: Desktop file – `C:\Hands-On-RPA-with-AA-Sample-Data\Chapter14_Chart.pdf`

   Like before, this file is not password-protected, so no credentials are needed.

   The properties should look as in the following screenshot:

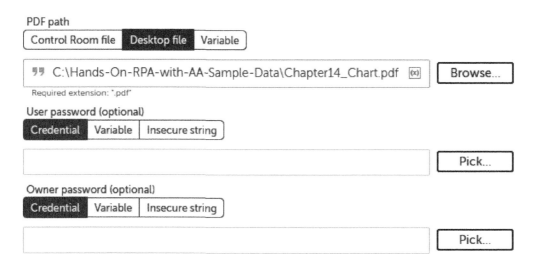

Figure 14.8 – PDF: Extract image – file properties

4. Click on **Save**.

5. Continue setting the properties. Next, specify the page range and the format of the image file. To do this, set the following properties for the **PDF: Extract image** action on line **5**:

Page range: **All pages**

Type of image to be converted to: **JPEG**

JPEG quality: 100

The properties should look as in the following screenshot:

Figure 14.9 – PDF: Extract image – output format properties

6. Click on **Save**.

7. The next properties to set are to specify the output folder for the image file. To do this, set the following properties for the **PDF: Extract image** action on line **5**:

Folder path: C:\Hands-On-RPA-with-AA-Sample-Data

File prefix: Chapter14_Chart

Overwrite files with the same name: *Checked*

The properties should look as in the following screenshot:

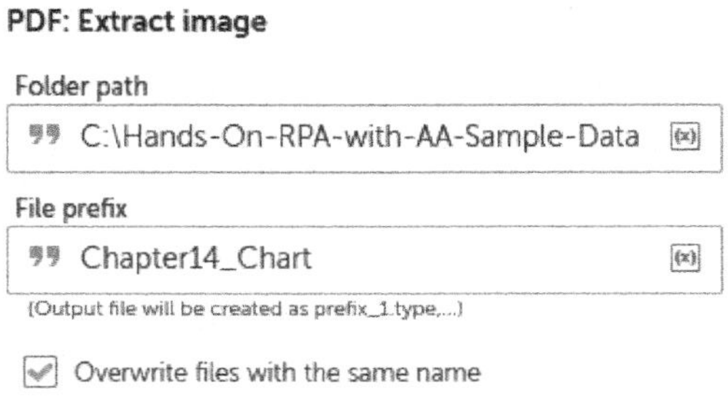
PDF: Extract image
Folder path
C:\Hands-On-RPA-with-AA-Sample-Data
File prefix
Chapter14_Chart
(Output file will be created as prefix_1.type,...)
Overwrite files with the same name

Figure 14.10 – PDF: Extract image – output file properties

8. Click on **Save**.
9. Finally, we need to specify the image resolution and the color for the output file. To do this, set the following properties for the **PDF: Extract image** action on line **5**:

   X Resolution(dpi): `200`

   Y Resolution(dpi): `200`

   Image output: **Color**

   Color property: **True color (32 bits)**

   The properties should look as in the following screenshot:

PDF: Extract image
X Resolution(dpi)
200
Y Resolution(dpi)
200
Image output
Color
Color property
True color (32 bits)
Grayscale
Color property

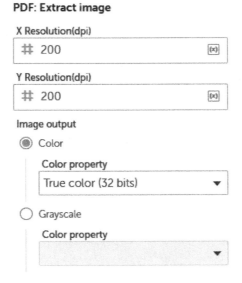

Figure 14.11 – PDF: Extract image – image resolution properties

10. Click on **Save**. The development interface for this section should look as in the following screenshot:

| 4 | 📝 Comment "------- Extract Image" | ⋮ |
| 5 | 📄 PDF: Extract image "C:\Hands-On-RPA-with-AA-Sample-Data\Chapter14_C..." to a JP... | ⋮ |

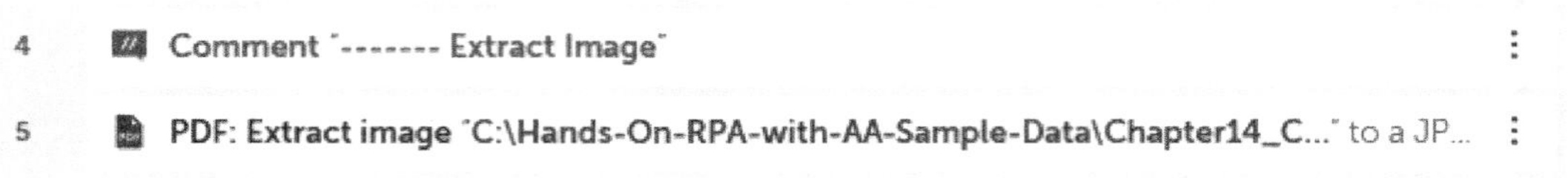

Figure 14.12 – Development interface

The extraction of an image is complete. Again, you can run the bot. When it's finished processing, you will have an output image file called `Chapter14_Chart_1.jpeg`. This file consists of the contents from the original PDF file. The output file should look as in the following screenshot:

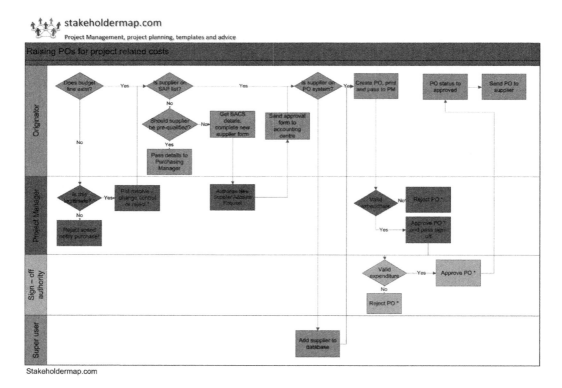

Figure 14.13 – Output image file

This walk-through has taught you how to extract an image from a PDF file. You have learned that the format can be modified, including the resolution and the file format. In the next section, you will learn how to split and merge PDF documents.

Splitting and merging documents

In this section, you will learn how to manipulate PDF files by means of splitting an existing file into multiple files and merging multiple files into a single PDF document. The walk-through will use the `Chapter14_Games.pdf` file, which is part of the GitHub repository.

Splitting a PDF file

The `Chapter14_Games.pdf` sample file that we will use is an eight-page document summarizing the contents of a book about retro arcade games. For this walk-through, the bot is tasked with splitting this document into eight separate PDF files, each file consisting of one page. Like always, let's begin by adding our comments:

1. Add a new **Comment** action just below line **5**, `"------- Split File"`, and click on **Save**.

2. To split the PDF file, add the **PDF: Split document** action just below line **6** so that you can start to set the properties.

3. Firstly, we need to specify the PDF file that will be used. To do this, set the following property for the **PDF: Split document** action on line **7**:

    PDF path: Desktop file – `C:\Hands-On-RPA-with-AA-Sample-Data\Chapter14_Games.pdf`

    Like before, this file is not password-protected, so no credentials are needed.

    The property should look as in the following screenshot:

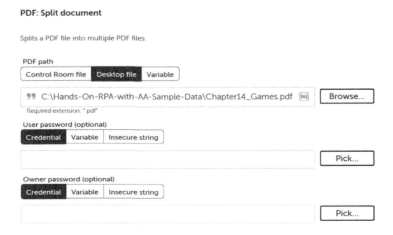

Figure 14.14 – PDF: Split document – file property

4. Click on **Save**.

5. Continue setting the properties. Next, we need to specify how the document is to be split. A number of options are available. In this case, we want to split it at each page. To do this, set the following property for the **PDF: Split document** action on line 7:

Output file creation options: Number of pages per extracted PDF – 1

The property should look as in the following screenshot:

PDF: Split document

Output file creation options

⦿ Number of pages per extracted PDF

    #   1   (x)

◯ Single file with selected pages

    "

    (e.g. 1, 3, 5-12)

◯ Blank page as a separator

◯ Bookmark level per file

    Bookmark Level

    #

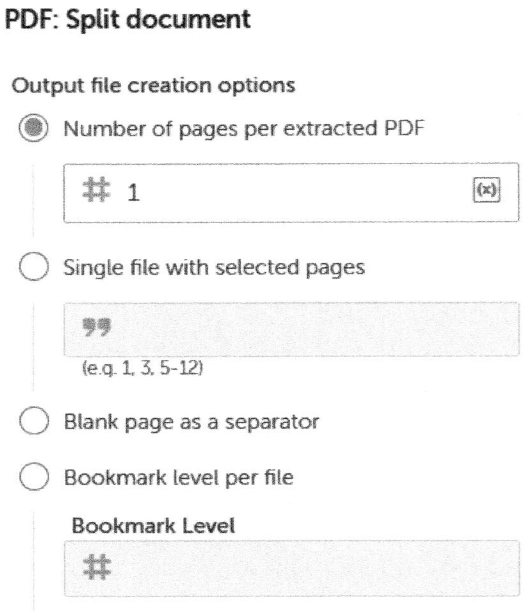

Figure 14.15 – PDF: Split document – file split property

6. Click on **Save**.

7. The final properties to set are to specify the output folder and the filename prefix. To do this, set the following properties for the **PDF: Split document** action on line 7:

Folder path: `C:\Hands-On-RPA-with-AA-Sample-Data`

File prefix: `Chapter14_GamesSplit`

Overwrite files with the same name: *Checked*

The properties should look as in the following screenshot:

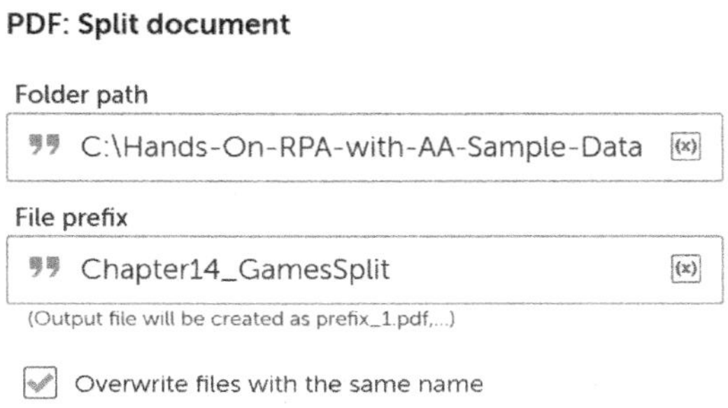

PDF: Split document
Folder path
C:\Hands-On-RPA-with-AA-Sample-Data
File prefix
Chapter14_GamesSplit
(Output file will be created as prefix_1.pdf,...)
Overwrite files with the same name

Figure 14.16 – PDF: Split document – output file properties

8. Click on **Save**. The development interface for this section should look as in the following screenshot:

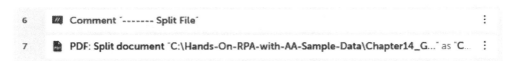

6
Comment "------- Split File"
7
PDF: Split document "C:\Hands-On-RPA-with-AA-Sample-Data\Chapter14_G..." as "C...

Figure 14.17 – Development interface

Right! You can go ahead and run your bot now. That was pretty straightforward, wasn't it? The original PDF file should be split into eight individual PDF documents, each with an increment counter suffix. All the newly created PDF files should be visible in the **File Explorer**:

Hands-On-RPA-with-AA-Sample-Data
File
Home
Share
View
« Local Disk (C:) › Hands-On-RPA-with-AA-Sample-Data
Chapter05_InputData.csv
Chapter08_InputData.txt
Chapter09_InputData.csv
Chapter10_SampleFile.xml
Chapter11_Catalog.xlsx
Chapter11_SampleData.xlsm
Chapter12_LoanData.xlsx
Chapter12_Template.docx
Chapter14_Chart.pdf
Chapter14_Chart_1.jpeg
Chapter14_Games.pdf
Chapter14_GamesSplit_1.pdf
Chapter14_GamesSplit_2.pdf
Chapter14_GamesSplit_3.pdf
Chapter14_GamesSplit_4.pdf
Chapter14_GamesSplit_5.pdf
Chapter14_GamesSplit_6.pdf
Chapter14_GamesSplit_7.pdf
Chapter14_GamesSplit_8.pdf
Chapter14_Letter.pdf
Chapter14_Letter.txt
21 items
8 items selected 39.8 KB

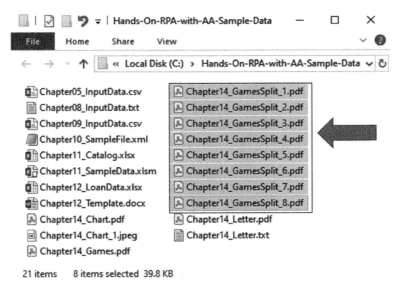

Figure 14.18 – Output PDF files

Awesome work! You have the skills to split a PDF document now. This can be a very useful action when automating tasks while working with PDF files. We will continue manipulating documents; in the next section, you will learn how to merge multiple PDF files into a single document.

Merging multiple PDF files

In this section, we will look at how to merge multiple files. It's a good job that we have just learned how to split a file, as now we have eight individual files to work with. For this walk-through, you will configure your bot to merge all eight `Chapter14_GamesSplit` files into a single PDF file. Like always, let's begin by adding our comments:

1. Add a new **Comment** action just below line **7**, "`------- Merge Files`", and click on **Save**.

2. To merge multiple PDF files, add the **PDF: Merge documents** action just below line **8**, so you can start to set the properties.

3. We need to specify the individual PDF files that we want merging together. To do this, click on the **Add PDF document** button from the properties of the **PDF: Merge documents** action on line **9**:

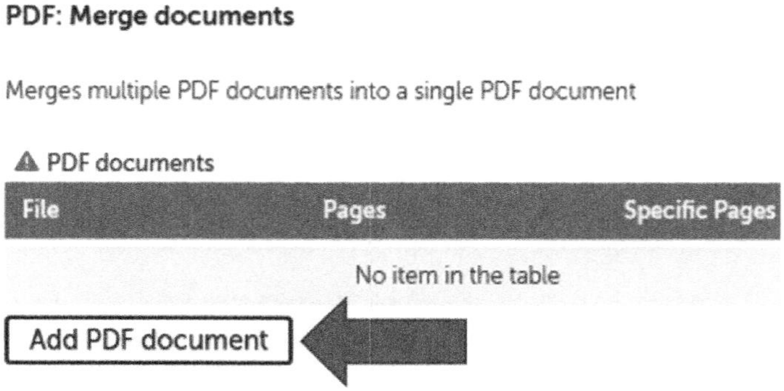

PDF: Merge documents

Merges multiple PDF documents into a single PDF document

⚠ PDF documents

File	Pages	Specific Pages
No item in the table		

Add PDF document ⬅

Figure 14.19 – PDF: Merge documents properties

4. The **Add PDF document** dialog box will appear. Here, you can specify the first document for merging. To do this, set the following properties in the **Add PDF document** dialog box:

PDF path: Desktop file – `C:\Hands-On-RPA-with-AA-Sample-Data\Chapter14_GamesSplit_1.pdf`

Pages: All pages

Like before, this file is not password protected, so no credentials are needed.

The properties should look as in the following screenshot:

Figure 14.20 – The Add PDF document dialog

5. Click on **Add**.

6. Repeat *steps 3* to *5* for each of the following seven documents:

    ```
    C:\Hands-On-RPA-with-AA-Sample-Data\Chapter14_
    GamesSplit_2.pdf
    ```

    ```
    C:\Hands-On-RPA-with-AA-Sample-Data\Chapter14_
    GamesSplit_3.pdf
    ```

    ```
    C:\Hands-On-RPA-with-AA-Sample-Data\Chapter14_
    GamesSplit_4.pdf
    ```

    ```
    C:\Hands-On-RPA-with-AA-Sample-Data\Chapter14_
    GamesSplit_5.pdf
    ```

```
C:\Hands-On-RPA-with-AA-Sample-Data\Chapter14_
GamesSplit_6.pdf
```

```
C:\Hands-On-RPA-with-AA-Sample-Data\Chapter14_
GamesSplit_7.pdf
```

```
C:\Hands-On-RPA-with-AA-Sample-Data\Chapter14_
GamesSplit_8.pdf
```

7. Click on **Save**. The **PDF: Merge documents** properties should look as in the following screenshot:

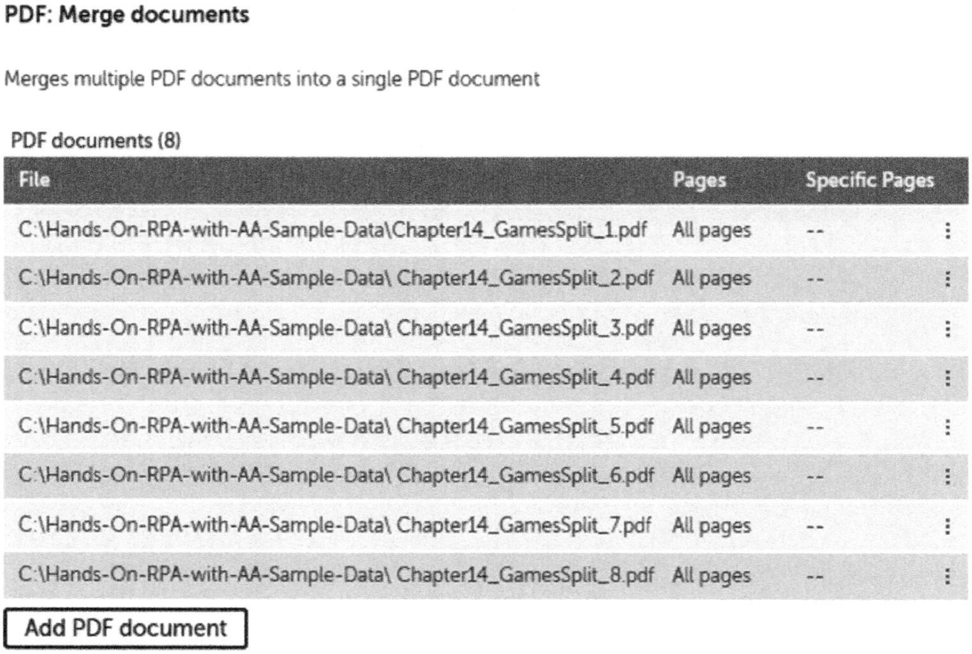

PDF: Merge documents

Merges multiple PDF documents into a single PDF document

PDF documents (8)

File	Pages	Specific Pages	
C:\Hands-On-RPA-with-AA-Sample-Data\Chapter14_GamesSplit_1.pdf	All pages	--	⋮
C:\Hands-On-RPA-with-AA-Sample-Data\ Chapter14_GamesSplit_2.pdf	All pages	--	⋮
C:\Hands-On-RPA-with-AA-Sample-Data\ Chapter14_GamesSplit_3.pdf	All pages	--	⋮
C:\Hands-On-RPA-with-AA-Sample-Data\ Chapter14_GamesSplit_4.pdf	All pages	--	⋮
C:\Hands-On-RPA-with-AA-Sample-Data\ Chapter14_GamesSplit_5.pdf	All pages	--	⋮
C:\Hands-On-RPA-with-AA-Sample-Data\ Chapter14_GamesSplit_6.pdf	All pages	--	⋮
C:\Hands-On-RPA-with-AA-Sample-Data\ Chapter14_GamesSplit_7.pdf	All pages	--	⋮
C:\Hands-On-RPA-with-AA-Sample-Data\ Chapter14_GamesSplit_8.pdf	All pages	--	⋮

Add PDF document

Figure 14.21 – The PDF: Merge documents properties

8. The final properties to set are to specify the single output file. To do this, set the following properties for the **PDF: Merge documents** action on line **9**:

Output file path: C:\Hands-On-RPA-with-AA-Sample-Data\Chapter14_
GamesMerged.pdf

Overwrite existing file: *Checked*

The properties should look as in the following screenshot:

PDF: Merge documents

Output file path

> 🔳 C:\Hands-On-RPA-with-AA-Sample-Data\Chapter14_GamesMerged.pdf (x)   Browse...

Required extension: ".pdf"
e.g. C:\Users\Admin\Test.pdf

☑ Overwrite existing file

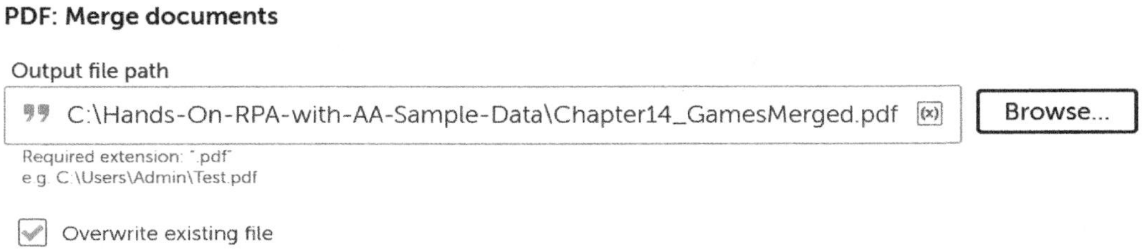

Figure 14.22 – PDF: Merge documents – output file properties

9. Click on **Save**. The development interface for this section should look as in the following screenshot:

| 8 | 🟦 **Comment** "------- Merge Files" | ⋮ |
| 9 | 📄 **PDF: Merge documents** into "C:\Hands-On-RPA-with-AA-Sample-Data\Chapter14_G... | ⋮ |

Figure 14.23 – Development interface

You are once again ready to test your bot. When your bot has finished, you should notice that a new PDF file, called `Chapter14_GamesMerged.pdf`, has been generated. This file is the result of all eight `GamesSplit` files being merged into a single file.

Fantastic work, you should now be able to confidently split and merge PDF documents. In the next section, we will take a look at PDF file security, specifically the encryption and decryption of files.

Encrypting and decrypting documents

Encrypted PDF files are widely used to protect sensitive data. Having the ability to automate encryption and decryption can be a key feature to aid automating manual tasks. In the following section, you will learn how to encrypt and decrypt PDF files using RPA. For this walk-through, we will be using the existing `Chapter14_Games.pdf` file from the GitHub repository.

Encrypting a PDF file

We will use our `Chapter14_Games.pdf` file and apply encryption to this document. Automation Anywhere allows you to apply one of the industry-standard encryption algorithms from RC4 40-bit, RC4 128-bit, or AES 128-bit. Like always, let's begin by adding our comments.

Let's start this walk-through by executing the following steps:

1. Add a new **Comment** action just below line **9**, " - - - - - - - Encrypt PDF File ", and click on **Save**.

2. To encrypt our PDF file, add the **PDF: Encrypt document** action just below line **10** so that you can start to set the properties.

3. Firstly, we need to specify the PDF file that will be used. To do this, set the following property for the **PDF: Encrypt document** action on line **11**:

   PDF path: Desktop file – C:\Hands-On-RPA-with-AA-Sample-Data\ Chapter14_Games.pdf

   The property should look as in the following screenshot:

PDF: Encrypt document

Figure 14.24 – PDF: Encrypt document – file property

4. Click on **Save**.

5. Next, we need to specify the password. There is an option of applying up to two passwords for your document. This includes a user password and an owner password. At least one of these must be set. We will apply a password to the **User password** property. To do this, set the following property for the **PDF: Encrypt document** action on line **11**:

   User password (optional): Insecure string – Password

   The property should look as in the following screenshot:

PDF: Encrypt document

User password (optional)

| Credential | Variable | Insecure string |

> 🔅 Password   [(x)]

Owner password (optional)

| Credential | Variable | Insecure string |

| | Pick... |

At least one password out of user password field and owner password
field needs to be added.

Figure 14.25 – PDF: Encrypt document – password properties

6. Click on **Save**.

7. Next, we need to specify which permissions the password applies to; for this
    example, we will apply permissions to all. To do this, set the following property for
    the **PDF: Encrypt document** action on line **11**:

    User Permissions to Apply: *Check all options*

    The property should look as in the following screenshot:

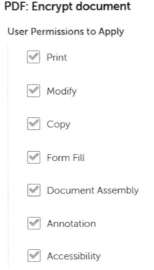

PDF: Encrypt document

User Permissions to Apply

☑ Print

☑ Modify

☑ Copy

☑ Form Fill

☑ Document Assembly

☑ Annotation

☑ Accessibility

Figure 14.26 – PDF: Encrypt document – permissions properties

8. Click on **Save**.

9. Now, we need to specify the level of encryption we want. For this example, we will apply RC4 128-bit encryption. To apply this to all, set the following property for the **PDF: Encrypt document** action on line **11**:

Encryption level: **AES 128-bit**

The property should look as in the following screenshot:

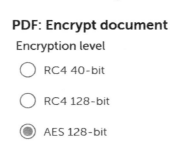

Figure 14.27 – PDF: Encrypt document – encryption type properties

10. Click on **Save**.

11. Finally, we need to specify the filename of the encrypted output file. To do this, set the following properties for the **PDF: Encrypt document** action on line **11**:

Save encrypted PDF as: C:\Hands-On-RPA-with-AA-Sample-Data\ Chapter14_GamesEncrypt.pdf

Overwrite files with the same name: *Checked*

The properties should look as in the following screenshot:

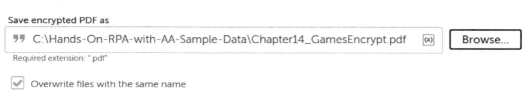

Figure 14.28 – PDF: Encrypt document – output file properties

12. Click on **Save**. The development interface for this section should look as in the following screenshot:

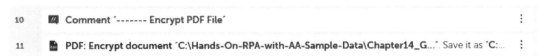

| 10 | 📝 Comment "------- Encrypt PDF File" | ⋮ |
| 11 | 📄 PDF: Encrypt document "C:\Hands-On-RPA-with-AA-Sample-Data\Chapter14_G...". Save it as "C:... | ⋮ |

Figure 14.29 – Development interface

Go ahead and run the bot. The bot will generate a file named `Chapter14_ GamesEncrypt.pdf`, which is password protected and encrypted. Try to open this file. It should prompt you for a password. We have set this to be `Password`. This leads us to the next section, where you will learn how to decrypt a PDF file.

Decrypting PDF files

We will continue with the bot by configuring it to decrypt a PDF file. It's quite handy that in the previous section an encrypted file was created. We can use this as our source file to decrypt. Like always, let's begin by adding our comments:

1. Add a new **Comment** action just below line **11**, "`------- Decrypt PDF File`", and click on **Save**.

2. To decrypt the encrypted `Chapter14_GamesEncrypt.pdf` file, add the **PDF: Decrypt document** action just below line **12** so that you can start to set the properties.

3. Firstly, we need to specify the PDF file that will be used. To do this, set the following property for the **PDF: Decrypt document** action on line **13**:

   PDF path: Desktop file – `C:\Hands-On-RPA-with-AA-Sample-Data\ Chapter14_GamesEncrypt.pdf`

   The property should look as in the following screenshot:

PDF: Decrypt document

Decrypts a PDF file.

PDF path

| Control Room file | Desktop file | Variable |

> C:\Hands-On-RPA-with-AA-Sample-Data\Chapter14_GamesEncrypt.pdf [x]   Browse...

Required extension: ".pdf"

Figure 14.30 – PDF: Decrypt document – file property

4. Click on **Save**.

5. Next, we need to specify the password. In the previous section, we set the password to be `Password`. To set this for decryption, set the following property for the **PDF: Decrypt document** action on line **13**:

    User/Owner password (optional): **Insecure string** – `Password`

    The property should look as in the following screenshot:

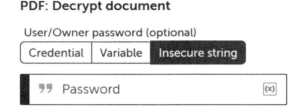

Figure 14.31 – PDF: Decrypt document – password properties

6. Click on **Save**.

7. Finally, we need to specify the output decrypted filename. To do this to all, set the following properties for the **PDF: Decrypt document** action on line **13**:

    Save the decrypted PDF as: `C:\Hands-On-RPA-with-AA-Sample-Data\Chapter14_GamesDecrypt.pdf`

    Overwrite files with the same name: *Checked*

    The properties should look as in the following screenshot:

Figure 14.32 – PDF: Decrypt document – output file properties

8. Click on **Save**. The development interface for this section should look as in the following screenshot:

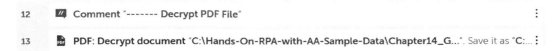

Figure 14.33 – Development interface

You have successfully configured your bot to decrypt a PDF encrypted file. Run the bot and you will notice a new file created named `Chapter14_GamesDecrypt.pdf`. This file is now decrypted. If you try and open it, it should just open without asking for any passwords.

One other thing to learn about the automation of PDF documents is that there may be instances where you need actual document properties. We will explore how to get these in the next section when we look at the PDF dictionary.

Using the PDF dictionary

As you have been progressing through the walk-throughs, you may have noticed an additional property at the bottom of the properties pane for all the actions referring to the `Dictionary` variable. Automation Anywhere has a pre-built `Dictionary` type variable for PDF documents. For each PDF document your bot reads, the `Dictionary` variable will store the following information:

Key	Value
pdfTitle	Document Title
pdfFilename	Document Filename
pdfSubject	Document Subject
pdfAuthor	Document Author

Figure 14.34 – PDF dictionary

In the following walk-through, you will modify the last **PDF: Decrypt document** action on line **13** to assign the dictionary details to a newly created variable. We can then use a message box to see the document properties.

Let's start this walk-through by executing the following steps:

1. Firstly, we need a `Dictionary` type variable to store the information. Create a `Dictionary` type variable called `dctPDF` and set **Type** to be **Dictionary** and **Subtype** to be **String**, as follows:

Figure 14.35 – Creating a Dictionary variable type

2. To assign the file properties to our newly created `Dictionary` variable called `dctPDF`, set the following property for the **PDF: Decrypt document** action on line **13**:

    Assign PDF properties to a dictionary variable (optional): dctPDF – Dictionary of Strings

The properties should look as in the following screenshot:

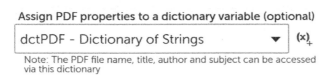

PDF: Decrypt document

Assign PDF properties to a dictionary variable (optional)

dctPDF - Dictionary of Strings   ▼ | (x)₊

Note: The PDF file name, title, author and subject can be accessed via this dictionary

Figure 14.36 – Assigning the PDF dictionary to variable

3. Click on **Save**.

4. To view the assigned values, add a **Message box** action just below line **13**.

5. For the **Message box** action on line **14**, set the following properties:

Enter the message box window title: PDF Dictionary

Enter the message to display: Title: |$dctPDF{pdfTitle}$|

Filename: |$dctPDF{pdfFilename}$|

Subject: |$dctPDF{pdfSubject}$|

Author: |$dctPDF{pdfAuthor}$|

The properties should look as in the following screenshot:

Message box

Displays a message box

Enter the message box window title

🔊 PDF Dictionary   [(x)]

Enter the message to display

🔊 Title: |$dctPDF{pdfTitle}$|
Filename: |$dctPDF{pdfFilename}$|
Subject: |$dctPDF{pdfSubject}$|
Author: |$dctPDF{pdfAuthor}$| [(x)]

Figure 14.37 – Message box properties

6. Click on **Save**. The complete development interface for this chapter should look as in the following screenshot:

Figure 14.38 – Development interface

7. When you are ready, please run the bot. The bot will now display a message box containing the document properties. It should look as in the following screenshot:

Figure 14.39 – Output message box

Great work! You can see all the property information that the bot has extracted from the file. The dictionary can be applied to all the PDF actions we have worked with, such as extracting text and images, merging and splitting files, and encrypting files.

Summary

In this chapter, you have learned how to add automation to your PDF-related tasks. The walk-throughs have enabled you to build a bot that performs many actions against PDF documents. This has included extracting text and images from PDF documents, as well as splitting and merging multiple documents. This chapter also demonstrated how to encrypt and decrypt files and how to get access to the document properties by using a `Dictionary` type variable.

In the next chapter, we will continue working with applications and automation. You will learn how to use RPA to help automate database-related manual tasks. You will also learn about connecting to databases. The walk-throughs will also explore how to perform SQL against databases, including `Insert` and `Delete` statements.

15
Working with Databases

In the preceding chapter, you learned how to include PDF tasks as part of your automation scope. Through the use of walk-throughs, you learned how to extract text and images from PDF documents. The chapter also included splitting and merging multiple documents into a single PDF file. We finished off the chapter with an explanation of how to encrypt and decrypt documents as well as how to use the `Dictionary` variable to get file properties.

In this chapter, you will learn all about automating tasks using databases. We will explore how to connect to different types of databases such as Access, SQL, and Oracle. We will also look at using connection strings to connect to data sources. The walk-throughs will guide you on how to work with your datasets. This will include reading, updating, inserting, and deleting your data. You will also learn how to execute SQL `Select` statements against your databases.

In this chapter, we will be using the following packages:

Figure 15.1 – Packages used in this chapter

The walk-throughs in this chapter will consist of demonstrating the different actions within the **Database** package. We will be using some files from the GitHub repository, which is part of the technical requirements. A sample each of the Access and SQLite databases are included in the GitHub repository and both are used as part of the walk-throughs. It is assumed that you already have a basic understanding of databases and SQL statements. You will learn how to configure an RPA bot to execute these statements.

In this chapter, we will cover the following topics:

- Connecting to, and disconnecting from, databases

- Reading data from databases

- Updating databases

Technical requirements

In order to install Automation Anywhere, the following are required:

- Windows OS version 7 or higher

- A processor with a minimum speed of 3 GHz

- A minimum of 4 GB RAM

- At least 100 MB of hard disk space

- Internet Explorer v10 or higher OR Chrome v49 or higher

- A minimum screen resolution of 1024*768

- An internet connection with a minimum speed of 10 Mb/sec

- Completed registration with Automation Anywhere A2019 Community Edition

- Successful logon to Automation Anywhere A2019 Community Edition

- Successful registration of a local device
- The successful downloading of sample data from GitHub
- An installed SQL or Oracle server (optional)
- Microsoft Access installed (optional)

Connecting to, and disconnecting from, databases

When working with databases, the first thing you would do with most development platforms is to establish a connection with the database. There are many types of databases that are used, the most widely used being the following:

- SQL or Oracle
- SQLite
- MS Access

A connection to all of these database types can be established using a **connection string**, which is also quite often used for bespoke or propriety databases. Automation Anywhere is designed to connect to the most common database types by just providing the key connection details, such as the server/database name and user credentials. It also provides the means to connect via a connection string. This removes any restrictions, allowing you to connect to any type of database for your automation needs.

As with most connections in Automation Anywhere, it uses a session to identify each connection. The **Database: Connect** action is used to create a database session. As with all sessions, they need to be closed once they are no longer required. With databases, a session is closed using the **Database: Disconnect** action. In the following walk-throughs, you will learn how to connect to the different types of databases and create a session. In particular, you will learn how to do the following:

- Connect to a SQL/Oracle database
- Connect to a SQLite database
- Connect to an Access database
- Connect using a connection string

As we have done previously, we will be using comments and steps to help structure all the actions. We will begin by building the initial skeleton using comments and steps:

Let's start this walk-through by performing the following steps:

1. Log in to **Control Room**.

2. Create a new bot and call it Chapter15 - Database Automation in the \Bot\ folder.

3. Add a new **Comment** action as "- - - - - - - - - - - - - - - - - - - -" on line **1** and click on **Save**.

4. Add a **Step** just below line **1**, set the **Title** property as "Connecting to Databases", and then click on **Save**.

5. Add another **Step** just below line **2**, ensuring it is within the **Step** on line **2**, set the **Title** property as "Connecting to a SQL/Oracle Database", and then click on **Save**.

6. Add another **Step** just below line **3**, ensuring it is within the **Step** on line **2**, set the **Title** property as "Connecting to a SQLite Database", and then click on **Save**.

7. Add another **Step** just below line **4**, ensuring it is within the **Step** on line **2**, set the **Title** property as "Connecting to MS Access", and then click on **Save**.

8. Add another **Step** just below line **5**, ensuring it is within the **Step** on line **2**, set the **Title** property as "Connect using Connection String", and then click on **Save**.

9. Add a new **Comment** action as "- - - - - - - - - - - - - - - - - - - -" on line **7** and click on **Save**. Your initial development interface should look like the following screenshot:

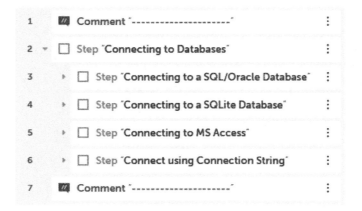

Figure 15.2 – Development interface

That's great! We now have a structure for our walk-through. The first connection we will look at is SQL and Oracle databases.

Connecting to a SQL/Oracle database

Two of the most popular enterprise-level database systems used are SQL Server and Oracle. As a system developer, you quite regularly need to build functionality that manipulates data stored on these databases. For SQL Server and Oracle, a few details are needed in order to establish a connection. These are the server name, database name, username, and password. In certain cases, you may also need to know the port number. In the following walk-through, you will learn how to create a session for a SQL Server and Oracle database.

Let's start this walk-through by performing the following steps:

1. To create our database session, drag the **Database: Connect** action just below line **3**, ensuring it is within the **Step** on line **3**. You are now ready to start setting the properties.

2. Firstly, we need to specify the **Session** details. To do this, set the following properties for the **Database: Connect** action on line **4**:

   Session name: db_Session

   Connection mode: **User defined** (*Default is used for connection strings only*)

   The properties should look like the following screenshot:

Figure 15.3 – Database: Connect properties

3. Click on **Save**.

4.   The next part is to specify the type of database we wish to create the session for. To do this, set the following properties for the **Database: Connect** action on line **4** *(values used are for representation only; please use values that are your own server settings)*:

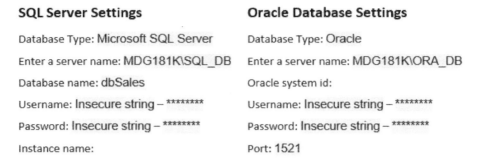

SQL Server Settings	Oracle Database Settings
Database Type: Microsoft SQL Server	Database Type: Oracle
Enter a server name: MDG181K\SQL_DB	Enter a server name: MDG181K\ORA_DB
Database name: dbSales	Oracle system id:
Username: Insecure string – ********	Username: Insecure string – ********
Password: Insecure string – ********	Password: Insecure string – ********
Instance name:	Port: 1521

Figure 15.4 – Sample database server settings

The properties should look like the following screenshot:

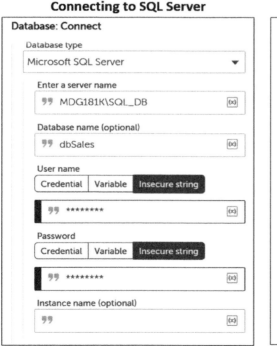

Figure 15.5 – Database: Connect – SQL/Oracle Server properties

5. Click on **Save**.

6. The session is now created. Once you have finished, you will need to disconnect from the database server. To do this, add the **Database: Disconnect** action just below line **4**, ensuring it is aligned to the **Database: Connect** action on line **4**.

7. Set the following property for the **Database: Disconnect** action on line **5**:

    Session name: db_Session

    The property should look like the following screenshot:

Figure 15.6 – Database: Disconnect property

8. Click on **Save**. Your development interface for this section should look like the following screenshot:

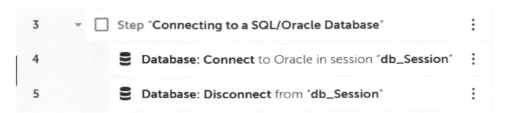

Figure 15.7 – Development interface

That's how we create a session to a SQL and Oracle database server. The example given here in the walk-through will only work when you use your own server and user credentials. If you don't have a SQL or Oracle server to connect to, you can always disable the **Step** action from line **3**. We will continue with connecting to a SQLite database in the next section. A sample SQLite database is included in the GitHub repository for the next walk-through. This database file is called Chapter15_SQLite.db.

Connecting to a SQLite database

Another lightweight database platform is **SQLite**. This is not an enterprise-level platform, but still proves to be a robust lightweight database. The following walk-through will show how to connect to a SQLite database. A sample database called `Chapter15_SQLite.db` is available as part of the GitHub repository.

Let's start this walk-through by performing the following steps:

1. To create the SQLite database session, drag the **Database: Connect** action just below line **6**, ensuring it is within the **Step** on line **6**. You are now ready to start setting the properties.

2. Firstly, we need to specify the session details. To do this, set the following properties for the **Database: Connect** action on line **7**:

   Session name: db_SqLite

   Connection mode: **User defined** (*Default is used for connection strings only*)

   The properties should look like the following screenshot:

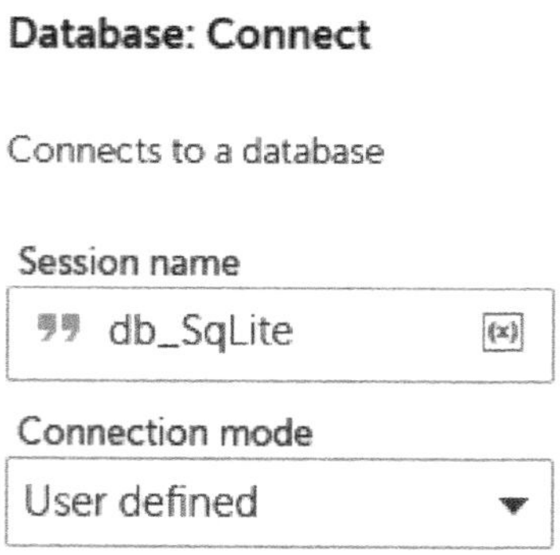

Figure 15.8 – Database: Connect properties

3. Click on **Save**.

4. The next part is to specify the type of database and location of the file. To do this, set the following properties for the **Database: Connect** action on line **7**:

   Database type: SqLite

   Database file path: Desktop file – C:\Hands-On-RPA-with-AA-Sample-Data\Chapter15_SQLite.db

   The properties should look like the following screenshot:

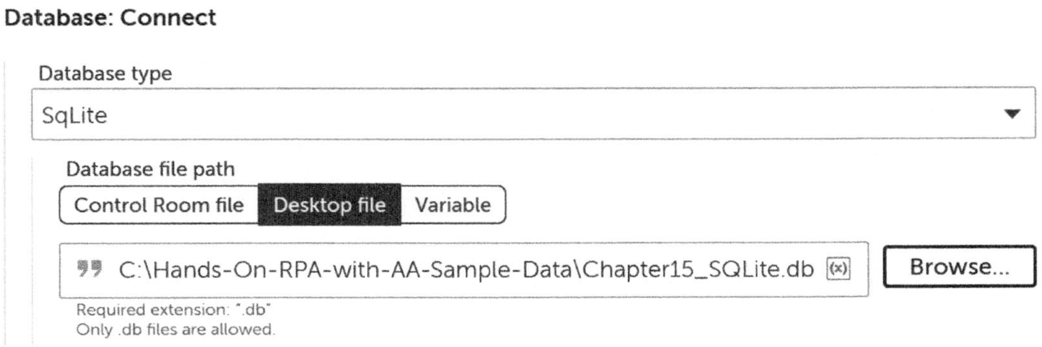

Database: Connect

Database type

SqLite	▼

Database file path

Control Room file **Desktop file** Variable

" C:\Hands-On-RPA-with-AA-Sample-Data\Chapter15_SQLite.db (x)   Browse...

Required extension: ".db"
Only .db files are allowed.

Figure 15.9 – Database: Connect – SqLite file properties

5. Click on **Save**.

6. The SQLite database session is now created. To disconnect, add the **Database: Disconnect** action just below line 7, ensuring it is aligned to the **Database: Connect** action on line **7**.

7. Set the following property for the **Database: Disconnect** action on line **8**:

    Session name: db_SqLite

    The property should look like the following screenshot:

    Database: Disconnect

    Disconnects from the database

    Session name
    " db_SqLite   (x)

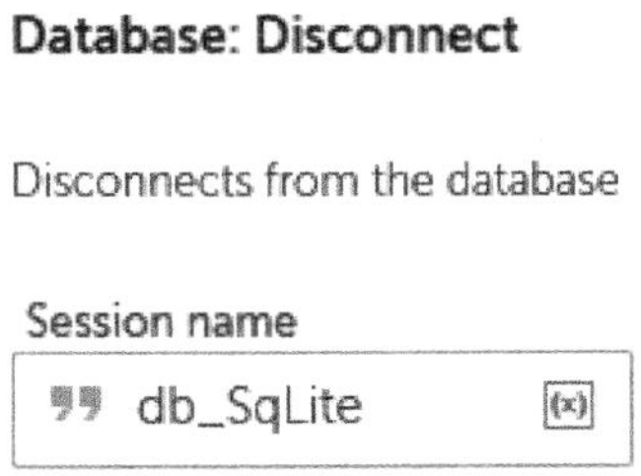

Figure 15.10 – Database: Disconnect property

8. Click on **Save**. Your development interface for this section should look like the following screenshot:

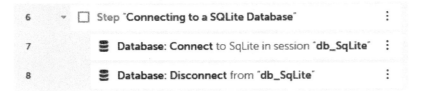

Figure 15.11 – Development interface

All done! You can run the bot to test it. It won't actually do anything visible, but we know it establishes a connection with our SQLite database and then disconnects.

Later in this chapter, you will learn how to read data after creating a session. Continuing with connecting with databases, we move on to Access databases in the next section.

Connecting to an Access database

Microsoft Access is part of the Microsoft Office suite and is a very popular database platform. A sample database, `Chapter15_Access.accdb`, is included in the GitHub repository. We will be connecting to this for the following walk-through.

Let's start this walk-through by performing the following steps:

1. To create the Access database session, drag the **Database: Connect** action just below line **9**, ensuring it is within the **Step** on line **9**. You are now ready to start setting the properties.

2. We first need to specify the session details. To do this, set the following properties for the **Database: Connect** action on line **10**:

    Session name: db_Access

    Connection mode: **User defined** (*Default is used for connection strings only*)

    The properties should look like the following screenshot:

Figure 15.12 – Database: Connect properties

3. Click on **Save**.

4. The next part is to specify the type of database and the location of the file. To do this, set the following properties for the **Database: Connect** action on line **7**:

Database type: Microsoft Access

Database file path: Desktop file – C:\Hands-On-RPA-with-AA-Sample-Data\Chapter15_Access.accdb

The properties should look like the following screenshot:

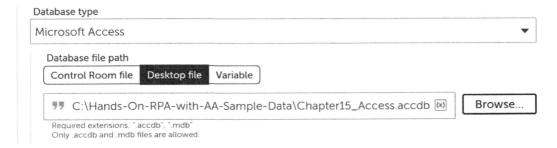

Figure 15.13 – Database: Connect – Access file properties

5. Click on **Save**.

6. We now have to add the **Database: Disconnect** action. To do this, add the **Database: Disconnect** action just below line **10**, ensuring it is aligned to the **Database: Connect** action on line **10**.

7. Set the following property for the **Database: Disconnect** action on line **11**:

Session name: db_Access

The property should look like the following screenshot:

Figure 15.14 – Database: Disconnect property

8. Click on **Save**. Your development interface for this section should look like the following screenshot:

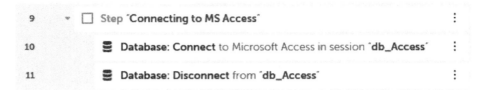

Figure 15.15 – Development interface

Now you know how easily a database connection can be established to a Microsoft Access database. In the next section, you will learn how to connect to a database using a connection string.

Connecting using a connection string

A connection string can be used to connect to all of the databases we have already looked at. It is commonly used by developers as a standard method of connecting to databases. Some bespoke and proprietary software vendors may provide a connection string to allow connectivity to a backend data store for their application.

In the next walk-through, we will use a connection string to establish a session. We will connect to an Excel worksheet using a database connection string. This also works as an alternative way to work with Excel spreadsheets. When using Excel as a database, the workbook represents the database and the worksheet represents the database tables. For this walk-through, we will use a connection string to create a session with the Chapter12_LoanData.xlsx file.

Let's start this walk-through by performing the following steps:

1. To connect using a connection string, drag the **Database: Connect** action just below line **12**, ensuring it is within the **Step** on line **12**. You are now ready to start setting the properties.

2. Firstly, we need to specify the session details. To do this, set the following properties for the **Database: Connect** action on line **13**:

    Session name: db_ConStr

    Connection mode: Default

The properties should look like the following screenshot:

Figure 15.16 – Database: Connect properties

3. Click on **Save**.

4. The next part is to specify the connection string. To create a connection to the Chapter12_LoanData.xlsx file, we will need to add this within the connection string. To do this, set the following property for the **Database: Connect** action on line **13**:

    Connection string: Provider=Microsoft.ACE.OLEDB.12.0;Data Source=C:\Hands-On-RPA-with-AA-Sample-Data\Chapter12_ LoanData.xlsx;Extended Properties="Excel 12.0 Xml;HDR=YES;IMEX=1";

    The property should look like the following screenshot:

Figure 15.17 – Database: Connect – Connection string property

5. Click on **Save**.

6. We now have to add the **Database: Disconnect** action. To do this, add the **Database: Disconnect** action just below line **13**, ensuring it is aligned to the **Database: Connect** action on line **13**.

7. Set the following property for the **Database: Disconnect** action on line **14**:

    Session name: db_ConStr

The property should look like the following screenshot:

Figure 15.18 – Database: Disconnect property

8. Click on **Save**. Your development interface for this section should look like the following screenshot:

Figure 15.19 – Development interface

Great work! You should now feel comfortable with establishing a database connection to different types of databases. Once we have created a session, we want to work with the data from our database. In the next section, you will learn how to read data from databases.

Reading data from databases

Naturally, the next stage is to access the data from our database. In this section, you will learn how to execute a SQL `Select` statement to retrieve data. A `Select` statement is commonly used among most databases.

Before we move on to the next section, let's disable our actions from the previous section. To do this, just click on the three dots on line **2**, select the **Disable** action, and then click on **Save**. This is designed to ensure that it doesn't interfere as we proceed with reading the data.

To read data, we will need to create a `Record` type variable to store each record. In the following walk-through, you will run an aggregated `Select` statement against the sample Microsoft Access database in the GitHub repository. This Access database has a table called `tblSales`, and the structure of the table is shown in the following screenshot:

Field Name	Data Type
ID	AutoNumber
Country	Short Text
Item Type	Short Text
Sales Channel	Short Text
Order Priority	Short Text
Order Date	Date/Time
Order ID	Number
Ship Date	Date/Time
Units Sold	Number
Unit Price	Currency
Unit Cost	Currency
Total Revenue	Currency
Total Cost	Currency
Total Profit	Currency

Figure 15.20 – Access database – table structure

For this walk-through, we will configure our bot to do the following:

- `Group by` the `Item Type` field
- `Count` the total `Item Type` records for each group
- `Sum` the `Units Sold` values for each group
- `Sum` the `Total Profit` values for each group

To achieve this, we will run the following SQL statement:

```
SELECT [Item Type] As Type, Count([Item Type]) as Orders,
Sum([Units Sold]) as Quantity, Sum([Total Profit]) as Profit
FROM tblSales GROUP BY [Item Type] ORDER BY [Item Type]
```

The bot will run the statement and retrieve the results in a CSV file as well as displaying a **Message box** for each record returned.

Let's start this walk-through by performing the following steps:

1. To keep our bot organized, let's begin by adding a new **Step** just below line **14** and setting the **Title** property to **Reading from Databases**.

2. Keeping up with tidy scene, it would make sense to collapse the **Step** in line **2**. Your development interface should look like the following screenshot:

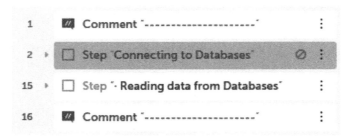

Figure 15.21 – Development interface

3. Click on **Save**.

4. As we will be reading records, we will need a Record type variable. Create a Record type variable and call it recData.

5. We are now ready to create our connection. Drag the **Database: Connect** action just below line **15**, ensuring it is within the **Step** on line **15**.

6. To create our connection, set the following properties for the **Database: Connect** action on line **16**:

Session name: db_Access

Connection mode: User defined

Database type: Microsoft Access

Database file path: Desktop file – C:\Hands-On-RPA-with-AA-Sample-Data\Chapter15_Access.accdb

The properties should look like the following screenshot:

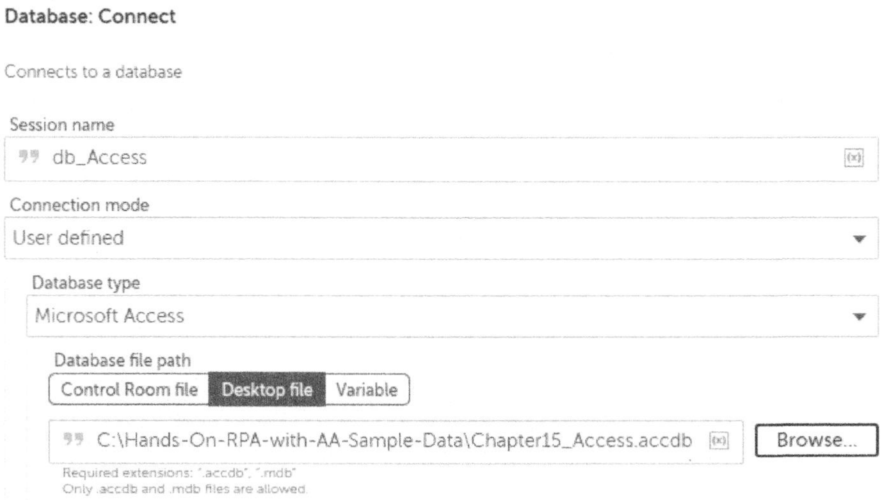

Database: Connect

Connects to a database

Session name

" db_Access

Connection mode

User defined   ▼

Database type

Microsoft Access   ▼

Database file path

Control Room file | **Desktop file** | Variable

" C:\Hands-On-RPA-with-AA-Sample-Data\Chapter15_Access.accdb [x] | Browse...

Required extensions: ".accdb", ".mdb"
Only .accdb and .mdb files are allowed.

Figure 15.22 – Database: Connect – Access connection properties

7. Click on **Save**.

8. Next, we add the action to read the data using the SQL statement and send the results to a CSV file. To do this, add the **Database: Read** action just below line **16**, ensuring it is aligned to the **Database: Connect** action on line **16**.

9. Set the following properties for the **Database: Read** action on line **17**:

   Session name: db_Access

   Enter SELECT Statement: SELECT [Item Type] As Type, Count([Item Type]) as Orders, Sum([Units Sold]) as Quantity, Sum([Total Profit]) as Profit FROM tblSales GROUP BY [Item Type] ORDER BY [Item Type]

   Export data to CSV: Desktop file – C:\Hands-On-RPA-with-AA-Sample-Data\Chapter15_Sales.csv

   Export data with header: *Checked*

   When saving: Overwrite existing file

The properties should look like the following screenshot:

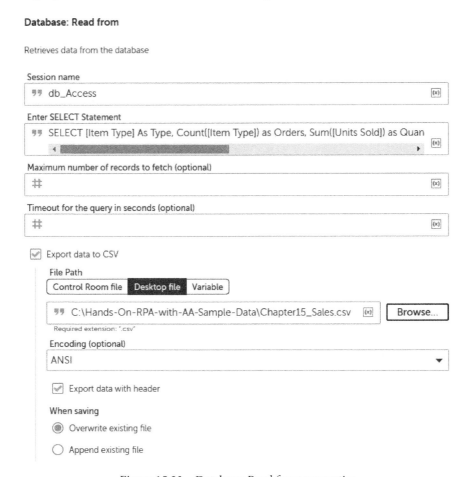

Figure 15.23 – Database: Read from properties

10. Click on **Save**.

11. At this point, the bot would have retrieved the full dataset from the SQL statement. As we want to see the data for each record, we will add a loop to iterate through our dataset. To do this, drag the **Loop** action just below line **17**, ensuring it is aligned to the **Database: Connect** action on line **16**.

12. Set the following properties for the **Loop** action on line **18**:

Loop Type: Iterator

Iterator: For each row in a SQL query dataset

Session name: db_Access

Assign the current row to this variable: recData - Record

The properties should look like the following screenshot:

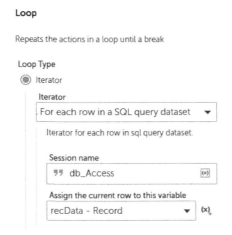

Figure 15.24 – Loop – SQL dataset properties

13. Click on **Save**.

14. We will also add a **Message box** so that we can see each record as the bot iterates through the dataset. To do this, add the **Message box** action just below line **18**, ensuring it is within the **Loop** action on line **18**.

15. Set the following properties for the **Message box** action on line **19**:

Enter the message box window title: Reading a SQL Dataset

Enter the message to display: Type: |$recData[0]$|

                    Orders: |$recData[1]$|

                    Quantity: |$recData[2]$|

                    Profit: |$recData[3]$|

Scrollbar after lines: 30 (*default value*)

Close message box after: *Checked*

Seconds: 5

The properties should look like the following screenshot:

Figure 15.25 – Message box properties

16. Click on **Save**.

17. The only action remaining is to add the **Database: Disconnect** action. To do this, add the **Database: Disconnect** action just below line **19**, ensuring it is aligned to the **Database: Connect** action on line **16** and not inside the **Loop** action on line **18**.

18. Set the following property for the **Database: Disconnect** action on line **20**:

    Session name: db_Access

The property should look like the following screenshot:

Figure 15.26 – Database: Disconnect property

19. Click on **Save**. Your development interface for this section should look like the following screenshot:

15 ▾ ☐ Step '· **Reading data from Databases'**	⋮
16 ⬚ **Database: Connect** to Microsoft Access in session "**db_Access**"	⋮
17 ⬚ **Database: Read from** database using the SQL statement "**SELECT [Item Ty**...	⋮
18 ▾ ↻ Loop : For each row in a SQL query dataset	⋮
19 🖻 **Message box** "Type: |$recData[0]$| Orders: |$recData[1]$| Quantity: |...	⋮
20 ⬚ **Database: Disconnect** from "**db_Access**"	⋮

Figure 15.27 – Development interface

That's how we retrieve and read data from a database. No matter how you have created your session, the preceding walk-through will work on all database types. Go ahead and run your bot. You should get a **Message box** for each record retrieved. A CSV file, Chapter15_Sales.csv, will also be generated with results. This output file should look like the following screenshot:

	A	B	C	D
1	Item Type	ORDERS	QUANTITY	PROFIT
2	Baby Food	7	40545	3886643.7
3	Beverages	8	56708	888047.28
4	Cereal	7	25877	2292443.43
5	Clothes	13	71260	5233334.4
6	Cosmetics	13	83718	14556048.66
7	Fruits	10	49998	120495.18
8	Household	9	44727	7412605.71
9	Meat	2	10675	610610
10	Office Supplies	12	46967	5929583.75
11	Personal Care	10	48708	1220622.48
12	Snacks	3	13637	751944.18
13	Vegetables	6	20051	1265819.63

Chapter15_Sales ⊕

Figure 15.28 – Output CSV file

Just out of curiosity, if you want to try reading data from the SQLite database or from an Excel workbook using a connection string, you can use the following connections and SQL statements to retrieve your dataset:

SQL statement to retrieve data using the Excel connection string used earlier:

```
Connection string: SELECT * FROM [Approved$$]
```
```
SQL Statement: SELECT * FROM [Approved$$]
```

The output CSV file should look like this:

	A	B	C	D	E	F	G	H	I	J	K	L	M
1	(Ref)	(Title)	(Forename)	(Surname)	(Address)	(City)	(County)	(Postcode)	(Amount)	(Term)	(Interest)	(Payable)	(Monthly)
2	Q298	Mr	John	Pince	21 Hobart !	Parkhar	Devon	EX39 5DJ	5000	24	0.034	5176.08	215.67
3	Q299	Mrs	Vannessa	Casper	45 Bradfiel	Newqua	Cornwall	TR7 1LS	3500	12	0.085	3657.12	304.76
4	Q300	Miss	Sarah	Mchughes	73 Parkfiel	Parwich	Derbyshire	DE6 1QN	7500	48	0.03	7961.76	165.87
5	Q301	Dr	David	Hawkin	30 Aughton	Norton	Staffordsh	WS11 9RH	8000	60	0.03	8616	143.6
6	Q302	Mr	Roger	Day	7 Richmonc	Hilton	Aberdeens	AB24 2RR	4000	36	0.085	4524.48	125.68

Figure 15.29 – Output CSV file using the Excel connection string

SQL statement to retrieve data from the sample SQLite database:

```
Connection string: SqLite Database - Chapter15_SQLite.db
```
```
SQL Statement: SELECT * FROM playlists
```

The output CSV file should look like this:

	A	B
1	PlaylistId	Name
2	1	Music
3	2	Movies
4	3	TV Shows
5	4	Audiobooks
6	5	90's Music
7	6	Audiobooks
8	7	Movies
9	8	Music
10	9	Music Videos
11	10	TV Shows
12	11	Brazilian Music
13	12	Classical
14	13	Classical 101 - Deep Cuts
15	14	Classical 101 - Next Steps
16	15	Classical 101 - The Basics
17	16	Grunge
18	17	Heavy Metal Classic
19	18	On-The-Go 1

Figure 15.30 – Output CSV file using the SqLite connection

Now that you know everything about retrieving data, let's make things more interesting. In the next section, you will learn how to run action queries against your database. This is updating records, inserting new records, and deleting records.

Updating databases

You have done a great job so far, but now we will actually start editing the data in our databases. You will learn how to execute the following types of SQL statements:

- `Insert`
- `Update`
- `Delete`

When working with databases, understanding how to update specific records, delete specific records, and append new records is essential. For the walk-throughs, we will continue working with the sample Access database. Instead of creating a connection for each statement type, it makes sense to just connect once for all of them as we're using the same database. We will begin by building the initial skeleton using the **Step** action.

Let's start this walk-through by performing the following steps:

1. Add a **Step** just below line **20**, set the **Title** property as `Updating to Databases`, and then click on **Save**.

2. Again, we will add our connection to the Access database, dragging the **Database: Connect** action just below line **21**, ensuring it is within the **Step** action on line **21**.

3. As you've done previously, set the following properties for the **Database: Connect** action on line **22**:

   Session name: `db_Access`

   Connection mode: **User defined**

   Database type: **Microsoft Access**

   Database file path: **Desktop file** – `C:\Hands-On-RPA-with-AA-Sample-Data\Chapter15_Access.accdb`

The properties should look like the following screenshot:

Figure 15.31 – Database: Connect – Access connection properties

4. Click on **Save**.

5. Add another **Step** just below line **22**, ensuring it is within the previous **Step** on line **21**, set the **Title** property as "Inserting data - INSERT Statement", and then click on **Save**.

6. Add another **Step** just below line **23**, ensuring it is aligned to the **Step** on line **23**, set the **Title** property as "Updating data - UPDATE Statement", and then click on **Save**.

7. Add another **Step** just below line **24**, ensuring it is aligned to the **Step** on line **24**, set the **Title** property as "Deleting data - DELETE Statement", and then click on **Save**.

8. Finally, add the **Database: Disconnect** action just below line **25**, ensuring it is aligned to the **Database: Connect** action on line **22** and not inside the **Step** on line **25**.

9. Set the following property for the **Database: Disconnect** action on line **26**:

Session name: db_Access

The property should look like the following screenshot:

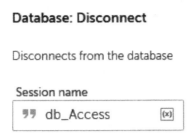

Database: Disconnect

Disconnects from the database

Session name

99 db_Access [x]

Figure 15.32 – Database: Disconnect property

10. Click on **Save**. Your development interface for this section should look like the following screenshot:

21	▾ ☐ Step "**Updating to Databases**"	⋮
22	🗄 **Database: Connect** to Microsoft Access in session "**db_Access**"	⋮
23	▸ ☐ Step "**Inserting data - INSERT Statement**"	⋮
24	▸ ☐ Step "**Updating data - UPDATE Statement**"	⋮
25	▸ ☐ Step "**Deleting data - DELETE Statement**"	⋮
26	🗄 **Database: Disconnect** from "**db_Access**"	⋮
27	📝 **Comment** "----------------------"	⋮

Figure 15.33 – Development interface

That's great! We now have a structure for our walk-through. We have a single connection and a single disconnect action. While the bot has the session open to the Access database, we can add the three different types of action statements. We will start with inserting data.

Inserting data

The Access database, Chapter15_Access.accdb, has a table called tblTypes. This table consists of all the product types sold. There is only one field in this table, called ItemType. Currently, there are 12 records in this table, as you can see:

Figure 15.34 – tblTypes table data

In the walk-through, our bot will insert a new type of product, Electrical. This will bring the total record count to 13. To insert this new record, the SQL statement would be as follows:

```
INSERT INTO tblTypes (ItemType) VALUES 'Electrical';
```

Let's start this walk-through by performing the following steps:

1. To add this Insert SQL statement, add the **Database: Insert/Update/Delete** action just below line **23**, ensuring it is inside **Step** on line **23**.

2. Set the following properties for the **Database: Insert/Update/Delete** action on line **24**:

    Session name: db_Access

    Statement: INSERT INTO tblTypes (ItemType) VALUES 'Electrical';

The properties should look like the following screenshot:

Database: Insert/Update/Delete

Executes a statement at the database

Session name

> db_Access   (x)

Statement

> INSERT INTO tblTypes (ItemType) VALUES 'Electrical';   (x)

Timeout for the query in seconds (optional)

\#   (x)

Figure 15.35 – Database: Insert/Update/Delete – Insert properties

3. Click on **Save**.

With the first SQL statement done, this will invoke the bot to add a new record in the tblTypes table. We will run the bot once all three statements are done. Let's now move on to the next one, where you will learn how to execute an **Update** SQL statement.

Updating data

For this walk-through, we will continue working with the tblTypes table. One item in the table is Fruits. We will configure our bot to update this value to Fresh Fruits. The SQL statement to apply this update would be as follows:

```
UPDATE tblTypes SET ItemType = "Fresh Fruits" WHERE ItemType =
"Fruits"
```

Let's start this walk-through by performing the following steps:

1. To add this Update SQL statement, add the **Database: Insert/Update/Delete** action just below line **25**, ensuring it is inside the **step** on line **25**.

2. Set the following properties for the **Database: Insert/Update/Delete** action on line **26**:

   Session name: db_Access

   Statement: UPDATE tblTypes SET ItemType = "Fresh Fruits" WHERE ItemType = "Fruits"

The properties should look like the following screenshot:

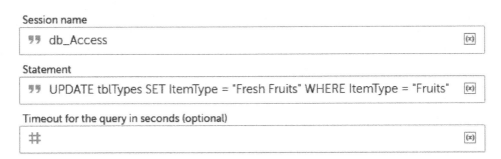

Database: Insert/Update/Delete

Executes a statement at the database

Session name

    🙿 db_Access   (x)

Statement

    🙿 UPDATE tblTypes SET ItemType = "Fresh Fruits" WHERE ItemType = "Fruits"   (x)

Timeout for the query in seconds (optional)

    #   (x)

Figure 15.36 – Database: Insert/Update/Delete – Update properties

3.   Click on **Save**.

Thus, the second SQL statement is done. This will update the Fruits value to Fresh Fruits in the tblTypes table. There is now one more SQL statement to do, and that's the Delete statement.

Deleting data

This is the final walk-through for this chapter; you will learn how to apply a Delete SQL statement. Again, we will work on the same table, tblTypes. In this example, we want the bot to delete the record where the ItemType value is Cereal. The SQL statement to apply this Delete statement would be as follows:

```
DELETE FROM tblTypes WHERE ItemType ="Cereal";
```

Let's start this walk-through by performing the following steps:

1.   To add this Delete SQL statement, add the **Database: Insert/Update/Delete** action just below line **27**, ensuring it is inside the **step** on line **27**.

2.   Set the following properties for the **Database: Insert/Update/Delete** action on line **28**:

Session name: db_Access

Statement: DELETE FROM tblTypes WHERE ItemType ="Cereal";

The properties should look like the following screenshot:

Database: Insert/Update/Delete

Executes a statement at the database

Session name

> db_Access   (x)

Statement

> DELETE FROM tblTypes WHERE ItemType ="Cereal";   (x)

Timeout for the query in seconds (optional)

(x)

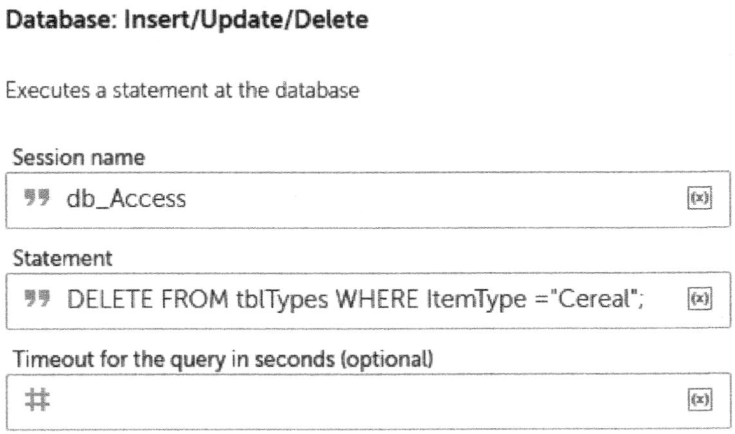

Figure 15.37 – Database: Insert/Update/Delete – Delete properties

3. Click on **Save**. The development interface for this entire section should look like the following screenshot:

21	▾ ☐ Step "Updating Databases"	⋮
22	⬓ Database: **Connect** to Microsoft Access in session "**db_Access**"	⋮
23	▾ ☐ Step "Inserting data – INSERT Statement"	⋮
24	⬓ Database: **Insert/Update/Delete** using the SQL statement "**INSERT INTO tblTypes (ItemType) VALUES 'E…**	⋮
25	▾ ☐ Step "Updating data – UPDATE Statement"	⋮
26	⬓ Database: **Insert/Update/Delete** using the SQL statement "**UPDATE tblTypes SET ItemType = "Fresh Fru…**	⋮
27	▾ ☐ Step "Deleting data – DELETE Statement"	⋮
28	⬓ Database: **Insert/Update/Delete** using the SQL statement "**DELETE FROM tblTypes WHERE ItemType =…**	⋮
29	⬓ Database: **Disconnect** from "**db_Access**"	⋮
30	▨ Comment "---------------------"	⋮

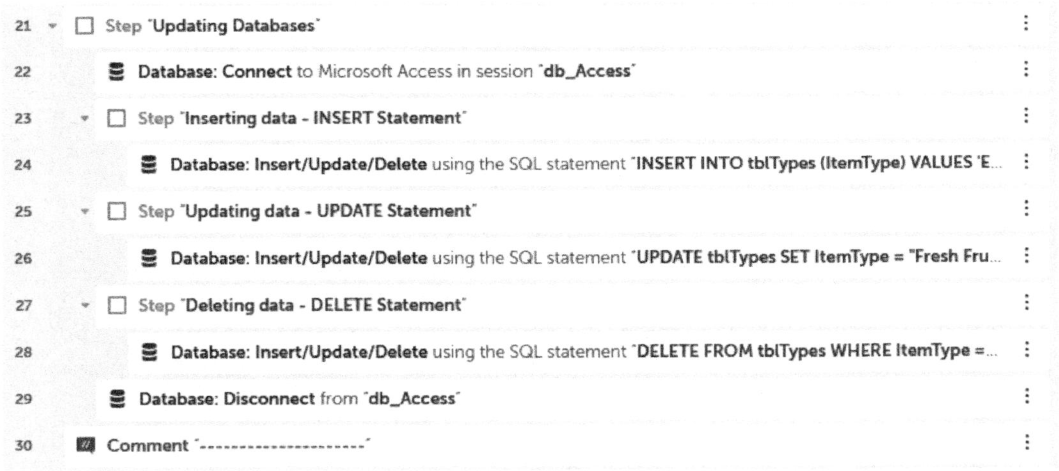

Figure 15.38 – Development interface

That's the final SQL statement! You now know how to automate all three of the SQL action queries. This will allow you to add RPA automation to your database-related manual tasks. Go ahead and run the bot. After the bot has completed, the `ItemTypes` table should be looking like this:

Figure 15.39 – tblTypes table data

You can see that a new record with the value `Electrical` has been inserted, the `Fruits` value has been updated to `Fresh Fruits`, and the record with the `Cereal` value has been deleted.

Summary

This chapter has taken you into the world of automation with databases. As you worked through the different walk-throughs, you have learned how to connect to various types of databases, including using specific connection strings. The chapter showed you how to connect to Excel as a database. Aside from connecting, you have acquired the skills needed to read, update, insert, and delete data from your databases. All this automation will help reduce the time you spend on manual tasks daily.

In the next chapter, we will move away from working with applications and start taking a look at building more efficient and robust bots. You will start by looking at how to build modular-based bots. You will learn how to create taskbots that are reusable and how to pass parameters between multiple taskbots.

16
Building Modular Bots and Sub-Tasks

The previous chapter was all about databases. It included a number of practical walk-throughs that demonstrated some of the automation actions available for your RPA projects. You learned all about connecting to databases such as SQL Server, Oracle, Access, and SQLite, and you even explored using connection strings. The skills gained there focused on reading and updating datasets from your database. Using the sample databases from the GitHub repository, the step-by-step instructions guided you on how to apply SQL `Select` statements, in particular, the `Select`, `Insert`, `Update`, and `Delete` statements.

This chapter moves away from Automation Anywhere actions and packages; here you will learn more about how to build a well-structured bot. As a good developer, you'll not only want your bot to perform its task without any issues, but you'll also want to build a bot that is easy to understand and is made up of small building blocks. This allows each block to work like a small sub-bot, making the whole thing a modular solution. The benefit of this is that as you build your library of small sub-bots, they can be reused without having to replicate the effort of building them.

For this chapter, you will be given a set process to design. We will examine this process and design an initial solution. You will then break the solution down into smaller bots that can work independently with a given set of parameters. The task itself will be working with databases and spreadsheets. All the files needed are included in the GitHub repository.

In this chapter, we will be using the following packages:

Figure 16.1 – The packages used in this chapter

The walk-throughs will take you through designing your sub-bots. This will result in building multiple bots that communicate with each other. You will also learn how to achieve this by passing parameters between them.

In this chapter, we will cover the following:

- Designing modular task bots

- Running sub-task bots

- Passing variables between main and sub-task bots

- A working example walk-through

Technical requirements

In order to install the Automation Anywhere Bot agent, you'll need the following:

- Windows operating system version 7 or higher

- A processor with a minimum speed of 3 GHz

- A minimum of 4 GB RAM

- At least 100 MB of hard disk space

- Internet Explorer v10 or higher, or Chrome v49 or higher
- A minimum screen resolution of 1,024*768
- An internet connection with a minimum speed of 10 Mb/sec
- A completed registration with Automation Anywhere A2019 Community Edition
- A successful login to Automation Anywhere A2019 Community Edition
- A successfully registered local device
- Successfully downloaded sample data from GitHub

Designing modular task bots

For this chapter, we will take a fictitious scenario where you are a bot developer tasked with building a bot. The walk-throughs will guide you from initial design to modular design right through to actually building the bot. In a nutshell, the task for your bot is this:

Extracting all the tables and data from a specific SQLite database to a new Excel workbook. The workbook should consist of a worksheet for each table in the SQLite database.

The following additional details are also given:

- The local repository location is `C:\Hands-On-RPA-with-AA-Sample-Data\`.
- The Excel spreadsheet should be named `Output.xlsx` and saved in the local repository folder. If this file already exists, it should be deleted and a new one should be created.
- The SQLite database file is available in the GitHub repository; it is named `Chapter15_SQLite.db`.
- Only the system tables should be extracted – system tables are prefixed with `sqlite_`.
- A new worksheet should be created for each table.
- Each worksheet should be named as its respective source table name.
- Only the first 20 records should be extracted for each table as this is only a prototype.

From the given specification, we have a concept of what actions the bot should perform. As we now have an understanding of databases and Excel, we can start by drafting an initial design. This should look as shown in the following figure:

1. Check if the Output.xlsx file exists.

    1. If it does, then delete the Output.xlsx file.

2. Open an Excel session with the Output.xlsx-xl_Session file.

3. Open a SQLite database session with the Chapter15_SQLite.db-db_Sqlite file.

    1. Retrieve all non-system table names from db_Sqlite to dataset-1.

        1. Loop through each table name from dataset-1.

        2. Retrieve a maximum of 20 records from current table name in dataset-1 to dataset-2.

            1. Create a new worksheet in xl_Session Excel session as current table name.

            2. Output dataset-2 to worksheet current table name.

            3. Close the db_Sqlite SQLite database session.

4. Close the xl_Session Excel session.

Figure 16.2 – Initial bot design

This design would serve its purpose and perform the task according to the specification. The drawback is that the bot would only work for the specified SQLite database. If a similar bot was needed to extract data to Excel from a different database, you would have to create a new bot. There really isn't any part of the design that could be extracted and reused without modification. If we built a skeleton of this design using Automation Anywhere with steps and comments, it would look something like this:

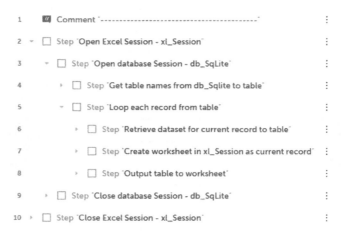

Figure 16.3 – The design template in the development interface

Taking the initial design, we can start breaking it down into smaller sub-tasks for our bot to perform. The idea is to create sub-bots that can be run from a main bot. Each sub-bot should be designed so it can be reused if needed by other bots in the future.

Looking at our scenario, we can break this down into one main task bot and three sub-bots. The three sub-task bots would perform independent tasks. These would be similar to the ones shown in the following figure:

Sub-Task Bot 1: Create a new Excel Workbook

1. Check if the output file exists.

2. If it does, then delete the output file.

    1. Create a new output file (opens a new session).

3. Close the Excel session.

Sub-Task Bot 2: Get non-system table names from SQLite database

1. Create a SQLite database session.

    1. Run a SQL statement to extract all non-system table names.

    2. Loop through each table name.

        1. Create a comma-separated string of all the extracted table names.

2. Close the database session.

Sub-Task Bot 3: Copy table data to a new worksheet

1. Create a SQLite database session.

    1. Run a SQL statement to extract data from the specified table.

    2. Create an Excel session to the specified workbook.

        1. Create new worksheet as table name.

        2. Export table data to worksheet.

    3. Close Excel session.

2. Close database session.

Figure 16.4 – Sub-task bot designs

With these three sub-task bots, our main task bot would be like the controller bot. It would run the sub-task bots in the correct order so the bot performs the complete process without any issues. The main task bot design would be as shown in the following figure:

Main-Task Bot: Export SQLite database non-system table data to Excel

1.   Run Sub-Task 1.
2.   Run Sub-Task 2.
3.   Assign comma-separated table names string to a list.
4.   Loop through table names list.
    1.   Run Sub-Task 3.

Figure 16.5 – Main task bot design

You should now have a much clearer idea of how to build modular bots. This example demonstrates how you can break a single bot into multiple smaller bots, where each bot performs a reusable task. The sub-bots are like building blocks ready to be utilized as and when needed. In the next section, we will look at how you can run these sub-task bots from within your main task bot.

Running sub-task bots

For our given scenario, the main task bot runs three sub-task bots. To run a sub-task bot from within your main task bot, you need to use the **Task Bot** package. This package contains actions such as **Pause**, **Run**, and **Stop**. The **Run** action will run another task. The configuration of this action includes the following:

- Specifying the location of the task bot

- Specifying any input variables

- Specifying the repeatable status of the task

When a sub-task is actioned, Automation Anywhere will run that task, and once it's completed, it returns back to the main task and continues from the next line. Later on in this chapter, there is a walk-through that will take you through building our bot for this scenario. You will build your sub-tasks and the main task. This will give you the practical knowledge of applying the **Task bot: Run** action. Often you will need to pass parameters to sub-tasks. In the next section, we will have a look at passing variables between main and sub-task bots.

Passing variables between main and sub-task-bots

We want each sub-task to work independently, but to do so they will need certain information. For example, the first sub-bot that creates the Excel workbook will need to know the full file path. This will allow it to delete the file if it exists and create a new one. So, the bot can perform this task for any given file path. Each sub-task can also output values; these always take the form of a `Dictionary` type variable. The name of the variable that is outputted is used as the key for this output dictionary. Whenever a variable is created, you will have noticed the **Use as input** and **Use as output** settings:

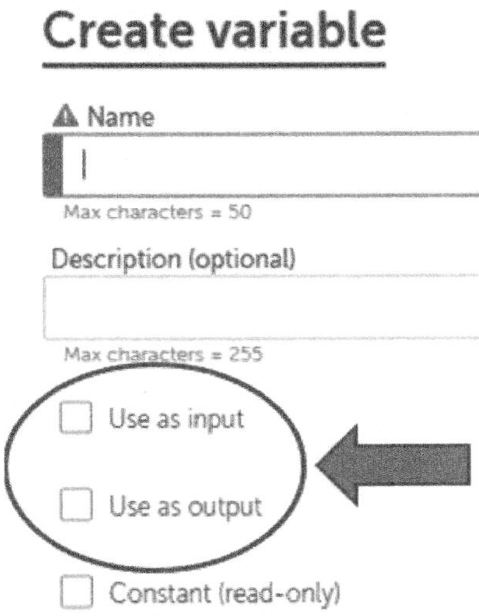

Figure 16.6 – The Use as input and Use as output settings

These settings define whether this variable will be provided as an input value and/or it will be outputted as part of the `Dictionary` variable to the calling task. The inputs and outputs for each task should be as follows.

Sub-task 1 – Create a new Excel workbook

This task will need the following inputs and outputs:

- **Inputs**: From the main task, the Excel file path as a `String` type variable – `strFile_OutputXL`

- **Outputs**: None

Sub-task 2 – Get the non-system table names from a SQLite database

This task will need the following inputs and outputs:

- **Inputs**: From the main task, the SQLite database path as a `String` type variable – `strFile_SqLiteDB`
- **Outputs**: To the main task, all the table names separated by a comma and stored as a single `String` type variable – `strTableNames`

Sub-task 3 – Copy the table data to Excel

This task will need the following inputs and outputs:

- **Inputs**: From the main task, a SQLite database path as a `String` type variable – `strFile_SqLiteDB`

  From the main task, an Excel file path as a `String` type variable – `strFile_OutputXL`

  From the main task, the maximum number of records to extract as a `Number` type variable – `numMaxRecords`

  From the main task, the table name as a `String` type variable – `strTableNames`
- **Outputs**: None

Main task – Export the SQLite database tables to Excel

This task will need the following inputs and outputs:

- **Inputs**: None
- **Outputs**: The SQLite database path as a `String` type variable – `strFile_SqLiteDB`

  The Excel file path as a `String` type variable – `strFile_OutputXL`

  The maximum number of records to extract as a `Number` type variable – `numMaxRecords`

  The table name as a `String` type variable – `strTableNames`

This clearly outlines the communication of variables between the tasks. We can see what inputs are needed for each task and what values will be outputted. We have a complete picture of what our main and sub-tasks should look like. In the next section, we can start actually building our modular bot.

Working example walk-through

You will now start building the modular task bot as described in our scenario. We have got the main and sub-bot designs to guide us. We will build four bots in total – one main task bot and three sub-task bots. For this scenario, we will use the sample `Chapter15_SQLite.db` database and will limit the records for each table to 20. Firstly, let's give our bots some names; we will name them as follows:

- `Chapter16_Sub_CreateNewExcel`
- `Chapter16_Sub_GetSqLiteTableNames`
- `Chapter16_Sub_CopySqLiteTableToExcel`
- `Chapter16_Main_SqLiteToExcel`

It always makes sense to start with the sub-tasks first. This will enable us to build the main task quickly as we bolt the smaller sub-tasks together. We will start the walk-through with the first sub-task bot, `Chapter16_Sub_CreateNewExcel`.

Building a bot – Chapter16_Sub_CreateNewExcel

This bot takes an Excel file path input and checks whether it exists. If it does, then this file is deleted and a new file is created.

Let's start this walk-through by executing the following steps:

1. Log in to **Control Room**.
2. Create a new bot and call it `Chapter16_Sub_CreateNewExcel` in the `\Bot\` folder.
3. Create a `String` type variable called `strFile_OutputXL` and set the following property:

   Use as input: *Checked*.
4. Click on **Create**.

5. Add a new **Comment** action as " - " on line **1** and click on **Save**.

6. Add a new **Comment** action as "`** Inputs: strFile_OutputXL`" on line **2** and click on **Save**.

7. Add a new **Comment** action as " - " on line **3** and click on **Save**.

8. Add a new **Comment** action as "`- - - - - - - - Check if file exists`" on line **4** and click on **Save**.

9. To check whether the Excel file exists, add the **If** action just below line **4**.

10. Set the following properties for the **If** action on line **5**:

    Condition: File exists

    File path: `$strFile_OutputXL$`

    How long you would like to wait for this condition to be true?: 0

    The properties should look as shown in the following figure:

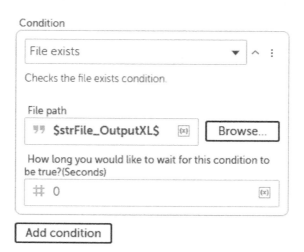

Figure 16.7 – If properties

11. Click on **Save**.

12. Add a new **Comment** action just below line **5** as "-------- Delete if file exists", ensuring that it is within the **If** action on line **5**.

13. Click on **Save**.

14. To delete the file, add the **File: Delete** action just below line **6**, ensuring that it is within the **If** action on line **5**.

15. Set the following properties for the **File: Delete** action on line **7**:

File: $strFile_OutputXL$

The properties should look as shown in the following figure:

File: Delete

Deletes a file

File

　　 🎵🎵 **$strFile_OutputXL$**　[x]　　 Browse...

e.g. C:\MyDoc*.doc

Figure 16.8 – File: Delete properties

16. Click on **Save**.

17. Add a new **Comment** action just below line **7** as "-------- Create new file", ensuring that it is not within the **If** action on line **5**.

18. Click on **Save**.

19. To create the Excel file, add the **Excel advanced: Create workbook** action just below line **8**.

20. Set the following properties for **Excel advanced: Create workbook** action on line **9**:

Session name: xl_Session

File path: $strFile_OutputXL$

The properties should look as shown in the following figure:

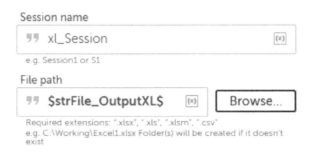

Figure 16.9 – Excel advanced: Create workbook properties

21. Click on **Save**.

22. To close the Excel session, add the **Excel advanced: Close** action just below line **9**.

23. Set the following properties for the **Excel advanced: Close** action on line **10**:

    Session name: xl_Session

    Save changes when closing file: *Checked*

The properties should look as shown in the following figure:

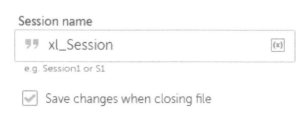

Figure 16.10 – Excel advanced: Close properties

24. Click on **Save**.

25. Add a new **Comment** action just below line **10** as " - " and click on **Save**. The development interface should look as shown in the following figure:

> ▶ Start
>
> 1   Comment "- - - - - - - - - - - - - - - - - - - -"
>
> 2   Comment "** Input: strFile_OutputXL"
>
> 3   Comment "- - - - - - - - - - - - - - - - - - - -"
>
> 4   Comment "- - - - - - - - Check if file exists"
>
> 5 ▾ ◇ If file exists at "$strFile_OutputXL$"
>
> 6   Comment "- - - - - - - - Delete if file exists"
>
> 7   File: **Delete** "$strFile_OutputXL$"
>
> 8   Comment "- - - - - - - - Create new file"
>
> 9   Excel advanced: **Create workbook** "$strFile_OutputXL$"
>
> 10 Excel advanced: **Close**
>
> 11 Comment "- - - - - - - - - - - - - - - - - - - -"
>
> ■ End

Figure 16.11 – The development interface

Great work! You have built your first sub-task bot. Whenever you need to delete an existing Excel workbook and create a new one, this bot will perform the task for you. Let's move on to the second sub-task bot for getting the table names from the SQLite database.

Building a bot – Chapter16_Sub_GetSqLiteTableNames

This bot connects to a SQLite database and then runs a SQL statement to get all the non-system table names. The statement we are using is as follows:

```
SELECT name FROM sqlite_master WHERE type='table' and name Not
Like 'sqlite%';
```

The bot will then loop through all the records, appending the value to a string while separating them with a comma. This string will be the output variable. We will begin by creating the variables and adding the comments.

Let's start this walk-through; follow the steps given here:

1. Log in to **Control Room**.

2. Create a new bot and call it `Chapter16_Sub_GetSqLiteTableNames` in the `\Bot\` folder.

3. Create a `String` type variable called `strTableNames` and set the following property:

   Use as output: *Checked*

4. Click on **Save**.

5. Create a `String` type variable called `strFile_SqLiteDB` and set the following property:

   Use as input: *Checked*

6. Click on **Save**.

7. Create a `Record` type variable called `recTableName` and click on **Save**.

8. Create a `Number` type variable called `numCounter` and click on **Save**.

9. Add a new **Comment** action as "`--------------------`" on line **1** and click on **Save**.

10. Add a new **Comment** action as "`** Inputs: strFile_SqLiteDB`" on line **2** and click on **Save**.

11. Add a new **Comment** action as "`** Outputs: strTableNames`" on line **3** and click on **Save**.

12. Add a new **Comment** action as "`--------------------`" on line **4** and click on **Save**.

13. Add a new **Comment** action as "`------- Initialize variables`" on line **5** and click on **Save**.

14. Add a new **Comment** action as "`-------- Get table names`" on line **6** and click on **Save**.

15. Add a new **Comment** action as "`------- Create comma separated string`" on line **7** and click on **Save**.

16. Add a new **Comment** action as "`--------------------`" on line **8** and click on **Save**; your initial development interface should look like the following figure:

Figure 16.12 – The development interface

17. Firstly, we must initialize the output variable by adding the **String: Assign** action just below line **5**.

18. Set the following properties for **String: Assign** action on line **6**:

    Select the source string variable(s) value (optional): *(null)*

    Select the destination string variable: strTableNames - String

    The properties should look as shown in the following figure:

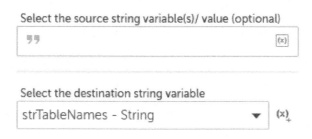

Figure 16.13 – String: Assign properties

19. Click on **Save**.

20. Next, we initialize our `numCounter` variable by adding the **Number: Assign** action just below line **6**.

21. Set the following properties for the **Number: Assign** action on line **7**:

    Select the source string variable/ value: 0

    Select the destination number variable: **numCounter - Number**

    The properties should look as shown in the following figure:

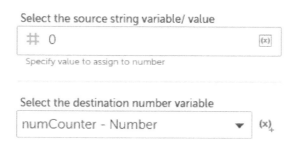

Figure 16.14 – Number: Assign properties

22. Click on **Save**. This section of the development interface should look as shown in the following figure:

Figure 16.15 – The development interface

23. Now we can start working with the SQLite database; first, to establish a connection, drag the **Database: Connect** action just below line **8**. You are now ready to start setting the properties.

24. Set the following properties for the **Database: Connect** action on line **9**:

    Session name: db_SqLite

    Connection mode: **User defined**

    Database type: **SqLite**

    Database file path: **Desktop file** – $strFile_SqLiteDB$

The properties should look as shown in the following figure:

Database: Connect

Connects to a database

Session name

    ❞❞ db_SqLite   [(x)]

Connection mode

User defined   ▼

    Database type

    SqLite   ▼

        Database file path

        | Control Room file | **Desktop file** | Variable |

            ❞❞ $strFile_SqLiteDB$ [(x)] | Browse... |

            Required extension: '.db'
            Only .db files are allowed.

Figure 16.16 – Database: Connect properties

25. Click on **Save**.

26. To run the SQL statement to get the table names, add the **Database: Read from** action just below line **9**.

27. Set the following properties for the **Database: Read from** action on line **10**:

Session name: db_SqLite

Enter SELECT Statement: SELECT name FROM sqlite_master WHERE type='table' and name Not Like 'sqlite%';

The properties should look as shown in the following figure:

Database: Read from

Retrieves data from the database

Session name

    ❞❞ db_SqLite   [(x)]

Enter SELECT Statement

    ❞❞ SELECT name FROM sqlite_master WHERE type='table' and name Not Like 'sqlite%';   [(x)]

Figure 16.17 – Database: Read from properties

28. Click on **Save**; this section of the development interface should look as shown in the following figure:

Figure 16.18 – The development interface

29. The bot needs to loop through the resulting dataset and create a comma-separated string. To do this, we start by adding the **Loop** action; drag the **Loop** action just below line **11**.

30. Set the following properties for the **Loop** action on line **12**:

    Loop Type: **Iterator**

    Iterator: **For each row in a SQL query dataset**

    Session name: db_SqLite

    Assign the current row to this variable: recTableName – Record

    The properties should look as shown in the following figure:

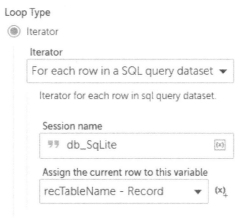

Figure 16.19 – Loop: SQL dataset properties

31. Click on **Save**.

32. As the bot is now in the **Loop** action, the counter needs to be incremented by adding the **Number: Increment** action just below line **12**, ensuring that it is within the **Loop** action on line **12**.

33. Set the following properties for the **Number: Increment** action on line **13**:

    Enter number: $numCounter$

    Enter increment value: 1

    Assign the output to variable: numCounter - Number

    The properties should look as shown in the following figure:

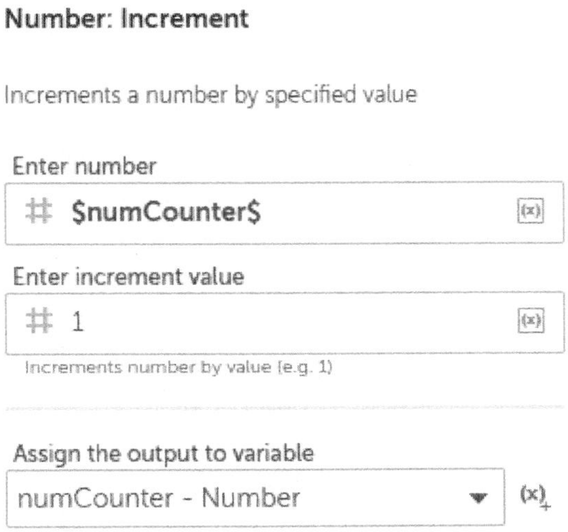

    Number: Increment

    Increments a number by specified value

    Enter number

    ⌗ **$numCounter$**   (x)

    Enter increment value

    ⌗ 1   (x)

    Increments number by value (e.g. 1)

    Assign the output to variable

    numCounter - Number   ▼   (x)₊

    Figure 16.20 – Number: Increment properties

34. Click on **Save**.

35. As we build the comma-separated string, we must ensure that no comma is added before the first value. To do this, add the **If** action just below line **13**, ensuring that it is within the **Loop** action on line **12**.

36. Set the following properties for the **If** action on line **14**:

    Condition: Number condition

    Source value: $numCounter$

    Operator: Equals to (=)

    Target value: 1

The properties should look as shown in the following figure:

Figure 16.21 – If properties

37. Click on **Save**.

38. Here, we assign the first value to the output string by adding the **String: Assign** action just below line **14**, ensuring that it is within the **If** action on line **14**.

39. Set the following properties for the **String: Assign** action on line **15**:

    Select the source string variable value: $recTableName[0]$

    Select the destination string variable: **strTableNames - String**

    The properties should look as shown in the following figure:

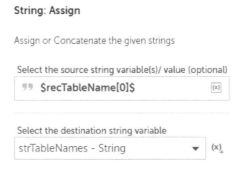

Figure 16.22 – String: Assign properties

40. Click on **Save**.

41. To add all the table names following the first record, add the **If: Else** action just below line **15**, ensuring that it is within the **If** action on line **14**, and then click on **Save**.

42. Continue to add the comma-separated values to the output string by adding the **String: Assign** action just below line **16**, ensuring that it is within the **If: Else** action on line **16**.

43. Set the following properties for the **String: Assign** action on line **17**:

    Select the source string variable value: `$strTableNames $,` `$recTableName[0]$`

    Select the destination string variable: **strTableNames - String**

    The properties should look as shown in the following figure:

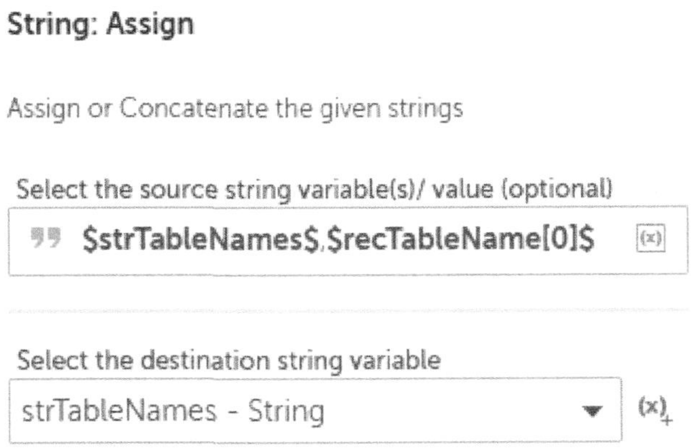

    ### String: Assign

    Assign or Concatenate the given strings

    Select the source string variable(s)/ value (optional)

    `$strTableNames$,$recTableName[0]$`   (x)

    Select the destination string variable

    strTableNames - String   ▼   (x),

    Figure 16.23 – String: Assign properties

44. Click on **Save**.

45. We can now close the session by adding the **Database: Disconnect** action just below line **17**, ensuring that it is not within the **Loop** action on line **12**.

46. Set the following properties for the **Database: Disconnect** action on line **18**:

    Session name: `db_SqLite`

The properties should look as shown in the following figure:

Database: Disconnect

Disconnects from the database

Session name

db_SqLite

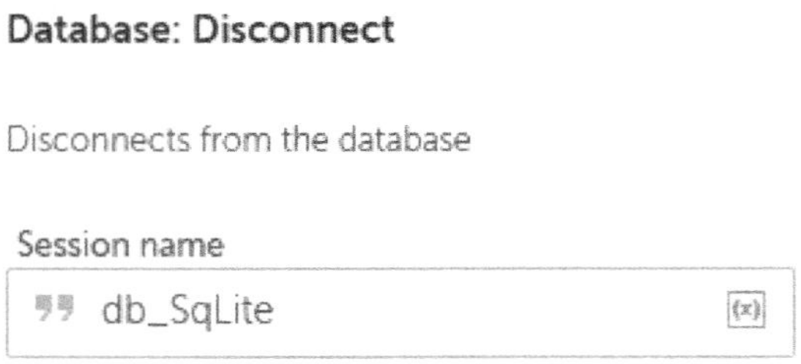

Figure 16.24 – Database: Disconnect properties

47. Click on **Save**; the development interface for this section should look as shown in the following figure:

11	Comment "--------- Create comma separated string"	⋮
12	Loop : For each row in a SQL query dataset	⋮
13	**Number: Increment $numCounter$ by 1** and assign result to a **$numCounter$** variable	⋮
14	If number **$numCounter$** Equals to(=) **1**	⋮
15	**String: Assign $recTableName[0]$ to $strTableNames$**	⋮
16	If: Else	⋮
17	**String: Assign "$strTableNames$,$recTab..." to $strTableNames$**	⋮
18	**Database: Disconnect** from "db_SqLite"	⋮
19	Comment "---------------------"	⋮

Figure 16.25 – The development interface

Good job! That's the second sub-bot built. This bot will extract all the non-system tables from any SQLite database. It just needs the database file path. The output should be a comma-separated string.

Next, we move on to the last sub-task bot; this is where the bot needs to produce the output data and file.

Building a bot – Chapter16_Sub_CopySqLiteTableToExcel

Here, the bot is given an Excel workbook, a SQLite database, and a table name. From this, the bot needs to connect to the database and extract data from the given table. It should then output all that data to a new worksheet on the given workbook. The SQL query that we will be using to get all the data is as follows:

```
Select * from $strTableName$
```

This bot will be broken down into two sections: the first will get the data, and the second will output the data. We will begin by creating the variables and adding some steps.

Let's start this walk-through by executing the following steps:

1. Log in to **Control Room**.
2. Create a new bot and call it Chapter16_Sub_CopySqLiteTableToExcel in the \Bot\ folder.
3. Create a Table type variable called tblTableData and click on **Save**.
4. Create a String type variable called strTableName and set the following property:

    Use as input: *Checked*.
5. Click on **Save**.
6. Create a String type variable called strFile_SqLiteDB and set the following property:

    Use as input: *Checked*.
7. Click on **Save**.
8. Create a String type variable called strFile_OutputXL and set the following property:

    Use as input: *Checked*.
9. Click on **Save**.
10. Create a Number type variable called numMaxRecords and set the following property:

    Use as input: *Checked*.

11. Click on **Save**.

12. Add a new **Comment** action as "`--------------------`" on line **1** and click on **Save**.

13. Add a new **Comment** action as "`** Inputs: numMaxRecords, strFile_ OutputXL, strFile_SqLiteDB, strTableName`" on line **2** and click on **Save**.

14. Add a new **Comment** action as "`--------------------`" on line **3** and click on **Save**.

15. Add a new **Comment** action as "`-------- Initialize variables`" on line **4** and click on **Save**.

16. Add a **Step** just below line **4**, set the **Title** property as **Retrieve data from table**, and click on **Save**.

17. Add another **Step** just below line **5**, set the **Title** property as **Output data to workbook**, and click on **Save**.

18. Add a new **Comment** action on line 7 as, "`-------------`" and click on **Save**; your initial development interface should look as shown in the following figure:

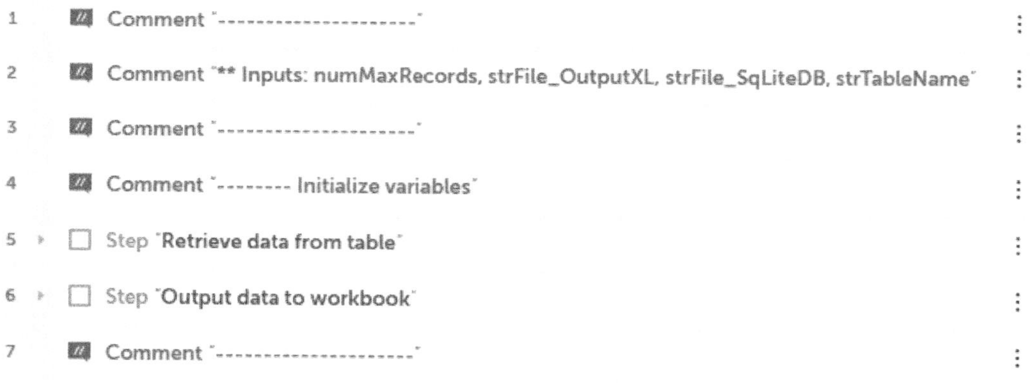

```
1      Comment "--------------------"                                              ⋮

2      Comment "** Inputs: numMaxRecords, strFile_OutputXL, strFile_SqLiteDB, strTableName"    ⋮

3      Comment "--------------------"                                              ⋮

4      Comment "-------- Initialize variables"                                     ⋮

5  ▸   Step "Retrieve data from table"                                             ⋮

6  ▸   Step "Output data to workbook"                                              ⋮

7      Comment "--------------------"                                              ⋮
```

Figure 16.26 – The development interface

19. To initialize our `Table` variable, add the **Data Table: Clear content** action just below line **4**.

20. Set the following properties for the **Data Table: Clear content** action on line **5**:

Data table name: tblTableData - Table

The properties should look as shown in the following figure:

Clears all content of the specified data table

Data table name

tblTableData - Table   ▼ (x)

Figure 16.27 – Data Table: Clear content properties

21. Click on **Save**; the development interface for this section should look as shown in the following figure:

4   Comment `-------- Initialize variables`   ⋮

5   Data Table: **Clear content** of data table $tblTableData$ ⋮

Figure 16.28 – The development interface

22. To establish the database connection, drag the **Database: Connect** action just below line **6**, ensuring that it is within the **Step** on line **6**.

23. Set the following properties for the **Database: Connect** action on line **7**:

Session name: db_SqLite

Connection mode: User defined

Database type: SqLite

Database file path: Desktop file – $strFile_SqLiteDB$

The properties should look as shown in the following figure:

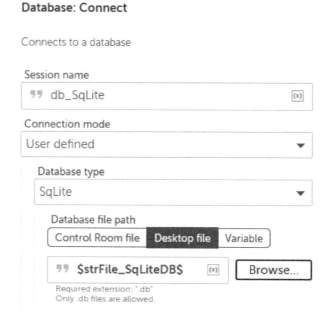

Figure 16.29 – Database: Connect properties

24. Click on **Save**.

25. Now we can configure the bot to extract the table data to a `Table` type variable. To do this, add the **Database: Export to data table** action just below line **7**, ensuring that it is within the **Step** on line **6**.

26. Set the following properties for the **Database: Export to data table** action on line **8**:

    Session name: db_SqLite

    Enter SELECT Statement: Select * from $strTableName$

    Maximum number of records to fetch (optional): $numMaxRecords$

    Assigned to: **tblTableData - Table**

The properties should look as shown in the following figure:

Database: Export to data table

Exports data from a database to a user specified data table

Session name

    　　 db_SqLite   (x)

Enter SELECT Statement

    　　 Select * from **$strTableName$**   (x)

Maximum number of records to fetch (optional)

    ⌗ **$numMaxRecords$**   (x)

Timeout for the query in seconds (optional)

    ⌗   (x)

Assigned to

    tblTableData - Table   ▼   (x)₊

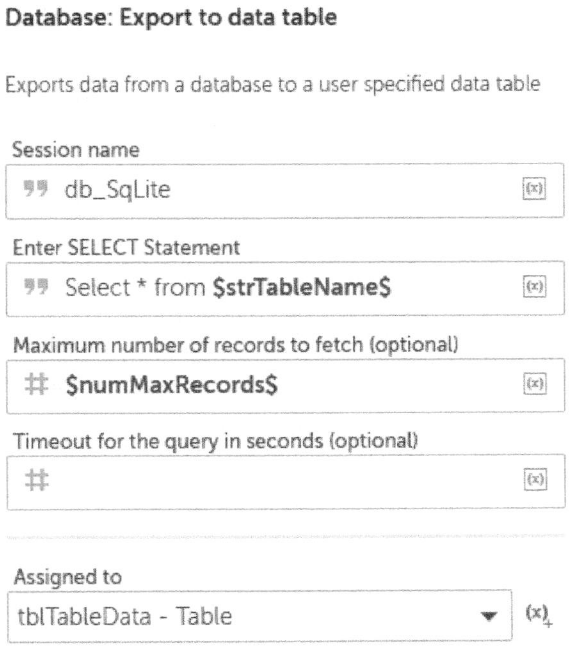

Figure 16.30 – Database: Export to data table properties

27. Now that the bot has this data assigned to a `Table` type variable, we can close the session by adding the **Database: Disconnect** action just below line **8**, ensuring that it is within the **Step** on line **6**.

28. Set the following properties for the **Database: Disconnect** action on line **9**:

Session name: db_SqLite

The properties should look as shown in the following figure:

Database: Disconnect

Disconnects from the database

Session name

    　　 db_SqLite   (x)

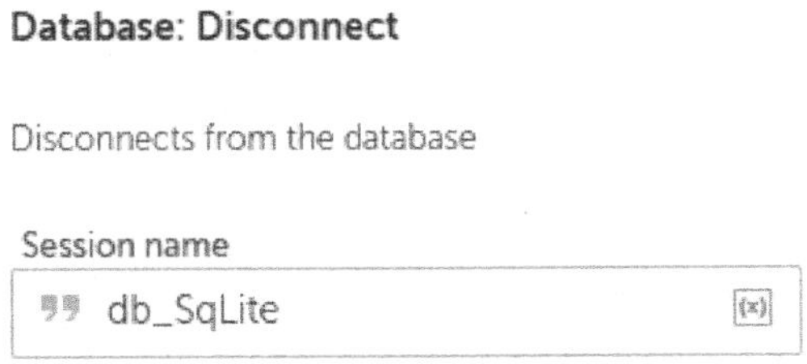

Figure 16.31 – Database: Disconnect properties

29. Click on **Save**; the development interface for this section should look as shown in the following figure:

6	▾	☐	Step "Retrieve data from table"	⋮
7		🗄	Database: **Connect** to SqLite in session "db_SqLite"	⋮
8		🗄	Database: **Export** to data table $tblTableData$ from SQL query "Select * from $strTableName$"	⋮
9		🗄	Database: **Disconnect** from "db_SqLite"	⋮

Figure 16.32 – The development interface

30. That's the first section done. We now have our dataset; to output it to our Excel workbook, we will begin by creating an Excel session. Add the **Excel advanced: Open** action just below line **10**, ensuring that it is within the **Step** on line **10**.

31. Set the following properties for the **Excel advanced: Open** action on line **11**:

    Session name: xl_Session

    File path: **Desktop file** - $strFile_OutputXL$

    Open in: **Read-write mode**

    The properties should look as shown in the following figure:

Excel advanced: Open

Opens an excel spreadsheet. This action works with xlsx, xls, xlsb, xlsm and csv files.

Session name

> 🔢 xl_Session   (x)

e.g. Session1 or S1

File path

| Control Room file | **Desktop file** | Variable |

> 🔢 $strFile_OutputXL$ (x)   Browse...

Required extensions: ".xlsx", ".xls", ".xlsm", ".xlsb", ".csv"
e.g. C:\Working\Excel1.xlsx

☐ Specific sheet name

> 🔢

e.g. Sheet1 or SHEET1

Open in

◯ Read-only mode

◉ Read-write mode

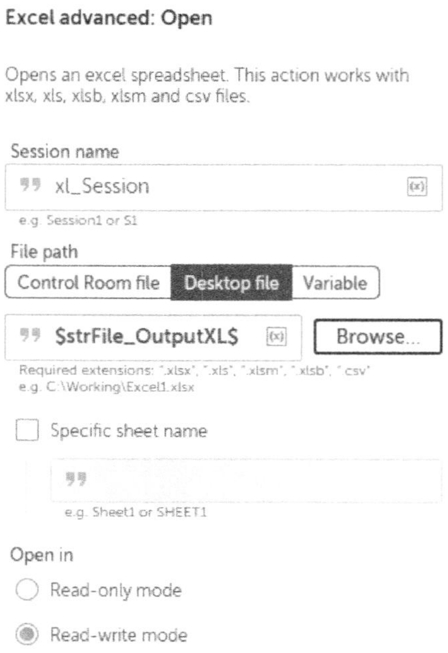

Figure 16.33 – Excel advanced: Open properties

32. Click on **Save**.

33. To create the output worksheet, add the **Excel advanced: Create worksheet** action just below line **11**, ensuring that it is within the **Step** on line **10**.

34. Set the following properties for the **Excel advanced: Create worksheet** action on line **12**:

Session name: xl_Session

Create sheet by: **Name** – $strTableName$

The properties should look as shown in the following figure:

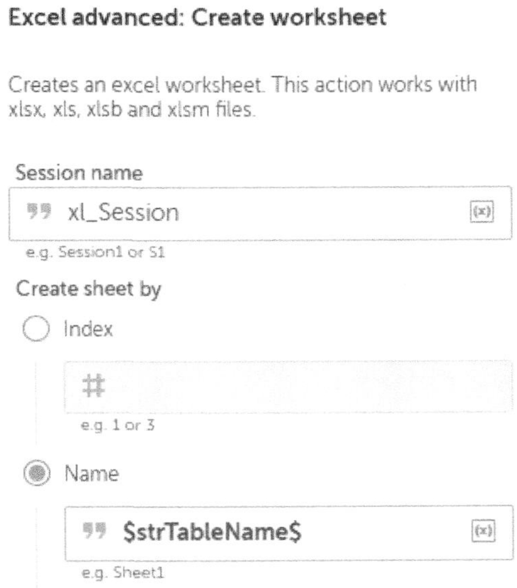

Excel advanced: Create worksheet

Creates an excel worksheet. This action works with xlsx, xls, xlsb and xlsm files.

Session name

    99 xl_Session   {x}

e.g. Session1 or S1

Create sheet by

◯ Index

    #

e.g. 1 or 3

◉ Name

    99 $strTableName$ {x}

e.g. Sheet1

Figure 16.34 – Excel advanced: Create worksheet properties

35. Click on **Save**.

36. To output the table data to this worksheet, add the **Excel advanced: Write from data table** action just below line **12**, ensuring that it is within the **Step** on line **10**.

37. Set the following properties for the **Excel advanced: Write from data table** action on line **13**:

Session name: xl_Session

Enter data table variable: **tblTableData - Table**

Enter worksheet name: **Specific worksheet** – $strTableName$

Specify the first cell: A1

The properties should look as shown in the following figure:

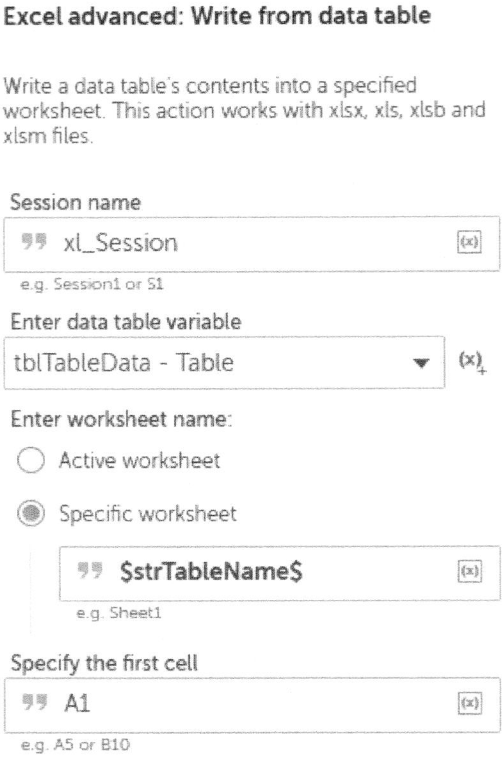

Excel advanced: Write from data table

Write a data table's contents into a specified worksheet. This action works with xlsx, xls, xlsb and xlsm files.

Session name

99 xl_Session   (x)

e.g. Session1 or S1

Enter data table variable

tblTableData - Table   ▼   (x),
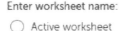

Enter worksheet name:

◯ Active worksheet

◉ Specific worksheet

    99 **$strTableName$**   (x)

    e.g. Sheet1

Specify the first cell

99 A1   (x)

e.g. A5 or B10

Figure 16.35 – Excel advanced: Write from data table properties

38. Click on **Save**.

39. Finally, we need to close the Excel session. Add the **Excel advanced: Close** action just below line **13**, ensuring that it is within the **Step** on line **10**.

40. Set the following properties for the **Excel advanced: Close** action on line **14**:

    Session name: xl_Session

    Save changes when closing file: *Checked*

The properties should look as shown in the following figure:

Excel advanced: Close

Closes an excel spreadsheet. This action works with
xlsx, xls, xlsb, xlsm and csv files.

Session name

    ⁹⁹ xl_Session   (x)

e.g. Session1 or S1

✓ Save changes when closing file

Figure 16.36 – Excel advanced: Close properties

41. Click on **Save**, the development interface for this section should look as shown in the following figure:

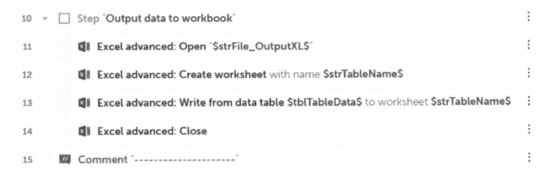

10	▼ ☐ Step "Output data to workbook"	⋮
11	Excel advanced: Open "$strFile_OutputXL$"	⋮
12	Excel advanced: Create worksheet with name $strTableName$	⋮
13	Excel advanced: Write from data table $tblTableData$ to worksheet $strTableName$	⋮
14	Excel advanced: Close	⋮
15	Comment "----------------------"	⋮

Figure 16.37 – The development interface

Awesome progress! All the sub-bots are now built. All we need to do now is to build the main bot so we can complete our bot. In the next section, you will build the main bot and run the sub-bots from within this main bot.

Building a bot – Chapter16_Main_SqLiteToExcel

You are now ready to integrate all these smaller bots to perform the overall task. We want our bot to run the first sub-bot, followed by the second sub-bot. We then need to take the output from the second sub-bot and split the comma-separated string into a list. The bot will then iterate through this list while running the third bot. You will get the practical experience of passing and receiving variables from these bots as we build. We will begin by creating the variables and adding some steps.

Let's start this walk-through by executing the following steps:

1. Log in to **Control Room**.

2. Create a new bot and call it `Chapter16_Main_SqLiteToExcel` in the `\Bot\` folder.

3. Create a `String` type variable called `strTableName` and set the following property:

   Use as output: *Checked.*

4. Click on **Save**.

5. Create a `String` type variable called `strFile_SqLiteDB` and set the following property:

   Use as output: *Checked.*

6. Click on **Save**.

7. Create a `String` type variable called `strFile_OutputXL` and set the following property:

   Use as output: *Checked.*

8. Click on **Save**.

9. Create a `Number` type variable called `numMaxRecords` and set the following property:

   Use as output: *Checked.*

10. Click on **Save**.

11. Create a `List` type variable called `lstTableNames` and click on **Save**.

12. Create a `Dictionary` type variable with a subtype of `String`, name it `dctTableNames`, and click on **Save**.

13. Add a new **Comment** action as "`--------------------`" on line **1** and click on **Save**.

14. Add a new **Comment** action as "`** outputs: numMaxRecords, strFile_OutputXL, strFile_SqLiteDB, strTableName`" on line **2** and click on Save.

15. Add a new **Comment** action as "`--------------------`" on line **3** and click on **Save**.

16. Add a new **Comment** action as "-------- Initialize variables" on line **4** and click on **Save**.

17. Add a step just below line **4**, set the **Title** property as **Create Output Workbook**, and click on **Save**.

18. Add another step just below line **5**, set the **Title** property as Get table names from SqLite database, and click on **Save**.

19. Add another step just below line **6**, set the **Title** property as Output to Excel, and click on **Save**.

20. Add a new **Comment** action as "----------------------" on line **8** and click on **Save**. Your initial development interface should look as shown in the following figure:

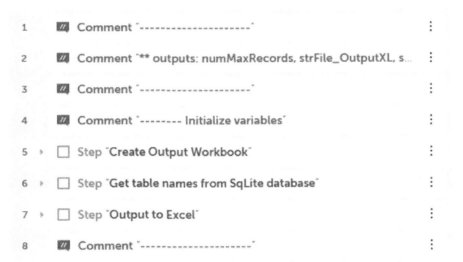

Figure 16.38 – The development interface

21. As we did before, we'll initialize the variables first. Add the **String: Assign** action just below line **4**.

22. Set the following properties for the **String: Assign** action on line **5**:

Select the source string variable value: C:\Hands-On-RPA-with-AA-Sample-Data\Chapter16_Output.xlsx

Select the destination string variable: strFile_OutputXL - String

The properties should look as shown in the following figure:

String: Assign

Assign or Concatenate the given strings

Select the source string variable(s)/ value (optional)

> C:\Hands-On-RPA-with-AA-Sample-Data\Chapter16_Output.xlsx   (x)

Select the destination string variable

strFile_OutputXL - String ▼   (x)₊

Figure 16.39 – String: Assign properties

23. Click on **Save**.

24. Continue initializing variables; add the **String: Assign** action just below line **5**.

25. Set the following properties for the **String: Assign** action on line **6**:

    Select the source string variable value: C:\Hands-On-RPA-with-AA-Sample-Data\ Chapter15_SQLite.db

    Select the destination string variable: strFile_SqLiteDB - String

The properties should look as shown in the following figure:

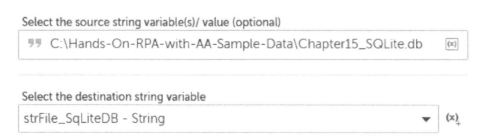

String: Assign

Assign or Concatenate the given strings

Select the source string variable(s)/ value (optional)

> C:\Hands-On-RPA-with-AA-Sample-Data\Chapter15_SQLite.db   (x)

Select the destination string variable

strFile_SqLiteDB - String ▼   (x)₊

Figure 16.40 – String: Assign properties

26. Click on **Save**.

27. Continue initializing variables; add the **Number: Assign** action just below line **6**.

28. Set the following properties for the **Number: Assign** action on line **7**:

    Select the source string variable value: 2 0

    Select the destination string variable: numMaxRecords - Number

    The properties should look as shown in the following figure:

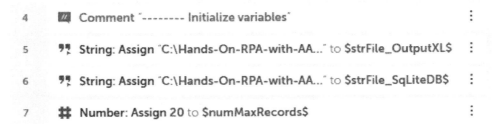

Number: Assign

Assigns user specified number to number variable

Select the source string variable/ value

| # 20 | (x) |

Specify value to assign to number

Select the destination number variable

| numMaxRecords - Number ▼ | (x)₊ |

Figure 16.41 – Number: Assign properties

29. Click on **Save**; this section of the development interface should look as shown in the following figure:

4	🖉 Comment "-------- Initialize variables"	⋮
5	🔢 String: Assign "C:\Hands-On-RPA-with-AA..." to $strFile_OutputXL$	⋮
6	🔢 String: Assign "C:\Hands-On-RPA-with-AA..." to $strFile_SqLiteDB$	⋮
7	# Number: Assign 20 to $numMaxRecords$	⋮

Figure 16.42 – The development interface

30. Now we can configure the bot to run our first sub-bot and pass the `strFile_OutputXL` variable as a parameter. To do this, add the **Task Bot: Run** action just below line **8**, ensuring that it is within the **Step** on line **8**.

31. Set the following properties for the **Task Bot: Run** action on line **9**:

    Task Bot to run: **Control Room file** – Bots\Chapter16_Sub_CreateNewExcel

    Input values: **Set strFile_OutputXL**: *Checked* - $strFile_OutputXL$

    Do not repeat: *Selected*

    The properties should look as shown in the following figure:

    Task Bot: Run

    Runs the selected task bot.

    Task Bot to run

    | Current Task Bot | Control Room file | Variable |

    Bots\Chapter16_Sub_CreateNewExcel   ✕   Browse...

    Input values

    ☑ Set strFile_OutputXL

        " $strFile_OutputXL$ (x)

    ◉ Do not repeat

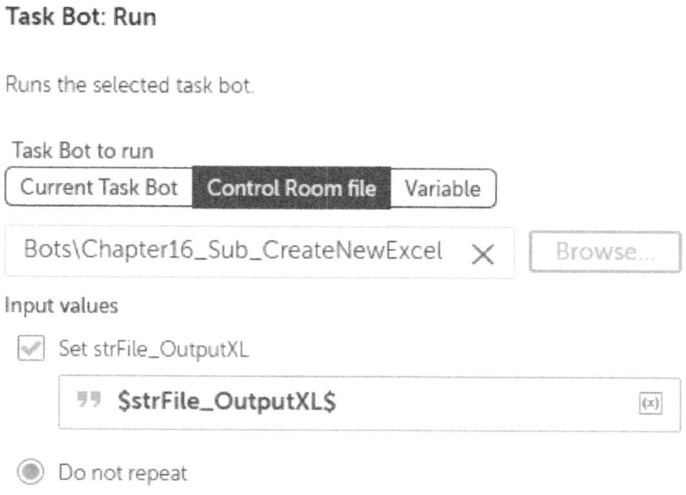

Figure 16.43 – Task Bot: Run properties

32. Click on **Save**; this section of the development interface should look as shown in the following figure:

Figure 16.44 – The development interface

33. Now it is time to call the second sub-task bot. To do this, add the **Task Bot: Run** action just below line **10**, ensuring that it is within the **Step** on line **10**.

34. Set the following properties for the **Task Bot: Run** action on line **11**:

Task Bot to run: Control Room file – Bots\Chapter16_Sub_GetSqLiteTableNames

Input values: Set strFile_SqLiteDB: *Checked* - $strFile_SqLiteDB$

Do not repeat: *Selected*

Assign the output to variable (optional): dctTableNames – Dictionary of Strings

The properties should look as shown in the following figure:

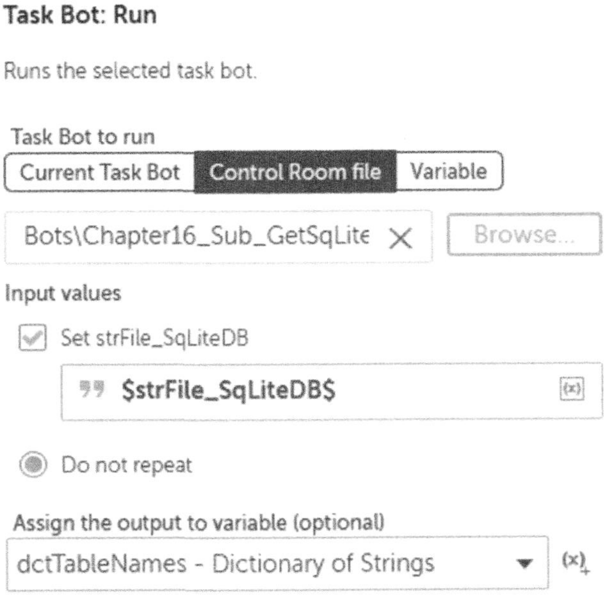

Figure 16.45 – Task Bot: Run properties

35. Click on **Save**; this section of the development interface should look as shown in the following figure:

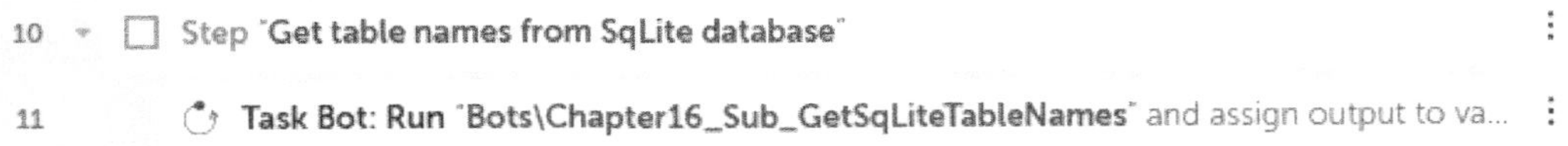

Figure 16.46 – The development interface

36. The second sub-task bot will return a comma-separated string containing the table names from our database. To process this, the string will need to be assigned to a `List` type variable; to do so, we add the **String: Split** action just below line **13**, ensuring that it is within the **Step** on line **12**.

37. Set the following properties for the **String: Split** action on line **13**:

    Source string: `$dctTableNames{strTableNames}$`

    Delimiter: `,` *(comma)*

    Delimiter is: **Not case sensitive**

    Split into substrings: **All possible**

    Assign the output to a list variable: **lstTableNames – List of Strings**

    The properties should look as shown in the following figure:

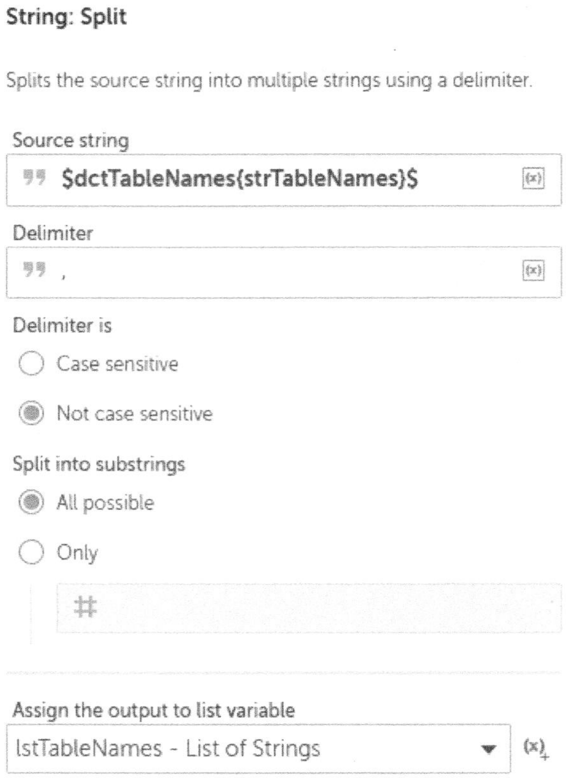

String: Split

Splits the source string into multiple strings using a delimiter.

Source string

    99 $dctTableNames{strTableNames}$ {x}

Delimiter

    99 ,   {x}

Delimiter is

○ Case sensitive

◉ Not case sensitive

Split into substrings

◉ All possible

○ Only

    #

Assign the output to list variable

    lstTableNames - List of Strings   ▼   (x)

Figure 16.47 – String: Split properties

38. Click on **Save**.

39. Next, we will loop through the table name list and pass this value with the database and output file to the final sub-task bot. To add the loop, drag the **Loop** action just below line **13**, ensuring that it is within the **Step** on line **12**.

40. Set the following properties for the **Loop** action on line **14**:

Loop Type: Iterator

Iterator: For each item in the list

List: lstTableNames - List

For: All items in the list

Assign the current value to variable: strTableName – String

The properties should look as shown in the following figure:

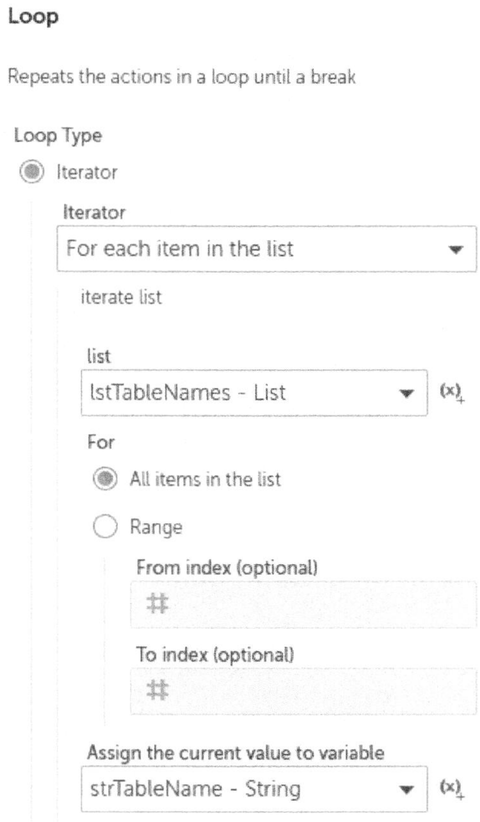

Loop

Repeats the actions in a loop until a break

Loop Type

◉ Iterator

Iterator

| For each item in the list ▼ |

iterate list

list

| lstTableNames - List ▼ | (x)

For

◉ All items in the list

◯ Range

From index (optional)

| # |

To index (optional)

| # |

Assign the current value to variable

| strTableName - String ▼ | (x)

Figure 16.48 – Loop – List properties

41. Click on **Save**.

42. To send these parameters to the final sub-task bot and run it, add the **Task Bot: Run** action just below line **14**, ensuring that it is within the loop on line **14**.

43. Set the following properties for the **Task Bot: Run** action on line **15**:

Task Bot to run: **Control Room file** – Bots\Chapter16_Sub_CopySqLiteTableToExcel

Input values: **Set strFile_OutputXL**: *Checked* – $strFile_OutputXL$

Set strFile_SqLiteDB: *Checked* – $strFile_SqLiteDB$

Set strTableName: *Checked* – $strTableName$

Set numMaxRecords: *Checked* – $numMaxRecords$

Do not repeat: *Selected*

The properties should look as shown in the following figure:

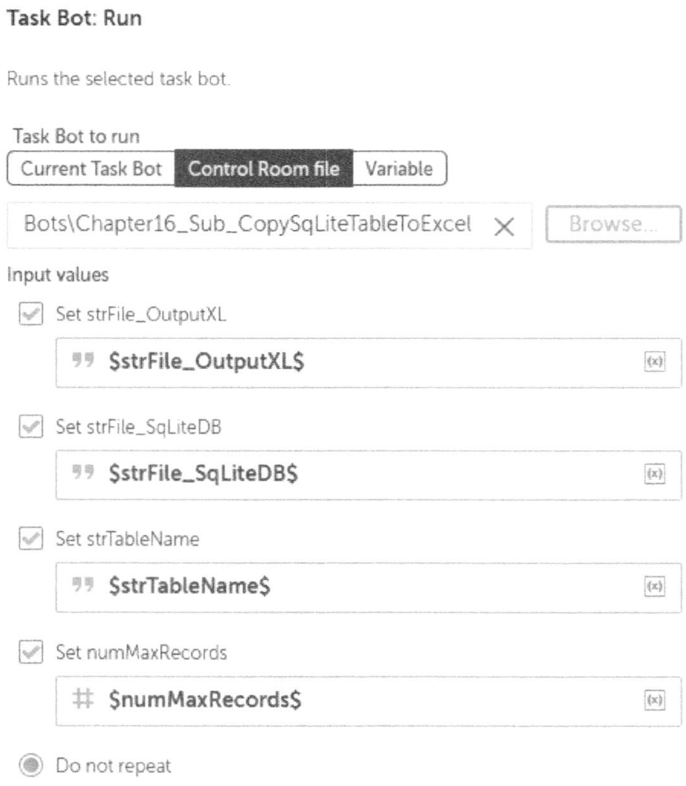

Figure 16.49 – Task Bot: Run properties

44. Click on **Save**. This section of the development interface should look as shown in the following figure:

Figure 16.50 – The development interface

Go ahead and run your main bot. It will run the sub-bots and perform the whole process, and the sub-task bots can be reused if needed. The output file should have multiple worksheets containing 20 records from each table. It should look like this:

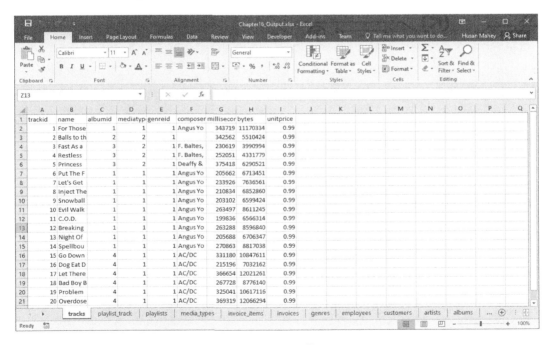

Figure 16.51 – Output file contents

That's all complete. You have done some fantastic work and have made great progress. You've just built a modular bot that runs three separate sub-task bots.

Summary

There has been a lot covered in this chapter, giving you the skills needed to understand and design modular bots. Taking this approach will be a stepping stone to having your own library of smaller sub-bots. This saves you from a lot of redevelopment effort, especially when automating larger and complete processes. You have learned how to run a sub-bot from within a bot, as well as how to pass parameters between these bots. The real-life scenario walk-through provided practical experience of how this actually works in the real world.

In the next chapter, we will be looking beyond Automation Anywhere. You will learn how to use external scripts, including VBScript and Python scripts, to enhance the functionality of your bots. You will also discover how to pass parameters between your scripts and your bot, opening up even more automation possibilities.

17
Running External Scripts

Previously, we looked at building modular bots and how to design efficient bots with reusable sub bots. The topics covered the approach to take when building modular bots, how to run sub bots from within the main bot, and also how you would pass parameters between these bots. There was also an extensive practical walk-through based on a real-life business scenario. A lot of valuable skills and experience were gained in the last chapter.

In this chapter, you will learn about how to expand on Automation Anywhere capabilities by running external components. There may be instances where you think a task cannot be easily automated using the actions available or it would take too many actions to achieve the required results. In these cases, it may prove easier to run a script such as a VBScript or a Python script. Well, Automation Anywhere allows you to run these as part of your overall RPA solution. You will learn how to run these scripts, including how to pass and receive values from them.

In this chapter, we will be using the following packages:

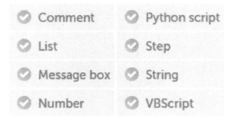

Figure 17.1 – Packages used in this chapter

We will look at the different types of scripts that can be executed as well as passing parameters. The walk-throughs will take you through each stage step by step, giving you valuable practical experience. Some sample scripts are included as part of the GitHub repository. These will be used in the walk-throughs.

In this chapter, we will cover the following:

- Running VBScripts
- Running Python scripts

For Automation Anywhere to run scripts, you have to first create a session with a script file or an inline script. Once a session is established, the script or functions can be executed. When finished, the session needs to be closed.

Technical requirements

In order to install the Automation Anywhere Bot agent, the following requirements are necessary:

- Windows operating system version 7 or higher
- A processor with a minimum speed of 3 GHz
- A minimum of 4 GB RAM
- At least 100 MB of hard disk space
- Internet Explorer v10 or higher or Chrome v49 or higher
- A minimum screen resolution of 1024*768
- An internet connection with a minimum speed of 10 Mbps
- You must have completed registration with Automation Anywhere A2019 Community Edition

- You must have logged on successfully to Automation Anywhere A2019 Community Edition
- A successfully registered local device
- Successfully downloaded sample data from GitHub
- Python version 2 or 3 installed

Running VBScripts

VBScripts are widely used by developers as they are easily written using any text editor, such as Notepad. A VBScript file will have the `.vbs` extension. This file may contain just a script or some functions and functions may return a value. Automation Anywhere allows you to import a VBScript file as well as letting you write the script inline within Automation Anywhere. You can also pass parameters to a script and receive a return value. In the next sections, you will learn all about importing a script file and inline scripting. You will also learn how to pass parameters to a script and get return values from functions. We can start the walk-through by building the outline using steps and comments.

Let's start this walk-through by executing the following steps:

1. Log in to **Control Room**.

2. Create a new bot and call it `Chapter17 - External Scripts` in the folder `\Bot\`.

3. Add a new **Comment** action as `"--------------------"` on line **1**, and click on **Save**.

4. Add a **Step** just below line **1**, set the **Title** property as `Running VbScripts`, and click on **Save**.

5. Add a new **Comment** action below line **2** as `"------ Importing a script file"`, ensuring it is within the **Step** on line **2** and click on **Save**.

6. Add a new **Comment** action below line **3** as `"------ Writing in-line scripts"`, ensuring it is within the **Step** on line **2** and click on **Save**.

7. Add a new **Comment** action below line **4** as `"------ Passing parameters"`, ensuring it is within the **Step** on line **2** and click on **Save**.

8. Add a new **Comment** action below line **5** as `"------ Returning value from functions"`, ensuring it is within the **Step** on line **2** and click on **Save**.

9. Add a new **Comment** action below line **6** as " - ",
    ensuring it is not within the **Step** on line **2** and click on **Save**. The development
    interface should look like this:

1	📄 Comment "- - - - - - - - - - - - - - - - - - - -"	⋮
2	▾ ☐ Step "Running VbScripts"	⋮
3	📄 Comment "- - - - - - Importing a script file"	⋮
4	📄 Comment "- - - - - - Writing in-line scripts"	⋮
5	📄 Comment "- - - - - - Passing parameters"	⋮
6	📄 Comment "- - - - - - Returning value from functions" ⋮
7	📄 Comment "- - - - - - - - - - - - - - - - - - - -"	⋮

Figure 17.2 – Development interface

We are now ready to start working with VBScripts. We will start with how to run
a script file.

Importing a script file

In order to make this guide as easy as possible, we will start with a simple *Hello World*
example. We want our VBScript to show a message box containing the text `Hello
World`. A VBScript file is available in the GitHub repository called `Chapter17_
HelloWorld.vbs`. You can run this file independently just by double-clicking on it.
The file only has one line of code as shown here:

Figure 17.3 – HelloWorld VBScript file

In the following walk-through, you will learn how to create a session and run this
script file.

Let's start this walk-through by executing the following steps:

1. To create our session with the script file, drag the **VBScript: Open** action just below line **3**, ensuring it is within the **Step** on line **2**.

2. Set the following properties for the **VBScript: Open** action on line **4**:

   New VBScript session: `vbs_Session`

   VB Script: **Import existing file**

   VB Script file: **Desktop file** – `C:\Hands-On-RPA-with-AA-Sample-Data\Chapter17_HelloWorld.vbs`

   The properties should look as shown in the following screenshot:

   VBScript: Open

   Opens a VBScript

   New VBScript session

   ```
   99  vbs_Session                                                    [x]
   ```
   Use the session name to refer to this file in other VBScript actions

   VBScript

   (●) Import existing file

   VBScript file

   | Control Room file | Desktop file | Variable |

   ```
   99  C:\Hands-On-RPA-with-AA-Sample-Data\Chapter17_HelloWorld.vbs  [x]    Browse...
   ```
   Required extension: ".vbs"

   ( ) Manual input

   Enter script here
   ```
   1
   ```

Figure 17.4 – VBScript: Open properties

3. Click on **Save**.

4. To run the script file, drag the **VBScript: Run function** action just below line **4**, ensuring it is within the **Step** on line **2**.

5. Set the following properties for the **VBScript: Run function** action on line **5**:

   VBScript session: `vbs_Session`

The properties should look as shown in the following screenshot:

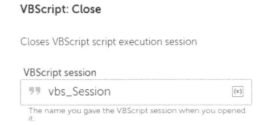

Figure 17.5 – VBScript: Run function properties

6. Click on **Save**.

7. We just have to close the session. Add the **VBScript: Close** action just below line **5**, ensuring it is within the **Step** on line **2**.

8. Set the following properties for the **VBScript: Close** action on line **6**:

    VBScript session: vbs_Session

    The properties should look as shown in the following screenshot:

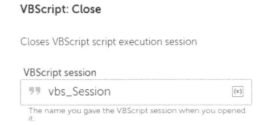

Figure 17.6 – VBScript: Close properties

9. Click on **Save**. The development interface for this section should look like this:

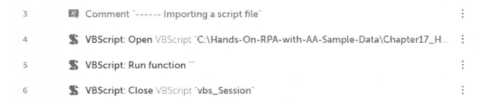

Figure 17.7 – Development interface

That's it – your bot will now run the VBScript file. Give it a test. The VBScript should show the following message box:

Figure 17.8 – Message box from an imported script file

In the next section, you will learn how to use inline scripting instead of using a script file.

Writing inline scripts

Instead of using a script file, you can write the lines of script directly within the action. In the following walk-through, we will demonstrate how to create an inline script to perform the same *Hello World* example as before.

Let's start this walk-through by executing the following steps:

1. Add the script line when you create the session by dragging the **VBScript: Open** action just below line **7**, ensuring it is within the **Step** on line **2**.

2. Set the following properties for the **VBScript: Open** action on line **8**:

   New VBScript session: vbs_Session

   VB Script: **Manual input**

   Enter script here: 1 msgbox "Hello World",,"In-Line Script File" (press *Enter* to enter new lines)

The properties should look as shown in the following screenshot:

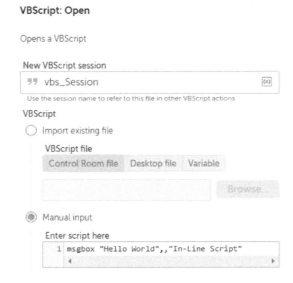

Figure 17.9 – VBScript: Open properties

3. Click on **Save**.

4. To run the script file, drag the **VBScript: Run function** action just below line **8**, ensuring it is within the **Step** on line **2**.

5. Set the following properties for the **VBScript: Run function** action on line **9**:

    VBScript session: vbs_Session

The properties should look as shown in the following screenshot:

VBScript: Run function

Executes a VBScript function

VBScript session

꠹꠹ vbs_Session   (x)

The name you gave the VBScript session when you opened it.

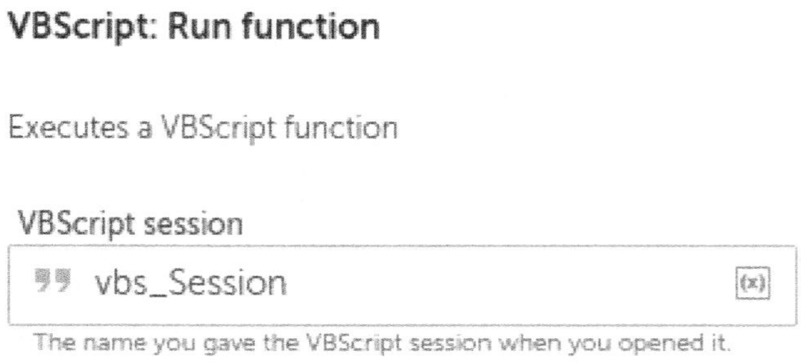

Figure 17.10 – VBScript: Run function properties

6. Click on **Save**.

7. We just have to close the session. Add the **VBScript: Close** action just below line **9**, ensuring it is within the **Step** on line **2**.

8. Set the following properties for the **VBScript: Close** action on line **10**:

   VBScript session: vbs_Session

   The properties should look as shown in the following screenshot:

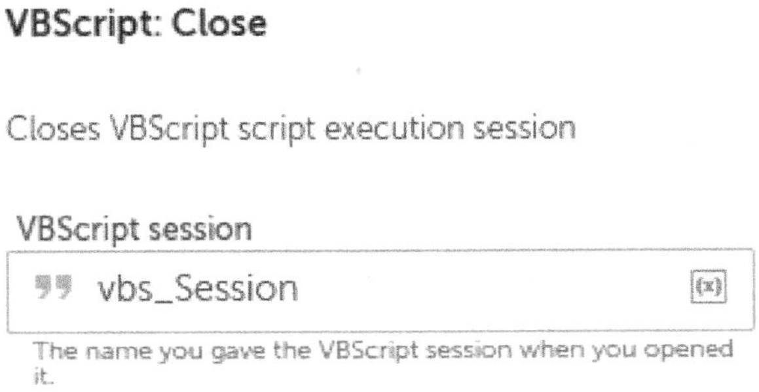

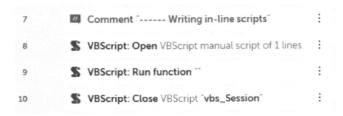

Figure 17.11 – VBScript: Close properties

9. Click on **Save**. The development interface for this section should look like this:

Figure 17.12 – Development interface

Although this is a simple one-line script, it demonstrates how to write your code directly within Automation Anywhere. When you run the bot, the VBScript will show the following message box:

Figure 17.13 – Message box from In-Line Script

We have looked at running scripts both from a file and inline scripting. In a number of cases, you will want to pass values to a script. In the next section, you will learn how to pass parameters to a script file.

Passing parameters

In this section, we will look at passing parameters. When passing parameters to a VBScript, they need to be in the form of a `List` type variable. A sample script file is included in the GitHub repository, which takes two parameters. This file is `Chapter17_InputParamters.vbs`. To use a parameter within a VBScript, you need to utilize the following syntax:

```
WScript.Arguments(0)
```

The index number (`0`) represents the item in the `List` and it uses a zero index, so the first value is indexed at `0`. The contents of the script file are as follows:

```
strValue01 = WScript.Arguments(0)
strValue02 = WScript.Arguments(1)
msgbox "Hello " & strValue01 & " " & strValue02,,"Input
Parameters"
```

For this example, we will create two `String` type variables and assign a first name and a surname as values. Then we will assign these `String` variables to a `List` variable before sending them to our script file.

Let's start this walk-through by executing the following steps:

1. Create two `String` type variables called `strFirstname` and `strSurname`.

2. Create a `List` type variable called `lstParameters`.

3. Assign the `strFirstname` variable with a value by adding the **String: Assign** action just below line **11**, ensuring it is within the **Step** on line **2**.

4. Set the following properties for the **String: Assign** action on line **12**:

   Select the source string variable(s)/ value (optional): Husan *(enter your first name)*

   Select the destination string variable: strFirstname - String

The properties should look as shown in the following screenshot:

String: Assign

Assign or Concatenate the given strings

Select the source string variable(s)/ value (optional)

> Husan   (x)

Select the destination string variable

strFirstname - String   ▼   (x)

Figure 17.14 – String: Assign properties

5. Click on **Save**.

6. Assign the `strSurname` variable with a value by adding the **String: Assign** action just below line **12**, ensuring it is within the **Step** on line **2**.

7. Set the following properties for the **String: Assign** action on line **13**:

Select the source string variable(s)/ value (optional): `Mahey` *(enter your surname)*

Select the destination string variable: strSurname - String

The properties should look as shown in the following screenshot:

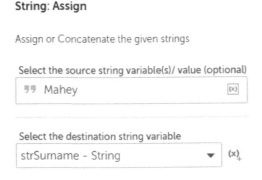

String: Assign

Assign or Concatenate the given strings

Select the source string variable(s)/ value (optional)

> Mahey   (x)

Select the destination string variable

strSurname - String   ▼   (x)

Figure 17.15 – String: Assign properties

8. Click on **Save**.

9. To add this variable to the **List** type variable, drag the **List: Add item** action just below line **13**, ensuring it is within the **Step** on line **2**.

10. Set the following properties for the **List: Add item** action on line **14**:

    List variable: **lstParameters - List**

    Item to be added: **strFirstname - String**

    Add Item: **To end of list**

    The properties should look as shown in the following screenshot:

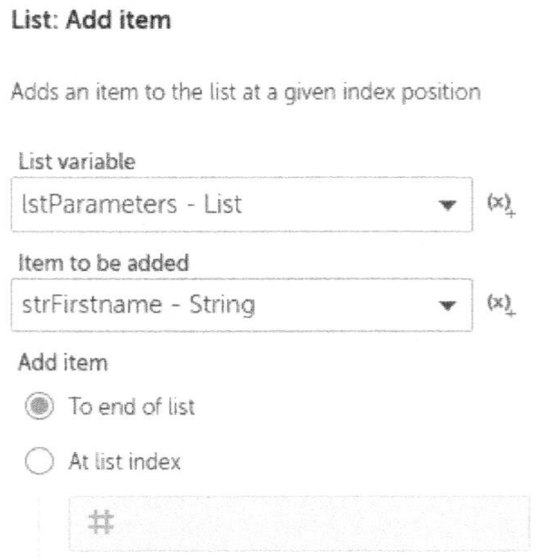

Figure 17.16 – List: Add item properties

11. Click on **Save**.

12. Add the `strSurname` variable to the `List` variable by repeating *steps 9* to *11* for the `String` variable `strSurname` just below line **14**.

13. We can now create our session by dragging the **VBScript: Open** action just below line **15**, ensuring it is within the **Step** on line **2**.

14. Set the following properties for the **VBScript: Open** action on line **16**:

    New VBScript session: `vbs_Session`

    VB Script: Import existing file

    VB Script file: Desktop file - `C:\Hands-On-RPA-with-AA-Sample-Data\` `Chapter17_InputParamters.vbs`

The properties should look as shown in the following screenshot:

Figure 17.17 – VBScript: Open properties

15. Click on **Save**.

16. To run the script file and pass the `List` type variable, add the **VBScript: Run function** action just below line **16**, ensuring it is within the **Step** on line **2**.

17. Click on **Save**.

18. Set the following properties for the **VBScript: Run function** action on line **17**:

VBScript session: vbs_Session

Parameters: **lstParameters - List**

The properties should look as shown in the following screenshot:

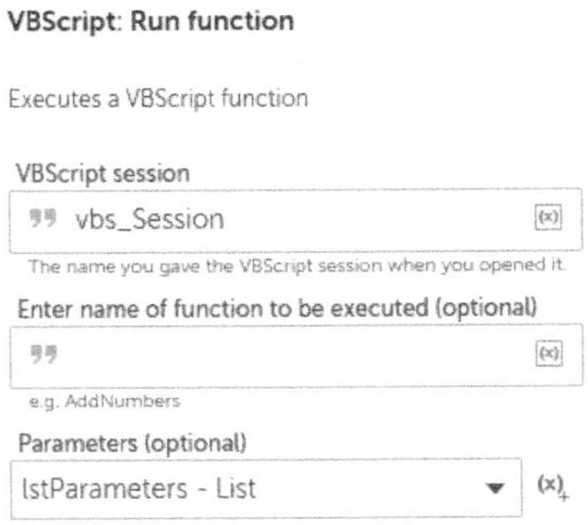

Figure 17.18 – VBScript: Run function properties

19. Click on **Save**.

20. We just have to close the session. Add the **VBScript: Close** action just below line **17**, ensuring it is within the **Step** on line **2**.

21. Set the following properties for the **VBScript: Close** action on line **18**:

    VBScript session: vbs_Session

    The properties should look as shown in the following screenshot:

Figure 17.19 – VBScript: Close properties

22. Click on **Save**. The development interface for this section should look like this:

11	📝 Comment "------ Passing parameters"	⋮
12	🔤 String: Assign "Husan" to $strFirstname$	⋮
13	🔤 String: Assign "Mahey" to $strSurname$	⋮
14	📋 List: Add item $strFirstname$ to $lstParameters$	⋮
15	📋 List: Add item $strSurname$ to $lstParameters$	⋮
16	📜 VBScript: Open VBScript "C:\Hands-On-RPA-with-AA-Sample-Data\Chapter17_...	⋮
17	📜 VBScript: Run function ""	⋮
18	📜 VBScript: Close VBScript "vbs_Session"	⋮

Figure 17.20 – Development interface

When you run the bot to test it, it will run the specified VBScript file, which should display a message box with the first name and surname. The values were passed from the bot to the script. This gives you an understanding of how to pass values from Automation Anywhere to a VBScript. In the next section, we will look at receiving values from a VBScript function.

Returning values from functions

With VBScripts, we know a function can return a value. You can also send a `Number`, `String`, or `Boolean` type variable to a function. In this section, you will learn about passing a parameter and receiving a result from a function within a VBScript. A sample script file is included in the GitHub repository; the file we will use is called `Chapter17_Functions.vbs`.

In this walk-through, we will run the function called `procSquareRoot`. This function takes a `Number` type variable and calculates the square root of this value. This value is then returned back to Automation Anywhere.

For this walk-through, we will create two variables, a `String` type for the output and a `Number` type for the input. Then we will assign these `String` variables to a `List` variable before sending them to our script file.

Let's start this walk-through by executing the following steps:

1. To store the input value, create a `Number` type variable called `numValue`.

2. To store the returned value, create a `String` type variable called `strReturnValue`.

3. Assign the `numValue` variable with a value by adding the **Number: Assign** action just below line **19**, ensuring it is within the **Step** on line **2**.

4. Set the following properties for the **Number: Assign** action on line **20**:

   Select the source string variable/ value: 25

   Select the destination number variable: **numValue - Number**

   The properties should look as shown in the following screenshot:

Figure 17.21 – Number: Assign properties

5. Click on **Save**.

6. We can now create our session by dragging the **VBScript: Open** action just below line **20**, ensuring it is within the **Step** on line **2**.

7. Set the following properties for the **VBScript: Open** action on line **16**:

   New VBScript session: `vbs_Session`

   VB Script: Import existing file

   VB Script file: Desktop file – `C:\Hands-On-RPA-with-AA-Sample-Data\Chapter17_Functions.vbs`

   The properties should look as shown in the following screenshot:

Figure 17.22 – VBScript: Open properties

8. Click on **Save**.

9. To run the function in the script file and pass the `numValue` variable and get the results to the `strReturnValue` variable, add the **VBScript: Run function** action just below line **21**, ensuring it is within the **Step** on line **2**.

10. Set the following properties for the **VBScript: Run function** action on line **22**:

    VBScript session: `vbs_Session`

    Enter name of function to be executed: `procSquareRoot`

    Parameters: numValue – Number

    Assign the output to variable: strReturnValue - String

The properties should look as shown in the following screenshot:

VBScript: Run function

Executes a VBScript function

VBScript session

> ⁇ vbs_Session   (x)

The name you gave the VBScript session when you opened it.

Enter name of function to be executed (optional)

> ⁇ procSquareRoot   (x)

e.g. AddNumbers

Parameters (optional)

numValue - Number   ▼   (x)₊

Assign the output to variable (optional)

strReturnValue - String   ▼   (x)₊

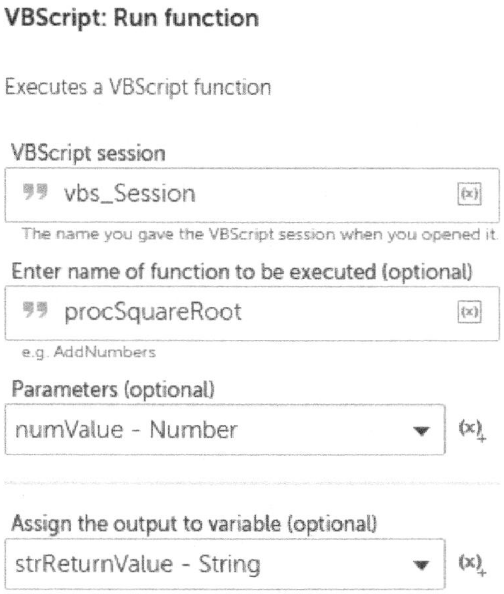

Figure 17.23 – VBScript: Run function properties

11. Click on **Save**.

12. To close the session, add the **VBScript: Close** action just below line **22**, ensuring it is within the **Step** on line **2**.

13. Set the following properties for the **VBScript: Close** action on line **23**:

    VBScript session: vbs_Session

    The properties should look as shown in the following screenshot:

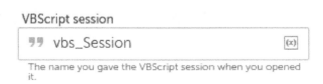

VBScript: Close

Closes VBScript script execution session

VBScript session

> ⁇ vbs_Session   (x)

The name you gave the VBScript session when you opened it.

Figure 17.24 – VBScript: Close properties

14. Click on **Save**.

15. Add a **Message box** to see the results returned by dragging the **Message box** action just below line **23**, ensuring it is within the **Step** on line **2**.

    Set the following properties for the **Message box** action on line **24**:

    Enter the message box window title: `Returning values from a VbScript`

    Enter the message to display: `Returned value: $strReturnValue$`

    Scrollbar after lines: `30`

    The properties should look as shown in the following screenshot:

Figure 17.25 – Message box properties

16. Click on **Save**. The development interface for this section should look like this:

Figure 17.26 – Development interface

Great work! That's all you need to know about VBScripts. When you run this bot, it should take the value of 25 from Automation Anywhere and pass it to the VBScript function. The function will calculate the square root and return the results back to Automation Anywhere. The following message box should appear showing the results:

Figure 17.27 – Message Box output

In the next section, we will explore running Python scripts.

Running Python scripts

Running Python scripts from Automation Anywhere uses the same principle as running VBScripts. Firstly, create the session, then run the function or script. You can pass parameters to the function or script. Finally, close the session once you have finished with it. For this walk-through, we will be replicating the same process as the previous task. The bot will run a function called procSquareRoot from the Python script file Chapter17_SquareRoot.py. The function takes a value as an input. It then calculates the square root of this value and returns the result. The contents of the Python file look like the following screenshot:

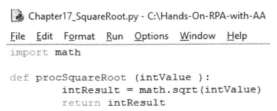

Figure 17.28 – Python script file (Chapter17_SquareRoot.py)

We will use the existing two variables, numValue and strReturnValue, for this walk-through. As we are using a Python script, please ensure you have Python installed on your workstation. You can download the latest version from https://www.python.org/downloads/. It is key that you know what version of Python you are using. For this example, it will be version 3.

Let's start this walk-through by executing the following steps:

1. Add a **Step** just below line **24**, ensuring it is not within the **Step** on line **2**, set the **Title** property as `Python Scripts`, and click on **Save**.

2. Assign the `numValue` variable with a value by adding the **Number: Assign** action just below line **25**, ensuring it is within the **Step** on line **25**.

3. Set the following properties for the **Number: Assign** action on line **26**:

   Select the source string variable/ value: `36`

   Select the destination number variable: **numValue - Number**

   The properties should look as shown in the following screenshot:

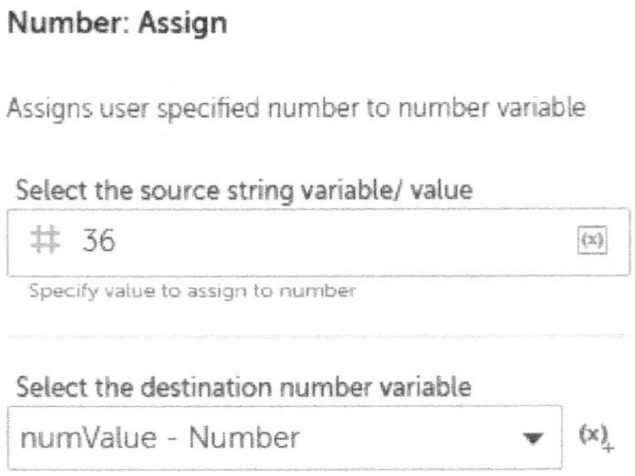

Number: Assign

Assigns user specified number to number variable

Select the source string variable/ value

    # 36   (x)

    Specify value to assign to number

Select the destination number variable

    numValue - Number   ▼   (x)

Figure 17.29 – Number: Assign properties

4. Click on **Save**.

5. We can now create our session by adding the **Python script: Open** action just below line **26**, ensuring it is within the **Step** on line **25**.

6. Set the following properties for the **Python script: Open** action on line **27**:

   New Python session: `py_Session`

   Python: Import existing file

   Python file: Desktop file – `C:\Hands-On-RPA-with-AA-Sample-Data\Chapter17_SquareRoot.py`

   Python runtime version: 3

The properties should look as shown in the following screenshot:

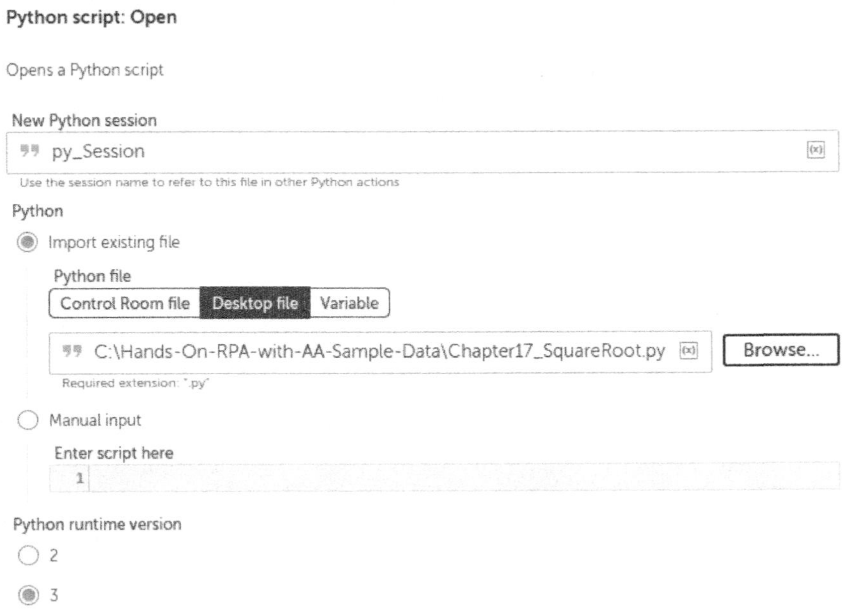

Python script: Open

Opens a Python script

New Python session

> py_Session   ⓧ

Use the session name to refer to this file in other Python actions

Python

◉ Import existing file

Python file

| Control Room file | **Desktop file** | Variable |

> C:\Hands-On-RPA-with-AA-Sample-Data\Chapter17_SquareRoot.py ⓧ   Browse...

Required extension: ".py"

○ Manual input

Enter script here

1 |

Python runtime version

○ 2

◉ 3

Figure 17.30 – Python script: Open properties

7. Click on **Save**.

8. To run the function in the script file and pass the numValue variable and get the results to the strReturnValue variable, add the **Python script: Execute function** action just below line **27**, ensuring it is within the **Step** on line **25**.

9. Set the following properties for the **Python script: Execute function** action on line **28**:

   Python session: py_Session

   Enter name of function to be executed: procSquareRoot

   Arguments to the function (optional): numValue - Number

   Assign the output to variable (optional): strReturnValue - String

The properties should look as shown in the following screenshot:

Figure 17.31 – Python script: Execute function properties

10. Click on **Save**.

11. To close the session, add the **Python script: Close** action just below line **28**, ensuring it is within the **Step** on line **25**.

12. Set the following properties for the **Python script: Close** action on line **29**:

Python session: `py_Session`

The properties should look as shown in the following screenshot:

Figure 17.32 – Python script: Close properties

13. Click on **Save**.

14. Add a **Message box** to see the results returned by adding the **Message box** action just below line **29**, ensuring it is within the **Step** on line **25**.

15. Set the following properties for the **Message box** action on line **30**:

    Enter the message box window title: `Returning values from a Python Script`

    Enter the message to display: `$strReturnValue$`

    Scrollbar after lines: `30`

    The properties should look as shown in the following screenshot:

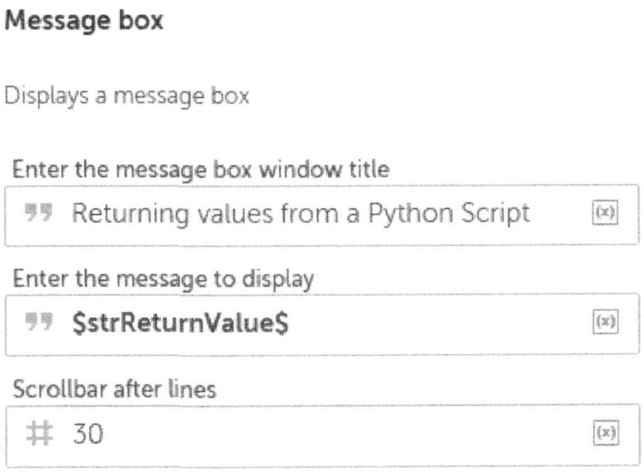

    Message box

    Displays a message box

    Enter the message box window title

    `Returning values from a Python Script`

    Enter the message to display

    $strReturnValue$

    Scrollbar after lines

    `30`

Figure 17.33 – Message box properties

16. Click on **Save**. The development interface for this section should look like this:

    25 ▾ ☐ Step "Python Scripts"   ⋮

    26   **#** **Number: Assign 36** to $numValue$ ⋮

    27   🐍 **Python script: Open** Python script "C:\Hands-On-RPA-with-AA-Sample-Data\Chapter17_...   ⋮

    28   🐍 **Python script: Execute function** "procSquareRoot" with parameter $numValue$ ⋮

    29   🐍 **Python script: Close** Python "py_Session"   ⋮

    30   🖻 **Message box** $strReturnValue$ ⋮

    31   ⁄⁄ Comment "--------------------"   ⋮

Figure 17.34 – Development interface

The bot is ready to run the Python script. You will notice how similar it is to running a VBScript. When you run the bot, the result should be a message box showing a result of **6.0** as this is the square root of 36, as shown in the following screenshot:

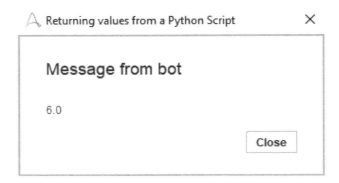

Figure 17.35 – Message box output

You can see how easily you can run external scripts using Automation Anywhere. Even when you may think certain tasks would require a lot of action using Automation Anywhere and would be better executed using a script, you can easily achieve them using RPA.

Summary

In this chapter, we looked at external scripts. There will be some exceptional instances when the actions within Automation Anywhere won't perform a specific action. An example could be calculating the square root of a value. In order to achieve this, we can still rely on Automation Anywhere to provide a solution. An ideal solution would be to use an external script. Whether it's a VBScript or a Python script, Automation Anywhere can handle it. You learned how to run scripts as well as how to pass parameters and receive return values. The step-by-step walk-throughs guided you through each stage and provided key practical skills, as well as boosting your confidence in working with RPA.

The next chapter will explore error management. You will learn all about handling exceptions and errors while your bot performs its tasks. Specifically, we will look at the different types of methods used to manage errors, such as **Try**, **Catch**, **Finally**, and **Throw**. The walk-through will demonstrate a real-life example showing how it all works. This will enable you to build a robust RPA solution.

18
Managing Errors

In the last chapter, you discovered how to run external scripts such as VBScripts and Python scripts. The walk-throughs showed how to call these scripts as well as how to send parameters with them, and finally get a result back to your bot. Having the ability to run scripts is a very useful tool to have in your automation toolbox. It opens up further automation opportunities, not limiting yourself only to the actions available in Automation Anywhere.

This brings us to the final chapter of the book; in this chapter, we will be exploring error management. I hear you say *my bots never have any errors, so error management is not needed!* I agree with you; I am sure your RPA skills and knowledge are impeccable. The most common errors are not necessarily caused by poor development but by invalid or incomplete inputs. Having robust error management will allow your bots to continue processing even when an error or exception is encountered.

With the help of the guided walk-throughs, you will learn how to implement an error-handling routine that will manage a real-life scenario as and when an error occurs. We will be looking at the following actions: **Try**, **Catch**, **Finally**, and **Throw**.

In this chapter, we will be using the following packages:

Figure 18.1 – Packages used in this chapter

There is a real-life scenario walk-through example in this chapter. The walk-through will take you through each stage step by step, giving you valuable practical experience. The input file needed for the walk-through is included as part of the GitHub repository.

In this chapter, we will cover the following:

- Error handling with A2019
- Understanding **Try**, **Catch**, **Finally**, and **Throw** actions
- Building an error-handling routine

Technical requirements

In order to install the Automation Anywhere Bot agent, the following requirements are necessary:

- Windows operating system version 7 or higher
- A processor with a minimum speed of 3 GHz
- A minimum of 4 GB RAM
- At least 100 MB hard disk space
- Internet Explorer v10 or higher or Chrome v49 or higher
- A minimum screen resolution of 1024*768
- An internet connection with a minimum speed of 10 Mbps
- You must have completed registration with Automation Anywhere A2019 Community Edition

- You must have logged on successfully to Automation Anywhere A2019 Community Edition
- A successfully registered local device
- Successfully downloaded sample data from GitHub

Error handling with A2019

Pretty much all development platforms will have some sort of error handling functions. Having error handling in your bots is crucial when building resilient automation. The purpose of managing any errors or exceptions is to keep your bot processing. As an example, if your bot is processing a large file unattended and there is an error within the first few records, your bot will stop processing and you won't be aware of this until you next check your bot. Having an error-handling routine should log the details of the invalid record and continue with the rest of the file until complete.

A bot works by executing a sequence of actions to complete a given task. While the bot is performing its task, an action may fail to complete. This could be caused by a number of factors, such as the following:

- Navigation on a web page where the page itself has been updated and the required controls have been renamed or removed
- A string value is present within a dataset where a number is expected
- The bot is unable to open a file as it may be locked
- A network failure
- The expected web page doesn't load for some reason

When such errors occur, the bot should be able to close the applications that have the issue and recover from the error elegantly. A bot should leave the workstation in the same position it was in before it started to run its task. Any applications or services that are used should be closed, leaving a nice clean desktop.

As a developer, you should also be thinking about using defensive coding. This is when you take a proactive approach rather than a reactive approach. An error-handling routine is a reactive approach as it will react to any errors that occur. Thinking proactively is using a mindset to predict any vulnerabilities in the code where the bot may be prone to an error. An example could be the bot being tasked with opening a file. In the event that the file is not present, an error would occur. A proactive approach would be to check first whether the file exists and only open it if it exists. This way the bot becomes more resilient and less prone to an error.

Automation Anywhere A2019 comes with an **Error handler** package. This package has four actions, which are designed to help build a robust error-handling routine:

Figure 18.2 – A2019 Error handler package

In the next section, we will look more closely into the preceding four actions. You will learn what they do and how to implement them for your bot.

Understanding Try, Catch, Finally, and Throw actions

The actions used for handling errors are all designed to manage different aspects of each error. We know a bot runs a sequence of actions. Each bot can have multiple error-handling routines. If there is a particular part of your bot that is vulnerable to an error, you would wrap those actions within a **Try** action. This would assign the action or actions as a block within the **Try** action. Any action within the **Try** action is managed by the error-handling routine. If any action was to fail from within the **Try** block, the bot would move directly to the **Catch** action for that error handler. Here, you would instruct the bot on what to do if an error was to occur. The most common actions would be to log the details to an error log file, maybe take a screenshot, or even send an email. The bot will continue to process any further actions in its routine without stopping.

All the actions within the **Finally** block are expected regardless of whether an error occurred or not. This would be a good place to close any open applications that were used. Since it is good practice to close them anyway, it would make sense to put these tidying up actions in the **Finally** block.

The **Throw** action is used to invoke an exception. This can be very useful when dealing with data. An example would be, say, your bot is processing a products file. This file is automatically generated and should not have certain products in it as they have now been discontinued. If such a product existed in this file, the bot would still process it as it wouldn't know it is an invalid entry. For this scenario, you could add a **Throw** action to identify such records and trigger an error. This way, you would still get an entry in the error log file of all the invalid records without processing them.

In the next section, you will be guided through a walk-through that will include adding an error-handling routine using the **Try**, **Catch**, and **Throw** actions.

Building an error-handling routine

You are probably keen to see the **Error handler** package in action. You will be guided through a step-by-step walk-through on building a fully functional bot. You will then introduce an error by editing the input file and creating an invalid record. This will result in the bot failing and stopping its processing midway as it encounters the invalid record. The walk-through will then take you through the process of adding an error handler routine.

This walk-through works with the file `Chapter18_Products.csv`. This file has a list of products within each business segment, and the contents look as shown in the following screenshot:

	A	B	C
1	Segment	Product	Price
2	Enterprise	Amarilla	125
3	Enterprise	Carretera	50
4	Enterprise	Montana	100
5	Enterprise	Paseo	15
6	Enterprise	Velo	350
7	Enterprise	VTT	40
8	Government	Amarilla	125

Figure 18.3 – Snapshot of the input file

For this scenario, the bot will perform the following tasks:

1. Read every record from the CSV file `Chapter18_Products.csv`.

2. Apply a `10%` discount to the price.

3. Create a new CSV file with updated prices called `Chapter18_UpdatedProducts.csv`.

This should be a relatively simple bot. From the tasks, we can identify a few variables that will be needed. We will need four variables:

- One `Record` type variable to read the product record
- One `String` type variable to assign the discounted price to be written to the new file
- Two `Number` type variables – one for the current price and the other for the calculated discounted price

We can start the walk-through by building the outline using steps and comments and creating the variables we will need:

1. Log into **Control Room**.

2. Create a new bot and call it `Chapter18 - Error Handling` in the `\Bot\` folder.

3. Add a new **Comment** action as "`--------------------`" on line **1** and click on **Save**.

4. Add a new **Comment** action below line **1**, "`------ create new csv output file`", and click on **Save**.

5. Add a new **Comment** action below line **2**, "`------ open products csv file and read each row`", and click on Save.

6. Add a **Step** just below line **3**, set the **Title** property as `calculate new price and update file`, and click on **Save**.

7. Add a new **Comment** action below line **4**, "`------ close products csv file`", ensuring it is not within the **Step** on line **4** and click on **Save**.

8. Add a new **Comment** action below line **5**, "`--------------------`", and click on **Save**. The initial development interface should look like this:

Figure 18.4 – Development interface

9. Create two Number type variables called numPrice and numNewPrice.

10. Create a String type variable called strNewPrice.

11. Create a Record type variable called recProduct. The variables should look as shown in the following screenshot:

Figure 18.5 – Variable interface

12. To create our new output CSV file, we will use the **Log to file** action. Starting with creating the file headers, drag the **Log to file** action just below line **2**.

13. Set the following properties for the **Log to file** action on line **3**:

File path: C:\Hands-On-RPA-with-AA-Sample-Data\Chapter18_ UpdatedProducts.csv

Enter text to log: Segment,Product,Price

Append timestamp: *Unchecked*

When logging: Overwrite existing log file

Encoding: ANSI *(default value)*

The properties should look as shown in the following screenshot:

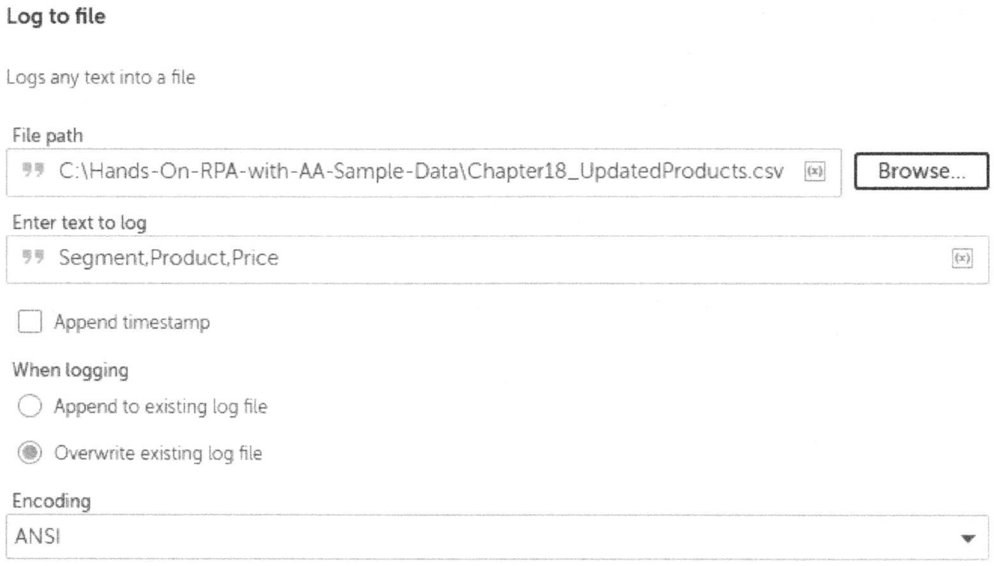

Log to file

Logs any text into a file

File path

> C:\Hands-On-RPA-with-AA-Sample-Data\Chapter18_UpdatedProducts.csv   [x]   Browse...

Enter text to log

> Segment,Product,Price   [x]

☐ Append timestamp

When logging

○ Append to existing log file

◉ Overwrite existing log file

Encoding

ANSI   ▼

Figure 18.6 – Create the output CSV file

14. Click on **Save**.

15. To create the session with our *products* CSV file, drag the **CSV/TXT: Open** action just below line **4**.

16. Set the following properties for the **CSV/TXT: Open** action on line **5**:

    Session name: csv_Session

    File path: **Desktop file** - C:\Hands-On-RPA-with-AA-Sample-Data\ Chapter18_Products.csv

    Contains header: *Checked*

    Delimiter: **Comma**

The properties should look as shown in the following screenshot:

CSV/TXT: Open

Opens a CSV/TXT file

Session name

    💬 csv_Session   (x)

File path

    Control Room file | Desktop file | Variable

    💬 C:\Hands-On-RPA-with-AA-Sample-Data\Chapter18_Products.csv (x)   Browse...

    Required extensions: ".csv", ".txt", ".tsv"

    ☑ Contains header

Delimiter

    ◉ Comma

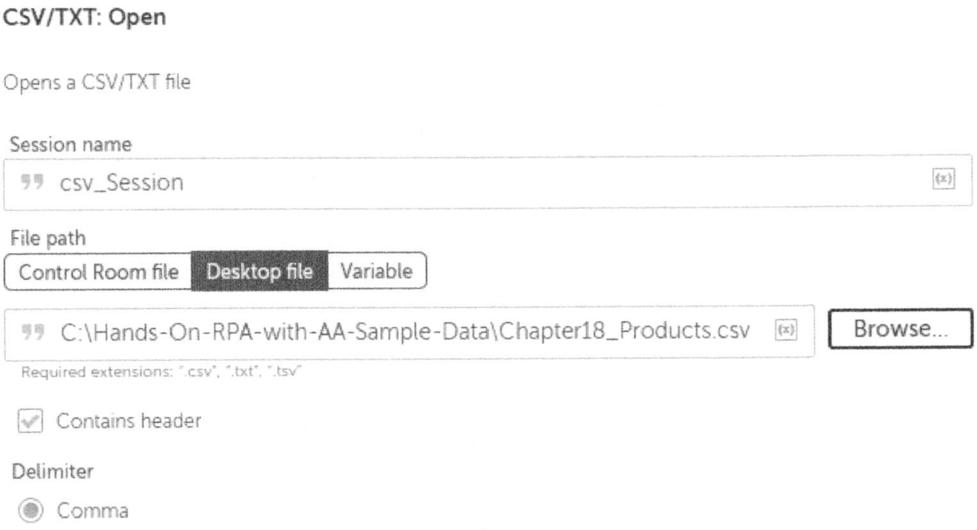

Figure 18.7 – CSV/TXT: Open properties

17. Click on **Save**.

18. To close the session that we have just created, drag the **CSV/TXT: Close** action just below line **7**.

19. Set the following property for the **CSV/TXT: Close** action on line **8**:

    Session name: csv_Session

    The property should look as shown in the following screenshot:

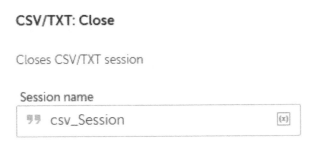

CSV/TXT: Close

Closes CSV/TXT session

Session name

    💬 csv_Session   (x)

Figure 18.8 – CSV/TXT: Close properties

Click on **Save**. The development interface for this section should look like this:

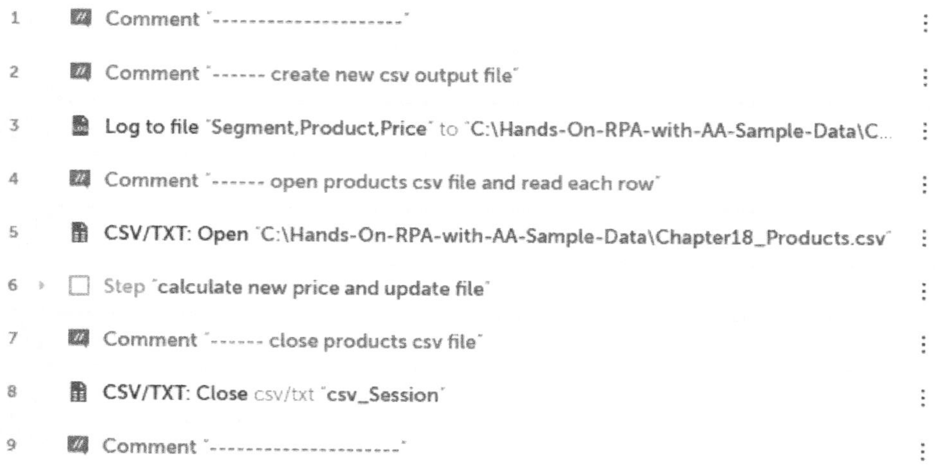

1   Comment `---------------------`   ⋮

2   Comment `------ create new csv output file`   ⋮

3   Log to file `Segment,Product,Price` to `C:\Hands-On-RPA-with-AA-Sample-Data\C...`   ⋮

4   Comment `------ open products csv file and read each row`   ⋮

5   CSV/TXT: Open `C:\Hands-On-RPA-with-AA-Sample-Data\Chapter18_Products.csv`   ⋮

6 › ☐ Step `calculate new price and update file`   ⋮

7   Comment `------ close products csv file`   ⋮

8   CSV/TXT: Close csv/txt `csv_Session`   ⋮

9   Comment `---------------------`   ⋮

Figure 18.9 – Development interface

20. Next, we can add the **Loop** to read each record from the *products* file. Drag the **Loop** action just below line **6**, ensuring it is within the **Step** on line **6**.

21. Set the following properties for the **Loop** action on line **7**:

Loop Type: Iterator

Iterator: For each row in CSV/TXT

Session name: csv_Session

Assign the current row to variable: recProduct - Record

The properties should look as shown in the following screenshot:

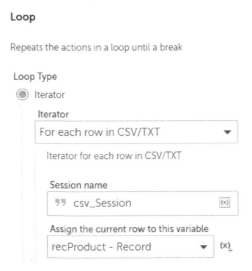

Figure 18.10 – Loop through CSV/TXT file properties

22. Click on **Save**.

23. `current price` is the third column in the CSV *products* file. This would give it an index value of **2**. To assign this value to our variable, add the **String: To number** action just below line **7**, ensuring it is within the **Loop** on line 7.

24. Set the following properties for the **String: To number** action on line **8**:

    Enter the string: $recProduct[2]$

    Assign the output to variable: **numPrice - Number**

    The properties should look as shown in the following screenshot:

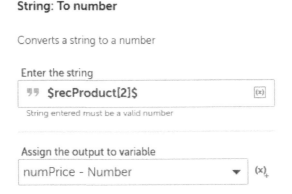

Figure 18.11 – String: To number properties

25. Click on **Save**.

26. The discounted price can now be calculated. To calculate and assign the new price to our variable numNewPrice, add the **Number: Assign** action just below line **8**, ensuring it is within the **Loop** on line **7**.

27. Set the following properties for the **Number: Assign** action on line **9**:

    Select the source string variable/ value: $numPrice$ * 0.9

    Select the destination number variable: **numNewPrice - Number**

    The properties should look as shown in the following screenshot:

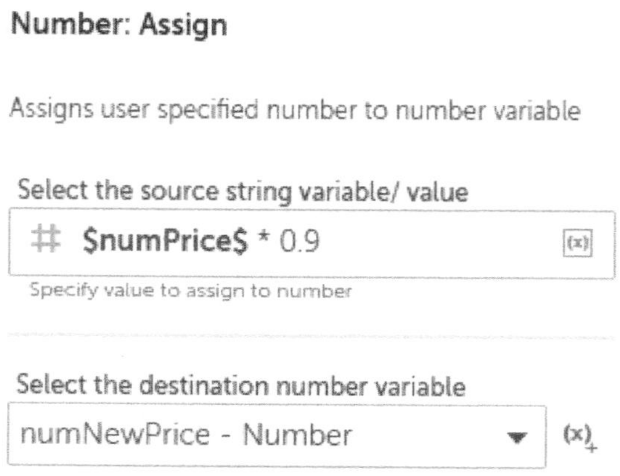

    ### Number: Assign

    Assigns user specified number to number variable

    Select the source string variable/ value

    ⌗ **$numPrice$ * 0.9**   (x)

    Specify value to assign to number

    Select the destination number variable

    numNewPrice - Number   ▼   (x)₊

    Figure 18.12 – Number: Assign properties

28. Click on **Save**.

29. As the new price will be saved to a file, it needs to be converted to a String. To do this, add the **Number: To string** action just below line **9**, ensuring it is within the **Loop** on line **7**.

30. Set the following properties for the **Number: To string** action on line **10**:

    Enter a number: $numNewPrice$

    Enter number of digits after decimal: 2

    Assign the output to variable: **strNewPrice - String**

The properties should look as shown in the following screenshot:

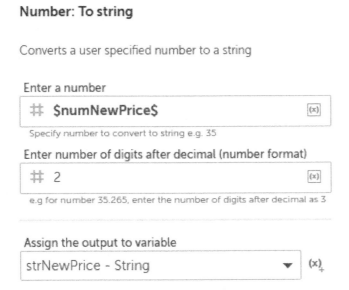

Figure 18.13 – Number: To string properties

31. Click on **Save**.

32. The last part is to append the record with the discounted price to the output CSV file. To do this, drag the **Log to file** action just below line **10**, ensuring it is within the **Loop** on line **7**.

33. Set the following properties for the **Log to file** action on line **11**:

    File path: `C:\Hands-On-RPA-with-AA-Sample-Data\Chapter18_UpdatedProducts.csv`

    Enter text to log: `$recProduct[0]$,$recProduct[1]$,$strNewPrice$`

    Append timestamp: *Unchecked*

    When logging: **Append to existing log file**

    Encoding: **ANSI** *(default value)*

The properties should look as shown in the following screenshot:

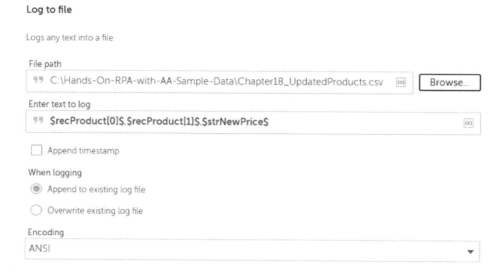

Figure 18.14 – Append to the output CSV file

34. Click on **Save**. The development interface for this section should look like this:

Figure 18.15 – Development interface

That's great work! You have now built the bot. This bot is should be working with no issues. Go ahead and run the bot. A file called Chapter18_UpdatedProducts.csv should be generated. This file will have the same records as the input file but with the new discounted price.

▲	A	B	C
1	Segment	Product	Price
2	Enterprise	Amarilla	112.5
3	Enterprise	Carretera	45
4	Enterprise	Montana	90
5	Enterprise	Paseo	13.5
6	Enterprise	Velo	315
7	Enterprise	VTT	36
8	Government	Amarilla	112.5

Figure 18.16 – Snapshot of the output file

This is all good – your bot will always work as long as the input file has no issues. But what will happen if the input file has an issue? How will your bot behave?

Modifying the input file and introducing an error

Let's have a look at what happens when we modify the input file and introduce an error:

1. Open the input file, `Chapter18_Products.csv`, in Notepad and delete the value `15` for the fourth record as shown here:

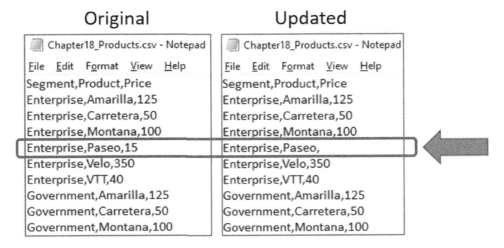

Figure 18.17 – Updated input file

2. Save and close the file.

The bot hasn't been modified in any way, only the input file has. This reflects a real-life scenario where your bot is dependent on some source data. Try running the bot again with the updated input file. While processing, the bot will fail. You will get the following message from Automation Anywhere:

Figure 18.18 – Error message from Automation Anywhere

The message refers to line **8**. This is when the bot assigns the price to the variable numPrice. Having this value as *null* has caused the bot to fail. Also in the message box, you will also notice that the bot stopped processing at the point of failure. The output file will only have three records in it. As soon as the bot encountered the error, it stopped.

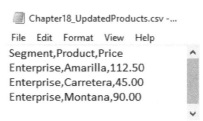

Figure 18.19 – Output file

Ideally, we would like our bot to log the error details in a file instead of a message box. Then it would be great if the bot continued with the rest of the records instead of just stopping. We will now continue with the walk-through.

In this walk-through, you will add an error handler that will manage the new error that we have introduced. To manage the error, we will need some additional variables. A Number type variable is needed to store the error line number. As this will also be added to a log file, a String type will also be required for the line number. Another String type variable will also be needed to store the error description.

We can start the walk-through by creating the variables we will need as follows:

1. Log into **Control Room**.

2. Create a `Number` type variable called `numErrLine`.

3. Create two `String` type variables called `strErrLine` and `strErrDesc`.

4. Lines **8** to **11** are when the bot is processing each record. This is what we want in our **Try** action for the error handler. Add the **Error handler: Try** action just below line **7**, ensuring it is with the **Loop** on line **7**, and click on **Save**. The development interface should look as shown in the following screenshot:

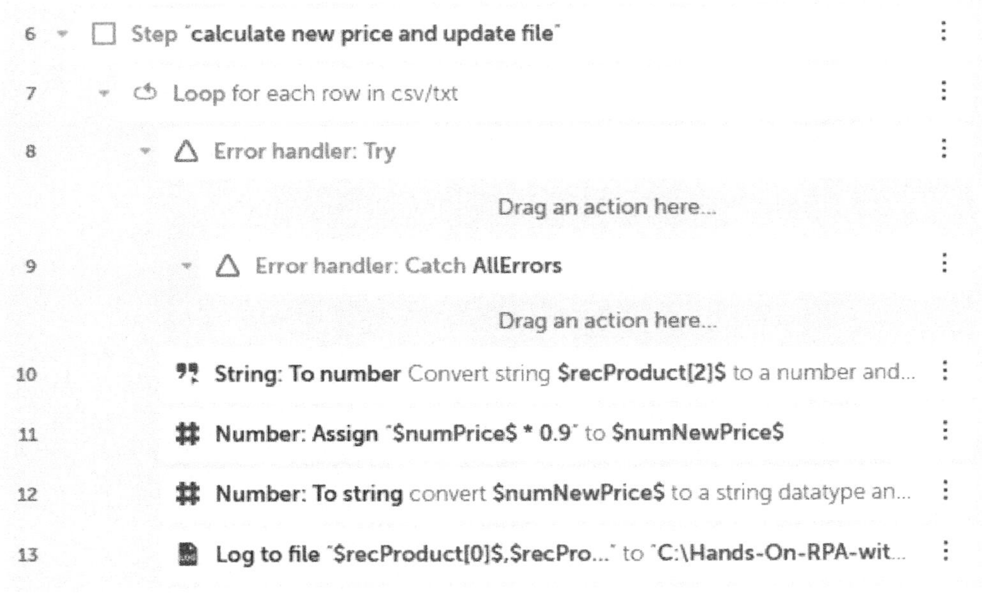

6	▾	☐ Step "**calculate new price and update file**"	⋮
7	▾	↻ Loop for each row in csv/txt	⋮
8	▾	△ Error handler: Try	⋮
		Drag an action here...	
9	▾	△ Error handler: Catch **AllErrors**	⋮
		Drag an action here...	
10		❞ **String: To number** Convert string **$recProduct[2]$** to a number and...	⋮
11		♯ **Number: Assign** "**$numPrice$** * 0.9" to **$numNewPrice$**	⋮
12		♯ **Number: To string** convert **$numNewPrice$** to a string datatype an...	⋮
13		▤ **Log to file** "**$recProduct[0]$,$recPro**..." to "**C:\Hands-On-RPA-wit**...	⋮

Figure 18.20 – Development interface

5. To add our processing lines within the **Error handler: Try** block, select lines **10** to **13** and drag them to just under line **8**, so they are within the **Error handler: Try** action on line **8**, and click on **Save**. The development interface should look as shown in the following screenshot:

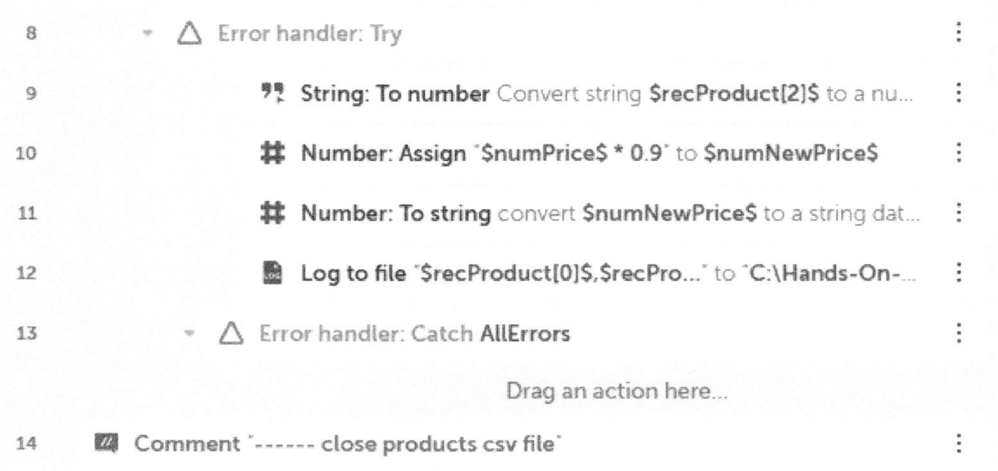

8	▾ △ Error handler: Try	⋮
9	🔢 String: **To number** Convert string $recProduct[2]$ to a nu...	⋮
10	⌗ Number: **Assign** `$numPrice$ * 0.9` to $numNewPrice$	⋮
11	⌗ Number: **To string** convert $numNewPrice$ to a string dat...	⋮
12	🖹 Log to file `$recProduct[0]$,$recPro...` to `C:\Hands-On-...	⋮
13	▾ △ Error handler: **Catch AllErrors**	⋮
	Drag an action here...	
14	🗎 Comment `------ close products csv file`	⋮

Figure 18.21 – Development interface

6. The error block has now been created. We need to instruct the bot on what to do if an error occurs from within the error block. To do this, set the following properties for the **Error handler: Catch** action on line **13**:

Exception: **AllErrors**

Assign exception message to: **strErrDesc - String**

Assign line number to: **numErrLine - Number**

The properties should look as shown in the following screenshot:

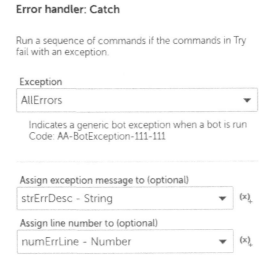

Figure 18.22 – Error handler: Catch properties

7. Click on **Save**.

8. All the actions within the **Error handler: Catch** block will be executed when an error occurs. We want the bot to output the error to a log file. The numErrLine variable will need to be converted to a String type variable for the log file. To convert this, add the **Number: To string** action just below line **13**, ensuring it is within the **Error handler: Catch** action on line **13**.

9. Set the following properties for the **Number: To string** action on line **14**:

    Enter a number: $numErrLine$

    Enter number of digits after decimal: 0

    Assign the output to variable: strErrLine - String

The properties should look as shown in the following screenshot:

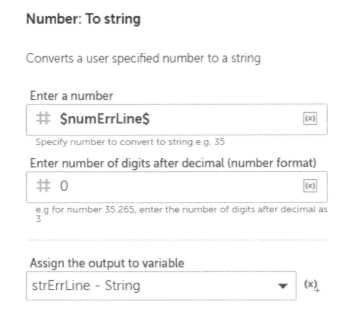

Figure 18.23 – Number: To string properties

10. Click on **Save**.

11. The last part is to append the invalid record to a log file. To do this, drag the **Log to file** action just below line **14**, ensuring it is within the **Error handler: Catch** action on line **13**.

12. Set the following properties for the **Log to file** action on line **15**:

    File path: C:\Hands-On-RPA-with-AA-Sample-Data\Chapter18_ErrorLog.csv

    Enter text to log: Desc: $strErrDesc$, Line: $strErrLine$, (Record: $recProduct[0]$,$recProduct[1]$,$recProduct[2]$)

    Append timestamp: *Checked*

    When logging: **Append to existing log file**

The properties should look as shown in the following screenshot:

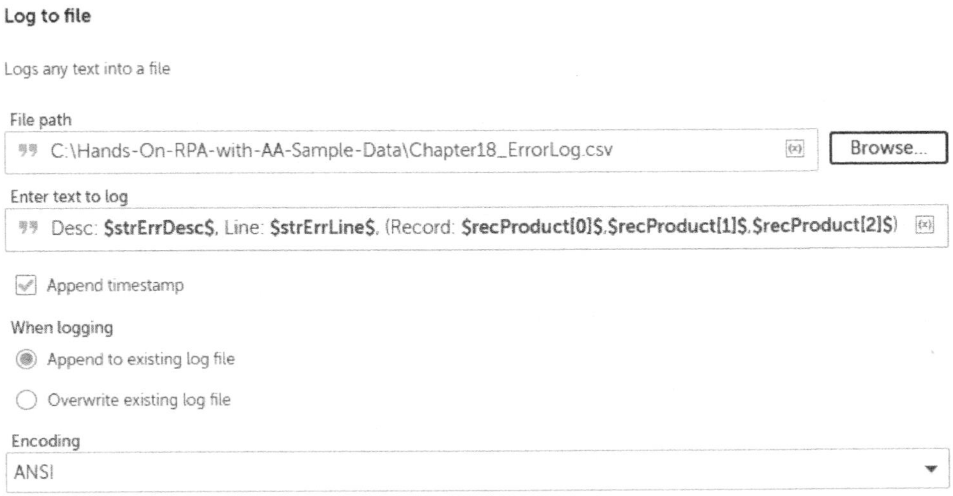

Log to file

Logs any text into a file

File path

99 C:\Hands-On-RPA-with-AA-Sample-Data\Chapter18_ErrorLog.csv   (x) | Browse... |

Enter text to log

99 Desc: $strErrDesc$, Line: $strErrLine$, (Record: $recProduct[0]$,$recProduct[1]$,$recProduct[2]$)   (x)

☑ Append timestamp

When logging

◉ Append to existing log file

◯ Overwrite existing log file

Encoding

ANSI   ▼

Figure 18.24 – Output to error log file

13. Click on **Save**. The development interface for this section should look like this:

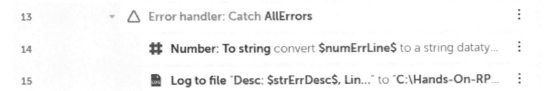

13	▼ △ Error handler: Catch **AllErrors**	⋮
14	**#** **Number: To string** convert $numErrLine$ to a string dataty...	⋮
15	**Log to file** "Desc: $strErrDesc$, Lin..." to "C:\Hands-On-RP...	⋮

Figure 18.25 – Development interface

You have now added an error-handling routine within your bot. If an error occurs while the bot is processing lines **9** to **12**, which make up our **Try** block, it will move directly to the **Catch** block on line **13**. The **Catch** block will log the details in our error log file, which is created if one does not already exist. Following the error, the bot will continue processing the rest of the input file.

14. Now run the bot once more. You will notice it will perform the task without an error occurring. Once it is complete, you can examine the files generated. The output file `Chapter18_UpdatedProducts.csv` will have all the records with the discounted prices, with the exception of the record we modified. The invalid record will not be present in the output file:

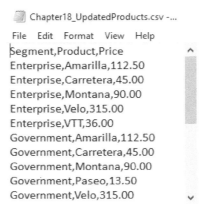

Figure 18.26 – Output CSV file

There will also be an error log file generated, `Chapter18_ErrorLog.csv`. This file will have the details of the error and the invalid record:

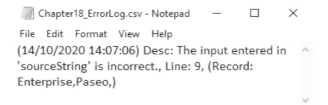

Figure 18.27 – Error log file

Great work! You have successfully added an error-handling routine. You can rest assured that your bot is more resilient and can handle files that may have invalid data.

Summary

This chapter has been all about building robust, resilient bots that can get up and continue even when they fall over. We have explored the **Error handler** package and the actions available. The walk-through provided the practical skills to actually build your own error-handling routine. Having a good error-handling routine is key to the success of your bots. No matter how great the functionality of your bot, one thing we cannot guarantee is the quality of any source inputs. A mechanism is needed to manage any anomalies in the best way possible. Using error management and some defensive coding is a step in the right direction.

This brings us to the end of this book. I hope you have enjoyed it as much as I enjoyed writing it. By following all the walk-throughs, you will have just over 20 bots already built, each one demonstrating some benefits of RPA. Hopefully, you have gained the skills and confidence to take you to the next step of your RPA journey. You are probably thinking about real-life scenarios where Automation Anywhere could help you save time and increase accuracy.

Other Books You May Enjoy

If you enjoyed this book, you may be interested in these other books by Packt:

Robotic Process Automation Projects

Nandan Mullakara, Arun Kumar Asokan

ISBN: 978-1-83921-735-7

- Explore RPA principles, techniques, and tools using an example-driven approach
- Understand the basics of UiPath by building a helpdesk ticket generation system
- Automate read and write operations from Excel in a CRM system using UiPath
- Build an AI-based social media moderator platform using Google Cloud Vision API with UiPath
- Explore how to use Automation Anywhere by building a simple sales order processing system

Robotic Process Automation with Blue Prism Quick Start Guide

Lim Mei Ying

ISBN: 978-1-78961-044-4

- Understand why and when you need to introduce robotic automation to your business processes
- Get up to speed with working with Blue Prism Studio
- Create automation processes in Blue Prism
- Make use of decisions and choices in your robots
- Understand how to use UI Automation mode, HTML mode, Region mode, and spying
- Discover how to raise exceptions
- Enable your robot to deal with errors

Leave a review - let other readers know what you think

Please share your thoughts on this book with others by leaving a review on the site that you bought it from. If you purchased the book from Amazon, please leave us an honest review on this book's Amazon page. This is vital so that other potential readers can see and use your unbiased opinion to make purchasing decisions, we can understand what our customers think about our products, and our authors can see your feedback on the title that they have worked with Packt to create. It will only take a few minutes of your time, but is valuable to other potential customers, our authors, and Packt. Thank you!

Index

Printed in Great Britain
by Amazon

70267660R00316